Phalanx Against the Divine Wind

Protecting the Fast Carrier Task Force During World War 2

Martin Irons

HOOSICK FALLS, NEW YORK
2017

This work was designed, produced, and published in
the United States of America by the

Merriam Press
489 South Street
Hoosick Falls NY 12090

E-mail: ray@merriam-press.com
Web site: merriam-press.com

The Merriam Press publishes new manuscripts on historical subjects, especially military history and with an emphasis on World War II, as well as reprinting previously published works, including reports, documents, manuals, articles and other materials on historical topics.

For more information about this book or other projects by the author, visit martinironsbooks.com.

The Jap plane headed away from the destroyer, then winged over in an Immelmann turn, and dived at the ship. Tackney swung his destroyer hard left while her automatic guns raked the plane. The "Judy," afire, crashed into the main radio-transmitter room. Up went an enormous gasoline fireball-an incandescent balloon that floated for a second, then splattered Haynsworth's superstructure with flame. Topside the ship became an inferno.

—Theodore Roscoe, *Tin Cans* (1953)

He shuddered and shook. The beer hadn't doused the flames. The conflagration still returned nightly. He emerged from the covers, feet to the floor, face in his hands. The old sailor went downstairs and made coffee. There'd be solace in the approaching daylight.

Dedicated to the sailors who took the USS Haynsworth to war,
Especially John McAllister Radioman Third Class.
Now we all shall know.
Baker Zebra

Well done

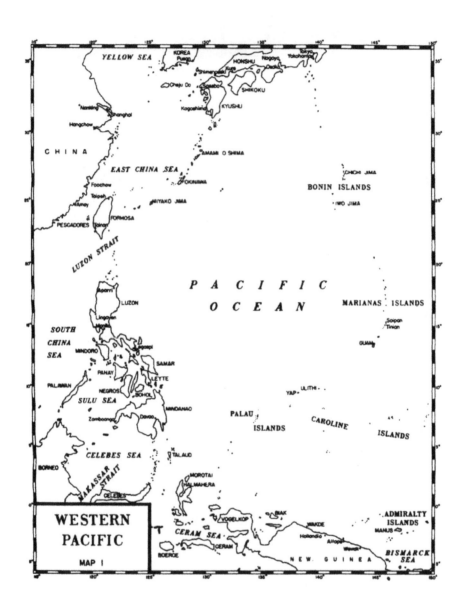

WESTERN PACIFIC

MAP 1

PHALANX AGAINST THE DIVINE WIND

Contents

Foreword

John McAllister S1c with niece, Joyce Gillespie (Walker)
at home on leave, September 1944.
(Courtesy of Brenda Walker)

THE SETTING FOR THIS BOOK is the Pacific theater during the last few years of the war, 1944-1945. At this point of the war Japan is losing more ground and sea space each day. Proud and stubborn fighters, they will not be defeated quietly or easily. Each engagement and battle will be hard fought, the Japanese fighting as if an individual victory just might be what is needed to turn the tide of the war back in favor of Japan. Many foes would have surrendered at this point, but not the tenacious Japanese. Short on money and expensive ammunition and fighting during a period when human loss was not a prominent factor in determining mission success, only whether or not the target was successfully neutralized, have resorted to employing cheaply built streamlined aircraft for the purposes of kamikaze missions; suicide flights made by relatively inexperienced and minimally trained pilots, intent on creating as much damage to the American fleet as possible. On April 6, 1945, the USS *Haynsworth* was struck and seriously damaged by a Japanese kamikaze.

The inspiration for this book was Jack McAllister, my great uncle, who as a young sailor was assigned to the *Haynsworth* from 1944-1946. A native of Newburgh, NY, he grew up along the shores of the Hudson River watching small freighters and river boats transport cargo on its waters between New York City and Albany. With this connection to the water and an aversion to the apparently harsh living conditions for soldiers depicted in popular war movies at the time, Jack knew that the Navy was the place for him to serve his country. A radioman striker, he trained with, worked alongside, and well knew the twelve of his shipmates that were tragically killed in the kamikaze attack, many of them being radiomen.

Jack was an amazing man who could spin yarns for hours discussing his time in the Navy, his life at sea, and the exploits of his ship and his shipmates. One subject he did tend to provide less detail about however was the kamikaze attack. Fate kept Jack physically off of the *Haynsworth* on the day of the attack, but I can assure you that he was onboard in an emotional and mental sense. Ties that bind sailors to their ships, and shipmates to shipmates, endure lifetimes, and once learning of that awful tragedy, Jack most certainly was mentally onboard *Haynsworth*, walking the passageways, imagining the call to General Quarters, envisioning the ensuing explosions, fire, and wreckage, and vividly recalling the faces of his fallen shipmates with whom he had shared so much.

Jack continued to serve in the Navy after World War II, returning to the Pacific theater less than a decade later in support of the Korean War. Afterwards he became a career firefighter, and I cannot help but wonder if his physical absence from the *Haynsworth* on April 6th, when he thought his ship and shipmates needed him most, may have inspired him to pursue a career in which he would always be there for others in similar need. When Jack passed in 1992, all that were left of his stories were what was remembered by family and friends that had listened to Jack wax poetically for hours over beers, narrating as if what was being told was happening at that very moment.

How this book happened is through Marty's persistent and impressive research of the Pacific theater; fleet operations and tactics; ship classes, capabilities, and operations; and never shying away from following leads to old sailors, destroyermen, shipmates and the families of Jack's shipmates. Countless hours of interviews have been so generously given to Marty by shipmates of Jack, surviving family members' records and recollections, and living veterans of the *Haynsworth*, sister ships, and ships of her squadron and task force. These men continue to give to their country today, providing a few last invaluable personal accounts that will sadly no longer be able to be heard within the next few years.

Countless books have been written about World War II and the Pacific theater of the war. What distinguishes this book from those of a similar topic is the personal emotion and connection that Marty possesses due to his close relationship with the inspiration for this book. What began as an organized collection of vignettes intended for the purposes of our family history grew into a noteworthy, relevant, and important work of naval history. You will not find many as personally involved, researched, and written as this.

—Commander Robert G. Walker, USN

Preface

THREE FADED UNIFORM CAMPAIGN RIBBONS. A few dozen old black and white photos, most without captions. A large manila envelope of old U.S. Navy personnel records. The physical mementos of a sailor sent to war.

So many of us wonder about our grandfathers, uncles, or father's service during the war. My wife and her family knew that her father was on a destroyer in World War II serving as a radioman. If that wasn't clear to an outsider, time spent at dinner with the family would allow a visitor to experience the reminder that Jack would levy at the audience when the conversation turned inane or trivial. "My ship was hit by a kamikaze!" It was startling enough to have its intended effect. His words were never an invitation to converse about the topic. Most veterans do not try to explain the battles they fought: the intended civilian audience just wouldn't grasp the significance of the details or have an appreciation of what had to be done in the horrors of war. Time spent at the VFW, American Legion or the Catholic War Veterans in the evenings allowed Jack to share the camaraderie and fraternal approval of his peers for service to his country.

In 1990 my wife took my father-in-law, John McAllister, to Boston for the second reunion with the crew of his World War II destroyer, USS *Haynsworth* DD-700. The experience was important enough to Jack that we brought him again to the next reunion in Florida, far from his native New York. Plans were made to attend the reunion again the following year but he passed away before the trip could be made.

What did my father-in-law do in the war? Moments with Jack and his shipmates laid the foundation for this book. What started out as a simple research project to present to my wife's family began to rapidly morph into a written account of an untold tale. The kamikaze attack of April 6-7, 1945 was the single largest raid of its type in World War II. So many ships were struck by the planes of the *Divine Wind*, the numbers rivaled the attack on Pearl Harbor. And, it was the destroyers in the waters off Okinawa Jima that bore the brunt of these attacks. With the encouragement and help of many of my father-in-law's shipmates, now in their 90's, the research took on a fever pitch. Survivors of passed shipmates and pilots also wanted to know more about what their fathers' experiences had been in World War II. Their help came in the fashion of oral tales, written journals, souvenirs, and photos taken aboard the *Haynsworth* during its crucial ten months in World War II.

The USS *Haynsworth* and her sister destroyers of Destroyer Squadron 62 faced typhoons, enemy mines, torpedoes and air attack. They screened the carriers, rescued pilots, shot down enemy planes, participated in bombardment actions, sank enemy picket ships and took prisoners on the high seas.

In their role as rescuers of the phalanx's pilots and aircrew, the destroyers accomplished tremendous feats that allowed the Fast Carrier Task Forces 38/58 to remain in the hunt. Rescues under difficult conditions were commonplace but since the war, few accolades have been awarded for their efforts. Without hesitation, sailors jumped into the seas with just a canvas harness and a length of rope to perform rescues that have become anonymous to history. The spotlight deserves to be turned in their direction.

Plans for the invasion of Okinawa included the Navy setting up radar picket stations around the island. Destroyers and other vessels would steam at specific locations to serve as advanced warning of enemy air attacks. One author described these destroyers as "sacrificial lambs." Ships at these locations took a tremendous beating and bore the brunt of kamikaze attacks. Their service has been well documented and serves as the foundation for several excellent books.

Less known and published was the service of the screening destroyers of the Fast Carrier Task Force. The destroyers of Task Force 58 also endured numerous kamikaze raids. The USS *Haynsworth* and other destroyers were often positioned far in front of the fleet on picket duty. Over half a century later, one of the surviving victims of the kamikaze raid stated it simply: "We were bait." After the twenty six U.S. Navy ships were damaged or sunk by kamikazes during the largest raid of World War II, the USS *Haynsworth* has rated just a few lines in books that explore the subject.

The crew considered the communal service aboard the confined spaces of a tin can, where the ship was always rolling, pitching, and diving when at sea, to be real sailing, not like the efforts of those aboard the larger cruisers, battleships, and carriers. For the *Haynsworth* sailors, all of this action took place in a relatively short period of time. Yet, the experience bonded together a crew of young men. For many, these bonds have lasted a lifetime.

Researching a book where the seventeen living survivors, the youngest member is eighty-nine at the time of this writing, yielded relatively few stories with one exception: the kamikaze attack against the *Haynsworth*. The living crew and the adult children of the participants almost verbatim reported similar tales of the attack, down to minute details.

Few of the sailors were immune to the psychological trauma arising from the kamikaze, from the radio striker Jack McAllister to the destroyer's captain, Cdr. Stephen Tackney. Some endured nightmares, other survivor's guilt, some chose to never speak of their service with their families. A war time crew is a close group but the attack served to make these bonds stronger.

In a letter post the war, the USS *Haynsworth*'s wartime Executive Officer Lt. Cdr. Scott Lothrop asked a writer to "Emphasize the individual and team bravery of the sailors and officers of our crew, even though the average age of the crew was between nineteen and twenty years old. Tell of the teamwork and patriotism of these men, who came from all parts of the country when they were called…And do not denigrate the Japanese in the telling. They were simply different and mistakenly led. And were brave in their own ways, even though different." I hope I have been able to complete that mission successfully.

Errors are mine and mine alone. I ask for the reader's indulgence in advance.

—Martin Irons
April 2017

Acknowledgements

SO many individuals and museums have given generously of their time, knowledge, and resources. This book could not have been written without their invaluable aid and contributions. Thanks go out but are not limited to: Rob Walker, Cdr., USN; Russ Padden (Sampson Webmaster); the late Howard Doble (USS *Haynsworth* webmaster); Linda Mital McConnell; Robin Reilly; Nick Zeoli RdM2c USS *Boston*; Bill Hillis; Paul Barbone; The Bryson Ley family; Jim Horn and the USS *Haynsworth* Association; the late David McComb (Destroyer History Foundation); Gus Scutari FC1c; Marianna Steele; Jim Schreffler; Karen Myreholt Shinn; Col. Justin 'Mac' Miller USMC (Ret.) VMF-217 and VMF-321; Bob Ammann and the other researchers of the Emil Buehler Library of the Naval Aviation Museum; Mrs. Margaret (Charles) Satterly; John Wheeler MD; 1st Lt. Philip Wilmot USMCR VMF-451; Chris Fahey, Planes of Fame Museum; Lt. David Oberholzer USN; Kimberly Kooyenga; The Flying Leatherneck Aviation Museum; Researchers at the National Archives in both Maryland and California; Morris Gillett CRT USNR; Ed Kelly; Nancy Matschat; LTC John Neal U.S. Army (Ret.); Capt. Army Dennett USN (Ret.); CDR Peter Lothrop USN (Ret.); Capt. Douglas Aitken USN (Ret.); the family of Admiral Stephen N. Tackney; Tim Rizzuto, ExecDir Destroyer Escort Historical Museum, USS *Slater* DE-766; Steve Kelly; Lt. Jack Melnick USNR (Ret.); and John O'Leary QM2c, USS *English* DD-696.

It is with regret that some of the sailors, pilots, researchers, and friends who have aided me have passed away since this project commenced. I wish them eternal fair winds and following seas.

Special thanks go to my dear friend Linda LiDestri who helped me figure out how to get this tale off the ways and into commission. Also, my friend, the late Dave DeMasi served as the illustrator and sidewalk editor. He is truly missed.

And finally, this book would not have been possible without the love and support of my wife, Ann McAllister-Irons

Author's Notes

THE tale is told in the local military time for the sake of consistency throughout the narrative. Unattributed quotes are taken from the official war diaries, deck logs, or action reports of that vessel. As with all reports taken in combat, there are occasionally differences in accounts written about a particular action. As much as possible, I have tried to reconcile the discrepancies by relying on official records and the words written seventy-two years ago in the sailors' diaries.

PART I

The War 1941-1944

THE BOY

Newburgh Waterfront

A ND HIS EYES FOLLOWED the freighters, tugs, and the ferry-boats as they crossed the mighty Hudson. Cruise boats like The *Dayliner Alexander Hamilton* brought thousands of passengers up the river from New York City. The freighters had crossed oceans to bring their goods north after having run the gauntlet of German U-Boats that owned the American coasts in the early part of the war. Tugboats, like those of the McAllister Tugboat Company of NYC, brought barges upriver loaded with fuel and other goods. At its widest point north of New York City, the mighty Hudson River flowed past this industrial river city set up on the hill. Over a mile from shore to opposite shore, steam powered ferries brought passengers and vehicles back and forth from Newburgh to Beacon. On warm days the wealthier citizens could be seen playing in their sailboats while fishermen in boats large and small set their nets or cast their lines. The river was alive, its mood changing with the moon, the time, and the weather. It was a stage for an infinite number of vessels representing the commerce of America. Its strength as an extension of the ocean held its lure tightly on the young man.

BATTLESHIP

Japanese battleship Yamato sea trials, 1941 (NARA 80-G-704702)

SUPERBATTLESHIP. Each time she returned from sea trials both sailors and dock workers at the naval base at Kure alike wondered in amazement at her size. This leviathan, whose keel was originally laid down at the Kure Naval Shipyards in 1937, was beyond anything anyone had seen. Powerfully built with a large Pagoda style superstructure, she was befitting both the Emperor and the Empire. The *Yamato's* superstructure towered eighty feet. She was the greatest battleship ever constructed, the crown jewel of the Imperial Fleet. At 71,000 tons, 840 feet in length and armed with the largest naval cannon ever forged, the *Yamato* and her twin sister, *Musashi*, were unequaled by any battleship in any navy.

Designed to not just compete but defeat battleships of any fleet, the *Yamato's* 18.1 inch cannon could fire projectiles twenty six miles. She bristled with an additional twelve 6.1 inch guns and twelve 5 inch guns. She was protected by numerous anti-aircraft guns. The *Yamato*, in theory, would be able to fight multiple battleships at a single time.

At this time in November 1941, America's biggest battleships were barely 600 feet in length with smaller cannon. Their twenty-one knot speed could not begin to match the speed of the twenty-seven knot *Yamato*. Built in secrecy, its immense size was flagrantly in violation of the Washington Naval Treaty that limited battleships to 37,000 tons and 16 inch guns. In 1936, Japan renounced the treaty and began planning to build a class of supreme battleships.

The *Yamato* represented the pride and aspirations of the Imperial Japanese Navy. Her efforts in World War II would come to symbolize the outcome of the entire Imperial Japanese Navy but not in a manner her admirals expected.

SUNDAY, DECEMBER 7ᵀᴴ

(McAllister Family Collection)

THE BANGING AT THE DOOR STARTLED THE FAMILY. Patriarch Edward McAllister put down his mandolin. Pot roast, potatoes, and pies, glasses of tea and beer, the remains of Sunday lunch, littered the table, a weekly tradition following Catholic Mass for the Irish-American family.

"Who could that be?" Mother Alvina wondered aloud. "There's plenty of food left, let'm in!" commanded Edward. Fifteen year old Jack, the youngest son, leapt to the front door of their Newburgh, New York home to find a neighbor out of breath.

"WAR! We're at war!" exclaimed their friend.

"With Germany?" asked the family.

"No," came the response. "Japan! They attacked our ships at Pearl Harbor!"

SEEKING REASSURANCE AND INFORMATION, the McAllisters, like the vast majority of Americans, listened to their radio the following day as President Franklin Delano Roosevelt addressed Congress:

> *Mr. Vice President, Mr. Speaker, members of the Senate and the House of Representatives: Yesterday, December 7th, 1941 — a date which will live in infamy — the United States of America was suddenly and deliberately attacked by naval and air forces of the Empire of Japan.*
>
> *The United States was at peace with that nation, and, at the solicitation of Japan, was still in conversation with its Govern-*

ment and its Emperor looking toward the maintenance of peace in the Pacific. Indeed, one hour after Japanese air squadrons had commenced bombing in the American island of Oahu, the Japanese Ambassador to the United States and his colleague delivered to our Secretary of State a formal reply to a recent American message. And while this reply stated that it seemed useless to continue the existing diplomatic negotiations, it contained no threat or hint of war or of armed attack.

It will be recorded that the distance of Hawaii from Japan makes it obvious that the attack was deliberately planned many days or even weeks ago. During the intervening time the Japanese Government has deliberately sought to deceive the United States by false statements and expressions of hope for continued peace.

The attack yesterday on the Hawaiian Islands has caused severe damage to American naval and military forces. I regret to tell you that very many American lives have been lost. In addition American ships have been reported torpedoed on the high seas between San Francisco and Honolulu.

Yesterday the Japanese Government also launched an attack against Malaysia.

Last night Japanese forces attacked Hong Kong.

Last night Japanese forces attacked Guam.

Last night Japanese forces attacked the Philippine Islands.

Last night the Japanese attacked Wake Island.

And this morning the Japanese attacked Midway Island.

Japan has, therefore, undertaken a surprise offensive extending throughout the Pacific area. The facts of yesterday and today speak for themselves. The people of the United States have already formed their opinions and well understand the implications to the very life and safety of our nation.

As Commander-in-Chief of the Army and Navy, I have directed that all measures be taken for our defense.

But always will our whole nation remember the character of the onslaught against us. No matter how long it may take us to overcome this premeditated invasion, the American people in their righteous might will win through to absolute victory.

I believe that I interpret the will of the Congress and of the people when I assert that we will not only defend ourselves to the uttermost but will make it very certain that this form of treachery shall never again endanger us.

PHALANX AGAINST THE DIVINE WIND

Hostilities exist. There is no blinking at the fact that our people, our territory and our interests are in grave danger.

With confidence in our armed forces—with the unbounding determination of our people—we will gain the inevitable triumph—so help us God.

I ask that the Congress declare that since the unprovoked and dastardly attack by Japan on Sunday, December 7th, 1941, a state of war has existed between the United States and the Japanese Empire.

In a little over thirty minutes, by almost unanimous vote, the Congress passed a declaration of war against Japan. Soon the McAllisters would send their sons to war. Their service flag, hung in the window of their home like millions of other American families, bore three blue stars for their sons. As the war progressed, thousands of these families replaced blue stars with gold stars in honor of their sons fallen in their fight for country.

ATTACK

THE TIDE HAD TURNED. By 1944, few Americans would have made the bet that the Japanese would win the war of the Pacific. Their defeat was not a matter of 'if' but rather 'when.' However this bet had not been a sure thing in the dark days after the surprise attack on December 7th, 1941, at Pearl Harbor.

The stage had been set years earlier. After spending ten years trying to conquer China, Japan's war machine was running short of oil. With the risk of Japan continuing its paths of conquest across Asia, the United States and the Allies sought to put a halt to Japan's efforts. An export block of vital steel and oil became part of an embargo forced on Japan. The Panama Canal, under U.S. control, was closed to Japanese flagged ships. While the plans achieved its initial goal of slowing down the Japanese, it also compelled Tokyo to seek new sources of oil and resources. If need be, they would be taken by force.

Japanese Admiral Isoroku Yamamoto was assigned the task of destroying the American Pacific fleet. By achieving this victory, the Japanese believed the United States, fearful of entering the war, would sue for peace.

Yamamoto, a graduate of the Japanese Naval Academy and later Harvard University, was familiar with America. The famous admiral had served in Washington DC as the military attaché for the Japanese Navy. Later he would be one of the key developers of Japanese naval aviation and would serve as an aircraft carrier commander.

The focus of Admiral Yamamoto's plan was to surprise the entire western fleet at anchorage. It was traditional that the U.S. Pacific fleet would maneuver at sea during the week and would return to port by Saturday. By sending in flights of torpedo planes, dive bombers, and fighters early on a Sunday morning, Yamamoto had hoped to catch the few but highly valuable U.S. aircraft carriers in port

Damaged USS Maryland BB-46, capsized USS Oklahoma BB-37
(U.S. Navy Photo by Harold Fawcett P3c)

GEYSERS AND FLAMES ERUPTED as the first wave of attackers flew over the anchorage early that Sunday morning. Japan's surprise attack on the US Navy's Pacific fleet sank or damaged twenty-one ships. The carriers, out at sea, escaped the raid while the battleships absorbed the brunt of the attack. All eight of the Pacific Fleet's battleships were heavily damaged, three sunk, and one capsized.

Trapped in the capsized USS *Utah* AG-16, five sailors were cut out of the hull. Like the six battleships that would be repaired, refurbished, and returned to fight in the Pacific, an electrician's mate on the former battleship would face the Japanese again while serving on a destroyer in the battle for Okinawa in 1945.

But, overnight the surprise attack changed the focus of the U.S. Navy's battle plans to one that made it stronger and faster. It was an unintentional consequence to Yamamoto's plan. And because of this effect, Japan would lose the war in the Pacific.

PACIFIC ISLAND HOPPING CAMPAIGN

THE ALLIES DEFEAT OF JAPAN IN WORLD WAR II WAS NOT BY CHANCE. A lethal combination of the foresight of military planners, U.S. Naval intelligence, the enormous capabilities of U.S. industrial production and the determination and efforts by a dramatically expanded military brought the dominant eastern tiger to its knees in less than four years. America's military anticipated the attack on the U.S. military in Hawaii as well as how they would defeat the Japanese in such a war as far back as 1904. The plan's code name was Orange. Quite simply its design was similar to a heavy weight fighter absorbing a strong blow from an opponent. The U.S. Navy would retreat to the west coast, regain its strength and then sail west to destroy the Imperial Japanese Navy in battle near their home islands. The plan was predicated on the American fleet being led into battle by its battleships. The planners had not considered the possibility that there would be no battleships available to lead the charge.

With the destruction of the battleship fleet and subsequent rise of the aircraft carrier, the U.S. Navy changed its battle tactics. An earlier attack by slow British biplane torpedo bombers at the Italian port of Taranto in 1940 had also demonstrated that large ships could be defeated by air attack. Rather than lines of dreadnoughts and support ships dueling opposing forces within visual sight by shell fire, the key to the future would be the use of carrier based airplanes. The battle field was no longer limited by the range of the cannons but by the aerial range of the fighters, dive bombers, torpedo bombers, and scout planes. The projection of power jumped from twenty miles to hundreds of miles with the change of tactics emphasizing aircraft carriers. Within seven months of the raid against Pearl Harbor, carrier fleets of the both the Japanese and American navies would engage in battle without any of the ships actually seeing the opposing force. Overnight on December 7th, the battleship had slipped from star player to supporting player in American naval tactics.

At the start of the war, America had just eight aircraft carriers. One was obsolete while four of the remaining seven were sunk in battles in 1942. But starting in that year and through the end of the war, twenty-six fleet carriers were launched by the U.S. Navy. Capable of turning thirty knots or more, these modern carriers were designed to carry large numbers of planes great distances and bring the fight to the enemy. They were augmented by dozens of light and escort carriers launched in the same period. Japan was able to only produce another twelve carriers during the course of the war to supplement the ten carriers that were available in 1941.

A large steam locomotive spends tremendous energy to move the first few feet but can rapidly gain speed once it gets moving. The American shipbuilding campaign was similar. Shipyards had to be expanded, equipment produced, workers hired, and vast numbers of sailors trained before new ships could be launched at an increasing rate. The *Essex* class carriers took on average eighteen months from the laying of the keel to the commissioning of the ship. Even though nine *Essex* class keels were laid down in 1941 and 1942, these ships were not available to fight until 1943 or later. A total of seventeen of these carriers were used in World War II along with nine of the smaller *Independence* class carriers. These carriers would form the nucleus of a new naval strategy: The Fast Carrier Task Force.

Charging into battle in 1944, the Fast Carrier Task Force was a collection of smaller carrier task groups. Each of the groups was configured so that they could work independently of each other or join forces to mass their lethal threat. The group had a core center of aircraft carriers. Protection against enemy heavy cannon was provided by battleships and cruisers. Their guns could blanket the sky with anti-aircraft fire. But it was the smallest warships in the groups, the destroyers that would provide the first line of defense against attacks from the air, the sea, or under the waves. Heavily armed, fast, and nimble, the destroyers performed tasks that kept the group in combat and the carriers safe from harm.

As the new carriers came on line, more destroyers were needed. America's ship yards laid the keels for hundreds of them. Correspondingly, the U.S. Navy needed sailors, hundreds of thousands of them.

SHANGRI-LA: THE DOOLITTLE RAID

AMERICA WAS REELING FROM THE PUNCHES THE JAPANESE HAD THROWN. After the attack at Pearl Harbor, the quick succession of losses at Wake Island, the Philippines, Hong Kong, and Guam had shaken America. The population was also nervous about the war against the European Axis powers. Since 1939 they had heard about the tremendous losses of Allied shipping to German U-Boats, the Blitzkrieg across Europe, and the collapse of the British Army at Dunkirk. There were continued rumors that the Japanese would attack the west coast. The U.S. Navy's fleets were reduced to older ships that had to fight wars across two oceans. The fighting spirit of America, which had soared for a few days after *The Day of Infamy* speech, had begun to sag under the realization that America's military was stretched very thin.

However, just two weeks after the Pearl Harbor attack, President Roosevelt gathered his Joint Chiefs of Staff. He expressed his wish that the Japanese home islands must be bombed at the earliest opportunity. Japan was thousands of miles from the nearest U.S. held airstrip, well beyond the range of even its great new bomber, the Boeing B-17 *Flying Fortress*. It was time for the military to put on its thinking caps to find a solution to the President's challenge.

An audacious plan to attack Japan was promoted by Admiral Ernest J. King: If carriers could get close enough to the Japanese home islands undetected then Army bombers could be launched, attack Japan, and fly to friendly airstrips in China. The plan was accepted but much work had to be done. No modern medium twin engine bomber had ever taken off from the relatively short runway of an aircraft carrier. The plane selected, the North American B-25 *Mitchell* bomber, had not been used in combat previously. With a wingspan of almost 68 feet, the bombers would be cramped on the 114 foot wide carrier deck of the USS *Hornet*.

The mission was assigned to the famed aviator and Army Air Corps Colonel Jimmy Doolittle. With less than two months to prepare for the mission, Doolittle trained his elite squadron of fliers with specially modified B-25 bombers. On April 1st, 1942 the men, supplies, and their bombers were loaded on the USS *Hornet* at the Naval Station Alameda near San Francisco. Theirs was a mission shrouded in secrecy.

The plan to launch the bombers 480 nautical miles from the Japanese home islands was foiled when a Japanese picket boat detected the U.S. forces. After a warning was radioed to the Empire by the enemy vessel, the decision was made to launch the bombers right away despite being 650 nautical miles from their targets.

The Doolittle Raiders traveled in small groups of two or four planes at low altitudes to Japan. Their bellies carried four 500 lb. bombs each. Military and industrial targets were bombed in several cities including Tokyo, Yokohama, Osaka, and Kobe. Despite obstacles caused by the early launching, most of the planes made it safely to China. One plane, low on fuel, was forced to land in the Soviet Union.

Though the tactical results were meager, the surprise attack was considered a great success. Japan was forced to divert military resources from other theaters back to the home islands for the duration of the war.

Much of the mission's details were kept secret from the U.S. public. The raid's success caused a great swell in both pride and morale for the American public. When asked where the bombers had been launched, President Roosevelt answered that the raid had come from 'Shangri-La,' the mysterious place of perpetual youth found in the book *Lost Horizon*.

But, it would be another three years before American fliers returned to attack Tokyo. When they did, enemy picket boats would again figure in the actions of the U.S. Navy.

Col. Jimmy Doolittle's Raiders on the U.S.S. Hornet.
(National Museum of the Air Force)

HALT: THE BATTLE OF THE CORAL SEA

THE U.S. NAVY HAD ANOTHER SURPRISE FOR ITS FOES. By mid-1942 the Japanese Army and Navy had expanded the reach of the empire to include most of the eastern Pacific. Aggressive expansion of their occupied territories included the Philippines, Formosa, French Indo-China, the Caroline Islands, the Solomon Islands, the Gilbert Islands, the Marshall Islands, Thailand, Singapore, Guam, the Dutch East Indies, Wake Island, Korea, and China. Australia stood alone as the major Allied power remaining against the Japanese onslaught. America had failed to crumble and negotiate as the Japanese military had hoped. Therefore the Japanese reasoned that the United States and its allies would use Australia as a springboard to launch attacks.

To prevent Australia from turning into a major Allied base, the Axis powers planned to invade Port Moresby in New Guinea and Tulagi in the Solomon Islands in May, 1942. Unknown to the Imperial Japanese Navy (IJN), American intelligence had cracked one of the major Japanese communication codes. A day into the invasion, American fliers from the USS *Yorktown* surprised Japanese forces at Tulagi. The naval aviators sank four Japanese warships and damaged four others with minimal losses to themselves. Though a tactical victory, the appearance of American naval fliers put the IJN on notice that an American fleet was in the area.

On the morning of May 7th, planes from the opposing forces spotted each other. By mid-morning attack forces were arriving on target. The Japanese forces mistook an American oiler as a carrier. Dive bombers successfully sank the oiler USS *Neosho* AO-23 and the destroyer USS *Sims* DD-409. However planes from the carrier *Lexington* ravaged the surprised Japanese carrier *Shoho*. After multiple bomb attacks, the carrier slipped beneath the waves.

The next morning, May 8th, both forces' aerial scouts spotted the opposing forces. Planes from the American fleet badly wounded the IJN carrier *Shokaku*. Unable to launch or recover planes due to damage, the wounded carrier withdrew from the battle before she could be sunk. About the same time, the American carriers were attacked by Japanese fliers. *Lexington* was hit by several bombs leading to crippling explosions when leaking aviation fuel tanks exploded. Two more bombs hit the *Lexington* during another attack. A single bomb pene-

USS Lexington burns after her crew has abandoned ship.
(U.S. Navy Photo NH 51382)

trated deeply through the *Yorktown's* flight deck down four levels. Its explosion caused damage to some compartments and death for sixty six sailors.

With heavy devastation to both carriers, the loss of the refueling oiler N*eosho*, and an undetermined number of Japanese carriers still at sea, the American task force withdrew from the Coral Sea. Fires and explosions continued to rock the *Lexington* and so she was finally abandoned and scuttled. The *Yorktown* was ordered to return to Pearl Harbor for repairs.

The Japanese invasion forces continued as planned until their reconnaissance planes discovered Task Force 16 east of the Solomon Islands. The presence of the task force was a ruse to disrupt the invasion plans. After being spotted, Task Force 16 turned back to Pearl Harbor. The Japanese command postponed the invasion due to the presumption of American forces in the area. Temporary became permanent.

The Battle of the Coral Sea was notable for several reasons. For the first time, attacking naval forces never had direct sight of each other. The battle also marked the first carrier force versus carrier force battle.

Though the allies lost a vitally important carrier (with another damaged), the Japanese also lost one carrier and a second was put out of commission. The loss of experienced pilots and crews as well took a toll on the IJN as well. With the invasion of the island of Midway planned for less than a month away, a third of Japan's planned carrier attack force was lost.

The Battle of the Coral Sea marked the first time Japanese aggression was checked by Allied Naval forces. The growing presence of American carriers would continue to dictate the battle of the Pacific as the opposing forces tangled for the next three years. And, along with the rise of the carrier, so did the importance of the destroyers' role increase.

MIDWAY

IT WAS TO BE PEARL HARBOR'S EPILOGUE BUT INSTEAD THE ATTACK BECAME ITS REVENGE. The enemy armada steamed east with six carriers, seven battleships, nine cruisers, twelve destroyers and thirty-five support ships. Its battle groups targeted Midway Island and the Aleutian Islands. Their ultimate goal was to surprise and sink the American aircraft carriers that that had escaped the Pearl Harbor raid six months earlier.

The author of the Pearl Harbor attack, Admiral Isoroku Yamamoto, wagered that an attack on American held territory would lure the remaining American carriers to battle. With the element of surprise and a superior force available for battle, the Imperial Japanese Navy should have held the upper hand. America had to be forced to come to the bargaining table to sue for peace. If the American carriers and the will of the American public could not be crushed then Japan would soon face a Navy that was already laying keels for hundreds of carriers, battleships, cruisers, destroyers, and submarines. Japan could not begin to compete with the industrial capacity of America. Yamamoto was eager to devastate the remains of the American Pacific fleet.

The Midway Atoll is a tiny coral island 1,300 miles west of Hawaii. Though strategically it would not provide great benefit to the Empire if captured, it was important for the United States Navy. Midway served to bridge the great distance to Japan as a staging area for American forces.

Simplicity was never an element of Yamamoto's battle plans. As dual lures to bring the American carriers to battle, one Japanese fleet would attack and invade the Aleutian Islands of Kiska and Attu while simultaneously another larger carrier fleet would attack Midway. Trailing at a great distance from the Midway carrier attack force was a group of battleships and cruisers. A small force of two battleships and a dozen destroyers would screen the four carriers bound for Midway. Though Yamamoto had a vast and potent force, it was separated into many pieces. The fragments were far from being as strong as the whole.

The plan's architect did not know that two crucial assumptions to the success in battle had already been lost before the attack began. American codebreakers were aware that an IJN operation was in effect but its details and location were not all accessible. Using some simple trickery, the American Naval codebreakers were able to discover the target of the attack by having the commander at Midway send an uncoded message that they were running short of fresh water due to machinery problems. The Japanese heard this message, forwarded it to their headquarters and so the Americans were able to confirm Midway was the target. The critical element of surprise was lost. It would prove fatal to the Japanese Navy.

With the loss of the two American carriers, *Lexington* and *Yorktown*, at the Battle of the Coral Sea, Yamamoto expected to face just the two remaining US carriers, *Hornet* and *Enterprise* but *Yorktown* was recalled for battle. The mighty carrier arrived at Pearl Harbor to find the shipyard ready to affect temporary repairs. *Yorktown* was back at sea within three days. Though outnumbered in carriers, four to three, the U.S. Navy had dramatically tilted its odds of victory.

Over 100 American aircraft were based at Midway. Some of these forces spotted and attacked the IJN invasion forces on June 3, 1942. The fight began in earnest the next day when the Japanese carriers sent attacks against the island. The first attack did not neutralize the American forces as the IJN had hoped so their reserve planes were readied for another bombing strike against the island. During this period, a Japanese scout plane detected at least one of the American carriers. The Japanese commander, Admiral Nagumo, was in a quandary. He needed to land his first flight, recover the combat air patrol, and load his second wave with torpedoes for attacks against the American ships.

As the first Japanese wave returned low on fuel, several waves of American dive bombers and torpedo bombers arrived over the Japanese fleet. The IJN, caught during refueling, had its planes fully gassed and armed on the flight decks and in the hangar decks of its carriers. In rapid succession the carriers *Akagi*, *Soryu*, and *Kaga* were hit by the American attackers. All three carriers rapidly became floating conflagrations. All three would be scuttled by the IJN.

The battle was not a one sided victory for the Americans. Planes from the remaining carrier, *Hiryu*, found the *Yorktown*. Two different waves achieved hits on the carrier and left it damaged and out of the fight. Retribution was achieved by *Enterprise's* planes when they bombed *Hiryu*. Like her sisters, the carrier was done. She would burn and sink after many hours.

The USS *Yorktown*, despite having been nearly abandoned and listing heavily, was still afloat. A Japanese submarine brought an end to her with two torpedoes. A third torpedo sunk the destroyer *Hammann* which had been lending assistance to the repair parties aboard the *Yorktown*.

USS Yorktown after being struck by second aerial torpedo
from planes of the carrier Hiryu, June 4, 1942.
(NARA 80-G-414423)

In a battle that had lasted a few days, the roles of dominance in the Pacific were reversed. Four of the six Japanese carriers that had attacked Pearl Harbor on December 7th were lost at Midway. Of great consequence for the IJN was the loss of hundreds of experienced carrier pilots, crews, and mechanics. The Japanese system of training would not allow for rapid replenishment within those ranks.

Of note, throughout the battle, Admiral Yamamoto was positioned on his flagship, the battleship *Yamato*. The greatest battleship in the Pacific was impotent as it remained hundreds of miles from the center of the fight. Tellingly it did not fire a shot in anger and had no impact on the course of Battle for Midway and the control of dominance in the Pacific.

Guadalcanal

THE DEFEAT OF THE JAPANESE ON LAND BEGAN AT GUADALCANAL. The island was one of the southern parallel Solomon Islands that extended from Rabaul south 800 miles. When American military leaders learned the Japanese were clearing the jungle to build an airstrip, the decision was made to prevent its completion. On August 7th, 1942, just eight months after the Pearl Harbor attack, U.S. Marines invaded the island and secured the airstrip during the first American amphibian operation of the war.

However, the Japanese were not easily defeated and fought viciously against the Marines (later joined by the U.S. Army) for what would be the war's longest land battle. Fought for six months under the primitive, hot, malarial conditions of the island, the fighting was often close up and hand to hand. The Japanese excelled at night fighting but their dependence on banzai charges handicapped their efforts. Great numbers of Japanese soldiers were slaughtered by machine gun fire as they charged behind a sword waving officer. It was a battle tactic of another era and made no sense in a time of machine guns, grenades, and mortars.

Regardless, the Japanese high command continued to reinforce the island and so lengthened the brutal campaign. By sending ships down the 'slot,' the sea pathway between the Solomon Islands, the Japanese Imperial Navy used the cover of darkness to bring reinforcements and supplies to Guadalcanal. Throughout the campaign the American navy ships and Army Air Corps, navy, and marine pilots tried to intercept the Japanese navy in the slot. An American and British force of destroyers and cruisers was defeated in the nighttime Battle of Savo Island, just off the northern tip of Guadalcanal. Four Allied cruisers were sunk, one cruiser damaged, and two destroyers damaged. The IJN suffered damage to just one cruiser.

The Battle of the Eastern Solomon Islands took place near the end of August. Both sides brought carrier forces to a battle that featured ship to ship, air to ship, and air to air fighting. Losses were felt by both sides. One of America's few remaining aircraft carriers, the USS *Enterprise*, was damaged while the Japanese carrier *Ryujo* was sunk. Coming on the heels of the loss of four carriers at Midway, Japan had lost thirty percent of its carrier strength in less than three months.

Yamato and sister ship Musashi at Truk in 1943.
(Yamato Museum PG071333)

The American carriers were stung, too. A week later, the American carrier *Saratoga* was torpedoed patrolling near the Santa Cruz Islands. On September 15 the American carrier *Wasp* was sunk patrolling the southeast of the Solomon Islands. The U.S. Navy was left with but one vital carrier in the Pacific, the USS *Hornet* of Doolittle Raiders fame. The great carrier fleet was still on the shipbuilders' ways.

While Admiral Yamamoto did send smaller battleships to bombard Guadalcanal, the massive *Yamato* stayed anchored in relatively safety at the Japanese base at the island of Truk. At a time when she was offensively superior to all American warships, a lack of ammunition for her main guns, a mighty thirst for oil and the fear of steaming in poorly mapped areas kept *Yamato* moored and away from battle. It was an opportunity squandered.

PART II

A Crew is Formed

In common with all persons in the Navy every enlisted man belongs to the armed forces which the nation maintains upon the seas. Membership in this military service calls for an unqualified realization by each man that there are essentially military duties which he is obliged to perform. Performance of these military duties by naval personnel is the difference which distinguishes the naval service from the merchant marine, and the bluejacket from the civilian.

—*The Bluejackets' Manual 1943*

THE RANKS OF THE NAVY WERE GROWING. As the number of new keels for aircraft carriers, battleships, cruisers, destroyers, destroyer escorts, and submarines increased rapidly, so did the training of America's young men into sailors. With less than 400,000 sailors in the ranks at the time of the attack at Pearl Harbor, the Navy would eventually mobilize over four million sailors by war's end. They came from all over the country to permanent Recruit Training Stations in San Diego, Orlando, Meridian, North Chicago, and Port Deposit in Maryland. Two other large Naval Training Bases were built to cope with the expansion of recruit training. One was in Farragut, Idaho, the other in upstate New York.

Sited on the east shore of Seneca Lake in the Finger Lakes region of upstate New York, Sampson Naval Training Base was constructed during 1942-43. Its mission was to train as many sailors as rapidly as possible. It was not designed to be a permanent facility unlike some of the Navy's other training facilities such as Great Lakes Naval Training Center on Lake Michigan or the facilities at Norfolk, San Diego, and Newport, Rhode Island. Built in just 270 days on 2,600 acres, the rough-hewn Sampson would contribute 411,000 sailors to the ranks before the war's end.

Just twenty two days after his eighteenth birthday, John McAllister received his notice from the local draft board. By the order of the President of the United States and the Selective Service System, 'Jack' reported to the auditorium of the Broadway School in Newburgh, NY, along with other draftees. After a brief physical it was determined that he was "Physically fit, acceptable by Navy, including Marine Corps, Coast Guard." Jack's brother, Bill, was already serving in the Navy aboard a destroyer. Having grown up in a river town and with enthusiastic reports about the Navy from his brother, Jack decided it was the Navy for him. His oldest brother served in the Army Air Corps. Ed McAllister had not shared tales of good food and a warm place to sleep.

The Navy officially inducted Jack six weeks later on March 24, 1944. McAllister recited the Oath of Allegiance: *I, John Albert McAllister, do solemnly swear that I will bear true faith and allegiance to the United States of America, and that I will serve them honestly and faithfully against all their enemies whosoever, and that I will obey the orders of the President of the United States and the orders of the officers appointed over me, according to the rules and articles for the government of the Navy.* McAllister quit his stock clerk job as preparation for his service.

Crowded aboard a train powered by an old steam locomotive, John was sent to the Sampson Navy Training Base (SNTB) for boot camp. It was a journey of nervous teenagers and young men who played cards on the train to kill time, told the boastful tales of youth, and also quietly wondered if they would be up for the challenge of being a sailor. Most had never sailed on a boat nor could the majority of these recruits swim. But, three years into the war, these boys knew of the tales and horrors of land battles in Africa, Italy, Guadalcanal, Kursk, and so many more. They were all aware of the horror of trench warfare in the Great War or World War I. They had heard the tales from their fathers and their uncles. They had grown up with movies like "All Quiet on the Western Front," "Sergeant York," and "The Big Parade." Life on a ship allowed at least that you would be clean, have a place to sleep, and regular meals. A good portion of the core of the crew of the future USS *Haynsworth* arrived in late March to find winter still holding firmly to its grasp of central New York.

Down the road from Newburgh, identical twins Charles and Ernest Satterly, of Meadowbrook, New York tried to join the service. While Charlie was accepted in the Navy, Ernie went to Williamsburg, Virginia, to join a Construction Battalion (Sea Bees). Upon arrival a heart murmur was detected and so Ernie was not allowed to enlist. Eager to serve, Ernie tried enlisting in the Army, Marines, and Coast Guard. All turned him down as did the Red Cross where he sought to be an ambulance driver. Finally, Ernie went to a local cardiologist who pronounced his heart as healthy. With the good news, Ernie finally joined the Navy. His first orders were to report to Sampson Navy Training Base.

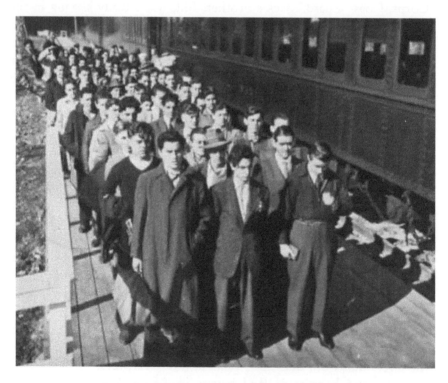

Recruits arrive at Sampson Naval Training Base
(Courtesy of Russ Padden)

BY THE THOUSANDS, the inductees arrived by bus and train at the gates of Sampson. The Navy was determined to strip them of their civilian identities and turn them into Able Seamen as rapidly as possible. The transformation from civilian to trainee was started im-

PHALANX AGAINST THE DIVINE WIND

mediately. The trainees said goodbye to their civilian clothes, stripped nude and stood in long lines to get their vaccinations. Corpsmen and doctors quickly probed them, checked them off as passed, and hustled them to their next station. Uniforms were gathered from supply clerks. Nakedness was replaced by skivvies. Moving down the line, gear was tossed at them while petty officers screamed at them that they were moving too slowly. It was also the first time, but certainly not the last, that they would pen their signatures to documents and manila cards stating they had received all their uniforms, whether they fit or not, and 'issue' gear.

Sampson Naval Training Station
(Courtesy of Russ Pudden)

The Navy then gave him his sleeping gear. In the tradition of the old navy: they issued him a hammock with a mattress, two mattress covers (sailors called them fart sacks), one pillow, two pillow covers, and two blankets. The Boot needed a place to store these items, so one of the first items issued to him was his Sea Bag. This cylindrical canvas sack of 26" x 36" had grommets on top through which the man wove a line to use as a draw string to close the bag and to hang it from a rack. As with everything else he got, he stenciled his name on the side of the bag. This bag was

his and his only. It was his entire and unique identity as an indi-
vidual among the mass of other men. When traveling, a sailor
rolled his mattress and sleeping gear inside the hammock which
he then wrapped around and secured to his sea bag. This pack he
slung up on a shoulder and marched off with all he owned. Before
rolling his mattress, however, a sailor laid out his bedding items
on the flattened mattress in a specific order according to regula-
tions.

Sampson Naval Training Station (Courtesy of Russ Padden)

Bernie Huntoon, a gunner's mate who later served aboard the USS
Holt DE-706, recalled his first day at Sampson. "We were told to fill
our seabag and our pillow case with our newly acquired gear. We were
told it should be dragged from station to station. As soon as we reported to the barracks, we were yelled at by our instructors for having
dirty seabags and so were made to clean them." Later, when studying
the *Blue Jackets Manual,* he would read, "*men must be careful to keep
their bags clean at all times. Never drag a bag along the deck.*"

The Bluejackets' Manual was the educational companion of all *boots.*
First published in 1902, it had been continually revised. McAllister
paid his ten bits ($1.25) for the 1943 eleventh edition of the 1,150 page
reference. While the book was broken down into eight main topics
(*Subjects All Enlisted Men Should Know, Deck Seamanship, Boat Seaman-*

*Firefighting training at Sampson Naval Training Station.
(Courtesy of Russ Padden)*

ship, Elements of Navigation and Piloting, Communications and Signals, Gunnery, Landing Force, and *Technical Features; Components of the Navy; Ship Facilities)* the book started simply with the lyrics to the *National Anthem.*

Their hair was shorn in just a few seconds. Coupled with their new appearance, boots also had to learn a new language: Navy. A room was no longer described by floor, walls, doors and ceiling. The navy translation was compartment, deck, bulkheads, hatches, and overhead. Compartments were connected by passageways. Besides their battlestation, the most important compartments to sailors were the head (toilet), and the mess (food). They slept on racks of metal tubes and canvas rather than beds. Supplies could be purchased at the canteen. Starboard was the right side of the ship, port was left, the bow was in front, and the stern brought up the rear. On the ship, 'front-center-back' were replaced with 'forward-amidships-aft/after.' With training at a furious pace, boots did not have to know daily time ashore was 'liberty' while extended time off the ship was 'leave.'

The Navy had its own alphabet: <u>A</u>ble, <u>B</u>aker, <u>C</u>harlie, thru <u>X</u>-ray, <u>Y</u>oke, and <u>Z</u>ebra. In addition, boots had to relearn time. Gone were the acronyms of a.m. and p.m. The Navy was on military time so the hours were numbered 00-24 rather than 1 through 12. The simple method of adding '12' to civilian p.m. times, followed by the minute as a group of four numbers designated the time. 1:17 a.m. became 0117. 5:34 p.m. became 1734. Midnight was 2400.

The day was broken up into six watches of four hours duration:

0000-0400 Mid-Watch
0400-0800 Morning Watch
0800-1200 Forenoon Watch
1200-1600 Afternoon Watch
1600-2000 Dog Watch
2000-2400 First Watch.

It was critical to remove the fear of fire from the trainees. Fire at sea could have deadly consequences so firefighting training was initiated at boot camp and continued throughout sailors' careers.

Even chow was a foreign experience: "We were served fried beans and potatoes for breakfast, which was a surprise," recalled Bernie Huntoon.

These were days initially defined by confusion and exhaustion. "All the days were full days," recalled Huntoon. "There was no walking, we had to 'doubletime' at all times." Chief Petty Officers, who never seemed to sleep were always 'motivating' the boots to learn more, do it better, and do it faster. Early on boots were told they were worth nothing but they had better adopt the U.S. Navy's ways. Their lives and the fate of their ships could be decided by the action of just a single sailor. As the days passed, the traditions of the U.S. Navy were reinforced. Each boot was forced to consider if he could measure up. Pride of being a sailor developed while individuality was replaced with a crew mentality.

While many sailors like eighteen year olds McAllister and Satterly had volunteered to enlist in the Navy when they were eligible, not all the 'boots' enjoyed their experience in the navy. "Ninety percent of the draftees didn't want to be there," recalled Huntoon.

As new warships were coming online daily, the need for sailors grew tremendously. The Navy launched 74 destroyers in 1944 alone and had 367 destroyers in service by year's end. This was triple pre-war

Able Seaman John McAllister 3rd row, 5th from right.
(McAllister Family Collection)

levels. Boot training for Tom Scott and Keith Myreholt (at Farragut) of the *Haynsworth* lasted eight weeks in 1943. With the demand for sailors, training had been pared down to six weeks from eight weeks when Bernie Huntoon arrived at Sampson in January, 1944. By the time Jack McAllister arrived in March of that year, it was further sliced to just four weeks.

After completing boot camp, orders were given out to the newly graduated trainees, now classified as 'Able Seamen,' for the next step in their training. McAllister showed his buddies the paper that held his future. "You are hereby ordered to report to the Destroyer Training Facility, Norfolk, Virginia." Destroyer!! The fastest ships in the Navy! The greyhounds of the ocean and guaranteed to be in the thick of battle!" Many of his peers from the spring companies of '44 were sent to Norfolk in preparation for the launching of the newest destroyers, the *Allen M. Sumner* class. And so after a few days of leave, the baby faced bluejacket reported to the Destroyer School at the Norfolk Naval Shipyard.

DESTROYER TRAINING: NORFOLK, VIRGINIA

T HE NEXT EVOLUTION FOR THE FUTURE TIN CAN SAILORS began at Norfolk. Here, they were instructed in the duties and expectations of destroyer service. Like other US destroyers, the training manual for the USS *Brush* DD-745 laid out the basics:

> *The Brush is organized on a departmental basis. It contains Operations, Gunnery, Engineering and Supply departments. Every officer and man aboard, except the Commanding Officer and the Executive Officer, who is the Captain's Chief assistant, is assigned to one of the departments.*
>
> *Each department is sub-divided into divisions to work responsibilities. Under the direct charge of a division officer, each division is composed of petty officers and non-rated men who are trained for-work in that particular division.*

Days aboard U.S. Navy ships were broken down into six watches of four hours duration:

> *For the performance of routine duty and to suit messing and sleeping arrangements, the crew works in shifts. Aboard the Brush the crew is divided into three watch sections. The normal duty watch lasts four hours. With the exception of the Commanding Officer and the Executive Officer, everyone on the ship is in a watch section.*

Each member of the crew was assigned a duty or a station for routine revolutions and every possible emergency. The ship's *Division Watch, Quarter, and Station Bill* specified each sailor's cleaning stations, lookout watch at sea and sentry watch while in port. During ships emergencies, each sailor was assigned positions for various emergencies such as fire, collision, rescue at sea and battle stations during General Quarters (GQ).

The destroyer and its crew operated within five conditions of readiness. Condition V was at the lowest risk of threat while Condition I was General Quarters or battle stations. When the alarm was sounded for General Quarters (Condition I) all watch stations were manned, all weapon systems ready to go, and damage control teams at maximum readiness. Additionally, the ship was designated as material condition "z." All watertight hatches and doors were secured. Repair lockers were manned with full fire and repair teams composed mostly of sailors with engineer ratings. These teams donned helmets, gloves, and a protective "flash" cream to protect from burns. Others however were assigned to be in the ships magazines or to serve as crew on the weapons. "When that bells rings GQ, everyone aboard ship has a station to go to, drop everything, you must go to your station," recalled the *Haynsworth's* Phil Goldstein GM2c. "You are being attacked."

After six weeks of training aboard destroyers at Norfolk, the sailors bound for the USS *Haynsworth* took trains to New York. There they reported to the Brooklyn Naval Yard a few days before the U.S. Navy's newest destroyer, the USS *Haynsworth*, was to be commissioned. They could not know it then but the destroyer would return from war in just ten months' time.

BATTLE OF THE PHILIPPINE SEA: THE GREAT MARIANAS TURKEY SHOOT

THE EMPEROR'S FORCES WERE GASPING. By 1944, the Imperial Japanese Navy's strength had diminished dramatically from its peak strength during the time of Pearl Harbor. Just two and half years earlier the IJN had been the greatest navy in the world but continued losses of capital ships combined with a lack of industrial capability to quickly replace them caused the tide to turn against the Imperial Japanese Navy long ago. Meanwhile American industrial capacity was able to increase production at even greater rates. With just eight carriers at the start of the war, America launched eighty three more carriers from 1942 to 1945. Japan on the other hand was only able to complete an additional ten carriers. In no other naval battle was this disparity more apparent than the Battle of the Philippine Sea.

Ever seeking a decisive victory over the Americans, the Imperial Japanese Navy placed their bet on a combined carrier and land based plane attack during the American invasion of the Marianas Islands. Guam, Saipan, and Tinian were among those islands whose airbases provided protection for the home islands. Their control was vital for security of the sea lanes. A reversal of ownership would allow the United States to develop airbases for its new long range bombers, the B-29 *Superfortress*. With a 4,000 mile flight range, Boeing's best would be able to regularly press attacks against the home islands.

Coming into the battle the U.S. Navy had an advantage in carriers (fifteen versus nine), battleships (seven versus five including the *Yamato*), submarines (twenty eight versus twenty four), and aircraft (956 carrier based versus 750 combined land and carrier based). While the Japanese were flying the same types of aircraft that attacked Pearl Harbor, the Americans had come to battle with more powerful, newer planes like the Grumman F6F *Hellcat* and the Chance-Vought F4U *Corsair* fighter planes. The American pilots were better trained than their rivals. With aviation fuel available, the American flyboys had hundreds of hours of airtime. The Japanese pilots were a mixture of grizzled, well trained veterans combined with many pilots that had been rushed through training with inferior aircraft and often minimal flight hours. But the numbers alone don't begin to explain the vast tactical advantage the U.S. had over Japanese. Military intelligence was still regularly intercepting and breaking Japanese coded radio transmissions.

And, in a string of running air battles beginning on June 19, 1944, the U.S. pilots decimated the pilots of the IJN (carrier based) and of the IJA (land based). While the U.S. lost forty-three planes to enemy action, the Japanese forces lost approximately 633 planes and two more irreplaceable carriers. Meanwhile the penultimate battleship, *Yamato*, never faced an enemy surface ship during the two day battle. Instead the only time it fired its guns was in error as a group of IJN fliers returned to the fleet.

The American's dominant victory will always be remembered by a description given by an American flier: "Hell, this is an old time turkey shoot."

USS *HAYNSWORTH* DD-700

USS Haynsworth in original camouflage paint scheme, 1944.
(National Archives 80-G Collection)

AMERICA'S INDUSTRIAL MIGHT WAS WITHOUT RIVAL. Anticipating the need for large numbers of destroyers to fight the two ocean wars, the United States Navy ramped up production. From 1940 to 1945 the ship builders of America turned out 368 destroyers. Japan in comparison was only able to complete forty four destroyers to compliment the eighty two they had built before their attack on Pearl Harbor. And by wars end, 106 of the 126, of Japan's destroyers were sunk. In comparison only fifty nine American destroyers were sunk in *both* the Atlantic and the Pacific during World War II.

At the start of World War II, dozens of new *Fletcher* class destroyers were under construction. They were significantly larger and more powerfully armed than their predecessors with five 5"/38 caliber guns in single mounts. At 2050 tons, they were able to turn up to 36.5 knots. Eventually 175 were built and served successfully throughout the war.

The next evolution of the destroyer was the *Allen M. Sumner* class. Based on the hull and propulsion systems of the *Fletcher* class, the new 2200 ton destroyers were more heavily armed. An additional 5"/38

PHALANX AGAINST THE DIVINE WIND

caliber gun was carried aboard along with 50% more 40mm anti-aircraft guns. Twin rudders replaced the single rudder of the previous class. No upgrade was made to the thin unarmored skin of the destroyers. They were commonly known among sailors as 'tin cans' for their thin steel hide. Shipyards building *Fletchers* were easily able to convert to construction of the new class. The Navy ordered seventy.

The contract for construction of the USS *Haynsworth* was awarded to The Federal Shipbuilding and Drydock Company, a division of the U.S. Steel Corporation. Federal Shipbuilding had been created during the First World War and with the coming of the Second World War was awarded contracts to build light cruisers and destroyers. Federal set a torrid pace for launching ships as evidenced by the five light cruisers and ninety two destroyers they constructed during the war. "On one day alone in May 1942, the company launched four destroyers. By 1943, Federal Shipbuilding was employing 52,000 people and building ships faster than any other yard in the world."

The keel of the *Haynsworth* was laid down on December 16, 1943. She was one of eighteen *Sumner* class destroyers built by Federal. Their hull numbers ranged from USS *Allen M. Sumner* DD-692 to USS *Hugh Purvis* DD-709. The *Haynsworth* was officially DD-700.

The destroyers coming down the ways late in the war were not dramatically larger or faster than their World War I forefathers and would have been easily recognizable to an earlier generation of bluejackets. The pencil style ratio of narrow width to length remained. Above the sea deck, the new cans' offensive capability created a profile that was more miniature battleship than the torpedo ships of the pre-Versailles Treaty.

The *Sumner Class* was designed from the beginning to integrate emerging radar and sonar technologies with both navigation and weapons systems. It pioneered a dedicated Combat Information Center (CIC) below the bridge and adjoining radio, radar, and sonar compartments. Various electronic nerve pathways-radio, radar, and sonar-merged in the compartment. Reports from lookouts were assimilated with the other intelligence by the CIC team. After threats were plotted, actionable intelligence was passed to the bridge that allowed a destroyer to navigate and fight a coordinated attack with other ships and planes. Fighters and the combat air patrol could be controlled from its facilities.

For DD-700, most of her senior officers were United States Naval Academy graduates or regular navy. Most of her younger officers and crew were part of the growing Navy Reserve. The new captain, Cdr.

Robert J. Brodie, Jr., arrived in February of 1944 to oversee the construction for the Navy. Brodie was an Annapolis graduate of the class of 1927. "Steve" as he was known, was described by his midshipmen peers thusly:

> *A natural aptitude for grasping and remembering all that he hears, sees, and reads, has carried him through the academic years with higher than average marks. Opportunity may knock but once, and that's all Steve needs, for he is always alert and having that desire to do something big. Bob is interested in politics and history and his ideas on the subject are sometimes astounding but very enlightening. A witty conversationalist until you get him talking about "old Kentuck." Then you might as well leave, for he goes on and on with facts and statistics proving that beyond the shadow of a doubt he comes from the state that ranks first in everything, from women to products. Steve has always a smile for everyone and has the welfare of his friends constantly at heart. A stern sense of duty makes him dictative at times, but when he gets this attitude we all know that he rates it. His character blends into one that will make him a good officer.*

Brodie's early Navy experience was service aboard two cruisers, three destroyers, the carrier USS *Saratoga* CV-3 and finally another destroyer, the USS *Cushing*. He was awarded his first command in 1942 when he was selected to captain the USS *Dallas* DD-199. Under Brodie, the *Dallas'* mission was to escort coastal shipping along America's eastern shores, Bermuda, Cuba, and the Caribbean. The Kentucky native went on to win the Navy Cross medal during the invasion of Africa. The citation read,

> *The President of the United States takes pride in presenting the Navy Cross to Robert J Brodie, Jr., Lieutenant Commander, U.S. Navy (Reserve), for extraordinary heroism and distinguished service in the line of his profession as Commanding Officer of the Destroyer U.S.S. DALLAS (DD-199), in action against hostile forces during the occupation of Port Lyautey, French Morocco, on 10 November, 1942. In a remarkable demonstration of seamanship and resourcefulness, Lieutenant Commander Brodie, proceeding with a detachment of raider troops across a treacherous bar through a heavy surf, entered the shallow Sebou River and by breaking a steel cable boom with the*

bow of his ship, forced his way, often literally ploughing through mud, ten miles up the river where he landed the raider troops at Port Lyautey airfield.

The raider detachment met up with a battalion of the US Army's 2nd Armored Division. By mid-morning the raiders had captured an airfield and P-40 *Warhawk* fighter planes from the escort carrier USS *Chenango* were able to land.

Brodie's second command was the newly commissioned destroyer USS *Ordronaux* DD-617 in 1943. This destroyer was involved in the invasion of Italy as well as patrolling harbors to prevent against attacks by Axis torpedo boats and submarines. After several convoy missions across the Atlantic, Brodie was relieved in January of 1944. His next assignment came in February when he was selected to captain the USS *Haynsworth*.

Brodie's second in command was Lieutenant Commander Scott Lothrop, United States Naval Academy Class of 1940. The *Haynsworth's* Executive Officer had served as the navigator while a lieutenant aboard the USS *Tarbell* DD-142. The old World War I era destroyer had been brought out of mothballs and recommissioned to serve as an escort to convoys crossing the Atlantic with needed weapons and materials for the Allied forces in Europe. Between assignments, Lothrop attended courses for his time leading the efforts in the CIC.

Gunnery officer Lieutenant Armistead "Army" Dennett reported for duty at the Office of the Naval District at Church Street in Manhattan in May. According to his peers at Annapolis, "Army is a deepwater man from Maine; he would rather sail than sleep. Since salt water was already long running in his veins, *Youngster Cruise* brought no new experience to this 'down-easter.' Years of boat handling and sailing had already given him his sea-legs."

With war looming, Dennett's graduation at Annapolis had been accelerated. Scheduled to originally graduate in the spring of 1942, the class received their commissions on December 19th, 1941, less than two weeks after the Pearl Harbor attack. At graduation he already had orders in hand to report to the destroyer USS *Benson* DD-421. This destroyer had already been in commission for two years before Dennett came aboard. She routinely patrolled the Atlantic and protected convoys of merchant ships from German U-Boat submarines. In 1943 she fought during the invasion of Italy and shot down an attacking Ger-

Left: Adm. Robert Brodie, postwar.
Center: Lt. Cdr. Scott Lothrop. (Courtesy of Cdr. Peter Lothrop, USN)
Right: Lt. Armistead "Army" Dennett, Gunnery Officer.

man fighter plane. At the time he left the *Benson*, Dennett had already sailed the Atlantic, the Mediterranean Sea, and the Panama Canal. His next mission would be to the Pacific where an entirely different form of enemy waited.

The Communications Officer was Lt. Robert P. Eshelman. Born in Ohio in 1916, Eshelman had just graduated from law school and joined the Naval Reserve when the Japanese attacked Pearl Harbor. As an ensign, he was assigned to the destroyer USS *Ordronaux*. By the time Eshelman came aboard the *Haynsworth* he was a veteran whose ship had shot down German fighters, escorted numerous convoys across the cold Atlantic and the Mediterranean Sea. Along with a group of other destroyers, the German U-boat 856 was spotted by the *Ordronaux* off Nova Scotia. After being forced to surface, the submarine was rammed by another destroyer. *Ordronaux* picked up many of the twenty eight survivors. It was his experiences and his abilities that had Brodie request Eshelman serve aboard his next command.

Lt. Leon Berk served as the ship's navigator. Berk, unlike the regular Navy Annapolis graduates, was a member of the Naval Reserve. Lt. Sidwell Smith was a young 23 year old Naval Reservist from Illinois.

In peacetime, a destroyer's company did not usually include doctors. But in time of war with the expectation of casualties in the fight against Japan, the U.S. Navy sent doctors to sea aboard the tin cans. Lt. jg. Allyn Bryson Ley (pronounced "lie") was fresh from his internship when he received orders to report to the USS *Haynsworth* as its medical officer. A graduate of the 1942 Columbia University College

*Newlyweds Lt. jg. Allyn
and Sydney Ley, 1944.
(Courtesy of the Ley Family)*

of Physicians, Ley was like many of his peers. With a war going on, they joined either the Army or the Navy. In February, 1944, he reported to the Federal Shipyard in Kearney. There Ley found just the keel laid on the ways. With time on his hands, Ley worked at the Brooklyn Naval Hospital "polishing my developing surgical skills."

While the majority of the destroyer's crew trained together in Virginia, a small nucleus of DD-700's crew was already in Kearney, New Jersey, during the construction of the new warship. Some, like Machinists Mate First Class Leon Kosloski, stayed at the St. Francis Hotel in nearby Newark, NJ. Gus Scutari FC1c reported for duty early in 1944. Since the *Haynsworth* was still being built, Cdr. Brodie asked the young sailor if he had family in the area. "Yes, sir!" responded Scutari. "Brooklyn, sir." The captain replied, "Good. Go see them every day and return to your ship every night."

Officers like Lt. Armistead Dennett had better billets. Without family in the immediate area, Dennett found a hotel room in Manhattan. Each day buses would arrive in Times Square to bring sailors over to Federal Drydock & Shipbuilding in Kearney. In the evenings, the Navy Service Club would arrange for officers to attend social events or visit Broadway. Despite the fact America was three years into a war that touched all fabric of American life, the mood in New York was festive according to Dennett.

Over in Kearney, daily roll call was held at 0800 Monday through Friday for the nucleus crew as the destroyer grew from a metal spine to a combat ship.

S HE WAS READY TO SLIDE DOWN THE WAYS by April of '44. An Associated Press account published stated:

DESTROYER ADDITION TO GROWING SEA POWER

*Heavy rain did not hinder the ceremonial launching of the
USS Haynsworth at the Federal Shipbuilding and Dry Dock*

Company at Kearney, N.J, April 15. Above, dock yard workers wave from the deck of the vessel as it goes down the ways following the christening in honor of the late Commander William McCall Haynsworth, Jr., by his widow, Mrs. Haynsworth, of 1015 L. St., N.W., Washington, D.C. Commander Haynsworth was lost August 23, 1943, when the destroyer Ingraham, which he commanded, sank following a collision in the North Atlantic while on convoy duty.

Launching April 20, 1944.

PHALANX AGAINST THE DIVINE WIND

Left: Mrs. Haynsworth christens the destroyer.
Right, Sponsor's party: First row, left to right: Lt. jg. Ann Heron White; Mrs.
Haynsworth, sponsor; Mrs. Walter C. White, and Ensign Mary Greenlead
White. Back Row: Stanley Williams Lenard, Walter H. White, A.S.., USNR,
and Donald Leroy Haynsworth. (Official US Navy Photo 80-G-385232)

Though the *Haynsworth* was nearly complete in early June of 1944, she had not been accepted by the Navy. Unfortunately a design flaw was discovered in earlier *Sumners*: the bridge was so low that it was difficult to see over the dual 5" cannon mount directly in front of it plus there were no decking off the bridge for the lookouts. By raising the bridge by eighteen inches and adding 'wings' to the pilothouse, it was easier for the crew and officers manning the bridge to see what was happening around them. Though he was not yet officially the Captain of the vessel, Brodie brought the destroyer over to the Brooklyn Naval Yard for the bridge retrofit. Gus Scutari FC1c recalled that, "we were

Courtesy of Mrs. Ralph Aakhus

sailing into the Naval Yard but technically we were not a Navy ship at that point."

The threat from enemy air power was countered with the addition of more guns. While at the Brooklyn Naval Yard, DD-700 had two sets of twin 40mm guns mounted behind the rebuilt bridge and ahead of the forward smokestack. These particular sets of guns would find themselves in the crosshairs of two kamikaze pilots in the months to come.

Brodie's ship had most of the modifications he requested completed ahead of schedule except for one. It was known that the additional armament of the new *Sumners* versus the previous *Fletcher* class would increase the weight of the ship. This additional tonnage shortened the cruising range. The Bureau of Ships had already made plans for a long-hulled *Sumner* to be built. The simple solution for the next generation of destroyers was to extend the destroyer fourteen feet amidships to hold extra fuel tanks to increase the range at sea. *Haynsworth* lore has it that the Bureau of Ships denied Brodie his request to have his ship cut in half and have the extra tanks installed. The need for destroyers and space at the Naval Yard were too great to consider slicing up a brand new destroyer.

The destroyer was dwarfed in her berth by her neighbor, the Navy's newest battleship, USS *Missouri* BB-63. The battle wagon's displacement at 52,000 tons was twenty times that of the destroyer. Both would serve together under Admiral "Bull" Halsey's command.

Just two weeks had elapsed since D-Day in Europe by the time the *Haynsworth* was finally commissioned on Thursday, June 22, 1944 at the Brooklyn Naval Yard. Her crew was comprised of 336 sailors and officers. Though some crew members were already in place, Seaman First John McAllister and majority of the new crew had just recently arrived at the Brooklyn Naval Yard from Destroyer Training at Norfolk.

While the Navy had pressing needs for its latest destroyer, the crew members also had needs of their own. Newlywed Seaman Second Class Bill Morton was late arriving back to Norfolk after his honeymoon. Returning five hours late to Norfolk earned him nine days restriction to post by his new Executive Officer, Lt. Cdr. Scott Lothrop. When they arrived in New York a few days later, Lothrop lifted the restriction so Mr. Morton could ensure the new Mrs. Morton was able to attend the ship's commissioning.

Also, on hand for the ceremony were representatives of the Navy, the new crew, family members, and invited guests, including Russian Princess Xenia Georgievna. Captain H. V. McKirttrick of the Third Naval District made his remarks to the gathered guests and crew:

> *Captain Brodie, Officers and men of the U.S.S. HAYNSWORTH: "It gives me much pleasure to be the representative of the Commandant today, and to take part in the commissioning of your fine ship for active fighting service. The news from the Pacific today of great damage to the Japanese fleet is enough to stir our imaginations. I am sure that you all are happy on this occasion-and proud too – proud of this fighting ship which you are the first crew to man. And you are prouder still that your ship will carry you into the battle line of our enemies – and you should be, for you are the fighting men of a fighting Navy.*

Your ship is a marvel of workmanship – the all American product of everything that is known about modern Naval warfare. The best of our country has been put into its construction – brain and brawn and material, in order that the HAYNSWORTH might be a masterpiece. Certainly no finer destroyer has been built, none more powerfully armed with offensive fighting punch.

But splendid man-of-war as she is – without help she is no fighter. You officers and men, as her crew, must make her that. The Navy expects each one of you individually and all of you together as a tightly-organized, well-trained combat crew to get the most out of your ship. You must lose no moment in mastering assigned duties, and getting yourselves geared to each other as a team. In this ship you have been given the best means to strike the enemy hard and swiftly; but you officers and men, as its fighting crew must supply the initiative, courage and cool determination that will allow your ship to deliver its fighting punch built into her.

Your Commanding Officer has already demonstrated his ability in this respect, so in that you are doubly fortunate.

Your ship is named in honor of Commander William McCall Haynsworth, Jr., U.S.N. He lost his life in 1942, when the destroyer he commanded sank following a collision in the North Atlantic while on convoy duty. "I am confident that you officers and men will do honor to his name to the United States Navy. "On behalf of the Commander in Chief, I welcome you to the Fleet and to active service. The best of luck and God's blessings to you all.

The future crew stood in orderly ranks pierside during the ceremony. Though there were many veterans, many of the crewmen were teenagers fresh to the Navy. It was considered that duty aboard a new warship was good duty. When Cdr. Brodie gave the order, "Set the watch," the crew rushed aboard. As the first crew on a newly commissioned ship, each sailor would forever own the title "plank owner." Though not an official Navy rank, the designation as a plank owner would be a label of pride for the crew. Nick Zeoli, RdM2c, recalled his experience coming aboard the new heavy cruiser, USS *Boston*, in 1943. "She was a brand new ship. I wanted to be the first guy of the crew to be aboard her. Would have been, too, except some big guy knocked me down. He was first, I was second aboard. I really wanted to be first."

The Commissioning Pennant was raised on the mast. The new crew stood assembled on the Main Deck. After Cdr. Brodie ordered "set the colors" the National Colors were raised on the mast, the union jack on the bow, the ensign on the stern.

From this point forward, the *Haynsworth* was on her path to war with Destroyer Squadron 62 and the Fast Carrier Task Force.

Left: Haynsworth, July 1944. (National Archives 80-G Collection)
Right: Forward 5-inch mount of Haynsworth. (Courtesy of Gus Scutari)

WARSHIP. The *Haynsworth*, like her all of her destroyer sisters, was the greyhound of the ocean. She could make 36.5 knots, the equivalent of 42 miles per hour. Her General Electric Turbines generated 60,000 shaft horsepower while twin rudders allowed her to turn tighter than the single rudder *Fletcher* class. This tremendous speed and high maneuverability allowed her to shepherd and protect the U.S. Navy's fast carrier groups. Crashed pilots and lost sailors bobbing on Pacific swells would come to appreciate these capabilities as well.

Armament aboard a destroyer was both offensive and defensive in design. The captain could call upon the three dual mounted 5"/38 caliber guns. These guns had a range of ten miles as well as a maximum ceiling of 37,200 feet. They were effective against shore, surface and air targets. Two sets of dual cannons were mounted forward while the third dual mount was aft. In the anti-aircraft mode, their bores belched shells capable of exploding when a plane was near. Other types of

Left: Haynsworth's twin depth charge racks on the stern, NY, 1944. (National Archives 80-G Collection)
Right: Mk.6 Depth Charge Cannon. (Courtesy USS Slater/Tim Rizzuto)

rounds were available for bombardment, illumination, and smokescreens.

Against submarines, destroyers could drop Mark IX depth charges or *ash cans* as they were commonly known. The wallop was provided by 200 pounds of explosive. Two gravity fed depth charge racks, one starboard side, the other port side, were mounted on the stern. Additionally, depth charges could be projected over the sides of the ship by the K-Guns. Mounted in two groups of three K-guns, a destroyer could place eight depth charges in a U shaped pattern against enemy subs, all detonating at a pre-determined depth.

Anti-aircraft protection included a dozen 40mm Bofors divided between two quad mounts and two twin mounts. Eleven 20mm Oerlikon machine guns were scattered across the destroyer. These crew served weapons were capable of firing over 120 rounds per minute.

In two sets of quintuple racks, *Sumner class* destroyers carried a total of ten 21" torpedoes. Each pivoting rack was mounted on top of the deck house, each aft of the two smokestacks.

But, a destroyer was more than just groups of weapons aboard a ship. In a 'Welcome on Board' pamphlet it stated, "The USS *Brush* is devoid of superfluous gear. Every available foot of deck or storage space serves some useful purpose." Packed within the *Sumner* class destroyers were machines ranging from scuttlebutts (water fountains) to

*John Magliocchetti S1c USS Haynsworth,
positioned on quad 40mm gun mount.*

*Magliochetti at a 20mm Gun station.
(Photos courtesy Marianna Steele)*

giant boilers. The amount of machinery on the vessel could fill an entire football field. High pressure tanks, blowers, fuel oil tanks, oil service pumps, lube oil purifiers, distillate condenser coolers, fuel oil heaters, water tanks, evaporators, electric radiators, steam radiators, steam air ejectors, radar, sonar, soot blowers, galley stoves and mixers, cannon shell hoists, radio transmitters, multiple Silex coffee makers, and much more. Storage space was filled with oil, water, food stores, ammunition, powder, repair supplies, anchor chains, and other items to keep the 336 man crew fed and ready for battle.

USS Dunlap DD-384 fires a practice torpedo, 1942 (NARA 80-G-418432)

Collision with another ship or fixed object. Explosion from an enemy weapon. Internal explosion. Weather damage. All of these situations could puncture the thin metal skin of a destroyer's hull. In-rushing water could cause the ship to lose stability, buoyancy, and the ability to maneuver. With this in mind, destroyers were designed so that if an outward compartment was punctured, the inward compartment would take over as the role of 'skin' for the ship. With compartments sealed off, as required during General Quarters, buoyancy could be maintained.

Destroyers were adept in many roles. They would shepherd convoys of slower moving vessels, both merchant and Navy. The twin rudders coupled with the speed of its engines allowed the *Sumners* to move quickly and nimbly when threats were detected. Radar and sonar allowed the *Sumners* to track subs at great range. Enemy submarines were deadly but slow. Being able to travel on the surface at around fifteen knots and less than ten knots submerged, subs were at a disadvantage when being hunted by destroyers and their little brothers, destroyer escorts.

In combat, the large capital ships, especially the aircraft carriers, would not stop to pick up a downed pilot, a man swept overboard, or anything else that would delay their mission or put them at risk for attack. Their fleet guards were the destroyers who were usually at the perimeter of the task group. If sonar detected a contact underwater, it was the destroyer whose job it was to locate and sink any submarine. If a pilot's plane crashed in the water or a man was lost overboard from any of the ships then it was the destroyers who would come to the res-

PHALANX AGAINST THE DIVINE WIND

cue. The tin cans' agility and ability were proven time and time again in the Pacific.

THE SOUL OF THE WARSHIP WAS NOT MADE OF ALUMINUM, STEEL OR CABLE. "Our crew, while young, was well-trained with a good sprinkling of the officers and petty officers drawn from war-experienced crews of other ships," boasted the Executive Officer. "Three and a half years of World War II had brought the US Navy from the debacle of Pearl Harbor to a ready, determined force of men and ships, Regulars and Reserves alike."

Phil Goldstein GM2c on 20mm gun. (Courtesy of Gus Scutari)

A. C. Pickens FC1c. (Courtesy of A. C. Pickens)

Raymond Techman, Baker Third Class. (Courtesy of Gus Scutari)

Seaman Henry Michalak. (Courtesy of Capt. Hank Domeracki USN)

Many of the crew didn't have high school diplomas. Coming out of the great depression and with the need for labor during the war, many young men left school to help put bread on the table for their families. "Doesn't mean they were stupid," stated radarman Nick Zeoli, "just means they weren't educated."

Though many of the enlisted crew were teenagers, some were 'older.' Gunners Mate Second Class Phil Goldstein married his high school sweetheart by 1940. With the war creating manufacturing jobs, Goldstein worked for Brewster Aviation on Long Island. The young man labored to manufacture airplane parts until he joined the Navy in 1943.

Seaman First Class Angelo Lizzari, hailing from Vermont, was a thirty seven year old married man with two kids. A baker in civilian life, the Navy saw fit to assign Lizzari to the deck crew.

Fireman Arthus Clarence "A.C." Pickens already had a family and worked in construction before he finally made the decision to join the Navy in 1944. At 26 years of age, he was an 'old man.' He wasn't alone in that age bracket as the petty officers were older than the newest sailors. Even then, A.C. was older than the majority of the officers aboard. He was often solicited for advice about the fairer sex by his younger peers.

The Communications Officer, Robert Eshelman, wasn't the only man aboard that Cdr. Brodie had transferred from his USS *Ordronaux* command to his newest command. Knowing a well fed crew was a happy crew, Brodie had Baker Third Class Ray Techman transferred to the *Haynsworth*. "His pies kept me alive," recalled Gunners Mate Phil Goldstein.

Two Navy Cross medal recipients were aboard the new destroyer. In addition to Cdr. Brodie, there was an experienced electrician's mate who not only had been in the war since the beginning but had also earned the Navy's second highest award for valor during combat for actions taken before the war was declared officially. Stationed at Pearl Harbor on the morning of December 7, 1941, John "Jack" Vaessen was in the bowels of his ship when the Japanese arrived early on that Sunday morning:

> *The President of the United States takes pleasure in presenting the Navy Cross to John Barth Vaessen, Fireman Second Class, U.S. Navy (Reserve), for exceptional courage, presence of mind, and devotion to duty and disregard for his personal safety while serving on board the Target Ship U.S.S. UTAH (AG-16), during the Japanese attack on the United States Pacific Fleet in Pearl Harbor, Territory of Hawaii, on 7 December 1941. Although realizing that his ship, the U.S.S. UTAH, was capsizing, Fireman Second Class Vaessen remained at his post at the for-*

ward distribution board after word had been passed to abandon ship, and kept the lights burning as long as possible. Trapped, he later was rescued through a hole cut in the bottom of the capsized target ship. The conduct of Fireman Second Class Vaessen throughout this action reflects great credit upon himself, and was in keeping with the highest traditions of the United States Naval Service.

Vaessen would have to perform some of the same actions a few months later while off the coast of Okinawa.

Another veteran of nearly the entire war, Arthur A. Goyer of up-state New York had volunteered just weeks after the Pearl Harbor attack. Having joining the Navy at the Boston Reception Station, he served on a variety of ships as a seaman before being trained as a radioman.

The plank owners included Seaman Henry Michalak. Hank, as he was known to his friends, "was a sailor's sailor. He liked to drink, loved beautiful women, had a tattoo, and didn't mind getting into fights."

Tom Scott recalled initially that, "It took quite a while from being assigned to the *Haynsworth* to being part of a crew, and the fact that the ship was not finished for weeks yielded little sense of being a crew." Days at sea and battles to come would forge the bonds of being a crew, bonds of comradery that would last a lifetime.

SEA TRIALS

USS Haynsworth, New York Harbor, 1944.
(National Archives 80-G Collection)

S HE WAS COMMISSIONED BUT WAS NOT YET READY
FOR WAR. The *Haynsworth* remained at the New York Naval
Yard for repairs and alterations for a month before she became a lethal
threat on July 23 when her full allowance of ammunition and pyro-
technics was loaded aboard while moored at Gravesend Bay, New
York.

Unlike a cargo ship with a central hold, bringing ammunition and
supplies aboard a destroyer required manual labor as just about all
supplies were moved by hand. While at Gravesend, Third Class Fire
Controlman Gus Scutari was perched on the top rung of a ladder to
pass 5" cannon shells. With his body poking through the hatch, he
passed the lethal ordnance to the next sailor down the ladder. One of
the fifty four pound shells slipped from the sailor's hands during the
exchange. The eyes of the sailors below widened, their heart rates accelerated as the shell rolled sideways down the ladder, clanging off each
step, until it bounced off the deck. Though supposedly inert without a
fuse, nonetheless the young sailors breathed a sigh of relief when the
impact did not cause an explosion.

Before the *Haynsworth* could start it sea trials, its magnetic signature had to be erased. After replenishment, the *Haynsworth* crossed the
Harbor of New York to the deperming station at Bayonne, New Jersey. Sailing between two docks, the destroyer was encircled by heavy

USS Haynsworth Division Inspection.
(Courtesy of Bill Vassey)

copper cables. High electrical pulses were transmitted through the cables to "deperm" the ship. The simple procedure provided a degree of safety against mines.

Fire belched from her guns for the first time on July 26th, a day before she started her shakedown cruise to Bermuda. Along the way she practiced anti-submarine runs with the Destroyer Escort USS *Maurice J. Manuel* against the Italian submarine *Goffredo Mameli*, one of a number of Italian Royal Navy pigboats sent to Bermuda after the armistice to assist in destroyer training. DD-700 finally moored in Bermuda on the last day in July of 1944.

For most of August, the *Haynsworth* trained in the Bermuda area with other destroyers including sister ship USS *Ault* DD-698. A destroyer tender there provided repairs and upgrades as needed. Harbored in the lagoon on the west side of the island, the destroyers departed each morning for training. Anti-submarine drills were run against another Italian submarine, the *Enrico Dandalo*. Practice torpedoes were launched, shore bombardments exercises with the 5" guns were held, smoke screens were created, tactical maneuvering with other ships practiced, battle problems were solved, night illumination rounds fired, rescues at sea drills run, and anti-aircraft drills held. Inspections, inspections, and inspections were the norm for the new crew.

Testing the rivets during depth charge practice off Bermuda, September 1944 (Left, Bill Morton Collection; right, courtesy of Gus Scutari.)

Depth charges were dropped not only as practice for anti-submarine warfare but also to check for hull integrity in the newly constructed ship. After an initial dropping of charges followed by pulsing concussions, a voice from below came over the sound powered phones. "Hey, we're sinking!" A few less than water tight areas received repair from the tender when they returned to Bermuda.

The klaxon's call was a constant refrain. Cdr. Brodie kept his warship at maximum offensive capability with the frequent calls to General Quarters. When called to GQ, sailors would drop what they were doing and hustle to their assigned battle stations. All weapons were manned and the number of sailors on watch was increased. Each sailor had to know instinctively what to do and where to go when GQ was sounded. They would remain at their battle stations until the command "all clear" was signaled. The calls to GQ would be frequent during the battles of the Pacific.

In addition to the attack drills, defensive tactics were practiced frequently. Damage control teams responded to the calls for damage repair. Paramount for the safety of the ship was ensuring watertight integrity, maintaining firefighting capabilities, and providing assistance to wounded personnel.

Damage control teams and equipment lockers were located in various areas of the ship. By staggering the teams and equipment locations, a redundancy was built into the system. A catastrophic event in one part of the ship could not eliminate the capabilities of repairing damage, saving the wounded, or battling fire. The repair parties were organized such that every area of the ship was protected by specific teams. The men performing damage control were trained to not only to use their equipment but to also understand the various systems of the ship they might encounter during their repair efforts. The frequent drills required by the *Haynsworth's* captain would be justified a few months later when the destroyer entered the fray in the Pacific.

Lt. jg. Ley's shipboard medical department was small but well stocked. With an apothecary cabinet similar to one found in a traditional pharmacy, a folding surgical table, an autoclave, and running water, Dr. Ley provided medical care for the 336 sailors and officers of the *Haynsworth*. This infirmary was located in the deck house between the two smokestacks with daily sick call at 0900 hours. Ley could also employ the officer's wardroom as an Emergency Dressing Station area. It had a folding surgical table with operating room style lights in the ceiling. Other emergency battle dressing stations were positioned aft in the deck house and in the mess hall forward. The medical department was rounded out by the three pharmacist mates aboard the *Haynsworth*, Arthur Bland PhM1c, James K. Jones Jr. PhM3c, and Norton E. Kessler PhM3c.

Emergency medical supplies were stored in various areas. The dispersal of duplicate medical supplies in several compartments was established so that in the case of battle damage, treatment supplies were available. Additional medical support was provided at sea by the larger ships that were to be part of the Pacific task forces that *Haynsworth* would join. The carriers and the battleships had advanced shipboard medical facilities with additional physicians, surgeons, and dentists aboard. Numerous sailors were highlined by the tin can to larger vessels when the medical needs of the sailor outstripped the care available by Dr. Ley and his team.

Sick bay.

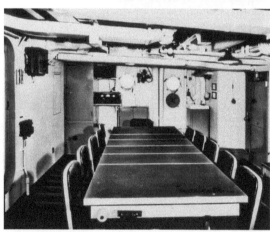

Officers Ward Room (Both courtesy of NavSource)

The time in Bermuda wasn't all training: "The pressure of hard shakedown cruising work was at intervals eased by good liberty, riding in horse drawn cabs and on bicycles, touristing up to the straw hill-shanties, trying to understand the native dialect, giving the children shiny new pennies and dimes."

The Destroyer Squadron (DesRon) 62 commander, Captain John M. Higgins, hauled his pennant down from his flagship, the USS *Ault*, when he transferred to the *Haynsworth* on August 5th. They finally returned to the New York Naval Yard on August 31st. Many of her crew were able to take leave and travel home for a few days. For most, it would be their last leave in the United States until after the battles of the Pacific were waged.

The first three weeks of September were spent preparing the USS *Haynsworth* for her first cruise. She was re-provisioned, repairs finished, ammunition restocked, and deperming completed. Additional crew members reported aboard on September 3rd including Radiomen Third Class Joseph Wilkerson and Donald Ward. The *Haynsworth* spent a few days off Long Island practicing anti-submarine warfare with the former Vichy French submarine *Argo*.

And, on September 20th, it was finally time for the *Haynsworth* to join the war.

DESTROYERS AND GOLIATH:
BATTLE OFF SAMAR ISLAND

USS Gambier Bay, CVE-73, and other warships
making smoke during the Battle of Samar.
(U.S. Navy Photo, U.S. Navy National Museum of Naval Aviation)

UNDETECTED, THE POWERFUL ENEMY CAVALCADE STEAMED EAST during the early morning hours of October 25th. The Japanese Center Force passed through the San Bernardino Strait into the Philippine Sea in its mission to attack and destroy the American landing forces. The battleship *Yamato,* along with three other battleships, six heavy cruisers, two light cruisers and eleven destroyers headed south along Samar Island. Fortune appeared to smile brightly on the Japanese Center Force.

As part of a plan to destroy the American invasion forces of the 7th Fleet, several Japanese task forces were sent simultaneously against Task Force 38. A diversionary group of Japanese carriers lurked near Luzon as a feint north of the American Third Fleet. Admiral William "Bull" Halsey felt he had little choice but to send his carriers to meet the threat but this decision caused the invasion force of smaller ships to

       PHALANX AGAINST THE DIVINE WIND

Tin cans lay a smoke screen while under fire.
(U.S. Navy Photo, U.S. Navy National Museum of Naval Aviation)

be left vulnerable without the fleet carriers to provide aerial protection.

The previous day Vice Admiral Takeo Kurita's attack force had been discovered in the Sibuyan Sea by American planes. The *Musashi*, sister ship of the mighty *Yamato*, was attacked repeatedly over several hours by fighters, dive bombers, and torpedo planes from the American carriers. The superbattleship absorbed nineteen torpedoes and seventeen bombs before finally succumbing to the damage inflicted from the air. Six hours after the attack began, the *Musashi* capsized and sank.

The next morning, believing that the Japanese attack force had been routed and was in retreat, Halsey took the bait. He sent his carriers north. He did not know that the Japanese carriers were mostly empty of pilots and planes. He had fallen into Vice-Admiral Takeo Kurita's trap.

Patrolling east of Samar was one of the American task units of the 7th Fleet. Task Unit 77.4.3, referred to as "*Taffy 3*," was a collection of six small escort carriers, three destroyers, and four destroyer escorts. They were one of three *Taffys* on station.

During a routine anti-submarine flight from the USS *St. Lo* CVE-63, a shocked American pilot discovered Kurita's forces just twenty miles from Taffy 3. At that point the American ships were already within reach of the guns of the battleships. Around 0700 *Yamato* fired her massive 18" cannon at the small group of American ships. The klaxons bellowed out the call to general quarters across the task unit's ships. Outgunned, Admiral Clifton Sprague turned his forces away from the enemy. Orders were given to get all planes in the air from the CVEs as the group headed towards rain squalls as cover.

Sprague's carriers were barely capable of twenty knots. They lacked armor, and carried little offensive punch in the way of cannon. The offense and defense for the CVEs was to launch their planes against the mighty IJN ships. Their mission: strafe the gunners and the command bridges of the mighty enemy force.

The American destroyers were quick but without armor. Their 5"/38 cannon and torpedoes had a range much less than the shells from the guns of the enemy battleships and cruisers. The destroyer escorts were slower, carried less cannon and torpedoes and were smaller than their bigger brother destroyers.

Like a small dog going after the throat of a large dog, Sprague's group would have to close with the enemy to give the vulnerable CVEs a chance to escape. The DDs and DEs of Taffy 3 made smoke to hide the carriers from the Japanese forces.

The last stand of the small American warships began. At the extreme range of their 5" cannon, USS *Johnston* DD-557 began its attack against the mightier enemy. Her guns bracketed the IJN cruiser *Kumano*. Forty five rounds hit their mark as fire emerged from the superstructure. Launching its torpedoes from extreme range, the *Johnston's* pressed attack caused the bow of *Kumano* to be blown off and the battleship *Kongo* to take evasive maneuvers. It was not a one sided fight. *Johnston* was hit by numerous shells including some 6" rounds from the *Yamato*. Despite the massive damage to the tin can, severe injuries to the captain, and many wounded and killed sailors, *Johnston* stayed in the fight.

Three other US destroyers and destroyer escorts-*Hoel, Heermann,* and *Samuel B. Roberts*-initiated an attack run against the Japanese force. They were joined by the wounded *Johnston.* By 0750 the air was filled by American planes from all three *Taffys* making attack runs against the larger enemy forces. Confusion reigned across the ocean battlefield with the rain squalls, smokescreens, and the aggressive assaults of American planes and destroyers. Thousands of 5" shells belched from their cannons. Many scored hits against the superstructures of several Japanese warships. Their torpedoes forced the Japanese to repeatedly change course but many still found their mark. Even the mighty *Yamato*, which had managed to score hits on the American ships, was forced to move away from the fight by their presence thus taking the attacking commander away from the scene of the battle.

Unfortunately for *Taffy 3*, the Japanese guns could still reach them. The destroyers *Johnston* and *Hoel* were eventually sunk as was the destroyer escort *Samuel B. Roberts*. The remaining DDs and DEs also absorbed hits from the Japanese force. Kurita's cruisers found their mark and sank the escort carrier *Gambier Bay*.

But, with concern of potential air attacks from the Fast Carrier Task Force, Kurita broke off the attack at 0920 and withdrew his forces, unaware that Halsey had moved his fleet carriers to the north. The Japanese forces had sustained great damage from *Taffy 3's* combined sea and air attacks. Three of its heavy cruisers were either sunk or crippled.

The *Yamato*, with the loss of the *Musashi* the previous day, was the largest battleship left afloat in the world. Despite her guns sinking the *Gambier Bay*, *Samuel B. Roberts*, and *Hoel*, the battleship was held at bay by pressed torpedo attacks and strafing runs on the bridge by the American fliers. Her combined weight and gun capabilities were more than equal to all of *Taffy 3*. Yet, *Yamato's* impact on the battle was not what had been envisioned by either her designers or her commanders.

As a portent of things to come, not long after the battle ended, the remaining escort carriers were attacked by the first coordinated kamikaze attack of the war. The exhilaration of escape from the mighty battleships and cruisers of the IJN was short lived. Less than two hours later *St. Lo* was sunk and five other CVEs of Task Group 77.4 were damaged. The battle off Samar had ended but the battle against the *Divine Wind* had begun. It was a battle that would last for another eight months. The *Divine Wind's* eventual toll would be more than 400 United States Navy ships damaged or sunk. The destroyers, like any forward scouting patrol, absorbed the brunt of attacks from the air so that the carriers' missions could continue. For the small boys, theirs was a mission of service and sacrifice.

In less than six months, the destroyers of Squadron 62 would be subject to a combined attack by the *Yamato* and the *Divine Wind*s.

PLANK OWNERS: FIRST MISSION

USS Haynsworth, 1944.
(Courtesy of NavSource)

LOOKOUTS SCANNED THE SEAS AND THE HEAVENS. The radar reached into the skies for telltale signs of long range bombers. Sonar sent its acoustic waves beneath the ocean hunting for metal reflections. Gun crews were at the ready. Between New York and England lay three thousand miles of ocean still regularly visited and hunted by German U-Boats. Though the success of the *Kriegsmarine* had waned as America sent more destroyers, destroyer escorts and small aircraft carriers into the Atlantic, none the less, in 1944 U-Boats were still a potent threat to Allied shipping. Two of these underwater killers had been sunk earlier in the year off America and Canada. Hitler and his submarine chief, Karl Dönitz, continued to have submarines built as fast as possible. Early in the war, German subs had patrolled and attacked the American coastline with near impunity. The fanatical fuehrer believed that this could be accomplished again with improved submarines.

RMS Queen Mary as troopship in World War II in New York Harbor.
(NARA 80-GK-5645)

The two most powerful men in the free world, Winston Churchill and President Franklin D. Roosevelt, had finished a five day meeting in Quebec on September 16th. The *Octagon Conference* was the second joint meeting held by the two heads of state in Quebec. By the conclusion of the conference, Churchill and Roosevelt had discussed the fate of Germany post the war. The Lend-Lease Agreements, where America supplied weapons to its allies, would be extended. When Churchill offered a British fleet for service in the Pacific theater, Roosevelt accepted the opportunity to supplement his forces. "We have agreed that the British Fleet should participate in the main operations against Japan in the Pacific, with the understanding that his Fleet will be balanced and self-supporting. The method of the employment of the British Fleet in these main operations in the Pacific will be decided from time to time in accordance with the prevailing circumstances."

When the meetings concluded, Roosevelt returned to Washington DC by train. Churchill also took the train as far as New York City. The rest of his journey would rely on the speed of the RMS *Queen Mary* and its shepherds to get him back safely to England.

FIRST MISSION. By late September of 1944 the *Haynsworth* was ready. Her crew had been assembled, her outfitting completed, and the full complement of fuel, ammunition, food, and supplies were aboard. Her Captain and the Navy had signed off on the final checks of her engineering and ordnance equipment. She was captained by an experienced captain, Commander Robert Brodie. The second in command, Executive Officer Lt. Commander Scott Lothrop, was young but a tested combat veteran. Though most of her crew were new sailors, they were prepared to take their place in the war.

Their inaugural assignment was of paramount importance: On September 20th, 1944 the USS *Haynsworth* was tasked with safely escorting the RMS *Queen Mary* with British Prime Minister Winston Churchill aboard back to England. The luxury liner had been converted to a troopship and was capable of speeds in excess of 30 knots. During her trans-Atlantic journeys, she usually traveled without escort. But, the memory of *Lusitania* nearly thirty years earlier had not been forgotten. The loss of nearly twelve hundred passengers and crew occurred close to shore when a German U-Boat sank her with one torpedo. The sinking helped draw America into World War I. With Churchill, the British's First Lord of the Admiralty in 1915, aboard the *Queen* Mary, no chances were taken that another lucky U-Boat would torpedo her, too.

The Cunard Lines flagship vessel was guarded by a triumvirate of destroyers: USS *Collett* DD-730, USS *Samuel N. Moore* DD-742, and the *Haynsworth*. The group hustled east at 27 knots. At flank speed, the destroyers' range was limited by their voracious appetite for fuel. The American sea guards rendezvoused with their British cousins midday on Thursday, September 21st near Nova Scotia. His Majesty's Royal Navy relieved Task Group 27.7 of escorting the *Queen Mary* back safely to the Great Britain. The American guards turned west back to New York.

WARTIME DUTY HELPED TO FORGE THE BONDS that transformed the *Haynsworth* sailors into a crew, a band of brothers. They would survive a lifetime but the visceral loyalty between the bluejackets was ignited by the *Queen Mary* escort mission. Fire Controlman Third Class Tom Scott recalled, "I think the fire control crew were about half new guys like me and half old salts. Everyone was easy to get along with. One of the First Class and one of the Second Class [fire controlmen] took charge and made assignments. Primarily we worked with each other and made other friendships 'accidentally.' I talked a lot with Ernie Satterly and also with gunner's mates, Charley Costello and Joe Dillon. An electrician's mate also worked in the 'plot' [the guns fire control center] when we were on watch. My partner then was John Friel. Being in the service was no big deal." Scott continued, "When any of us were together, we talked."

The seas along the route to Nova Scotia were much stronger than those routinely encountered near Bermuda. "Most of the crew had not developed their 'sea legs' and so seasickness was rampant," recalled Scott. Some sailors never fully adjusted to life at sea including Marion Parker GM3c. "He was the only man aboard ship that was seasick when in port," remembered his buddy, Phil Goldstein GM3c. The bridge had a simple pendulum gauge to measure how far a ship in high waves rolled to its side. The officers called it by the official name, clinometer. The sailors knew it as the 'puke meter.'

FOLLOWING THE SUCCESSFUL COMPLETION OF HER FIRST MISSION, the *Haynsworth* returned to New York on September 23rd. She berthed at the 35th street pier temporarily until she was to begin her transit to the Pacific. For her crew, it would be their last opportunity for liberty on the east coast until the spring of 1946, a last chance for the bluejackets to carouse in the sights and sounds of the Big Apple.

In the weeks that followed the USS *Haynsworth's* arrival, the nature of war in the Pacific took a deadly new turn.

STORM WINDS GATHER

THE NOOSE WAS TIGHTENING. As the Empire's perimeter was continually shrunk by the allies, it became apparent to the Japanese high command that long range U.S. Boeing B-29 bombers would soon be stationed within bombing distance of the Japanese home islands. As protection for the homeland against future attacks, the Imperial Japanese Navy organized the *Air Group 210* on September 15, 1944. Attached to the 3rd Air Fleet, this large air unit of carrier fighters, interceptors, night fighters, reconnaissance planes, carrier bombers, and carrier torpedo planes was stationed at the Meiji air base in the Aichi Prefecture near Nagoya. Before year's end, this training unit would be called on to defend the homeland islands from air attacks. Come 1945, the *Air Group 210* would fly against the Allied forces invading the Ryukyu Islands as part of the *Divine Wind*.

PACIFIC BOUND

FINALLY BOUND FOR THE PACIFIC, the *Haynsworth* departed Brooklyn on September 25th. The *Collett* was still with her as they steamed to Delaware Bay to join other vessels heading west. Destroyer Squadron 62 sisters USS *Charles S. Sperry* DD-697 and USS *Waldron* DD-699 were in attendance. Task Group 27.3 was rounded out by the cruiser USS *Pasadena* CL-65 and the new battleship, USS *Wisconsin* BB-64.

USS Wisconsin leaving the Philadelphia Naval Shipyard, September 1944.
(U.S. Navy Photo)

The largest battleships ever commissioned by the U.S. Navy were of the *Iowa* class. The *Iowa, New Jersey, Missouri,* and *Wisconsin* were 887 feet long with a 108 foot beam while weighing in at 52,000 tons. Fast and well-armed made them suitable for service with the fleet carriers. They could turn thirty knots, unlike the older Pearl Harbor fleet battleships, while serving as massive cannon platforms, floating fortresses. The main batteries were three turrets of triple mounted 16"/50 caliber guns. Each 16" gun, forged at the Watervliet Arsenal in upstate New York, could hurl a 2,700 lb. shell twenty miles. The secondary batteries were ten twin 5"/38 guns flanking the superstructure. As defense against enemy planes, each warship bristled with eighty 40mm Bofors cannons and forty nine 20mm Oerlikon guns. Their duties included shore bombardment and anti-aircraft protection for the carriers

USS Haynsworth in the Panama Canal, October 12, 1945
(Henry Michalak S1c photos, courtesy of Capt. Hank Domeracki)

and the fleet. But, as the carriers were the queens, two more *Iowa* class battleships keels that had been laid were never completed.

The task group entered the Panama Canal on October 2nd. After passing through the locks near the Port of Cristobal, the task unit headed west. The transit through the forty-eight mile canal took just four and a half hours. Sonarman Bill Morton admitted that he was, "amazed at the engineering of the canal, how narrow it was for the size of the ships passing through and the number of gun emplacements whittled out of the jungle for its protection. The locks were a marvel and some ships were towed through by the 'mules' with inches to spare on either side. I spent most of the transit on the gun director ra-

PHALANX AGAINST THE DIVINE WIND

dar watching it unfold. I could see the remains of the canal abandoned by the French when malaria stopped them.

"My gawking got me the worst sunburn I had in the Navy. In the tropics the sun is closer and the humidity increased the intensity of the ultra violet light." While Morton was enthralled by the geography, Carpenters Mate Second Class Ed Mital was impressed by the large swarms of mosquitoes that descended on the ship as it made the passage.

The first port of call was at Balboa. Moored at Pier #1 Naval Ammunition Depot the group spent two days, "lying off Panama City while the crew had liberty in this city of friendly people and a hundred nationalities, scarce whiskies and rare perfumes." Signalman John Vasquez recalled that they were cautioned not to drink while on liberty. "Since it was just a caution and not a command, very few of us heeded the advice."

Liberty in the Navy was, "an interesting adventure" recalled Bernie Huntoon. "There were 'cathouses' [brothels], tattoo parlors, bars and not much else. Being from rural Vermont I wondered if the American public knew what was here." Keith Myreholt noted in his journal, "Arrived Panama. Made two liberties." From Marion Parker, "We stayed there for three days and I had liberty. Some of the city was beautiful but part of it was the scum of the earth."

Balboa was known as a sailor's town. Sonarmen Bill Morton, Charlie Gruber and Ed Maugel, along with Machinist Mate 'Ole' Olsen hired a cab driver to show them the sights of Panama City. After seeing the Presidential Palace, they were driven past the areas that gave Balboa its reputation: "He took us by the dens of iniquity for which Panama was famous. *The Coconut Grove* (3 Ways $3) and then passed the *House of Love* ($6). It was almost palatial in its pink stucco surrounded by a high, vine-covered stucco wall with an arched entrance. The bar in it was all mirrors and had every race and size girl represented. We didn't stop.

"We finished off the evening when our driver dropped us at sunset in front of the El Rancho, a Latin/American night club situated on the highest point of Panama City overlooking the bay. The moonlight streaming across the little islands dotting the bay made me wish Mae [his wife] was there to enjoy it with me."

Not satisfied to pay for transportation, Torpedoman Third Class Ed Kelly and a buddy stole a car. Apprehension was swift. After their arrest, the two sailors protested to the authorities it had been a misunderstanding. The alibi proffered was that they were simply FBI agents impounding the car of a communist. The ship's brig and a lost stripe awaited them. And liberty for the crew came to an abrupt conclusion.

Before they left Panama, two Army officers and twenty five soldiers came aboard the *Haynsworth* as passengers enroute to the west coast. After staying for several days to take on fuel and supplies, Task Unit 12.9.1 left Balboa. Come October 4th they entered the Pacific Ocean on their way to San Diego and the shooting war in the Pacific. Their wait for action was not long.

ALARM! After a summer of training with French and Italians submarines, excitement was high on October 9th when the *Haynsworth's* sonar caught the echo of an underwater boat. In the early days of the war, Japanese subs had probed the American West coast, sinking merchant freighters, sending reconnaissance planes aloft, or occasionally shelling inland.

With the klaxon's call to General Quarters, sailors scrambled through hatches and across the decks to their battlestations. Chipping and painting came to a halt as the bluejackets donned helmets and lifejackets, ammunition lockers were unlatched as the guns were manned. Extra lookouts scanned the waves for the telltale wake of a periscope and torpedoes. Doors and hatches were 'dogged,' pharmacist mates moved to different battle dressing stations, damage control teams remained at the ready while the torpedo men stood prepared at the tubes and alongside the depth charge racks and guns. The pulse of the warship rose.

Sonarman Bill Morton described the action in the sonar hut:

> On the 4-8 watch at 1625 I picked up contact on what sounded like a school of fish. I kept checking it until I turned it over to "Chollie" Gruber, SoM3c. I asked if he wanted to report it but he said no but after listening for a while I asked Mr. Berk to check it. He said to report it and then investigate it. We lost it on the 14k kilocycle [sonar] stack and picked it up on the 30kc stack at a range of about 1200 yards. It was only 15 degrees off the bow and had a definite submarine echo. General Quarters was sounded and I had to go to the fantail where I was the gun captain on the three twin 20mm guns. We made four runs dropping depth charges each time. The first time was only two charges because the racks jammed. The second time was nine charges and the third and fourth were eleven each. After we dropped the last pattern, screw [propeller] noises were heard but they said it was

the 'foxer gear' [a device to distract sound directed torpedoes which might be fired at the ship] but I was on the fantail and the foxer gear had never been streamed.

Though twenty four depth charges were dropped, no oil slicks, flotsam or other telltale signs of sinking rose to the surface. Stated Vasquez, "With the war waiting for us, we couldn't wait around to see if we had sunk the sub or not."

Depth charge from the Haynsworth goes off. (Courtesy of Gus Scutari)

THEIR LAST LIBERTY IN THE STATES came after the *Haynsworth* was redirected to the port at San Pedro, California. While she was moored to re-provision and take on fuel, many of her crew had just enough time to explore Los Angeles and Hollywood. For the young men that had completed training at Sampson and Norfolk a few months earlier, the chance to investigate and let loose in America's movie capitol, Hollywood, the town made famous by Paramount and Metro Goldwyn Mayer, was an exciting opportunity. In the previous months, the movie industry had released *The Fighting Sullivans*, *Thirty Seconds over Tokyo*, *Going My Way*, and *Laura*. Betty Grable was gracing the screen in *Pin Up Girl*. John Wayne's *The Fighting Seabees* was a popular tale. The seamen were less eager to see Alfred Hitchcock's *Lifeboat*.

Hobart MacLaughlan S1c and John McAllister on liberty in Los Angeles, October 13, 1944. MacLaughlan was killed during the kamikaze attack on April 6, 1945. (McAllister Family Collection)

As small groups of friends ventured through tinsel town, many visited iconic sites. Grauman's Egyptian Theatre and The Chinese Theatre were popular attractions. Some headed to the famous Hollywood Canteen. Founded by actors Bette Davis and John Garfield, the club was frequently staffed by famous Hollywood celebrities. For sailors heading overseas, the price of admission was borne by their blue uniforms. Besides the free food and entertainment, many held the hope they could dance with the likes of Bette Davis, Lauren Bacall or Martha Raye. Recalled John Vasquez, "We didn't get to see any movie stars that day."

For buddies Jack McAllister of New York and Hobie MacLaughlan of Maine, part of the day was spent touring Los Angeles, visiting the local USO, bending an elbow at local taverns. After a day of carousing and fun, two bits bought them a souvenir photo from a booth before it was time to return to their destroyer.

The *Haynsworth* cast her lines two days later en route to Pearl Harbor. For some of the sailors, their final days in the United States had come to an end. They would never make the return voyage to America.

KAMIKAZE: *DIVINE WIND*

A kamikaze just before impact against the USS White Plains CVE-66 on October 25, 1944.

STRANGULATION. Coral Sea. Midway. Guadalcanal. New Guinea. Rabaul. Tarawa. Battle of the Mariana Islands. Island after island, battle after battle, the Japanese military suffered defeat. With each loss, the Empire was cut a little deeper and bled a little more. Its defensive perimeter continued to shrink. American subs were wreaking havoc on commercial shipping of raw resources to the home islands. It had become increasingly difficult for fuel to be obtained for Japan's trucks, planes, and ships. Japan's industrial complex was unable to keep up with the loss of equipment, planes, and ships. The IJA and IJN could not train enough new pilots to replace the thousands lost during the war.

The expansion of the Empire by Japan early in the war was a liability by 1944. Without safe sea lanes, Japanese ships could not reinforce their soldiers and sailors at the far end of the supply lines. Without a large air cargo capability, Japan could not easily bring resources to bear from the air. The military was withering. American strategic planners often bypassed Japanese held islands that held little tactical or strategic value.

Having not won a decisive battle against the American fleet since Pearl Harbor three years earlier, desperation to slow the Allied advance had taken hold of the Japanese military's planning. The military had showed its willingness to put up stubborn defenses without consideration for surrender. On the tiny island of Tarawa in the Gilbert Islands, U.S. Marines fought against an entrenched Japanese garrison for seventy six hours during November of 1943. At the end of the battle, only seventeen of 2,619 IJA soldiers surrendered. The rest were all killed or committed hari-kari to avoid capture.

The American juggernaut could not be slowed down. With each passing month, the American fleets grew larger in size and capability. It was apparent that the Americans would soon return to the Philippines as General Douglas MacArthur promised during March of 1942. Following that invasion, American would invade the large islands Iwo Jima and Okinawa to build bases for long range bombers to attack the Japanese home islands. From these bases the American military would prepare the eventual invasion of Japan.

By summer of 1944, a *Special Attack Corps* or *Tokubetsu Kōgeki tai* was formed. Known as *Kamikazes,* translated as '*Divine Wind*,' these units started as a volunteer group of IJA officer pilot trainees. The IJN units were formed with volunteer pilots. Their formation marked the first organized attempt at training flyers to deliver lethal blows to the enemy that also required the pilot to specifically crash his plane into an enemy ship. Previously pilots whose planes were severely damaged or who had suffered substantial wounds had turned their planes into weapons by crashing into ships. This was not by order but rather the pilot making a spontaneous decision based on the culture of the samurai, *bushido.*

The essence of the kamikaze attack was simple: Pilots would fly planes that were fully fueled and usually armed with a high explosive bomb into navy ships. They were given additional training as to recognize the ships by class. While the IJA planes would target troop and convoy ships, the IJN would put its focus on the American carriers. If a carrier could be struck near the forward deck elevator, it would put the ship out of commission for flying operations. If the attacker's bombs could explode amongst planes on the deck or below in the hangar deck, great fires fueled by aviation gas and weapons could ignite. If a powder magazine below decks could be ignited, the potential

USS Franklin and USS Belleau Wood afire
after kamikaze hits, 30 October 1944.
(NARA 80-G-326798)

for mass devastation was created. Diving from high altitudes, the kamikazes used the advantage of height and speed to crash into ships from the stern.

An advantage that Japan held in the fight against the invasion of the Philippines was their nearly sixty airfields spread across the islands. Luzon, the focus of the invasion, had over two dozen airfields. Many of the IJN pilots had significant combat experience which allowed them to use their flight skills to evade American fighters and anti-aircraft fire.

The operation started officially on October 25, 1944 during the Battle of Leyte Gulf. Within a short time, many American ships fell victim to the pilots of the *Divine Wind*. In the initial period of October 25-30, 1944, two fleet carriers, one light carrier, and seven escort carriers had been struck. Within a few weeks, four more fleet carriers and another light carrier became victims. Additionally numerous other ships had been hit by the kamikazes as well. By the middle of February, 1945, over one hundred fifty American ships had become victims of the kamikazes. Of this group, twenty six had been sunk. While many were smaller merchant and troop ships, larger American warships were still the key targets. Over thirty destroyers, destroyer minesweepers, and destroyer escorts were victims during this period. Foreshadowing the fate of Destroyer Squadron 62, the original ship in the class, USS *Allen M. Sumner* DD-692 was struck on January 6, 1945. Fourteen of her sailors were killed and nineteen were injured.

The payoff for the Japanese military was immediate and tactically important. For the loss of a plane and a pilot, an American fleet carrier with ninety planes could be put out of action. The initial success of the *Tokubetsu Kogeki tai* encouraged the Empire to not only continue their efforts but to also expand the scope of the program. Resources were used to train suicide swimmers, manufacture suicide boats, and build manned torpedoes (*Kaiten*).

There was a tradeoff. While American factories produced hundreds of planes daily, the Japanese were faced with continued declining aviation production. Third Fleet Commander Admiral William Halsey commented on this trade off: "*While planes were expendable, pilots are not. Long before these attacks, it was clear that the quality of Jap pilots was degenerating. We suspected that we had killed off their good ones, deep into the reserves, and the kamikazes confirmed our suspicions...To me, the kamikaze was a weapon not of inspiration, but of desperation-an unmistakable sign that the Japanese war machine was close to collapse.*"

PHALANX AGAINST THE DIVINE WIND

DESTINATION PEARL HARBOR

Maui, October 27, 1944 Navy Day.
(McAllister Family Collection)

"MAN THE RAILS!" The command beckoned the sailors topside as the USS *Haynsworth* steamed into Pearl Harbor on October 20, 1944. The excitement of entering the Navy's center of Pacific Fleet operations replaced the tedium of transit. Noted Bill Morton, "Most of the travel was the monotonous routine of daily ship duty: watches, scrape paint, and pass the time."

Frank Studenski S1c, of the heavy cruiser USS *Boston*, described his own ship's arrival at Pearl: "This morning the coast line of Oahu Island came into view, with Diamond Head standing out above the horizon. On entering Pearl Harbor we passed through torpedo nets that are opened and closed by tugs. This is a beautiful island with high mountains in the background. We passed through the channel into the large bay filled with ships at anchor or tied to piers. Ford Island is on one side and the repair yard is on the other. On our way in signs of the attack could still be seen. The water and shore line was covered with a lot of oil." Studenski related the most visible reminder of the attack against Pearl Harbor: "The Arizona is alongside the pier, on the in-board side, looking over the side we can make out the outline of the hull...A lot of oil is seeping out of the *Arizona*."

Gone from battleship row and the drydocks were the six other battleships damaged during the attack in December 1941. Though it had become a carrier war, the firepower of the battleships was needed, especially in the first critical years of the war.

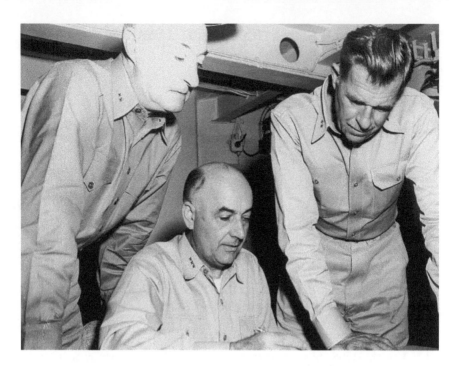

Adm. John Martin Higgins (right) 1950. (NARA 80-G-668791)

On the opposite side of Ford Island, electrician mate Jack Vaessen's USS *Utah* remained capsized, many of its crew forever entombed inside.

The *Haynsworth* moored along the side of her sister *Sumner* destroyer, USS *Charles S. Sperry*, in the Middle Loch of Pearl Harbor. The two destroyers were the latest Destroyer Squadron 62 members to arrive on station.

Composed of nine sequential *Sumner* class 2,200 ton destroyers built by Federal Shipbuilding & Drydock Company, DesRon 62 was divided into two Destroyer Divisions, (DesDiv) 123 & 124. During most of 1945 the destroyers worked as a group screening the Fast Carrier Task Forces of the 3rd and 5th Fleets.

DesDiv 123: Commander John Higgins
DD-696 English
DD-697 Charles S. Sperry
DD-698 Ault
DD-699 Waldron
DD-700 Haynsworth

DesDiv 124: Commander R.M. Smith
DD-701 John W. Weeks
DD-702 Hank
DD-703 Wallace L. Lind
DD-704 Borie

USS Gwin screening USS Hornet on April 18, 1942

The pennant of Commander Destroyer Squadron 62 (ComDesRon 62) flew from the *Ault*. Captain John Martin Higgins, Annapolis class of 1922, commanded the squadron. During the battles of World War II, Captain Higgins had served on numerous ships including battleships and destroyers. At its outbreak, he was the captain of the destroyer USS *Gwin* DD-433, one of several cans that screened the USS *Hornet* during the Doolittle mission in April of 1942.

Coming aboard the USS *Ault* after its commissioning in 1944, Captain Higgins spent the balance of the year training the new *Sumners* destroyers to work as part of a larger group. After each of the destroyers had completed its shakedown cruise and all fitting was completed, it was then sent to Pearl Harbor to join the squadron. *Ault* was the first. The final destroyer to join the DesRon 62 was USS *Borie* on January 26, 1945 at the Ulithi Atoll.

The focus in the Pacific Theater was very different than the Atlantic. Rather than anti-submarine warfare (ASW), the focus was mostly on anti-aircraft drills and protection of the aircraft carriers. "Officers from other ships told us that we had been goofing off in the Atlantic.

'You are in a real war now with kamikazes' we were told," remembered Lt. Armistead Dennett.

Their two month station at Pearl was a period of intense training. The weapons systems were tested, anti-aircraft drills by the gun crews were run repeatedly, and shore bombardment by its 5"/38 caliber guns was practiced. At night 5" starshells were fired for illumination of targets as part of night battle practice. Radar calibration practice was also held while anti-submarine warfare runs were completed along with simulated submarine attacks by a US submarine. Some of the days and nights involved torpedo tracking and firing exercises in coordination with other ships from Pearl as well as DesRon 62's own destroyers. Smoke screen drills were part of the efforts. The squadron's drills continued the development of novice destroyer crews into crews prepared for the battles that lay ahead.

The hard work by Commander Brodie's boys paid off. "Here we went through more firing and beach bombardment. For we had to qualify for the fleet and was one of the first of the DDs to do so," boasted Seaman Marion Parker of the *Haynsworth*. But, aboard the *Lind*, Bob Plum FC2c griped, "Work has decreased, drills have increased. Not enough sack time."

T HE INAUGURAL STRIKES OF THE *DIVINE WIND* had blown against American warships in Philippine waters just a few weeks earlier. In the span of four weeks, dozens of warships were hit by the suicidal raiders. The attacks were not included in CINCPAC Navy Department communiques or press releases. But, news of this magnitude always made its way to the scuttlebutt. "As reports were received of action in the Philippines, she wondered how soon she would be pulling up the hook. She had not long to wait" wrote USS *Charles. S. Sperry's* John Casey.

To ward off the determined foe and protect the carriers, changes in US Navy tactics were necessary. In a message to Vice Admiral John McCain, Commander of Task Force 38, tactics of the new aerial threat were reviewed:

> *Coordinated simultaneous approach by several four to eight plane groups. Approach bearings indicate probably different take off points. Radar detection at average forty miles. All groups seen by radar were intercepted, average twenty miles. Probability that some approached too low for detection by present radar equipment in time to intercept. Total of twenty-one shot down by in-*

tercepting fighters, however immediate dispersal and evasive tactics when tallyhoed prevented 100 percent kill. This resulted in singles coming through to suicide dive on carrier decks. AA shot down ten. Three evidently not hit before dive into deck. Hancock AA disintegrated plane less than 2000 feet above deck, fuselage and wing falling on deck, bomb and engine a near miss on port side. Two planes which dived on Intrepid came in low at less than fifty feet through screen. Two attackers on Cabot came in at same altitude, one hit by Cabot AA a near miss, other diving into deck.

With the surprise success of the suiciders, it was expected that this new threat would continue to threaten the carriers and other warships. In the message, requests were included to increase the number of radar picket ships as well as increase the percentage of carrier fighter planes (VF) in each carrier air group.

Experience with advanced radar pickets covered by CAP [combat air patrol] indicates immediate need for at least five CL [light cruisers] equipped with SP radar so that interceptions may be made at greater range from force. Greatly increased number of VF [fighter planes] needed to insure 100% kill on interceptions and still satisfy requirement of VF sweep, strikes and continuing target CAP.

In response, the *Haynsworth* and other DesRon 62 cans' destinies were altered by the installation of new equipment. A few specially trained officers joined the ship's company in mid-November. The 'fighter director' equipment installed over the balance of the month included two new types of radar: The SC-3 or 'sugar charlie' radar was used to track aircraft. Its antenna, looking like an old box spring, was attached to the top of the mast. Its companion was the SG or 'sugar george' surface search radar. It was used to track ships, land masses, and aircraft. The installation of Electronic Countermeasure (ECM), also known as the "Identification Friend or Foe" (IFF) equipment, provided identification of American planes on the radar screens. The fixes and upgrades of additional radar, radio, and radar counter measure equipment led to designation of these destroyers as "Fighter Director Ships."

The culmination of advanced electronic warfare hardware, task force tactics, and the purpose built Combat Information Center creat-

USS Charles S. Sperry, postwar. On top of the mast is SG surface radar. The larger rectangular antenna below is the SC-3 for detection of planes and ships at long range. Note sailors performing routine painting on deck.

ed a state of the art destroyer. The CIC was a small compartment adjacent to both the bridge and the radio shack. While previous genera-

PHALANX AGAINST THE DIVINE WIND

Cdr. Robert Brodie.
(Bill Morton Collection)

tions of destroyers had their chart rooms converted to CIC's, the *Sumners* were the first generation of destroyers with a purpose built CIC, the ship's nerve center. Ships movements, enemy planes and other vital information was tracked and plotted. The additional radio allowed the ship to speak directly to fighter teams while the radar counter measures could be used to detect or jam enemy radar. Fighter director officers were trained in the use of this equipment to coordinate fighter interception against enemy air attacks. "They spoke their own language," recalled Lt. Dennett, the *Haynsworth's* gunnery officer. "We didn't have much interaction with them except in the galley."

As the destroyers of Squadron 62 prepared for service with the carriers, most days though "the Silex coffee makers were the most important pieces of equipment on the ship," recalled Radioman Third Class Harold Bly.

The time spent at Pearl Harbor wasn't all war preparation. Movies were shown most nights on the destroyer. Liberty allowed the *Haynsworth* sailors time for purchasing needed items for sailing and souvenirs. Lt. Armistead Dennett recalled that the Pearl Harbor Officers Club had the longest and most crowded bar he had ever seen. Many of the sailors ventured into town when on liberty. Marion Parker's journal noted that there was, "LOTS OF LIBERTY in Pearl Harbor but it wasn't so hot. Too many service men. One trip out to the Waikiki Kei Beach and the Royal Hawaiian Hotel which I enjoyed very much." Signalman John Vasquez's recollection was that, "Waikiki was a sailors' town. When we first came to town we found a line of 100 to 200 sailors outside of a building. Asking what was going on, it was explained this was a whorehouse. Then it was explained there were just three girls working to handle the line of sailors. We kept just walking. I didn't want my mom disappointed in me."

Nick Nicotra,
Jack McAllister,
John Magliocchetti,
John Mandola.
(Courtesy of Marianna
Steele)

Left: John Dyer at U.S. Naval
Training School for Radio,
Bedford Springs, PA.
(Courtesy of Helen Dyer
Richmond)

Right:
Ralph K. Aakhus RdM3c.
(Courtesy of Ralph Aakhus)

The preparations for battle included changes to the muster. When the request came down from the fleet for two of his seamen with high aptitude to be trained as Radio Strikers, Brodie chose friends from the deck division, John McAllister and John Magliocchetti. The striker role, similar to being an apprentice, allowed them to train in a position that could earn them the rating of radioman third class. The two seamen were transferred off the *Haynsworth* to attend Radio Striker School at Camp Catlin, Pearl Harbor for eighteen weeks of training. Jim Lail, RM3c was transferred off the ship at the same time. Replacing him was Radioman Third Class John Dyer who came aboard November 12th and Francis Kenney, Seaman First Class.

The twenty year old Dyer had just returned from deployment with USS *Richard W. Suesens* DE-342 near the Philippines. The former telegrapher for the Delaware & Hudson Railroad had joined the Navy a year after the Pearl Harbor attack. Enlisting in Albany, New York, near his home in Plattsburgh, he originally served with convoy escorts traveling to North Africa and Sardinia. Radio striker candidate Dyer was sent to the U.S. Naval Training School for Radio at Keystone Schools, Bedford Springs, Pennsylvania. This wartime training facility was erected in the Bedford Springs Hotel. The civilian amenities were retained while the radio strikers spent four months learning Morse code, use of radios and typing. Eventually he was transferred to the Pacific where he served as the personal radioman for the Commander of Destroyer Escort Division 69. When he was transferred to the *Haynsworth* in late 1944, there was no way of knowing then that it would be an assignment of fatal consequence.

Another addition to the crew was Radarman Ralph Aakhus. Known as 'Horse' because of his strength, Aakhus transferred aboard on December 9th after serving duty as a land based radarman on Tarawa Island. A four week course at Ford Island helped him make the transition from land to sea based radar. After coming aboard at noon, Aakhus was tasked with scraping paint until 2100 that evening. With berthing at a maximum due to a full wartime compliment of crew, Aakhus slept in the mess hall. The coolness and the proximity of food made the temporary bunking assignment tolerable.

WARRIOR SEAMAN

Cdr. Stephen Noel Tackney.
(Courtesy of David Tackney)

"I RELIEVE YOU, SIR!" The orders were read, salutes were exchanged. In a brief change of command ceremony on December 14th, a new commanding officer reported aboard to replace Cdr. Brodie who had been promoted to command Destroyer Division 24.

Lt. Cdr. Stephen Noel Tackney USN, Annapolis Class of '28. Tall but lean, his clothes draped his lanky frame. To a sailor under his command, Tackney was stern but occasionally a glimpse of his sometimes rebellious Irish sense of humor flashed in his eyes. Just as he was sparse of frame, so was Tackney with words. The thirty-eight year old captain "was a standoffish guy but a good leader. He had a job to do and so did it. He was not outgoing," related Harold Bly TM3c. "The officers from the Naval Academy were stricter than their Reserve Officer peers."

Born of a first generation Irish-American family with seven children that had settled in Brooklyn, Stephen lost his father, John, when he was just ten years old. To provide for her children, his mother, Katie, became the housekeeper for the Bishop of New York. The efforts of her employer led to a path of service to the Lord for four of her children: two of Stephen's brothers became priests, two sisters became nuns. Though young Stephen excelled at Brooklyn Prep during high school, the Bishop did not see a path to the priesthood in the future for his housekeeper's third son. Discipline was his greatest need.

The Bishop's influence reached all the way to Annapolis, Maryland. Eighteen year old Tackney was admitted to the United State Naval Academy in 1924.

Acclimation was difficult for the son of immigrants, especially as he was not born of a navy family. At that point in his life, Tackney did not bleed blue though that would change to a certain extent over the decades. He had neither connections in the Navy nor coin in his pocket. Moving from his lower middle class Catholic neighborhood to enter a world so culturally different than his own, Tackney struggled attempting to make the change. His grades lagged during his plebe year, the first year, while his actions brought him 'before the mast' on numerous occasions.

The academy court-martials prosecuted by his classmates led to various penalties. At one point charged with *chicanery* (a charge invented to prosecute his actions), Tackney faced the private support of his peers but the public condemnation of actions unspoken of outside the fraternity of the midshipmen. He was sentenced to spend time on an old prison barge moored in the Eastern Bay, sustained by just bread and water.

By his second year, the midshipman from Brooklyn had gotten serious with his studies and began to excel academically. For sport, he was a field athlete, javelin and hammer his instruments. Come 1928, Tackney had earned both his diploma and a coveted class ring. A commission as an officer in the United States Navy came with the sheepskin, the opening steps for a long career. The future warrior seaman left Annapolis, the seas and U.S. Navy warships awaiting him.

Tackney's assignments were varied, each bringing him experience and lessons for his role as the captain of the *Haynsworth*. He served aboard the battleship USS *Maryland* BB-46, spent three years as the executive officer of a gunboat on the Yangtze River, was the engineering officer for the first destroyer to use a super-heated steam boiler system and commanded a fleet oiler. Between assignments, he taught at the United States Navy Post Graduate School at Annapolis.

On a sunny Hawaiian Sunday morning, Tackney was startled by the sounds and smoke rising from Pearl Harbor, the enemy planes flying over the island. Living on Oahu and married with two children by December 7, 1941, Tackney's wife, Priscilla, was pregnant with their third child when Japanese dive bombers, torpedo planes, and fighters attacked the Pacific Fleet. His dual concerns were for the ships and their crews and the eventual evacuation of his family to the mainland.

Tackney's old assignment, the battleship, *'The Fighting Mary,'* was wounded but not mortally but it was hard to tell that morning. Thick black smoke accompanied the fires and explosions that emanated from the battlewagons. The water of the harbor was fouled with oil, bodies floating in the thick flotsam. The battleship USS *Nevada* had been grounded, the only battleship to get underway during the attack. Three cruisers, many destroyers, and a few old destroyer-minesweepers were also able to get underway and head to sea. It was a meager battle force.

By the morning of the December 8ᵗʰ, it was apparent that three battleships and the *Utah* were sunk or capsized. *Nevada* was grounded and would remain that way for several months. The *Maryland, Pennsylvania*, and the *Tennessee* were wounded but would head to the west coast for repairs before the month was over. The U.S. Navy had become the defensive team.

With wars now raging across the world and two oceans, all available U.S. Navy ships had been put in commission. Lt. Cdr. Tackney's time had come. He received orders to take command of the USS *Gamble* DM-15, one of the few ships to steam from Pearl Harbor on December 7th. When Tackney boarded the seaplane tender USS *Wright* AV-1 in early April 1942 for transport to the South Pacific and his new command, the departing sight of Pearl Harbor still showed five battleships sunk, capsized, or grounded.

It was a time of uncertainty: The Imperial Japanese Navy owned the Pacific. Fears of a Japanese invasion of Pearl Harbor, Midway, and possibly the west coast of America were on the minds of all those who served the Navy. The Navy was engaging the IJN in mortal engagements throughout the South Pacific. Skilled night fighters, the Japanese warships preyed on their American counterparts while their veteran pilots dueled in the daytime skies. The Philippines had capitulated. Australia lay under the threat of Japanese invasion.

The U.S. Navy's keel, pushed down by the attacks, was finally beginning to right itself. Colonel Doolittle was taking his raiders to Tokyo while the *Wright* was crossing the equator en route to Suva, Fiji. Tackney would be on hand three years later when the U.S. Navy finally returned to attack the city of the Emperor.

After Tackney took command of the *Gamble* in mid-April, 1942, the old 'four piper'-as the four smoke stack World War I vintage destroyers were known- was off to the first American invasion in the Pacific, Guadalcanal. While there, she rescued American airmen, lay mines, and transported Japanese prisoners.

It was a challenging period. The old *Gamble* had spent almost as much time out of commission as she had commissioned over the twenty-four years. Inactivity for extended times, moored in mothball fleets, did not serve to keep her in top shape but her crew made do with what they had. Lt. Cdr. Tackney described this period of command the most difficult of his long career.

Tackney and his crew made their mark when the former destroyer (DD-123), still carrying anti-submarine weapons aboard, sank the Japanese submarine I-123-ironically modeled from the German submarine U-125 awarded to Japan after the First World War-during action off Guadalcanal. The action earned Tackney a Navy Cross.

After the *Gamble* returned to Pearl Harbor for repair and weapon upgrades in December, 1942, Admiral Chester Nimitz himself pinned the medal on the thirty-seven year old skipper. The award stated, "*for extraordinary heroism and distinguished service in the line of his profession as Commanding Officer of the Destroyer-Mine Layer USS Gamble (DM-15), while escorting supply ships supplying newly seized bases in the Solomon Islands Area on 29 August 1942 Lieutenant Commander Tackney skillfully located a Japanese submarine in the vicinity. He made persistent and determined attacks for her for four hours until oil and wreckage convinced him the submarine had been destroyed.*"

Though the Navy Cross would forever standout on Tackney's uniform, when he was relieved of command of the *Gamble* in March, 1943, it was the knowledge that he had brought his entire crew home safely that mattered most to him.

After another stint teaching at the Navy Post Graduate School, Tackney was selected to command the USS *Haynsworth*. He had just a few days to become acclimated. His new ship was twice the tonnage of the *Gamble* with a crew three times the compliment of the old WWI vintage minesweeper. Though the two ships had comparable speed, the new *Sumners* were heavier armed than the old converted destroyer. With an integrated Combat Information Center, new radar, a fresh crew, and a high speed young executive officer, Tackney commanded a potent, state of the art weapon.

The demands of command would make Tackney a ghost on his own ship. He would rarely be seen by this crew who didn't have reason to be on the bridge but the former Engineering Officer was not above going below decks to oversee the progress of repairs.

And, as he had with the crew of the *Gamble*, Lt. Cdr. Tackney was determined to bring his new crew through the war safely, too. But, there was the *Divine Wind*, equally as intent on preventing any American warship safe passage in the final battles of the Pacific.

DEPARTURE

SINGLE UP ALL LINES! PREPARE TO CAST OFF!" Three years post the surprise attack of 1941, much had changed during the war and at Pearl. The water no longer had the sheen of oil. New modern warships were moored throughout the harbor. Four of the battleships damaged in the attack had been repaired, modernized, and were serving the fleet near the Philippines. A fifth, the *Nevada*, was in California for upgrades but would soon be sortieing to the battles of the Pacific.

Initially, Destroyer Squadron 62 was slated to join 7th Fleet for service with amphibious forces preparing for the invasion of Luzon but a few days before departure their orders were changed. Instead of being under General MacArthur's control, the squadron was ordered to join Admiral Halsey's Third Fleet.

After their final repairs had been completed by the tender USS *Yosemite* AD-19, the DesRon 62 *Sumners* departed Pearl Harbor in small groups in the waning days of '44 (The exception was the *Borie*, still in San Diego). Clearing the harbor channel and the torpedo nets, the small task units set a western course that would eventually bring them to Ulithi.

The *Haynsworth* weighed anchor on Saturday, December 16. Her magazines were filled with ammunition, the holds with food and gear, the tanks topped with oil, the refrigeration compartment with fresh meat, fruit, and vegetables. Spare parts were loaded and her new radar gear had been tested repeatedly. The bluejackets and officers of the *Lucky 700* had taken their final liberties ashore. Last letters from the tropical paradise had been penned to parents, girlfriends, and wives.

She was joined by her sister *Sumner* destroyer USS *Charles S. Sperry* DD-697 and the light cruiser USS *Flint* CL-97. They served as an escort for the attack troop ship USS *Barrow* APA-61 which was on its way to the island of Eniwetok.

What the future held was the subject of conjecture for the young bluejackets: "When the *Ault* went to sea again, her personnel began to think more about the active part they would certainly have in Pacific operations. In the months past, our forces had pushed up from the Solomons, past Rabaul, past Truk, past the outposts of the Japanese Empire, and were firmly established on Guam and Saipan in the Marianas; Task Force 58 [Fast Carrier Task Force] had gone dauntlessly on sorties into territory the Japs had believed would never be threatened by American forces."

But, as they left Hawaii, the *Haynsworth's* gunnery officer, Lt. Armistead Dennett observed, "We had a grim feeling as we passed by the sunken battleship *Arizona* on our way out of Pearl Harbor to head west to the fight."

A RITE OF PASSAGE OCCURRED for the bluejackets as the caravan crossed the International Date Line at 2300 on December 19th. The 180° longitude vertical axis separated today from yesterday as they sailed west and so a day was lost in the journey. All those aboard who had never previously crossed into the IMPERIAL DOMAIN of GOLDEN DRAGON were issued cards inducting them "into the silent mysteries of the FAR EAST." On behalf of the Golden Dragon, August Ruler of the 180th Meridian, the Executive Officer Scott Lothrop affixed his signature.

While en route, Lt. Cdr. Tackney received word that he would wear three matching gold braids on his sleeves and silver oak leaves on his collar. The warrior seaman had been promoted to Commander.

PAST THE CRUMBLING RAMPARTS OF THE EMPIRE steamed the warships. The outer reaches of Japanese held territory had been slowly pushed back since their pinnacle in 1942. The Americans had captured or bypassed numerous enemy held islands and atolls. Eniwetok atoll, halfway between Hawaii and Australia, had been captured in February of 1944. As the *Haynsworth* entered the anchorage, the sailors on deck were greeted by the sight of hundreds of Allied vessels. Fifty miles across, the atoll served as a forward base for naval operations in the south Pacific. Their visit was brief. After refueling and gunnery practice on the 23rd, the destroyer was back at sea on Christmas Eve.

While Gene *Kelly's Christmas Holiday* brought crowds to movie theaters back in the states, the small caravan of ships spent Christmas at sea. Assigned *first* watch from 2000 to 2400 on Christmas Eve, Radarman Aakhus wrote his family about the evening: carols were sung for a few hours; Some Christmas candy and cups of coffee helped them to stay awake on watch. A miniature pine tree brought aboard by Ed Maugel SoM3c served as the lone Christmas tree for the new crew. "Full holiday routine" recalled Sonarman Third Class Bill Morton. As celebration of the holy day, less crucial tasks were not assigned and a special meal was prepared by the cooks and the bakers like Ray Techman Bkr2c. Ed Mital CM2c reminisced, "We were all dreaming of

Above: Imperial Domain of Golden Dragon Card. (McAllister Family Collection)

Right: Ed Maugel SoM3c and the Haynsworth's only Christmas tree. (Courtesy of Edwin Maugel)

a white Christmas and the folks back home, although we were still happy. Happy to be alive."

As Christmas turned into December 26th, the crew of the *Haynsworth* was just days away from combat. "Passed 300 miles from Jap held Truk Island. Spotted Jap plane seventeen miles from us," recorded Morton. The plane stayed outside of the effective range of the tin can's guns. In the near future, not all of the enemy planes would keep their distance.

"December 27th. Passed Guam early this morning. Did not stop but dropped off transport that was with us." After refueling, the *Haynsworth* and *Sperry* departed the next day. "At midnight we passed eighty-seven miles from Saipan and at 0700 we were twenty-six miles from the Jap held Rota Island."

Their next stop would be the Navy's staging area at the Ulithi atoll. Waiting there was the famous Task Force 38, Admiral William 'Bull' Halsey's Fast Carrier Task Force.

ULITHI BOUND

A small part of the U.S. Navy's Third Fleet at Ulithi Atoll anchorage, 1944.

IT WAS A VIEW WITHOUT EQUAL. As far as the eyes could see, hundreds of ships greeted the *Haynsworth* as it arrived at Ulithi in late December, 1944. The Third Fleet filled the deep water harbor protected by the reefs of the atoll. Just as Doolittle's Raiders flew from Shangri-La, there seemed to be no port visible. No rows of docks, no fuel tanks, and no large cranes to offload and load vessels were apparent. Fire Controlman Tom Scott recalled that "the anchorage at Ulithi was so big you could not see all the ships there, let alone all those of your own task group."

Realizing the need for a deep water port to base its ships for the future attacks on the Philippines as well as Japan and its nearby islands, the U.S. Navy seized the atoll of Ulithi from the protective force of three Japanese soldiers in September, 1944. The four hundred locals were rounded up and relocated to another island while the Navy secretly set the stage to construct a protected forward base on the postage stamp islands. The tiny atoll, 1300 miles south of Tokyo, was the new home of the largest assemblage of naval ships ever gathered.

The ports capabilities contrasted with the Navy's desperate existence in the dark days of early 1942. Lt. Cdr. Tackney's USS *Gamble* led a nomadic existence in the South Pacific. When and where the next replenishment of fuel, ammunition, and especially food would arrive was an uncertainty. "When the minecraft had left Pearl Harbor, the sailors were assured they would be gone for a few weeks at most and would shortly return to Pearl Harbor for more supplies. Believing this, many of the ships had given away supplies to various Marine units that were also short of food. As it worked out, no supplies were forthcoming for the minecraft until December of 1942." Replacement parts for the old machinery of the junkyard navy were non-existent. When the fresh water evaporators broke down, Tackney sent shore parties out on the whaleboat into the streams of the Solomon Islands. Filling barrels with water during the daytime, the boilers would be brought back on line at night in preparation for enemy engagements. While on the islands, food was scrounged where it could be found. It was a common sight to see fishing lines laid over the stern in attempts to catch tuna, dolphin, or even barracuda. "The cooks did a tremendous job with what they had to work with, but even a dedicated chef can only do so much with dehydrated cabbage and potatoes."

Two years later, Destroyer Squadron 62 was greeted by a supply line that reached across the Pacific to ensure the bluejackets could focus on battle without the worry of their next meal,

> *Within a month of the occupation of Ulithi, a whole floating base was in operation. Six thousand ship fitters, artificers, welders, carpenters, and electricians arrived aboard repair ships, destroyer tenders, floating dry docks. USS AJAX had an air-conditioned optical shop, a supply of base metals from which she could make any alloy to form any part needed. Many refrigerator and supply ships belonged to three-ship teams: the ship at Ulithi had cleaned out and relieved sister ship No. 2 which was on the way back to a rear base for more supplies while No. 3 was on the way out to relieve No. 1. Over half the ships were not self-propelled but were towed in. They then served as warehouses for a whole system of transports which unloaded stores on them for distribution. This kind of chain went all the way back to the United States. The paper and magazines showed England sinking under the stockpile of troops and material collected for the invasion of Normandy.*

The Okinawa landings were not so well documented but they involved more men, ships, and supplies-including 600,000 gallons of fuel oil, 1500 freight cars of ammunition, and enough food to provide every person in Vermont and Wyoming with three meals a day for fifteen days. The smaller ships needed a multitude of services, the ice cream barge made 500 gallons a shift, and the USS ABATAN, which looked like a big tanker, really distilled fresh water and baked bread and pies. Fleet oilers sortied from Ulithi to refuel the combat ships a short distance from the strike areas. They added men, mail, and medical supplies, and began to take orders for spare parts.

Rear Admiral Beary's Logistics Support Group, Task Force 30, was based there. The actors for the Fast Carrier Task Force 38 were carriers, battleships, cruisers and destroyers. The stage hands were Beary's ships that provided everything needed so that the show could go on, even six thousand miles from the shores of America. Ammunition ships, reefers (store) ships, survey vessels, floating hospitals, cargo ships, tugboats and destroyer tenders for repair. Gasoline tankers brought fuel for planes of the carriers.

The slow sailing support group was a tempting target to Japanese aerial predators and submarines. For protection, the support vanguard was protected by its own guard of escort carriers, destroyers and destroyer escorts. The 'jeep' carriers brought replacement aircraft and pilots. But to keep the task force hunting, especially the thirsty destroyers, it was Beary's fleet oilers that carried the most precious commodity.

"We arrived at Ulithi Island to join the Third Fleet. There were a couple of hundred ships here. We expect to shove off in the morning but don't know, as yet, where to," wrote Bill Morton aboard the *Haynsworth.* The ship took what Admiral Beary and Ulithi had to offer: "We are topping off provisions and ammunition, refueling. We left Ulithi with Task Force 38-Task Group 38.2 for fast carrier attacks on several points unknown at present. Expect to be under weigh approximately twenty days."

The next three weeks would bring the task force two enemies: The Japanese and the weather.

PART III

Fast Carrier Task Force 38

The Hoplite Phalanx of ancient Greece was a nearly impregnable military formation. Rows upon rows of farmer-soldiers formed into a rectangular formation, its perimeter protected by overlapping shields. Large spears emerged ahead of the front rank. Behind the shields, each hoplite carried a short sword. Helmets and armor provided protection to the wearer. Enemies that got past the porcupine defense then had to penetrate the armadillo exterior of heavy shields. At the same time, the phalanx was advancing, scattering the enemy by its sheer mass. Enemy formations stood in terror at the sight of the phalanx.

JOINING THE PACIFIC FLEET

USS Haynsworth taken from the USS Sangay AE-10.
(Courtesy of NavSource)

THE PACIFIC WAS A BATTLEFIELD WITHOUT EQUAL, an expanse of several million square miles stretching east from the coast of the United States and west to China, Malaysia and Australia. Battles centered around the islands of Micronesia, Melanesia, and Polynesia as well as the Philippines, Formosa (Taiwan) and the Ryukyu Island chain south of Japan. As the war advanced, the Japanese perimeter became its noose.

The United States Navy developed a twentieth century phalanx to project force and attack the expanded Japanese Empire. The U.S. Navy built this formation around a new battle concept: The Fast Carrier Task Force. The Task Force (TF) was composed of multiple Task Groups (TG). The task groups worked both independently of each other and in cooperation depending on the mission. Within each TG were several carriers along with battleships and cruisers for their protection. The final punch of the TG was the numerous destroyers assigned for protection. All of these warships were capable of thirty plus knots. The older slower pre-Pearl Harbor battleships were relegated to the slower invasion forces.

A task group traveled in a large circular pattern composed of concentric rings. This tactic of defense was developed between the wars by

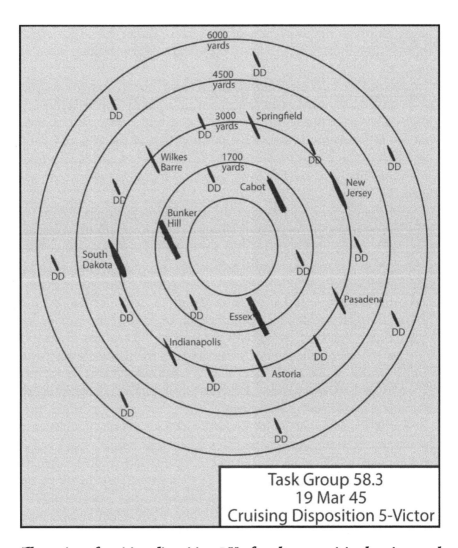

Illustration of cruising disposition 5-V after destroyers joined cruisers and battleships surrounding the carriers Essex, Randolph, and Bunker Hill. (USS Bunker Hill CV-17 Action Report 14 March-14 May 1945)

Commander Roscoe MacFall. At the center of the group were the carriers with outlying rings of cruisers and battleships. An outermost ring of destroyers enveloped the entire group. The destroyers were the first rampart of protection against submarines, warships, sea mines, and enemy aircraft. Finally, destroyers with extra radar-fighter director capabilities, like the *Haynsworth*, were sent forward of the group on 'picket' duty. Depending on the potential threats, several destroyers could be positioned well forward of the screen. At night the pickets might return to the protection of the screen. Either way, the destroyers were usually the first to greet the enemy. Warm feelings were not mutual.

The task group's steaming arrangement of circles was not designed to be an iron sea turtle that journeyed in a purely defensive posture. Historian Walter Borneman wrote, "Halsey had shown that far from hiding carriers behind battleships, putting them at the core of a small, nimble task force capable of moving at thirty knots yielded an offensive capability that could strike surprise tactical blows almost anywhere."

For the carriers, the greatest threat to the task group was by air. The screen normally cruised at disposition 5-Roger (5-R), a circular pattern that extended 6000 yards from the center of the group. There were several advantages to this formation. The entire group of ships could pivot or turn as one with no loss of position. Additionally, mutual protection was created by the concentration of overlapping gunfire provided by the ships. Like a phalanx, the task group would close in on itself when confronted with the enemy. At cruising disposition 5-Victor (5-V) the radius of the group dropped by half as the destroyers joined on the capital ships. This change reduced the area of the task group by seventy-five percent. Like the Greek phalanx, penetrating the screen was hazardous for the enemy.

By 1944 the few remaining pre-war carriers had been supplemented by new carriers of three classes: Fleet, Light, and Escort. The small escort carriers (CVE) were neither fast nor large but could bring naval air power anywhere on the water. They were utilized in submarine hunter-killer units, to protect replenishment vessels like the oilers as well as invasion forces, and to bring replacement pilots and planes to the larger carriers. The light carriers (CVL) were an expedient redesign of cruisers that were under construction. They were fast and could be built quicker than the fleet carriers. Their relatively small size and flight deck limited their plane compliment to about 40% of the fleet carriers. The larger fleet carriers (CV) of the *Essex* class were the most modern carriers in the world at the time of their construction. They could achieve over thirty knots while their nearly 900 foot long flight decks carried over ninety planes with a mixture of fighters, bombers, and torpedo planes. They were the belles of the ball.

As early as 1921, Army aviator General William 'Billy' Mitchell demonstrated that aerial attack could sink a capital ship. In a test of aviation capability, bombs were dropped against the captured German battleship *Ostfriesland*. Ruptured hull plates caused the sinking of the old dreadnaught as well as an eventual change in U.S. Navy tactics of defense. Two decades later, obsolete British torpedo biplanes crippled the *Bismarck*, the German's state of the art battleship. Come World War II, wherever American carriers would go, so would protective air cover.

Admiral Halsey kept potent aerial weapons in his quiver: The group's own planes flew the Combat Action Patrols (CAP) to protect the ships. During daylight, except on days of nearly typhoon conditions, a CAP flew over the task group. Throughout the day, additional CAPS would be launched and recovered aboard the carriers. The fighters, torpedo planes, dive bombers, and scouts, painted dark blue atop, became known as the 'big blue blanket.'

Japanese raiders sent to attack the task force had to evade the ever-present flights of fighters hovering overhead in the combat air patrols. The modern Grumman F6F *Hellcats* and Chance Vought F4U *Corsairs* flew from the nine large fleet carriers and six light carriers. The smaller escort carriers provided Grumman F4F *Wildcats* and F6F *Hellcats* for air protection as well. The *Hellcats* and *Corsairs* were superior to nearly every plane in the Japanese air inventory. *The Hellcats*, flown strictly by Navy pilots, had a 13:1 kill ratio against the fabled but older Japanese A6M *Zeroes/Zekes*.

The General Motors FM-2 *Wildcat* was General Motor's version of the venerable Grumman F4F *Wildcat*. Though the design predated the war, this sturdy small fighter was more than equal to most Japanese planes. It forged a 6.9:1 kill ratio against the enemy in battle. Though replaced on the larger carriers by the *Hellcat* as the war progressed, the *Wildcat* continued to serve in a variety of roles with the smaller CVEs.

The Vought F4U *Corsairs* were flown by both Navy and Marine units as well as British and New Zealand air squadrons. It also had an outstanding combat record against the Japanese air arm achieving a 12:1 kill ratio against the *Zero*. With its distinctive bent wing structure, six machine guns, and the ability to carry rockets, bombs and napalm, Japanese soldiers referred to the plane as "whistling death." Originally rejected by the U.S. Navy due to the difficulty of landing them on carriers, the 'big nose bird' achieved great success with land based Marine fighter squadrons fighting in the South Pacific like Major Greg 'Pappy' Boyington's Black Sheep squadron. As the menace of Japanese pilots hurling their planes into the fleets carriers grew, the U.S. Navy reconsidered the use of the plane aboard its carriers. By the Iwo Jima invasion, both navy and marine squadrons were flying the mighty *Corsair* from the carrier decks in fighter squadrons (VF/VMF) and fighter-bomber squadrons (VBF).

Large Grumman TBM/TBF *Avengers* carried either bombs or torpedoes as part of the torpedo squadrons (VT). They lumbered through the air at just 126 knots. Equally large Curtiss SB2C *Helldivers* served the bomber squadrons (VB). They were not much faster than the *Avengers* but as their named suggested, they served the role as dive bombers. Through 1944, the carriers carried equal mixtures of fighter squadrons, torpedo bomber squadrons, and dive bomber squadrons. The composition of the mix began to change post the initial kamikaze attacks. Fighters were forced to shoulder a heavier load.

The Fast Carrier Task Force took to battle in the late summer of 1943. As new *Essex* class carriers, fast battleships, and destroyers came online in 1944 and 1945, the task force and its four task groups grew in both size and potency. In preparation for the invasion of Okinawa in 1945, Task Force 58 would swell to seventeen carriers, over a hundred vessels, and nearly eighty-eight thousand officers and sailors.

Operation FLINTLOCK/CATCHPOLE in January-February, 1944 allowed the Americans to capture the island of Eniwetok in the Marshall Islands. This atoll was used as a staging area for the attacks against the Mariana Islands. These operations were followed immediately by Operation HAILSTONE. Truk Island in the Caroline Islands was a major Imperial Japanese Naval base. On February 17-18, 1944, the Fast Carrier Task Force raided the island in hopes of catching numerous large Japanese warships within the atoll. Though the IJN ships had left the atoll the week earlier, the air raids destroyed the majority of the Japanese planes as well as sinking dozens of other ships. The raid effectively neutralized Truk as a major threat to the allies.

The Fast Carrier Task Force returned to Pearl Harbor after the Truk raid but set out again in late March for attacks on the Island of Palau in the Caroline Islands. Operation DESECRATE I brought five fleet carriers and six light carriers for three days of attacks against shipping at Palau and a one day raid on the atoll of Ulithi. Like the attack on Truk, dozens of Japanese ships were sunk by the raiding American fliers.

The Allied landings during the Western New Guinea Campaign jumped off in early April, 1944. Task Force 58 was on hand to ensure domination of the sky and the sea, as well as protecting the invasion ships during Operations RECKLESS and PERSECUTION. The juggernaut that was the Fast Carrier Task Force continued to extend its reach as it attacked Japanese forces across the western Pacific through the end of 1944. The ability of the task force to bring hundreds of planes to bear against targets of its own choosing was evidenced during Operation FORAGER. By capturing the Mariana Islands, the American Navy planned to set up bases for its ships as well as airfields for long range Boeing B-29 bombers. The American invasion lured the Japanese Navy out of protective hiding. The outcome in the air was the 'Great Marianas Turkey Shoot,' a lopsided victory for the 'big blue blanket.'

The task force returned to Eniwetok at the end of August for rest, repair, and reprovisioning. At the same time, its command was transferred to Admiral William Halsey. Aggressive and scrappy, Halsey had cut his teeth as a destroyer captain and later as a destroyer squadron commander. As his star shined, 'Bull' earned his pilot's wings at age fifty-two so he would be eligible to command one of the U.S. Navy's first carriers, the USS *Saratoga* CV-3.

With the change in command, came a new designation: Task Force 38. Their next assignment was to assist General MacArthur make good on his promise to return to the Philippines. Operation KING II departed Eniwetok at the end of the August. On its way to the Philippines, it made numerous attacks against installations and airfields on other islands. Iwo Jima, Chichi Jima, and Palau came under attack from TF 38. It was on September 2nd, 1944 that a young Navy pilot, Lt. jg. George Bush, was shot down in a bombing attack against a radio station. Flying with VT-51 aboard the USS *San Jacinto* CVL-30, the future president's plane was hit by anti-aircraft fire. Bailing out of his flaming *Avenger*, Bush was later rescued by a submarine. His aircrew did not survive.

The Japanese forces in the Philippines were subject to attack for four weeks before TF 38 steamed to Okinawa for a quick strike October 10th. After refueling, the task force returned west to the Philippines to continue attacks there as well as against Formosa.

It was in late October that kamikazes began to target the carriers and ships of the 3rd and 7th Fleets. By the end of October, the *Divine Winds* had struck the carriers *Intrepid*, *Franklin*, *Belleau Wood* and seven escort carriers. At the cessation of KING II on November 25th, the carriers *Lexington II*, *Essex*, *Hancock*, and *Cabot* had also been bloodied by the pilots of the *Tokubetsu Kōgeki tai*. The bruised Fast Carrier Task Force returned to Ulithi at the beginning of December.

Roaring out of Ulithi a week later, Task Force 38 turned its sights on the Philippines and the invasion of Mindoro as part of operation LOVE III. Charged with suppressing enemy air attacks from nearby airfields, the task force was expected to strike on December 14-16 while Vice Admiral Thomas Kinkaid's 7th Fleet invaded Mindoro. Post the three days of attacks, Halsey planned to have his force refuel on December 17th and then be prepared for three more days of attacks on December 19-21. Staying on plan, the TF 38 steamed east three hundred miles to link with TG 30.8, Captain Jasper Acuff's At Sea Logistics Group, after the attacks on December 17. After three days of attacks, Halsey's destroyers were especially low on oil. The fuel served a dual purpose: energy for propulsion and weight for ballast.

A typhoon was the uninvited guest to Halsey and Acuff's rendezvous. As the weather deteriorated, Halsey repeatedly tried to have his ships refuel while shifting the task force's position. The ships took a beating, several destroyers were lost, many were damaged and mission capability was diminished. During the fury of the storm, sailors were swept overboard, planes were wrecked in their hangars and on deck, and equipment was damaged or lost.

Halsey himself wrote in his autobiography, "No one who has not been through a typhoon can conceive its fury. The 70 foot seas smash you from all sides. The rain and the scud are blinding; they drive at you flat-out, until you can't tell the ocean from the air...What it was like on a destroyer one-twentieth the *New Jersey's* size, I can only imagine. I was told that some of them were knocked down until their stacks were almost horizontal and were pinned there by the gale, while water rushed into their ventilators and intakes, shorting the circuits, killing their power, steering, lights, and communications, and leaving them to drift helplessly."

As the storm lost its fury, rescue operations were commenced. Small groups of survivors were recovered while the ships finally were able to get their fill of fuel. Rather than turning west to the Philippines, the force set its sights on repair at Ulithi to the south. Finally, on December Christmas Eve, the storm battered armada entered the protective waters of Ulithi.

A belated Christmas gift from Admiral Chester Nimitz to the veteran task force was the seven new, clean state of the art destroyers that formed the nucleus of Destroyer Squadron 62. Halsey probably took little notice of their arrival on December 28th as his focus was elsewhere. Admiral Nimitz had arrived to hold a Court of Inquiry to determine the facts of *Typhoon Cobra*. Nimitz, who had just received his fifth star and promotion to Fleet Admiral, was present for several days of testimony. In the end, the Commander in Chief Pacific Fleet and the Court of Inquiry were reluctant to pin the blame for the loss of the destroyers on Halsey.

With orders to sortie from Ulithi and fulfill the carefully laid operational plans, Task Force 38 would soon be back in the hunt.

Task Force 38: Halsey's Hammer

"Murderers Row" Third Fleet aircraft carriers at anchor in Ulithi Atoll, 8 December 1944, during a break from operations in the Philippines area. The carriers are (from front to back): USS Wasp, USS Yorktown, USS Hornet, USS Hancock and USS Ticonderoga.

BOLTING FROM ULITHI after less than a week's time to repair and re-provision, Admiral William 'Bull' Halsey's naval hammer, the Fast Carrier Task Force 38, set its sights on Luzon as part of Operation MIKE I. Commanded by Admiral John 'Slew' McCain, TF 38 was the most dominant naval force ever assembled, a steel armada of mighty fleet carriers, heavy warships, and a protective screen of destroyers. Their mission: launch carrier airstrikes against Luzon then attack Japanese held Formosa and Indo-China during Operation GRATITUDE.

The armada was composed of four task groups. Destroyer Squadron 62 was assigned to Task Group 38.2 along with carriers USS *Lexington II* CV-16, USS *Hornet* CV-12, USS *Hancock* CV-19 *(McCain's flagship)*, and USS *Independence* CVL-22. Protection of the valuable flattops was afforded by the *Iowa* class battleships USS *New Jersey* BB-62 (Admiral Halsey's flagship) and USS *Wisconsin* BB-64; the cruisers

***Admiral John S. McCain, Sr., confers with Admiral William Halsey, Third
Fleet Commander, December, 1944. (U.S. Navy Photo)***

USS *San Juan* CL-54, USS *Wilkes-Barre* CL-103, USS *Pasadena* CL-65,
and USS *Astoria II* CL-90; and the destroyer screen Task Unit 38.2.3
with members Destroyer Squadrons 52 and 62 (less *Wallace L. Lind*
and *Borie*). Adm. Gerald Bogan commanded TG 38.2.

Lt. Richard Bullis, the navigator of the USS *Waldron*, described the
phalanx's departure:

> *Leaving Ulithi, the destroyers left first and made a sweep out-
> side the atoll and got into formation with the cruisers, then the
> battleships, and finally the carriers. The carriers were always pro-
> tected in the center of the group. We usually traveled in a circu-
> lar formation. Under non-combat, the destroyers might be ten*

miles out from 'the guide.' The guide was usually the battleship New Jersey which Halsey was riding. In combat we would close in about two miles from the guide, and the cruisers would move in closer to the battleships and the carriers forming a very tight-knit task group to protect against air attack. This closing formation was a remarkable procedure.

Down the chain of command, the view of the common bluejacket differed from those of the brass. As the task force sortied, Haynsworth Radarman Third Class Ralph Aakhus reported that "they are at sea again looking for trouble."

TO COUNTER THE AERIAL THREATS of attacking enemy planes and kamikazes, new tactics had been developed by the staffs of Admirals John S. McCain and Bill Halsey. The trident included short, medium, and long-range defenses: At short range, the collective overlapping anti-aircraft firepower of a task group's phalanx would put up a lead and explosive shield in the air.

Medium range defenses had a two part plan: the Combat Air Patrol would be sent out further and at higher altitudes away from the center of the task group. This tactic would close the time to interception of enemy marauders. The plane going into the fight with the highest altitude was the plane with the tactical advantage.

Radar was the second part of the medium range defenses. Detection of enemy warships and planes would occur earlier as destroyers were sent out of the phalanx as radar scouts on picket duty. Halsey, an old destroyer man himself, said after the war, "If I had to give credit to the instruments and machines that won us the war in the Pacific, I would rank them in this order: submarines first, radar second, planes third, bulldozers fourth." The USS *Haynsworth* and the tin cans of Destroyer Squadron 62 would spend much time proving Halsey correct.

The third tine of the trident, the long range defense, was the conversion to a "constant CAP." Halsey described this tactic as flights that "entailed keeping a blanket of fighters over all enemy airfields on a twenty-four hour, heel-and-toe schedule." An increased air presence also meant more take offs, more landings, more planes in the air, and an increased amount of pilots having to land in the ocean.

THE OPERATION UNFOLDED AT FORMOSA'S DOORSTOP on the last Sunday of '44. The first plane launches began before the sun's arrival. For the crew of the *Haynsworth* the period of training and drills had been replaced by days of combat. The warship was now part of the shooting war. As such, Lt. Cdr. Lothrop provided guidance to the crew through his daily set of Morning Orders:

Task Force #38 is under way for a fast carrier attack against FORMOSA. Expect to be in enemy-searched waters approximately 2400 31 December and more or less continually from that time on.

It is the C.O.'s desire that when off watch, the bulk of the crew is expected to sleep and rest except for a reasonable amount of up keep, maintenance and cleanliness.

While on watch, you must be on your feet and alert. Save your 'caulking-off' for your off watch hours. The point is made strongly that every man topside on watch is a lookout; that, particularly, those men assigned as lookouts and those given assigned sectors regardless of what four ring circus is going on behind them. It is a human trait to gape at an accident or a spectacle, but the principle of diversion of attack direction is an old favorite trick of the Japs. You must stay in your own sector, reporting everything you see.

No further information will be put out just in case you should fall overboard into enemy hands. It is better you should not know too much too far ahead.

SPEED AND STEALTH, coupled with an overwhelming air superiority, were the calling cards of McCain's task force as an effective, free ranging threat against the Japanese Empire. To keep air supremacy at its peak, pilot and aircrew rescue was given a high priority.

While land based squadrons in the Pacific had 'dumbo' rescue amphibious planes and 'crash' rescue boats assigned to recover plane crews that went down, McCain's only amphibious planes were the few Vought OS2U *Kingfishers* carried as observation planes by the cruisers and battleships. They were not designed to be put down in the heavy swells of the ocean. For some missions, lifeguard submarines would be posted off the shores of task force targets, ready if needed to recover pilots but often a downed pilot could become a needle in an aquatic haystack.

It would not be until the invasion of Okinawa that the Fast Carrier Task Force would eventually have larger dumbo planes and lifeguard submarines on a regular basis. For the phalanx to stay in the hunt then, it would be required of the destroyermen to rescue pilots

*USS Haynsworth
on plane guard duty.
(Courtesy of Gus Scutari)*

and crews whose planes could not put their tailhook and wheels on the safety of the carriers' wooden decks. Planes could be replaced but a man that could drop an aircraft on a carrier's bucking deck was hard to come by. The U.S. Navy put a heavy emphasis on recovering pilots and aircrew at sea, even the Marine flyboys. Attrition could be great: On missions against well defended targets, a dozen or more planes could be lost in a day.

In TG 38.2, DesRon 62 and its sister squadrons 42 and 57 had the primary rescue duty of downed airmen or sailors lost overboard within the phalanx. Rescue swimmers, like the *Haynsworth's* Bill Vassey S1C, Harrison Beasley RT2c and Henry Michalak S1C, took to the sea with just a lifeline to retrieve sailors, aviators, and a select few of the Emperor's Imperial Japanese Navy. For the pilots (and the destroyermen), the recovery of aircrew from the unforgiving Pacific was a morale booster, a reminder that despite wounds or damage to their planes, pilots had a chance of survival.

During flight operations, one or two destroyers would serve as 'plane guard.' "We could either be ahead or astern of the carrier. When we were ahead of the carrier, it was to recover pilots that could not stay airborne after attempting takeoff. Astern we recovered pilots whose landing was poor or those so severely damaged they could not land on the carrier, "recalled Lt. Armistead Dennett. "Only about 50% of those that went in the water were we able to actually recover."

RESCUE OPPORTUNITIES PRESENTED THEMSELVES IM-MEDIATELY. During the first day at sea, Ensign John Buttler attempted to land his fighter aboard the USS *Hancock*. After a hard touchdown, the fighter bounced over the wire cable barriers and plowed into planes positioned ahead on the flight deck. Facing a four ton fighter landing on him, a deckhand instinctively jumped into the Pacific. Within minutes the USS *Ault* had safely recovered the sailor. The next day, December 31st, a torpedo bomber from the *Hancock* crashed 1000 yards off the *Hank's* post quarter of. Two minutes later the Grumman *Avenger* had sunk, though her crew was able to escape the plane. Proceeding at top speed, the *Hank* slowed then tossed lines over to the aircrew. Pilot Lt. jg. Jim Cuff, Gunner Thomas Dickie AMM1c, and Radioman Victor H. Holland ARM2c were safely rescued. The crew stayed as guests for two days until they could be returned to the carrier. It was early in the mission, but destroyers of Destroyer Squadron 62 had already proved their ability to fulfill the role of task group lifeguards.

THE SACRIFICES OF THE AMERICAN PEOPLE after three years at war had brought positive results as 1944 ended. Despite the rationing of many food items, rubber, gasoline, metal, and other essential goods plus a lack of young male labor, the home front had risen to the occasion. In 1944 alone, America had produced nearly twelve thousand tanks, ninety-six thousand planes, six fleet carriers and seventy-four destroyers. Allied forces had invaded Europe. The Germans were being pushed back to their own country's border. Japan's stronghold on the Far East was withering. The industrial might of America coupled with the strength of its military and support services meant that it was not a matter if American and the Allied forces would win the war, but when.

Commander of the Third Fleet, Admiral Bill "Bull" Halsey, sent New Year's greetings to his task force via Talk Between Ships (TBS) voice radio. He encouraged the bluejackets and officers under his command to fight harder the next year: "This is Blackjack himself. Your work so far has been superb. I expect even more. Keep the bastards dying!"

All who heard Halsey's message hoped that 1945 would be the last year of the war. Ralph Aakhus had suspicions that the *Haynsworth*, "will probably stay out here a year or more which I hope is not true." Though the tide for the battle of the Pacific had turned against the Japanese years earlier, they were still a dangerous foe. Island invasion after island invasion by the Allies showed that the Japanese were ready to fight to the very last man. Rather than surrender, Japanese soldiers would turn to suicidal actions. Iwo Jima and Okinawa were being transformed into island fortresses awaiting the eventual invasion of the Allies. Small Japanese held islands were turned into volcanic 'aircraft carriers.' The Allies plan was to invade Kyushu in November 1945 followed by more main Japanese home island invasions in 1946. There was still a feeling amongst the men serving in the steel fleet of the Allies that the war might even stretch until 1950.

The kamikazes' tally by the end of 1944: one hundred U.S. Navy vessels had fallen victim to the Japanese military's new weapon. Twenty ships were sunk. In just ten weeks' time, the *Divine Wind* had touched sixteen carriers and seventeen destroyers. The fight for the control of the Pacific had taken a new direction, a path that would directly influence the battles of the Fast Carrier Task Force and the destroyers of Squadron 62 in the months to come.

1945

DesRon 62 Destroyers in the Pacific.
(Henry Michalak photo, courtesy of Capt. H. Domeracki USN)

FOR TASK FORCE 38, NEW YEAR'S DAY 1945 was marked by just the turn of the calendar page. With the *Haynsworth* and the other destroyers positioned in a circular screen around the heavy units, TF 38 was on the move for attacks against Formosa and Luzon. Many of the ships had already won numerous battle stars in the fight for control of the Pacific. As the caravan proceeded to meet its tankers for refueling, the carriers launched planes against the task force's destroyers. The mock attacks by eight planes-known as *mousetrap* drills- were countered by drills aboard the ships. The USS *Ault*, with ComDesRon 62 Capt. Higgins aboard, acted as the destroyers' controller. The anti-aircraft firing drills lasted two hours. Finally, a radar jamming exercise was carried out late in the afternoon. The days were coming soon enough when the planes diving out of the sky towards the task force would wear angry red meatballs instead of white stars.

While an army traveled on its stomach, the navy traveled by the depth of its fuel bunkers. Like a hungry dog never knowing when its next meal would come, destroyers topped off their fuel tanks whenever they could. January 2nd brought calm seas to Task Force 38 so refueling with the four oil tankers went normally. Bill Morton wrote, "Refueled several hundred miles off Formosa. It is said the Japanese know we are coming and are ready. What they are going to do about it I don't know. We'll probably find out tomorrow. Word was passed about 1700 we were to make our first attack early tomorrow morning." With the cessation of fueling efforts, the task force went to 'flank' speed of twenty-five knots as it sped to Formosa. The green tin can sailors were about to be put to the test.

Before dawn on January 3rd, fighter strikes were launched from the carriers *Lexington*, *Hancock*, and *Hornet*. "Very bad weather for dive bombing attacks. Altitude visibility only about 1500 feet," noted Morton. The targets for the day were airfields on southern Formosa and the Pescadores Islands. The mission: suppress land based enemy aircraft by a continuous patrol of fighter planes throughout the day. At night the carrier *Independence* launched planes for 'heckler' missions over the enemy airfields plus to keep a combat air patrol over the task force.

Death often arrived without notice or expectation. The *Hank* had ended 1944 rescuing pilots and crew. 1945 found the *Hank* in this role again but she wouldn't have the same luck as a few days earlier. During carrier launches, a plane crashed 500 yards from *Hank's* starboard beam. By the time DD-702 had arrived there was nothing to be found of either the plane or the pilot. During flight launches, Fighting Squadron Seven also lost a pilot when his *Hellcat* experienced a power failure during takeoff from the *Hancock*: Ensign Charles D. Siegenthaler "attempted to stop the plane from rolling down the deck, but was not successful. It plunged into the wild, dark sea and Ensign Siegenthaler was not seen to leave his plane when it sank."

In a crash, pilots faced the violence of impacting the deck and steel barrier cables of the carrier or the power of the seas. Often pilots impacted instruments in the cockpit and had but a few seconds to escape their flying steeds despite suffering from facial injuries and disorientation. Aviators were weighed down by, "a hunting knife, a thirty-eight caliber revolver, one and two cell flashlights, a pencil flashlight, waterproof charts, flags, whistles, heavy Marine shoes, vitamin capsules, first aid kit, Mae West life jacket, parachute harness, chart board, helmet and goggles, flight suit, very pistol and flares, dye marker, and a back pack which contains 'K' rations, machete, malted milk tablets, jack knife, whet stone, mosquito net hood, poncho, water, first aid kit, fishing tackle, more flares, smoke bombs, twine, matches, compass, gloves, and various other useful items. Each man also has a one-man raft secured to his parachute pack." Many planes that went into the seas entered at angles that made escape difficult.

Ault had better luck in the beginning of the year saving pilots than the *Hank*. DD-698 was named for Commander William B. Ault, the commander of USS *Lexington's* Carrier Air Group 2. During the Air Battle of the Coral Sea, Cdr. Ault led an attack against the enemy carriers. The skilled twenty-five year Navy veteran bombed one of the Japanese carriers on 8 May 1942 but the intense anti-aircraft fire returned by the Japanese warship injured his gunner, William T. Butler ARM1c, and himself. With the *Lexington* sunk and his plane running low on fuel, the *Yorktown* could not find the CAG 2 commander on their radar. They wished him "good luck." Ault was never recovered. He was posthumously awarded the Navy Cross for extraordinary heroism.

Three years later, the USS *Ault* was on station to save pilots in distress. Running out of fuel before he could land his fighter, Ensign L. Ray was recovered after water landing his plane on the *Hancock's* starboard bow. Anti-aircraft fire over the target had reached up and found its mark. A TBM crew from the carrier *Hornet* had its hydraulics shot out during the strike against targets on Formosa. Mid-afternoon as the strike was being recovered, Ensign Thomas Adams put his *Avenger* down on the waves. Johnny on the spot, *Ault*, rescued the pilot and his crew, Thomas Fanger ARM1c, wounded in the thigh by flak, -a Purple Heart award to follow- and William Corley AMM1c. The return of the Fighting Squadron Seven and Torpedo Bomber Squadron Eleven pilots demonstrated the destroyers' lifeguard abilities to the birdmen.

The *Haynsworth* was ready for that role, too.

RESCUE AT SEA

Left: Lt. jg. Donald Seiz. (Courtesy of Peggy Seiz Turner)
Right: VT-20 TBM. (Courtesy of the National Navy Aviation Museum)

EVERYTHING WAS AGAINST THEM. Damage from anti-aircraft batteries. One wheel locked up in the wing and the other locked down. No way to land on their carrier. Deep in enemy territory. The waves below them had been getting bigger all day. The choice was easy, but not desired. Lt. jg. Donald Francis Seiz knew that landing in the ocean was his only option.

January 3rd, 1945 started as a strike day for Lt. Seiz and his TBM-1C crew as part of Task Force 38's attacks against targets on Formosa and Luzon. American forces would be landing ashore at Lingayen Gulf in less than a week's time. Airstrikes were sent against Japanese airfields, communication facilities, and supply lines despite adversity in the skies: "A cold front moved slowly across Formosa during the morning and southeastward past the task force the following night. This front caused numerous squalls and heavy overcast conditions at the launching point all day. Flying conditions in the launching area were unfavorable and only slightly better at the target. The afternoon strike was called back due to weather conditions."

Despite the poor weather, the two days of attacks had been successful. Twenty-one enemy ships had been sunk or destroyed, while another fifty-eight had been damaged. On the ground eleven locomotives, four tank cars, and several freight cars were destroyed. Additionally, a railroad bridge, warehouse, fuel depots, and ammunition dumps all over Formosa were left in ruins. Lt. Seiz's squadron, VT-20, had sunk a 1500 ton ship.

There was still enemy opposition to contend with. Despite the fact that few enemy planes rose to challenge the strike force, enemy anti-aircraft fire exacted its revenge against the American fliers. In all, seventeen planes were lost in combat that day.

After jettisoning his torpedo, Seiz prepared to put the bomber down in the Pacific. He recalled the radio operator, John Francis Brady ARM3c, from the belly back to the top. Gunner Clifford Gallant AMM3c was already topside in the turret at the rear of the large crew canopy. Seeing a destroyer nearby, Seiz ran through the checklist to put the bomber down in the ocean. Flying parallel to swells, Seiz extended the flaps and then slowed the huge plane by first throttling back and reducing the rpm to the Wright R-2600 14 cylinder radial engine. If the speed fell below 70 knots, the Avenger might stall and nose over into the ocean; it was essential to keep the plane above stall speed while keeping the nose elevated. No different than a carrier, except there was no one waiting in the ocean to assist if the landing went awry. He attempted to keep the plane upright as he landed in the troughs of the large waves. Seiz knew that the *Avenger* was rugged, and if he hit the water just right, they should be okay.

The *Avenger* TBF/TBM torpedo bomber was a beast of a carrier aircraft. It dwarfed the other planes on deck. Designed to carry a torpedo or a 2000 pound bomb load in an internal bomb bay, the Avenger was almost forty-one feet long. Unfolded, it wings spanned fifty-four feet. It weighed over 11,000 pounds empty and nearly 17,000 pounds fully loaded. Machine guns were mounted in her wings, a dorsal turret at the end of the cockpit, and a ventral mount in the belly. She was the biggest plane that resided on the 147 foot wide carrier USS *Lexington*. The crews that flew her referred to the bomber as the 'pregnant turkey.'

The Grumman TBF-1C's underside was lightly armored. The main landing gear was tucked into the wing, but still remained exposed. Accurate anti-aircraft fire damaged Lt. Seiz's landing gear. One strut hung limply, while the other remained stuck in its wing compartment.

Lt. Seiz successfully flew slowly down the length of the waves before he cut the ignition to the large radial engine. With a smooth landing on the water, the pilot and his crew of two escaped the airplane and boarded their life raft. As the waves bounced the raft, the crew spread dye in the water to mark their position.

The USS *Haynsworth* was steaming 70 miles from Formosa when lookouts on the bridge spotted an American plane in trouble. The Officer of the Deck, Lt. Leon Berk, USNR, ordered, "Engines ahead full." Berk's goal was to maneuver the *Haynsworth* between the wind and the TBF's crew, while keeping the aircrew forward of the ship's beam.

Recovering aircrew while under the pressure of group operations was not new to Cdr. Tackney. On the same day in 1942 when his command, the destroyer minesweeper USS *Gamble*, was hunting the Imperial Japanese Navy submarine I-123, Tackney was tasked with rescuing a pilot and airmen stranded on a Japanese held island near Guadalcanal.

Attacking the Japanese Advance Force of ten cruisers and eight destroyers, two TBF *Avengers* of Torpedo Squadron 8 came under attack from two Japanese *Zero* fighters. Lt. jg. Edward "Frenchie" Fayle 'won' his battle when his turret gunner, Edward Velasquez ARM3c, traded fire with Pilot Officer First Class Iwaki Yoshio, an ace with eight kills to his credit and a TBF killer to boot-he had bagged three VT-8 *Avengers* during the battle of Midway. Yoshio did not survive. Fayle had to ditch his plane near Nura Island after sustaining damage in the battle and running short of fuel to return to the USS *Saratoga*. An allied coastwatcher alerted the Navy of the collection of sailors now gathered on Nura. The *Gamble* safely rescued Fayle, Velasquez, Robert Minnig S1c, and J. R. Moncarrow ARM3c.

Just a few weeks into his next command, Tackney had the *Haynsworth* proceeding on various courses and speeds until it was on station within ten minutes. They arrived to find the fliers already in their inflatable raft but the *Avenger*, while remaining afloat for nearly four minutes, had already started the slow descent to Davy Jones' locker.

When a call went out for a volunteer to swim out to the aircrew, Seaman Bill Vassey answered, "I'm ready." As a young man on the family farm in South Carolina, Vassey had learned to swim in the pond on their property. The lanky bluejacket climbed down from the starboard dual 40mm gun. The eighteen year old sailor found himself being lowered into the ocean, a line tied around his waist. Like a young Buster Crabbe preparing to swim in the Olympics, Vassey jumped into the Pacific.

Cargo nets were lowered over the side to facilitate the recovery. Swimming out to the aircrew, Vassey brought each of them back to the hemp rope on the side of the tin can. By 1430, all three were aboard. The *Haynsworth's* doctor, Lt. jg. Ley pronounced that the, "pilot and crew [were] in good condition."

VT-8 Lt. jg. E. Fayle top row, 2ⁿᵈ from left.
(Courtesy of the Museum of Naval Aviation)

Bill Vassey S1c at left.
(Courtesy of Bill Vassey)

Crew of a VT-31 TBF Escaping 6 August 1943

Despite the damage and loss of the plane, the mission was a success. "We are reported to have lost twenty planes but nothing official. We sent six TBFs after three Jap transports. They said one of the transports was low in the water and the other two were burning badly. Large fire and explosions were seen over the target" entered Seaman Morton's into his secret journal. "As yet, task force has encountered no attacks from planes or enemy task forces. I hope our luck holds."

Seiz and his two crewmen were later returned to their carrier to rejoin their squadron, VT-20. Less than two weeks later, January 16, 1945, Seiz did not return from his mission against Hong Kong. In a telegram, the Navy notified the family of his status: missing in action. Lt. jg. Donald Francis Seiz was declared dead by the Navy on January 17, 1946.

TASK FORCE 38 DISHED OUT PUNISHMENT WITH NEAR IMPUNITY. After two days of air attacks, the Commander in Chief of the Pacific, Fleet Admiral Chester A. Nimitz, issued a communiqué that totaled the score: 111 enemy aircraft destroyed with an additional 220 planes damaged. The air attacks sank twenty-seven ships and damaged another sixty-eight. Very few enemy planes rose to challenge the fleet and of those that did, did so without result.

Strikes continued on January 4th and then the task force set course for Luzon in the Philippines as the weather deteriorated. "These raids were made against the airfields, shipping and strategic enemy installations as a softening up measure for the amphibious operation against Luzon, scheduled for January 9th." *Haynsworth's* Bill Morton noted, "Sent over two more strikes this morning. The weather all night had been clear and would have made a perfect day for bombing but when morning came, it clouded up. Visibility closed in to 500 feet and below that over the target. It varied from 0 to 2,000 [feet] around us. We secured from GQ about 0930. I slept till 1115 then got up for chow. I was nearly in the mess hall when the general alarm sounded. A Japanese twin engine bomber had been sighted. Several other groups of planes (unidentified) were reported ranging from five miles to seventy-eight miles. Evidently none of them could find us because not a shot was fired. Several mines were sighted and exploded that had evidently been laid by mine laying aircraft or subs during the night. It was definitely confirmed we only lost seven planes yesterday. We secured about 1430. We are to retire to the fueling rendezvous tonight. We refuel tomorrow but after that, what? I don't know." Past what was listed in the daily Morning Orders, the bluejackets were not in a 'need to know' status.

The USS *Wallace L. Lind* DD-703 joined Task Group 38.2 on January 5 to bring DesRon62 to nearly full strength. Eight of her nine

USS Hancock CV-19, USS English DD-696, USS Enterprise CV-6 January 5, 1945. (NARA 80-G-470281)

destroyers were engaged as part of the eighteen destroyer screen protecting TG 38.2. Only the USS *Borie* DD-704, still training in the waters off Oahu, had yet to join her sister destroyers.

In the late afternoon, the task force turned its course to Luzon upon completion of refueling. The sailor's perspective was caught by Morton. "We are moving down to Luzon for neutralizing strikes on her airfields. It is rumored that it is to be a softening up of it for an invasion by the 7ᵗʰ Fleet. Then it is said, we will move back to Formosa on the inside next to China to try and keep her planes on the ground. The weather has cleared up and we are going within thirty-five miles off the coast of Luzon so I figure we will catch Hell but good."

SUPPRESSION AND DESTRUCTION OF ENEMY AERIAL ASSAULTS against the landing forces was the mission on Saturday, January 6ᵗʰ. The targets: enemy airfields on northern Luzon. The enemy's focus was not on McCain's carriers. "We received no attack from the Japs because they are too busy with the 7ᵗʰ Fleet."

Positioned as a carrier plane guard, the USS *Charles S. Sperry* aided a plane crew from the USS *Lexington*. Lt. Robert E. McHenry, Edward

Butler ARM2c, and Carroll Fletcher AMM2c ditched their TBF Grumman Avenger at 1430 close to the destroyer. "Coming about to windward she rescued the pilot and crew from the grasping sea. Both pilot and crew were uninjured despite the fact the plane made a very hard landing, sinking almost instantly." McHenry, a member of Torpedo Squadron 20, had been previously credited with a torpedo hit against the *Yamato's* sister ship, *Musashi,* on October 24, 1944 during the Battle of Leyte Gulf. It took nineteen torpedo strikes and seventeen bombs to finally sink the leviathan battleship. McHenry's actions in the face of strong anti-aircraft fire earned him a coveted Navy Cross. For Vice Admiral John S. McCain, the rescue kept one more experienced pilot and aircrew on the roster.

CRUCIAL WATER DISCIPLE HAD DETERIORATED aboard Cdr. Tackney's vessel after seven days in combat. Personal use had risen so much that the crew was put on water restriction for five days. Fresh water for the boilers took precedence over bluejacket cleanliness.

Aboard ship, issues for the sailors often took on a more personal nature. For radarman Aakhus, there were two battles: one against the Japanese and one against a case of 'jungle rot' picked up on previous duty. Twice a day the radarman visited Dr. Ley's sick bay for treatment of infected feet. Despite wearing wooden shower shoes and regular medical treatment, the problem would not resolve. Some battles were violent but brief. Others, like Aakhus' personal affliction, were a daily struggle.

The crew found Lt. Cdr. Lothrop's posted Morning Orders to be interesting souvenirs of their time at sea during combat, especially as personal logs were not supposed to be written by the crew. In his Morning Orders, Lothrop reminded the crew to leave them posted at least until the next morning had arrived before adding them to their locker stash.

WEATHER CONDITIONS WORSENED late on the 6th and remained poor through the 7th. Strong winds and heavy waves at the bow resulted in damage to many of the tin cans. Task Force Commander Adm. McCain slowed the formation speed to seventeen knots to prevent further damage to the destroyers but the typhoon took a toll on the fleet. Whereas the *Sumner* class' design predecessor, the *Fletcher* class destroyers, had two singly mounted 5" guns on the bow, the dual 5" mounts of the *Sumners* made them especially bow

Protective "bloomers" on a Sumner class destroyer can be seen on both front 5" gun mounts

heavy. This extra weight forward drove the *Sumners* deeper into the heavy seas.

Capt. Higgins' squadron took a beating. The USS *John W. Weeks* lost the 'bloomers'-the protective canvas shrouds over the guns-from the forward #1 5" guns. Refueling efforts by the destroyers from the heavies were difficult at best. Aboard the *Sperry,* "wind and weather conditions extremely poor making fueling almost impossible. Cast off from USS *Hancock* after parting three fuel hoses." The waves were strong enough that the forward #1 5" mount was damaged on the *Sperry.* Seaman Bill Morton of the *Haynsworth* recorded, "The weather was extremely rough and several cans split seams and had to turn back to a repair group since they were taking on water and were unable to maintain the pace." A victim of the storm, the USS *Hunt* DD-674, was detached to Ulithi for repair of damage incurred by the pounding seas. The winter storms off Formosa offered no mercy to the metal ships.

For the novice crews, the previous days "were excellent indoctrination. Overshadowing and generally eliminating most thoughts about impending action was the more immediate weather instigated action constantly proposing new problems of substitution and repair."

A S VICE ADMIRAL KINKAID'S SEVENTH FLEET INVA-SION FORCES WERE UNDER HEAVY AERIAL ATTACK, the planned airstrikes against Formosa, were scrubbed. Course was reset for Luzon to provide air cover on the morning of the 7th.

On Sunday, the weather had improved enough that most of the targets had good visibility, a winter rarity for the pilots of Task Force 38. Heavy air attacks were directed against Clark Field, north of Manila. Reconnaissance showed that 155 Japanese planes were reveted there. With the 'big blue blanket' over the airfields, few Japanese planes rose to take the challenge. Despite a lack of aerial response from the enemy, eighteen American planes along with most of their pilots and crew were lost to combat. The tradeoff was uneven. Though seventy-five Japanese planes were destroyed on the ground, none contained pilots.

Despite the strikes, the tin cans had numerous roles to fulfill. The *Sperry* served duty again as one of the plane guards. During the day's launches, one of the most experienced pilots in the task force got into trouble. Lt. John E. Nearing USNR had already completed three combat tours with time in VF-2 and VF-12. With four years of flying experience under his belt, it was a loss when Nearing's VF-20 *Hellcat* failed to get airborne as it cleared the deck of the USS *Lexington*, plunging into the heavy waves of the Pacific. Despite the proximity of the *Sperry* and the USS *Tingey* DD-539, rescue efforts were in vain. The twenty-five year old New Jersey native was not recovered.

Seas remained rough so fueling attempts were halted after the *Waldron*, *Charles S. Sperry*, and *Ault* parted fuel lines sent from the heavy ships. By the conclusion of two days of pounding seas, five of the nine destroyers of DesRon 62 had buckled gun shields and/or guns jammed in elevation at the forward dual 5" mounts.

Continued poor weather and prolonged periods at sea took a toll on carrier planes and air groups. Knowing that their fleets would be at sea for long periods of time in the push against Japan, the U.S. Navy had floating depots ready. Escort carriers were available to the task force as a source of replacement planes and pilots.

The *Sperry* transferred pilots from the fleet carriers *Hornet* and *Hancock* to the escort carriers USS *Shipley Bay* and USS *Kwajalein*. The pilots ferried replacement aircraft back to their respective carriers. *Hancock's* pilots brought back six F6F *Hellcats* to partially replace the eight that already been lost since New Year's Day. Flight operations had caused the loss of five *Hornet Hellcats* in the same time period. Their replacement allotment was just four new fighters.

SETTING SAIL FOR FORMOSA, the task force fed from the fleet oilers on the 8th. Even on days without air missions against the enemy, both carriers and destroyers were busy. The USS *Hancock*'s deck log recorded the numerous destroyers that tended to task group needs:

0845 DD-670 *Dortch* alongside to transfer Officer Messenger (O.M.) mail

0849 Came alongside AO-62 *Taluga* to fuel.

0907 DD-558 *Laws* alongside to transfer photographic material and one war correspondent

0946 DD-697 *Sperry* alongside to receive replacement pilots for transfer to CVE

1000 DD-702 *Hank* alongside to transfer radar material

1010 DD-744 *Blue* alongside to transfer O.M. mail.

1307 DD-703 *Lind* alongside to transfer personnel

1408 DD-538 *Stephan Potter* alongside to transfer O.M. mail

1422 DD-696 *English* alongside to transfer six passengers

1455 DD-793 *Cassin Young* alongside to transfer O.M. mail

1508 DD-697 *Sperry* alongside to deliver six new pilots

1532 DD-701 *Weeks* alongside to transfer U.S. and O.M. mail

1550 DD-535 *Miller* alongside to transfer O.M. mail

PILOT SALVATION BY THE TIN CANS CONTINUED. The USS *Wallace L. Lind* was already well versed in rescuing aircrew. In December, while serving as plane guard for the carrier *USS Enterprise*, *Lind* rescued the crews from one fighter and two torpedo bombers. Northeast of Luzon in the Philippines, *Lind* sent the rescue swimmers after another pilot. Ensign P. King from Fighting Squadron Eleven made a water landing after failing to get airborne during launch. The *Hellcat* pilot was quickly rescued and returned to the *Hornet* while his plane slowly descended 2300 fathoms to the ocean's floor.

The scenario was repeated the next day when Cdr. George DeMetropolis' *Lind* rescued Ensign John H. Buttler of Fighting Squadron 7 after an airstrike against Formosa. For Buttler, "hard luck seemed to dog his whole time with squadron. His engine quit when he was at angels 5. It was perhaps well that he landed downwind toward a DD in view of the heavy seas running. After encountering considerable difficulty in extricating himself from his plane, whose canopy had jammed in an attempt to jettison it, he swam to the surface and was picked up by a DD."

The *Charles S. Sperry* saved one herself, a fighter pilot from the carrier USS *Hornet*. His plane afire, he crashed in the middle of the task group.

A DMIRAL HALSEY SENT A MESSAGE TODAY indicating he expects to seek out and find big targets for a surface engagement in a few days. Ready yourself and the ship," advised the *Haynsworth's* executive officer in his daily bulletin to the crew. "In order to keep phone circuits clear, lookouts shall not report movements or sightings of planes they are positive are friendly. Report all doubtful sightings and all enemy plane sightings as 'BOGIES.'" Lothrop offered counsel on the 7th Fleets invasion: "Thought for the day as our amphibious forces make a landing on LUZON. *Put the screws on LUZON.*" Finally, he returned to the issue of water use, "The need for water conservation is far more than just water shortage. Every extra gallon you use of water wastes extra gallons of fuel burned. If operations materialize, we are going to need every bit of oil we have." Somewhere out there potentially were the surviving battleships of the Japanese fleet.

The next day airstrikes against Japanese airfields on Formosa were conducted. Mother Nature had no intention of making things easy for the task force. Winter weather at sea again remained poor. A few bogies ventured out over the fleet but no attacks were made. Course was set to the southwest as the fleet prepared to cover the American invasion at Lingayen in southern Luzon.

"I saw Admiral Halsey when we refueled from the *New Jersey*. Word was passed to get plenty of sleep because we would need it the next few days because we would meet the enemy for sure," wrote Bill Morton. "It's a funny thing because I'm not too nervous. Perhaps it is because I don't allow myself to think about it too much. I've got to live through it."

The crew of the *Haynsworth* was just ten days into their one hundred days of combat.

M AN YOUR BATTLESTATIONS!" Early on the 9th of January, the USS *Charles S. Sperry* reported a possible submarine contact to the TG Commander at 0332. Just 900 yards from the screen, the contact posed an imminent threat to the task group. Under the cover of darkness, submarines ran on the surface at night to recharge their batteries. The four carriers loomed as prize targets to any enemy submarine. Responding to Rear Admiral Bogan's orders, Task Group 38.2 executed an emergency turn away from the contact while two radar equipped torpedo planes were launched immediately.

Cdr. Harry McIlhenny ordered his bluejackets aboard the *Sperry* to drop depth charges at 0355. Though initial results of the attack were negative, Cdr. Tackney's *Haynsworth* was ordered to investigate with

USS Borie fuels from the battleship USS New Jersey. (National Archives)

Sperry while the rest of the TG continued in a direction 60 degrees away.

Tackney already had one Japanese sub sinking under his belt and a Navy Cross on his dress whites to show for it. His destroyer mine-sweeper USS Gamble had been in the Solomon Islands on August 24, 1942, when the enemy was spotted: "As soon as it was sighted, the sub dove, and the *Gamble* took off in hot pursuit, her sonar pinging away, and the entire crew at General Quarters. Three times the *Gamble* passed over the sub's location and each time she laid a nice string of depth charges that exploded at various depths." After several hours of chasing the sub and dropping additional patterns of charges, an officer saw "an air bubble six feet in diameter break the surface" along with sections of deck planking and oil bubbles." Lt. Cdr. Tackney had sunk just the twelfth Japanese submarine to that point during the war.

The opportunity to sink a second sub was presented to the new captain of the *Haynsworth*. On the bridge, Cdr. Tackney ordered the lee-helmsman, "Signal all engines ahead flank speed- EMERGENCY, make turns for 30 knots." In response, the lee-helm pushed both the port and starboard handles on the Bendix Engine Order Telegraph from the setting *Ahead Standard* to *Ahead Flank* while passing through *Ahead Full*. Immediately he pulled the handles back to *Ahead Standard* and then again immediately back to *Ahead Flank*.

The rapid change of settings on the EOT set off a flurry of bells ringing down below in the heart of the tin can. Known as an 'all ahead Bendix' order amongst the bridge and engine rooms, the officers and crew knew that Tackney wanted more speed and he wanted it straight away. In rapid response the throttle men shifted the EOT answer indicator on the throttle board to *Ahead Flank* as a signal that the order was received.

The destroyermen felt the warship lean in response to the hard turns of the twin rudders. As the speed increased, the vibration of the screws' increased rpm rippled through the metal decks of the destroyer. In the darkness, sailors raced across the ship to man their battle stations in response to the bong-bong-bong of the klaxon. The torpedomen along the depth charge racks and the 20mm men behind them witnessed the destroyer's rooster tail grow, the churning frothy phosphorescent wake that grew with the knots.

"At 0345 this morning they called 'stand by for submarine attack.' Everyone promptly went to GQ only to find out another ship had had a contact and lost it so we went back to bed with the GQ team of Sonar and the depth charges remaining on alert," Morton wrote in his journal. Cdr. Tackney simply logged 'Negative results.' Finally, after eight hours of searching, the hunter-killer group of two DesRon 62 destroyers rejoined the task group.

WHILE FIVE AIRSTRIKES WERE LAUNCHED against Formosa, a Mitsubishi Ki-46 *Dinah* reconnaissance plane found itself in the crosshairs of both the destroyers and the CAP. The deck gun crews held their fire as two CAP fighters chased the *Dinah* across the clouds before shooting her down just over the horizon.

Once again, the seas attacked the fleet: "The weather was rough and tons of water were cascading across the lower decks. Spray was coming over the bridge at each wave. It was whipped by a high wind that made it feel like sleet," reported Morton. The sonarman's assessment of the situation was prescient. "It looks to me like Admiral Halsey is trying to bait the Japanese Navy out for a final battle. At present we are going to meet a convoy of Japanese reinforcements. I hope we get them."

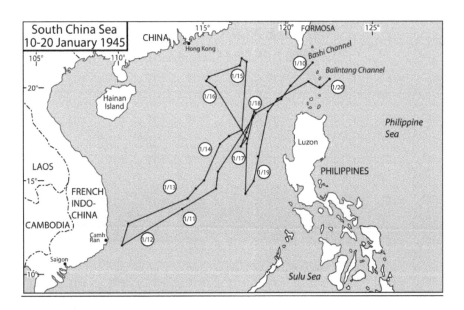

The USS Lexington movements with Task Force 38 within the South China Sea, Asia's cauldron, during operations 10-20 January 1945. (Adapted from USS Lexington Action Report: December 20, 1944 Through January 22, 1945: Strikes Against Formosa, Luzon, Indo-China, Hong Kong, Okinawa)

"YOU WILL NOT GET OUT ALIVE"
THE SOUTH CHINA SEA

USS John W. Weeks.
(Jim Tshanz photo courtesy USS John W. Weeks Association)

WELCOME TO THE SOUTH CHINA SEA," Tokyo Rose greeted the Fast Carrier Task Force over the radio. "You will not get out alive."

Admiral Halsey had long desired the chance to enter the South China Sea with his hammer. American submarines and long range patrol bombers had already closed off the open expanses of the Pacific Ocean to the Empire. Just the Sea of Japan, the East China Sea, the Yellow Sea, and the South China Sea remained for the Emperor's fleet to roam. Reports suggested that some of the remaining IJN battleships would be found in the South China Sea. In addition, the sea was ringed with Japanese airfields and installations. Targets were ripe for the picking.

In the opening moves of nautical chess, the destroyers served as pawns. DesRon 62 mates *Ault, Charles S. Sperry, Waldron* and *John W. Weeks* led Task Force 38 through the narrow Bashi Channel separating Formosa and the Philippines into the South China Sea, Asia's caul-

USS Waldron underway July 1944. Note crew at all weapons stations. (U.S. Naval Historical Center #NH96832)

dron. This was the furthest west any Allied ships had ventured since the war started.

In an unusual move, the fleet oil tankers followed the Fast Carrier Task Groups into the eye of the needle rather than remaining at a distant point away from Japanese planes. Admiral Halsey's fleet had planned to take up residence in the cauldron.

In the South China Sea, Task Force 38 was surrounded by Japanese held territory. Enemy planes had the potential to emerge from any direction. "It was a bold action; anything might have happened; we were ready for it." From the viewpoint of the common bluejacket, Bill Morton wrote, "We are now bottled up, more or less, with the Japanese on four sides of us. We are supposedly going after a 100 ship Jap convoy that is bringing up reinforcements to Luzon. They say the biggest ships of the convoy are cans so it ought to be duck soup for us since we have cans, cruisers, wagons, and aircraft carriers."

The Japanese reconnoitered the fleet as several bogies penetrated the airspace. "This morning our planes shot down two Jap planes. One of the ships hit another one but it came on for about fifteen miles. When it burst through the clouds it was a ball of fire. It tried to crash dive on a carrier and the pilot bailed out." Sonarman Morton noted,

"It was, at first, thought to be one of ours but they found a Jap life raft and chute so it was confirmed as definitely Japanese."

The fast oiler task group topped off 38's tanks on Wednesday the 10th but bogies appeared. "While at precautionary General Quarters, one enemy plane was shot down in flames over the formation. Planes of the task force continued their strikes against the enemy during the day." -

While Admiral McCain's forces had come through the day un-scathed, the invasion forces of the 7th fleet had suffered dearly. Kami-kaze plane and suicide boat attacks struck eleven ships. Nearly one hundred sailors were killed, over two hundred were wounded.

THE SMALL DOGS WERE ALWAYS HUNGRY. The next day was used to refuel and accomplish other tasks. The USS *Hank*, af-fectionately known as the *Happy Henry*, was used to transfer war cor-respondents from ship to ship on the 11th. After picking up Keith Wheeler and William F. Marion from the USS *Hornet* CV-17, she de-livered them to the heavy cruiser USS *Boston*. Correspondents were always popular guests aboard the warships. Tales of battle action by the common seamen might eventually find their way stateside to mag-azines or local newspapers.

The USS *Wallace L. Lind* served as the task group's mailman. Cdr. George DeMetropolis' ship distributed sacks of mail to the other war-ships as airstrikes against Formosa and Saigon were launched. The long and hard days at sea for the crew could often be monotonous. Corre-spondence from home was a welcome relief, even just temporarily, for the bluejackets. Every few weeks, mail would be forwarded to the ship and letters home sent off. Due to the risk of classified information be-ing leaked-'*loose lips sink ships*'-officers censored the letters before they left the ship. Some sailors had prearranged codes with their families at home so they would know where their sailor was sailing. Those that had not created ways to encrypt their messages and gave out too much information, sent home letters with passages blacked out or removed by razors.

THERE WERE NEVER ENOUGH DESTROYERS AVAILA-BLE but the screen swelled to twenty-one tin cans with the arrival of Destroyer Squadron 61. With the risk of enemy air attacks increas-ing, Captain J. Womble had five destroyers sent out to serve as picket ships including DesRon 62 members *Hank, Waldron, English* and

Lt James L. Hooper in-flight photo, VT-11 Avenger, USS Hornet CV-12. (Courtesy of Jim Hooper)

Haynsworth. Stationed twelve to twenty-five miles from the task group, the tin cans became the guard dogs on the flanks.

Late afternoon, three enemy aircraft were spotted approaching the formation. None survived. *Haynsworth* bluejacket Bill Morton detailed the action: "Two *Zekes* were reported to our CAP coming in low and fast on one of our pickets. The general alarm was sounded and when I arrived at my GQ station they had been downed already (sic) and you could see where they were burning on the water at the horizon's edge." The trident defense continued to exact a toll on the enemy.

The 11th ended with the task force proceeding on a southwesterly course for strikes the next day at Camranh Bay. "In South China Sea, about 225 miles west of Manilla, about 400 miles east of Japanese Indo-China. After fueling expect to proceed south [at] a high speed, possibly for engagement with a force reported south of us," noted Seaman Marion Parker. Third Fleet Commander "Bull" Halsey's message to his ships regarding the mission was simple: "You know what to do-Give them Hell- God bless you all. Halsey"

ADMIRAL McCAIN'S CARRIERS TARGETED FRENCH IN-DO-CHINA with strikes against Saigon and Camranh Bay on Friday, January 12th. The US Navy had hoped to find major vessels of

Lt James L. Hooper in-flight photo, VT-11 Avenger, USS Hornet CV-12. (Courtesy of Jim Hooper)

the Japanese Navy but few capital ships were found, the IJN battle-ships having fled for safer anchorage. "Admiral Halsey says today is the day of golden opportunity," was the daily annotation in Parker's journal. But, with heavy resistance expected, the *Haynsworth's* executive officer tempered the crew's optimism: "Just to strike a cheery note on the Morning Orders, this is one day to keep yourself completely clothed and buttoned up with your lifejackets handy."

Task Force 38's sledgehammer attacked targets along 420 miles of coastline. It was a maximum effort: 1465 sorties were flown by the carrier pilots with the 850 planes that were available that Friday in January. For the airedales, it was a very successful day. The results of the raids against Axis shipping delivered a staggering punch to the enemy. Forty-four ships were sunk including fifteen IJN ships plus a dozen oil tankers. The airstrikes concluded with heckler air sweeps sent against targets in Saigon.

On picket duty, *English's* radar detected an 'enemy' vessel. The submarine USS *Rock*, serving on pilot lifeguard duty, heard the destroyer request permission to fire on an enemy sailboat. With permission received, DD-696 fired thirty-four rounds from her 5 inch cannon at a range of 4000 yards. Poor marksmanship and good fortune allowed the 'sailboat' to submerge rapidly to a depth of 300 feet. After a period of time, the periscope was extended. Seeing that the coast was clear, the submarine surfaced. Its commander decided that a torpedo run by an American sub against an American tin can would not benefit the war effort.

Serving again as a carrier plane guard, the USS *Hank* retrieved another TBM Grumman *Avenger* crew from the South China Sea. At 0915 the big torpedo bomber crashed after takeoff 4000 yards off the starboard bow of the destroyer. By 0925 the *Hank* had pulled pilot Ensign Thomas R. Jones, radioman Max A. Eckels ARM3c, and gunner Dean P. Kenny AMM3c from the ocean. The aircrew from Torpedo Squadron 7 would be transferred back to the *Hancock* along with two injured *Hank* crew members on the 14th.

Admiral McCain's forces met very little aerial resistance. The *Divine Wind* had avoided the cauldron. Instead Imperial warriors flew their steeds towards the ships of Admiral Kinkaid's 7th Fleet off the eastern coast of the Philippines. Nine ships of the invasion forces were struck by day's end. It would be a harbinger for the future invasion of Okinawa.

REPLENISHMENT AT SEA

*A Sumner class destroyer attempts to refuel on January 13, 1945.
(NARA 80-G-299869)*

ROUGH WINTER WEATHER PREVENTED AIRSTRIKES on
January 13th. Structural damage of the thin skinned destroyers'
bulkheads was the norm for the day. The force of the heavy waves had
unexpected reactions aboard the USS Waldron: "0320–Depth charge
projector [K-gun] was fired accidentally by heavy seas. Depth charge
did not detonate being set on 'safe.'" On the Haynsworth, Morton
recorded his impressions, "We were driving into the wind all night
which batters the devil out of a ship. One of the other ships lost
mount #1 (5" turret) over the side. All we got was the guard around a
couple of 40mm guns smashed. It was so rough they didn't even have
the routine GQ this morning."

Squadron 62 Commander John Higgins urged his destroyer captains, "Repairing storm damage will require effort normally far beyond
the capacity of the ship's forces. We are on the first team and expected
to do the impossible. Keep bailing, keep shoring, and when the time
comes, keep shooting."

The purported range of a *Sumner* class destroyer was 6,000 nautical miles at fifteen knots. The reality was that a fully *loaded Sumner* had a range of just 3,600 nautical miles at fifteen knots but the Fast Carrier Task Force frequently traveled at speeds greater than twenty knots. For the carriers, increased speeds eased the launching of their planes. For all the ships, higher speeds allowed them to outrun enemy submarines, shorten travel times and maneuver more quickly against enemy aircraft. However, these speeds led to fuel bunkers that emptied quickly on the destroyers. The *Sumners* could hold but 500 tons of fuel. Fuel oil not only provided energy for the hungry boilers of the destroyers, it also served as ballast to the ship. Fuel replenishment was vital and necessarily frequent. If the destroyers could not refuel from the oilers, they could top off their tanks from lines extended by the fleet carriers or the battleships.

The U.S. Navy had learned first-hand during the typhoon of December, 1944 what could happen to a destroyer low on fuel. The USS *Spence* DD-512 was unable to refuel due to the high seas and winds of *Typhoon Cobra*. With her fuel bunkers less than 15% filled, *Spence* was top heavy and foundered in the storm. She was lost along with most of her crew. Two other TF 38 destroyers low on fuel suffered various degrees of damage from the typhoon as well.

Captain Acuff's Task Group 30.8, the Fast Refueling Group, rendezvoused with Task Force 38 in the South China Sea on the 13th. Composed of two escort carriers, eight destroyers, and six fleet oilers, the FaReGrp had supplied Task Force 38 since the start of Operation MIKE, the Invasion of Luzon. The encounter with the storm was the worst weather they had experienced since *Cobra* the previous month.

Cold. Tired. Wet. Winter seas were punishing for the crews of the DesRon 62's destroyers as they attempted to bring fueling lines aboard. Capt. Higgins' destroyers left the circular screen in an attempt to refuel but were not fully successful. Replenishment at sea (RAS) required tremendous effort and teamwork between the crews of two ships as the tin cans bobbed up and down in high waves. On the blustery Saturday in January, the challenges to the sailors were both fatigue and Mother Nature herself.

One by one, destroyers left the circular screen of the task group in attempts to fuel their bunker tanks. The destroyers approached the oilers at a speed slightly faster than the oiler. As the ships ran parallel courses to each other, 140-180 feet abeam of each other, the destroyer reduced speed to line up with the oiler. Running at thirteen knots, the oiler sent three lines across to the destroyer. One line was used to gauge distance between the ships while the other two span-wires were used to bring the refueling rigs to over to the receiving vessel. Crews of approximately ten sailors were positioned fore and aft to receive the lines. Helmeted and wearing life jackets, the crews connected the span-wires to a pelican hooks and then the lines were pulled taut so that the fueling nozzle and hose could be brought across from the oiler. Hung from a boom on the oiler, some slack was maintained in the fuel lines. Manhandled by the destroyer's sailors, the nozzles were seated into bellmouth assemblies to receive the fuel. It was not unusual for lines to part. If the fuel hose parted, bunker oil would be splashed on the crew, the deck, and into the sea. "As crew members we participated in all crew activities like helping with fuel lines, wondering how frustrated the officers were when things didn't go right," recalled Tom Scott. It was easy in stormy seas to spill the heavy fuel over the deck and the ship.

The destroyers' deck crews were subjected to the South China Sea's punishing winter weather. "By that day, the forward five-inch gun bloomers had been shredded; green seas had reached the main battery director; thirty degree rolls had been reached and passed; shoes had been dyed white, and clothes hardened into boards by seas which saturated every part of the ship; water sloshed from side to side in living compartments; shoes left on the deck filled and overflowed; shower clogs floated with the tide. The wind was then near typhoon velocity; the very high seas covered mount two and after-fueling station with increasing regularity, sweeping over the quarter deck and aft, knocking men off their feet, parting fuel lines and hoses," recorded the *Sperry*.

With the heaving seas, trouble came quickly to the sailors on several destroyers being refueled. Aboard the rolling and pitching *Haynsworth*, a sailor in the refueling party was hurt. Ralph Aakhus RdM3c recounted, "It was in the South China Sea during the end of the typhoon when Don [Karos RdM3c] received an injury. We were side by side when a refueling line flew out of control and hit him in the face. He had some teeth knocked out and was generally banged up." The 'Bloody W,' as her crew nicknamed the *Waldron*, also had several sailors who suffered broken arms and legs in the storm.

Haynsworth's Seaman First Class Marion Parker wrote, "We were to take on fuel and it was a job. A boy was washed over the rail from the 703 [*Lind*]." On the USS *Wallace L. Lind*, Bob Plum FC2c, was called to his position at the fantail fueling station. Out on deck without his life jacket, Plum found a life vest left by a navy pilot who was rescued by the *Lind* the previous day. "We had managed to attach the

Left: Don Karos RdM3c. (Courtesy of Don Karos Family)
Center: Marion Parker. (Courtesy of Sylvia Parker Lowder);
Right: Bob Plum FC2c. (Courtesy Plum family)

after fuel line to the bulkhead when it suddenly became detached due to the force of the sea between the carrier and the destroyer, and caught our Exec around the neck and pinned him to the starboard K-Gun depth charge racks. I saw this and was mesmerized, when I saw the same line caught me around the waist and pinned me to the lifeline near Mount 3 [5"/38]. A Gunners Mate, recognizing my situation, cut the lifeline which immediately flipped me overboard and into the sea."

The twenty-six year old Plum was quick to open the dye marker on the pilot's lifejacket. Despite releasing the bright green dye into the sea, the fleet did not initially see him in the heavy waves. Plum, also, had trouble seeing the ships unless he was carried to the crest of a wave. "It is strange what goes through your mind," recalled Plum. "First there was fear, then came panic, and I guess finally despair. I thought of my wife and baby and wondered if I was going to make it."

Several ships went by without spotting him, but a lookout on the *Haynsworth* caught sight of Plum. After forty-five minutes adrift in the storm, he was brought aboard. Missing the tips of two of the fingers of his right hand, Plum was brought to Lt. Ley for treatment. Lt. Cdr. Lothrop's stateroom, near the sickbay, was pressed into service as a hospital room. Plum was unable to walk due to injury to his back, a result from being pinned between the fuel line and the deck metal wire lifeline.

A clarinet player in the *Lind's* band, Plum was anxious to save his fingers so Dr. Ley treated him with just Vaseline wrapped in gauze and tapes. Plum was later transferred to a destroyer tender where a surgeon was able do minor surgery to preserve his fingers. The founder of the

Bob Plum FC2c of the USS Wallace L. Lind behind the 'N'.

The Lind Jammers.
(NARA 80-G-373775)

'Lind Jammers' was able to return to both his military and musical roles aboard the *Lind*.

"It was subsequently reported that twelve men were washed overboard that day from different ships," Plum testified. "Only two were rescued. [Cdr. Tackney] later acknowledged that it was this dye marker that made all the difference in seeing me at all."

WHILE THE STORM POUNDED THE THIRD FLEET, the *Divine Wind* struck three more victims of the Seventh Fleet near the Philippines.

A THREAT ON THE HORIZON early on the 14th, forced the *Hank* to investigate. It turned out to be a small fishing boat. "Five men, believed to be Japanese, brought on board. No evidence of radio, radar, or military equipment found on board. Destroyed boat with gunfire. 1043 Transferred mail and prisoners to USS *New Jersey* (BB-62)." The prisoners turned out to be Chinese fisherman. Pulled from the South China Sea's bounding waves, they were transferred from their one cylinder engine boat to the two hundred twelve thousand shaft horsepower battleship.

The fleet oiler *Nantahala* AO-60 dropped out of formation overnight due to engine problems. The destroyers *Haynsworth* and *Sperry* were detached to protect the valuable oiler and stayed with her through the night. After *Nantahala's* engines were repaired, all three ships slowly plowed their way through the waves to rejoin the protection of the fleet. The day ended with calmer seas allowing the destroyers to finally fill their fuel tanks with black gold.

While Vice Admiral John McCain requested cancellation of all strike missions due to weather, Admiral Halsey wanted to take advantage of the task force's position. Targets were ripe for attack along the coastal perimeter of the South China Sea. Strikes were sent against the Chinese coast, facilities on Formosa and the harbors at Takao and Toshien. Also, the opportunity to find and engage enemy battleships was too big for Admiral Halsey to pass up.

Fighter opposition had been light the entire mission but on the 15th numerous enemy planes were in the air. "On General Quarters from 0645 to 2000," noted Marion Parker of the long day. "One fighter & four torpedo planes broke through our fighter screen. Two were shot down and the others turned tails."

Despite conditions not ideal for flying, the carrier strikes were directed against enemy shipping in the Pescadores Islands on the western side of Formosa as well as Swatow on the eastern coast of China. After two airstrikes, the remaining flights were cancelled as a precaution due to the weather. Despite the adverse flying conditions, the missions were successful. Two enemy destroyers were sunk as well as an enemy tanker. In the air, sixteen enemy planes were downed by the navy fliers. Another eighteen were knocked out by aerial strikes against airfields. The tradeoff was the loss of a dozen American planes.

TODAY WE STRIKE AT HONG KONG but the weather is bad and clouds are low," recorded the *Haynsworth's* Marion Parker on the 16th. "The first planes over the target report, target clear. Thirty-six ships sunk & lots of small craft. Several locomotives shot up, dock and Navy yard. Supply warehouse bombed." Task Group 38.2 launched four air raids throughout the daylight hours against Hong Kong and the Hainan Island area of the South China Sea. The results were meager for the effort with just a few ships attacked and a baker's dozen enemy planes downed. McCain's carrier air groups losses totaled nearly fifty American planes written off due to operational problems or flying through the gauntlet of accurate anti-aircraft fire ringing Hong Kong's harbor.

USS Hancock recovering aircraft in the South China Sea, January 1945.
(NARA 80-G-470280)

After several months of flights in this area, the enemy was familiar with the tactics of the American flyers. "AA was hellish, both in volume and in its precise barrage which would cover the exact areas where the planes had to enter to deliver their attacks. After three weeks of continuous combat and flying the availability of planes was low, too low to deliver a knock-out punch to the enemy," cited a Carrier Air Group 7 report. "Give us carrier planes with improved performance. If we are to continue to dig the enemy out of his foxholes, wherever he may be, we must have better implements. The SB2C, the TBM, and the F6F-5 are obsolescent, overloaded planes. If we cannot have these new planes, then send us more and better replacement pilots, because, by God, we will need them."

With the first launches of the day, *Hank* was stationed as plane guard number one when a F6F spun into the ocean during takeoff. With the *Hellcat* burning on the water 2000 yards ahead, *Hank*'s captain, Cdr. George Chambers ordered flank speed for the rescue while the deck force hoisted a cargo net overboard. Rescue swimmers with lifelines stood by the ready. Within ten minutes, Ensign Royce Carruth was saved from the Pacific. The twenty-three year old Texan flier would stay overnight as a guest aboard his rescuer until he could be returned to the *Hancock* the next day.

For the tin can sailors focused on their duty, what would happen next was mostly conjecture. Keith Myreholt RM3c wrote, "Still looking for the Jap Fleet."

STORM: NATURE'S HAMMER

THE BAROMETER CONTINUED TO DROP over the next three days. Starting on January 17, DesRon 62's tin cans experienced their first Pacific winter storm. Winds climbed as did the waves. The tempest screamed and howled as the ships moaned, their metal structures aching in the seas. Sustained twenty-four to thirty knots winds with seas so violent that fleet speed was reduced to eight knots to prevent damage to the ships. No airstrikes were launched. Combat Air Patrol (CAP) planes were kept aloft but Halsey's efforts to find the Japanese dreadnoughts and their caravan were futile.

In heavy seas, large capital ships like the battleships, fleet carriers and cruisers were fairly stable though nausea did afflict some sailors. Aboard the 894 foot fleet carrier USS *Hancock*, Phil Mulé AMM3c mused, "While some of the crew was seasick, it just meant more food for the rest of us."

But, the pencil thin destroyers though were always rolling and bobbing to some extent. Heavy seas increased that tendency, especially for the newer destroyers. Additional weaponry forward also created a high center of gravity as the *Sumners* weighed nearly ten percent more than the *Fletcher* class ancestors. The extra guns and related compartments built during the retrofit at the Brooklyn Naval Yard compounded the nose heavy aspect of Captain Higgins' destroyers.

The storm's pounding seas pushed the destroyers into deep rolls. The tin can sailors held their breath as their ship leaned to the side, waiting for the destroyer to right itself. Deeper sways caused longer recovery times until the deck returned momentarily to level. Pushed to the side, water could enter ventilators and rip equipment from their mounts. The waves created additional topside weight. Seas flowing into the ship could cause electrical shortages. Without electrical power, the pumps ceased their work, air stopped being circulated, radio and radar systems were put out of action, steering was lost. With water seeping through the vents into the engine compartments, a loss of steam could cause a loss of propulsion. Without the ability to make headway in the seas and wind, survival in the storm was a constant thought in the minds of the blue jackets. A destroyer without electricity was a dying ship.

A month earlier, Third Fleet lost three destroyers in a storm that became known as "Halsey's Typhoon." Seven additional destroyers were so badly damaged they were detached from the warzone for major repairs. The news was kept under cover by the U.S. Navy with no official communiqué from CINCPAC released about the loss of the tin cans in *Typhoon Cobra*. Rumors of the catastrophe escaped and circulated through the scuttlebutt meetings that never made the Executive Officer's Morning Orders.

Twelve months earlier, most of the Haynsworth's crewmen were living in their hometowns, many still attending high school. Just six months previously, the new destroyer ventured out into the warm summer waters of the Atlantic for its shakedown cruise. A winter storm in the unforgiving Pacific was a different proposition.

The cruel sea took its vengeance on the crews as the nautical roller coaster took its toll on the ship. Pharmacist Mate Second Class James Jones, Jr., recalled, "The storm was so bad that even seasoned seaman would vomit continuously. There was so much sickness that the decks were very difficult to walk on due to all of the vomit."

"One can lost two men. We had several injuries," were Bill Morton's remarks for that day. "Last night the sea was so rough we had to strap ourselves in our bunks," noted perpetually seasick Marion Parker. Radarman Ralph Aakhus wrote of the January storm, "It's been rough but this is the roughest yet. Half the time we are standing on our heads and the other half lying on the deck. We had a 45 degree roll once that evening. When the seas are that bad you strap yourself in your bunk and tie all furnishings to the bulkhead." Clay Lutz WT3c tried an alternate bunk: "I slept spread eagle on a mess hall table."

"Baby flat tops are taking an awful pounding. So are we." Carpenters Mate Second Class Mital noted that, "Ship rolled from 55 to 60 degrees all night." The rumor spread that three other destroyers were lost to the seas. With the *Sumners* rolling so much, the gossip found purchase amongst the crews. Mital reflected, "It pays to pray."

The 18th of January offered no relief from seas for the sailors of the task force. As the smallest combat ships in the Fast Carrier Task Force, the destroyers took the greatest pounding. The storm took a toll on both men and ships. The *Haynsworth's* Bill Morton's observed:

> *Battling heavy seas on the edge of a hurricane. High winds and swells forty to fifty feet high. Took a 56 degree roll last night (she was only built to take 61). Didn't get much sleep because it was so rough. Do not know where we are going now. The Haynsworth lost its motor whaleboat and all the life line stanchions ripped from the deck perimeter. It was rumored three destroyers turned turtle with all hands lost. We started splitting*

with a break from the main deck aft of the quarter deck extend-
ing across the first superstructure deck and down into the main
deck. After the storm had subsided a bit I walked out there and
when we would plow into a wave it would gap at least 6 inches.
For several days you ate standing up in the mess hall with your
arm around a stanchion and a cup of coffee in one hand and a
sandwich in the other. If you were lucky enough to have a bunk
against the bulkhead you could shorten the chain so it formed a
"V" with it. Then you could slide the mattress in that area and
get some rest...every time the screws came out of the water I
thought we would shake apart. We were lucky to come
through...we came out alive.

One of the towering waves crashed down on the *Haynsworth* like a demolished building. "Grab ahold of something," warned Signalman John Vasquez to the sailors on watch. His words were swallowed by the cacophony of the storm. Vasquez wrapped his arms around the ladder on the mast. The *Haynsworth*, pounded and covered by the tons of seawater collapsing down on the ship, took a deep roll. Vasquez' feet were no longer on the deck. As the ship was pushed down and to its side by the wave, Vasquez swung freely above the churning ocean. The roll was the greatest this young crew had experienced. Vasquez was told later that if the *Haynsworth* had leaned just another degree or two she would have foundered and been lost.

"We had a 52 degree roll," recorded Marion Parker. "The sea was so rough and the weather bad, that we did not strike. We rolled along and waited for the weather to break. Boy this is a rough sea. Some of the life rafts & lines are gone."

Twenty-two year old Ralph Aakhus wrote to his family about the tempest: "you couldn't see the ship next to you. They sailed the ships by the radar blips to avoid collisions. So many were seasick that there weren't many to plot the course. The Lieutenant Commander [Lothrop] was there [in the Combat Information Center] most of the time with three or four others. Some were running scopes and some were plotting. You couldn't go topside because there was three feet of water running over the decks most of the time. We heard that one destroyer escort had run out of fuel and was lost with all hands. You took on water for ballast as the fuel was used up, but you had no steerage without fuel. After the storm we were close enough to see lights, which they figured was the Chinese mainland."

USS Marshall DD-676 of the destroyer screen 38.2.3 fuels from an oiler in the South China Sea. (NARA 80-G-431087)

The storm took its toll on all, both officer and bluejacket. The Executive Officer, Lt. Cdr. Lothrop, despite his youth, was a seasoned sailor who had been at sea fighting for three years. As the XO of the USS *Tarbell* DD-142 during 1942, he had to endure the long moments as the destroyer maneuvered against two torpedoes fired in their direction by a U-Boat. One torpedo missed, one hit the destroyer but did not explode. Yet, even Lothrop was not immune to being afraid at sea: "Fear is a very personal thing. And coping with it is, too. So maybe, being truthful with myself, the fact that even at my levels of experience there was fear will be of help to others in coping...We are not all heroes. Some of us are just ordinary people."

Despite the storm, there was some good news. "Tonight's communiqué: We have sunk 130 ships," noted Seaman Parker.

THE FLEET FINALLY FED THE SMALL DOGS on the 19th. After riding out the storm for several days, the first order of the day was to add black ballast to the destroyers. "Refueled for the biggest part of the day," was Marion Parker's simple assessment.

But, the weather remained poor, waves were strong and enemy aircraft were within striking distance. "May have trouble getting out," penned Radioman Keith Myreholt about exiting the South China Sea. Tokyo Rose offered similar sentiments recalled Admiral McCain post the action. "We don't know how you got in, but how the hell are you going to get out?"

W E WERE ATTACKED BY PLANES." After three weeks in combat and ten days in the South China Sea, January 20th marked the first air attacks against Higgins' Destroyer Squadron 62. Steaming near Luzon, strikes were conducted against Luzon and Formosa but in the skies over Task Group 38.2, the CAP drove off or destroyed the raiding Japanese planes that ventured near except one. After penetrating the aerial shields of the phalanx, the Japanese invader was finally repulsed by intense anti-aircraft fire. Aboard the *Haynsworth*, Bill Morton recounted the action: "The firing was beautiful to see with the 40mm going into the air in almost a solid stream. It was like the sentence of death punctuated with the flash of larger guns." The final count was ten raiders shot down and two probables. *Haynsworth's* crew were kept at General Quarters for four hours during the action.

Exiting the cauldron, Destroyer Division 123's *Ault*, *Haynsworth*, *Sperry* and *English* became the spearhead for the task force at 1530. As Task Unit 38.2.6, the destroyers entered the *Balintang Channel* to conduct visual, radar and sonar sweeps before the rest of the task force, moving in protective phalanx groups, threaded the needle. Marion Parker GM3c recorded, "Late in the afternoon started out of China Sea though we expected trouble for it is only twenty-six miles wide."

Steaming into the channel at 1900, the foray was completed by 2200 without enemy air or sea defenses being detected. Admiral Halsey recalled, "The night promised to be rugged. But just as we entered the channel, the wind and sea abated, and we sprinted through safely."

Despite the odds against them and Tokyo Rose's warning, Task Force 38 retired from the *South China Sea* at dawn. Life in the enemy's cauldron caused great pain for the Japanese defenders while Halsey's ships came away bruised but not beaten. Carpenter Mate Second Class Edward Mital's opinion of their time in the stormy South China Sea: "We were lucky."

T HE *DIVINE WIND* BLEW ACROSS THE TASK FORCE the next day, trailed by the bloom of black clouds. Off the coast of

USS Ticonderoga CV-14 after kamikaze attack.
(U.S. Navy National Museum of Naval Aviation photo)

Formosa, Task Group 38.1, sailing north of TG 38.2, became the target for Japanese attackers. The carrier USS *Ticonderoga* CV-14 and the destroyer USS *Maddox* DD-731 were hit by kamikazes while the carrier USS *Langley* CVL-27 absorbed an attacker's bomb. Though the *Ticonderoga* was saved, she was out of the war for four months while repairs were made. She was detached from the task group to return to Ulithi with escort provided by the USS *Halsey Powell* DD-686. The punishment was not evenly traded. For the sacrifice of three pilots and their planes, the *Tokubetsu Kōgeki tai* had taken a fleet carrier and its one hundred planes out of the hunt.

At the same time, Formosa was hit heavily by the task force as a total of seven strikes were sent aloft. "Our planes really went to town," wrote Gunners Mate Marion Parker after a day spent in the metal confines of the aft 5" mount. "We were at General Quarters from 1200 to 2200. The Jap planes came after us. Eight Zeroes and six bombers were shot down." The jousting of DesRon 62 against the kamikazes would only intensify as their time with the Fast Carrier Task Force increased.

Damage control parties fight fires on the USS Hancock.
(NARA 80-G-301150)

In the *Haynsworth's* task group, the USS *Hancock* was severely damaged after one of its VT-7 torpedo bombers was recovered on deck. At 1328 the TBM-3 *Avenger* of Lt. jg. Carrol Dean, with his crew of Fred Blake ARM2c and Edward Zima AOM2c aboard, landed and taxied forward. Without warning, two armed 500 lb. bombs in the plane's bomb bay dropped to the deck. The explosion caught many of the deck crew and others on the island superstructure out in the open. The aftermath was measured by sixty one deaths, ninety one injured, and a 10' by 16' hole in the flight deck. The detonation's force caused three planes to be destroyed, damaged multiple compartments and started fires on several decks. With a ship full of planes, munitions, and high octane gas, it was imperative for the damage control teams to act quickly to prevent the conflagration from growing.

The action by the crews as well as maneuvering by the captain to drain the ship of water from firefighting efforts, saved the carrier. By 1406 the fires were extinguished and by 1510 temporary repairs to the flight deck were completed. Both the *English* and the *Charles S. Sperry* came to the *Hancock's* aid as she left the formation to deal with the emergency. Higgins' destroyers stayed with the *Hancock* until she resumed her position in the task group at 1500.

During the day's missions, the crew of the *Haynsworth* stayed at their battle stations for nine hours. "About 1830-1900 a plane approached on our starboard side and we started firing on it. It burst into flame and tried a suicide dive on a tin can but couldn't make it and crashed into the water," observed Bill Morton. For the sonarman and his fellow bluejackets, long days kept at General Quarters had become the norm without a let up in sight.

YESTERDAY WAS ONLY A TASTE OF THINGS TO COME," the *Haynsworth's* exec reminded the crew on Monday, January 22nd, "Today is another strike day." But after several weeks of battling the Japanese and the weather, Marion Parker GM3c's perspective was that, "today is a lovely day. The sun is bright and the air is cool. As yet no Japs have come out after us but it is only 4 P.M. and we may have trouble yet. Radio Tokyo said that they believed we had three task forces in and around Formosa and they had sunk three of our large carriers and a destroyer. They did hit two of our carriers and a DD and one of our planes exploded while landing and set another carrier on fire. The *Ticonderoga* had to turn back but the others were able to stay with us."

Parker continued, "Our planes also struck at Okinawa in the Ryukyu Islands group, which is 350 miles from Japan." After airstrike and photo strikes against Okinawa Jima, TG 38.2 set course for Ulithi. The *Haynsworth* was sent out in harm's way ahead of the TG. Once again, Cdr. Tackney's destroyer drew the sentry's role as a radar picket ship.

The next day, the *Haynsworth* returned to the group from its picket station. "We were to finish fueling this morning or early afternoon but couldn't find the tankers. We were assigned as a mail ship again until 1500. The whole torpedo deck is stacked three deep with mail bags. There is about the same amount on the quarterdeck. There was only one good bag out of all this for the *Haynsworth* crew," recorded Morton. After distributing mail to the ships of TG 38.2, the *Haynsworth* intercepted TG 38.3 to act as mailman for that group on the 24th.

The anticipation of mail call could quickly be replaced by heartbreak in the letters from home. Ed Maugel SoM3c, like many of his bluejacket peers on the *Haynsworth*, received sad news about this time. Maugel's brother, Robert, was killed in Belgium at the beginning of the Battle of the Bulge in early December as Allied forces tried to repel a surprise German offensive. Maugel would not be the only *Haynsworth* sailor to learn of the death of a sibling serving their country while the destroyer was in the midst of its own fight.

But during the time that *Haynsworth* was acting as squadron postman, her squadron mate *Borie* was undergoing its baptism of fire near Iwo Jima. Cdr. Noah Adair's destroyer "was attacked by enemy planes which were trying to break up our bombardment position. An enemy plane came in from the East, passed over the USS *Gwin* and headed directly for *Borie*. As the enemy [Nakajima divebomber] *Jill* cleared over the *Gwin* she was met squarely by the first salvo from our 5"/38 and plane burst into flames at it crashed into the water about two miles ahead. Once again we turned to our bombardment course and proceeded towards Iwo Jima. A fierce duel between the heavily fortified shore batteries and the task group was encountered, and because of the heavy shore fire and reduced visibility caused by overcast skies and rain, the shore bombardment was discontinued and the task group reformed and retired." Just a few days into her wartime mission, *Borie* had escaped harm's way. She would remain a target of enemy planes right up until the very end of the war.

Task Force 38 rendezvoused with the fleet oilers early on the morning of January 23rd as the Task Force set sail to return to Ulithi. Without expectation of enemy air attacks, focus aboard the *Haynsworth* returned to basic maintenance: "Up all hammocks. Air bedding...Concentrate on scrubbing exterior bulkheads, [gun] mounts with soap and FRESH water...go easy on water, but get salt, fuel oil, and rust streaks cleaned off...touching up rust spots with chromate." Sweepers would man their brooms.

On their journey for some well-deserved rest, Seaman Parker noted that, "Our planes sunk 250,000 tons of shipping in the China Sea while out the twenty-nine days. We are headed back to the briar patch."

COMMANDER TACKNEY'S RESCUE SWIMMERS GOT THE CALL while en route to Ulithi on January 25th. A torpedo bomber from the USS *Enterprise's* VT(N)-90 was returning from an antisubmarine patrol when it nearly collided with another plane. As Ensign Knox O. Scott attempted to bring his *Avenger* back aboard he was given landing clearance by the Landing Signal Officer but at the same time a disabled fighter flew right over his bomber. Scott, unclear whether the *Hellcat* was attempting to land ahead of him or was simply out of control, landed the *Avenger*. "His hook caught on a wire on

Left to right: William D. Crowley ARM3c, Ens. Knox Scott, Eugene Wengler ARM3c. (Courtesy of Mike Wengler)

landing but his plane went over the side and broke in half. The empennage remained on deck but the forward part went into the water."

The plane plunged into the ocean 2000 yards ahead of the *Haynsworth*. "Late this afternoon a TBF fell and we went to the rescue of the crew. We picked up the pilot & gunner but the radioman went down with the plane," recorded Parker in his journal. The bomber sank rapidly. Knox and twenty year old Eugene Wengler ARM3c struggled to free the unconscious second radioman from the sinking wreckage. Finally, the twenty-one year old pilot decided the rescue attempt had to be aborted. Knox and Wengler escaped and were pulled from the seas by the rescue swimmers but several minutes later an underwater explosion shook the *Haynsworth*. The *Avenger's* depth charge had detonated at a predetermined depth, eliminating the slim chance that the other radioman, William D. Crowley ARM3c, might have survived.

For the young crew lining the rails, it was difficult to watch Crowley disappear under the waves. It was their first time seeing death close up while in action but it would not be their last.

T HEIR FIRST BATTLE STAR. Come afternoon, DesRon 62 entered the lagoon at Ulithi and ended its participation in Operations MIKE I and GRATITUDE. Other than the *Borie,* all of Captain Higgin's destroyers were decorated for their baptism under fire. A source of pride for the *Haynsworth* crew, the award read:

30TH DECEMBER 1944 – 25TH JANUARY 1945. THIS VESSEL IN COMPANY WITH TASK FORCE #38 IN SOUTH CHINA SEA AND IN SUPPORT OF LANDINGS ON LUZON. TASK FORCE #38 CARRIED OUT STRIKES AGAINST FORMOSA, LUZON, CAMRANH BAY, HONG KONG, HAINAN AND OKINAWA GUNTO. DURING ONE PERIOD THIS VESSEL WAS PICKET STATION 15 MILES OFF THE JAP STRONGHOLD AT CAMRANH BAY

For the DesRon 62 destroyers, the first exposure to the *Divine Wind* was minimal. The USS *Maddox* and the USS *Ticonderoga* were the only TF 38 casualties during their mission. The brunt of the kamikazes' attacks had been directed at the invasion forces of the Seventh Fleet off the Philippines. Though the killing wind blew lightly during DesRon 62's month in combat, the cost of battle was high for the task force. Over two hundred carrier aircraft were lost in the span of several weeks. The few kamikaze attacks took the lives of 205 sailors. The balance sheet, often measured in machines and not men, was in the Americans' favor. Over 600 hundred Japanese planes had been destroyed along with over 300,000 tons of shipping. Halsey's team, with DesRon 62 aboard, was getting the job done.

Admiral John S. McCain.
(NARA-80-G-308510)

PRAISE WAS SENT BY THE TASK FORCE COMMANDER, Admiral John McCain, to the officers and crews of Task Force 38: "Only Navy pilots could have flown the weather, wrecked and killed as you have done these past weeks. Only Navy Captains could have delivered on the line with superb seamanship required. Only the Navy of the United States could have maneuvered and fought through this last campaign. Thank you one and all."

Third Fleet Commander William Halsey also had high praise for his sailors: "I am so proud of you that no words can express my feelings. This has been a hard and historic operation. At times you have been driven almost beyond endurance, but only because the stakes were high, the enemy was as weary as you were, and the lives of many Americans would be spared in later offensives if we did our work well. We have driven the enemy off the sea, and back to his inner defenses. Superlatively well done. Halsey."

The crews of the DesRon62 destroyers were also able to bask in the Fleet Admiral Chester Nimitz' praise. In a press release dated, January 28, 1945, the Commander in Chief, Pacific Fleet and Pacific Areas paid homage to the men of Task Force 38: "The Third Fleet in the last four months has hit the enemy hard in the Philippines, the Ryukyu Islands, Formosa, Indo-China and South China. It has demolished and damaged aircraft, ships and land objectives to a degree which has materially reduced Japan's ability to make war. It has paved the way for and covered the Philippine re-occupation. It has written proud pages in our nation's history. Well done to the officers and men of these gallant fighting forces."

Finally, proud words were delivered to the officers and crew of the *Haynsworth*: "The Captain and the Executive Officer wish to add their thanks, though our individual part may have been small, our performance of the jobs assigned to us have been excellent. Our snap and speed at fueling in any kind of weather is a credit to the ship. A fine spirit is shown each time we fuel and it is an indication that we have a far better sense of cooperation required between divisions than many others of our type. Good work. Keep it going."

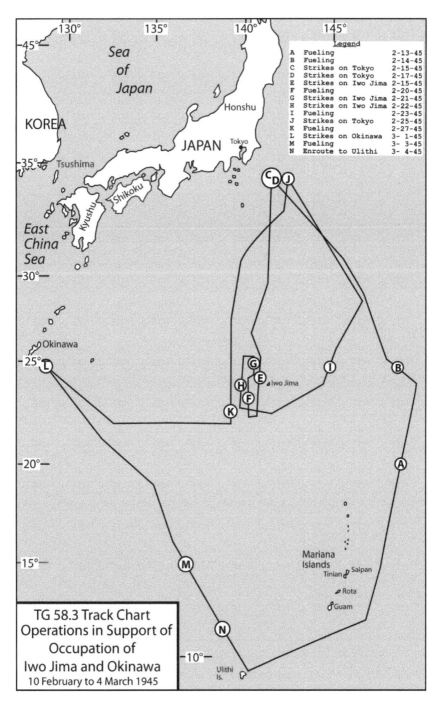

Mission track of Task Group 58.3: Operation in Support of Occupation of Iwo Jima 10 February to 4 March 1945. (Commander Task Group 58.3: Report of Air Operations Against Japan, Bonins, Ryukyus 16 February-1 March 1945)

Part IV

Fast Carrier Task Force 58

Destroyers have become the all purpose ships of the Navy. They are a gradual development from the small speed boat, which was envisioned as the logical torpedo conveyor when the torpedo was invented. As time and trial went on the torpedo boat merged into the destroyer, resulting in the present type. They do not have as a great a cruising radius as the larger types but are valuable as anti-submarine, anti-aircraft and anti-torpedo screens for them.

—Bluejackets' Manual 1943

PREPARE FOR BATTLE

Warship assemblage at Ulithi. (NARA 80-G photo)

R EPAIR, RE-PROVISIONING, RECREATION, AND REST became DesRon 62's focus after four weeks of combat. The *Haynsworth* had sailed 10,558 miles since joining the Third Fleet.

En route some basic 'housekeeping' was done of the ship's food stores. "We dumped our meat so we can get fresh meat. The old meat is mutton. Cheesecloth is wrapped around the meat but it has turned green." Declared radarman Ralph Aakhus, "I'll never eat mutton again!" The Minnesota native wrote again on February 7th: "Busy taking on stores. It went pretty fast because it was 'all hands turn to.' I got plenty to eat such as oranges, apples, and juice. You know the cases break open now and then."

For some of the sailors, the stormy seas in January exacted a toll. Marion Parker never fully developed his 'sea legs.' The winter storms and towering waves caused him to be "really sick when on a strike," remembered his buddy Phil Goldstein. "He was given the choice of being transferred to shore duty but refused. He said, 'I came aboard with the original crew and I am staying until the end.'"

Over the next two weeks, various ships of the squadron moored along destroyer tenders for repairs and updates. The needs of the *Haynsworth, English, Ault* and *Waldron* were attended to by the tender USS *Prairie* AD-15. Despite having to scrape and paint while in port, there was time and opportunity to get a Coke and some ice cream. "Movies were shown including *Shine on Harvest Moon* and *Golden Saddles* with John Wayne. It rained a few times during the shows but we sat through it. When you haven't seen one for some time a little rain doesn't bother you," reflected Aakhus. While there, the crew was able to spend some time on shore with sand at their feet and beers in their hands. Noted Marion Parker, "I had two liberties while in port Feb. 4th & 8th on island of Mog-Mog."

A month past Christmas and nearly six weeks since leaving Pearl Harbor, mail from that period finally caught up with the *Haynsworth*. Radarman Ralph Aakhus was the beneficiary of a month's worth of correspondence as the recipient of thirty-five letters. Mail brought tales of family and neighbors, updates of home. For a few moments paper and ink allowed the bluejackets to escape back into the comfort of the world they knew, the minutiae of family life. It also served as a stark reminder of the contrast in life aboard ship versus the comfort of home.

During the two weeks at Ulithi the squadron took part in anti-aircraft firing practice and various individual daily escorts for some of the larger vessels. The *English* left Ulithi on the 8th of February to escort the USS *Indianapolis* CA-35 to Saipan. The cruiser would become a ship of notoriety in the months to come. She served as the flagship for Admiral Spruance, was struck by a kamikaze, and later delivered the atom bombs to the island of Tinian

LAUNCHING, FLYING, AND LANDING A 2000 HORSEPOWER PLANE on a short, narrow runway could be perilous. Carrier landings have been referred to as controlled crashes. Pilots had to line themselves up, descend to the correct altitude, reduce airspeed to just above a stall, shut off the engine, and drop on the carrier's stern when approved by the landing signal officer despite the carriers moving up and down and side to side. If all went well, the tailhook trailing behind the rear wheel snagged an 'arresting' wire to prevent the plane from crashing into planes parked forward on the carrier's deck. All this occurred while the plane's nose was pointed up high enough that the propeller did not hit the deck. Under the best of circumstances, it was a difficult job. For the carrier pilots, a landing could go south quickly.

Plane guard operations continued for the destroyers during their time at the atoll. Commander Noah Adair's *Borie* was on hand February 8th when one of these landings went awry. The carrier USS

The USS Bunker Hill as seen through the sights of the gun director atop the #2 mount as the Haynsworth served plane guard duty. (Courtesy of Gus Scutari)

Cowpens (affectionately known as the *Mighty Moo* by its crew) was launching planes for training. The *Borie* had the plane guard duty. Coming in for a landing, Ensign Bruce Garlock was given the 'wave off' signal at the last moment. Attempting to apply power to his F6F *Hellcat* and get back in the air, Garlock's plane struck a gun sponson. The force of the impact plus the crash into the ocean caused his arm to be severed above the elbow. Despite the traumatic injury he managed to free himself from the plane and assist in his own rescue when the *Borie* came close aboard. The next morning the pilots of the Fighting Squadron 46 made Garlock an official member of the *Dunkee Club* when he left the ship's sickbay and came to breakfast.

Tom Scott recalled one day as the *Haynsworth* served as plane guard. From his position in the fire director tub, he recalled, "The *Haynsworth* was with a carrier while planes were returning from a mission. This was normal duty for periods of takeoffs and landings. A Grumman TBM landed on the deck and 'bounced' up veering to the right. It turned and went nose first into the water. The fleet kept on the move but we spent quite a while circling the area in case of survivors. That was unlikely given the plane's trajectory."

PHALANX AGAINST THE DIVINE WIND

OPERATION JAMBOREE: ATTACKS AGAINST JAPAN

"Task Force 58 gets underway from Ulithi on February 10, 1945." Taken from the USS Bunker Hill, this photo shows CAG-84 Corsairs spotted forward. Ahead of the Bunker Hill are (left to right) Cowpens, Essex, Pasadena, and Astoria.

THERE WAS A CHANGE IN COMMAND AFTER TASK FORCE 38 RETURNED TO ULITHI as Admiral Raymond Spruance relieved Admiral Halsey and thus Halsey's Third Fleet became Spruance's Fifth Fleet. Though the ships remained the same, the command style shifted. The aggressive "Bull" Halsey led as a bolder presence than the more measured and less demonstrative Spruance. Regardless, both admirals were eager to win the war in the Pacific.

After nearly two weeks of preparation, Task Force 58 sortied from Ulithi on February 10th for Japan and the commencement of Operation JAMBOREE. TF 58 was the most powerful fleet to ever sail the world. With the addition of a fifth task group, the force embarked with eleven fleet carriers, six light carriers, eight fast battleships, sixteen cruisers and seventy three destroyers. With enough planes to darken the skies of the Empire, Vice Admiral Mitscher's phalanxes could strike at will. In contrast, just two years earlier, the U.S. Navy was down to its last fleet carrier operating in the Pacific.

Their mission was to "destroy enemy aircraft, aircraft facilities and naval forces in TOKYO area; support landing operations on IWO JIMA by direct air support and surface bombardment; and provide photographic coverage and air reconnaissance in order to assist the capture and occupation of IWO JIMA." The task force was also given the mission of a carrier plane attack around Tokyo. Raids against the seat of the Empire would divert enemy resources from the main goal of invading Iwo Jima, an island just 600 miles southeast of Japan.

Rear Admiral Frederic Sherman commanded TG 58.3. Assigned were the fleet carriers USS *Essex* CV-9 and USS *Bunker Hill* CV-17 plus USS *Cowpens* CVL-25. They were supported by the battleships *South Dakota* and *New Jersey* plus five cruisers.

For the destroyers, DesRon 62 Commander Capt. Higgins was promoted to Commander of the destroyer screen, Task Unit 58.3.4. His tin cans were assigned the duties of anti-aircraft and antisubmarine screening for the operation. Destroyer Division 109 of DesRon 55 (DDs *Porterfield*, *Callaghan*, *Cassin Young*, *Preston II*, *and Irwin*) was attached with DesRon 52 to fill out the screen. All totaled there were nineteen destroyers protecting the flattops.

From the seaman's perspective of Task Force 58's re-entering the ring, Marion Parker wrote that "left Ulithi with 5th Fleet for something big as yet know not what." Fire Controlman Tom Scott pondered "I was aware that the first question asked as we left the harbor was not 'Are we there yet?' but 'When do we get back?'"

TO INCREASE THE PUNCH OF TASK FORCE 38, two squadrons of Marine *Corsair* F4U fighter planes had been brought aboard a carrier in January. Flying from the USS *Essex*, the Marine pilots proved that the potent attack planes that had ruled the skies from land bases in the Solomon Islands could also fight at sea. Eight marine and navy *Corsair* fighter and fighter-bomber squadrons became part of Admiral Spruance's arsenal before TF 58 stormed out of Ulithi, replacing some of the bomber and torpedo planes. As the battles progressed and the *Divine Wind* blew stronger, sailors of the ships of the task force would be comforted by the sight and sounds of the bent wing birds overhead.

The first day out of Ulithi, February 11th, was a day of exercises at sea for the task group: At 0900 the carriers launched eight fighters as the combat air patrol (CAP) to protect the fleet from both aerial and

Ensign Peter Kooyenga standing at the far left.
(Courtesy of Kimberly Kooyenga)

sea enemy predators; Four fighters were sent up as the antisubmarine patrol (ASP); Anti-aircraft firing practice was held by the ships; *Sperry* took the role as plane guard while twelve other destroyers steamed in the expanded 5-Roger disposition, a circular pattern 6000 yards from the center of the formation.

The *Hank* and the *Lind* were sent to investigate a potential sub contact while the *Porterfield* rescued a pair of squadron mates. Ensign Peter Kooyenga's Grumman F6F *Hellcat* crashed ahead of the formation at 1510. After three hours in the air, his tanks ran dry before he could be recovered by the carrier. Ensign Alfred Adair, also water landed his *Hellcat* at 1814. As part of the last CAP of the day, Adair's Hellcat crashed on final approach. Kooyenga, a 1939 Golden Gloves boxer, and Adair were highlined back to the *Cowpens* on the 13th. Both pilots became official members of the Fighting Squadron 46's '*Dunkee Club*.'

TARGET: TOKYO

A Japanese picket ship destroyed by the USS Haynsworth 16 February 1945. (Courtesy of the USS Haynsworth Association)

THE UNITED STATES NAVY RETURNED UNINVITED TO BOMB JAPAN for the first time since Doolittle's Raiders had attacked Tokyo three years earlier. "Iwo Jima was about to be taken. To minimize Jap air threat from the north and to create a diversionary threat of our own, the force proceeded directly to the Tokyo area. There was the greatest excitement when that objective was announced. To have sailed boldly into the South China Sea had seemed brazen enough; now we were on our way to the very heart of the Empire. The Tokyo area had not hitherto fore been struck from the sea. If we could get away with this, we were nearer the day of victory than we had dared hope!"

In 1942 the Raiders were supported by just two carriers, four cruisers, and eight destroyers. Admiral Spruance's Fast Carrier Task Force with its four task groups was seven times the size of its predecessor. By the end of the 14th, the task force was just 700 miles from Japan. *Haynsworth's* Marion Parker logged, "Taken from the morning orders this morning we are about 330 miles east of Iwo Jima in the Bonins. This task force is headed up to conduct carrier strikes against Tokyo and other targets near Tokyo in the Honshu area. We will if necessary go in very close. It is getting colder by the hour and this afternoon foul weather clothing was given out."

USS Lexington 14 February 1945. (NARA 80-G-431091)

In preparation for the attack, the *Haynsworth* completed tasks, both important and mundane. Gun drills were held for the 5" crews, sailors were ordered to air out their bedding on the fantail as this might be the last opportunity to do so for some time, and 'Doc' Ley and his pharmacist mates held first aid lectures for the crew. Cdr. Tackney had his damage control parties' drill again and again. The days would soon be long and dangerous.

The tempo for the operation changed on the 15th as the task force charged toward its important target. Parker penned in his journal, "Morning orders: Top off with fuel today from carrier *Bunker Hill.* Bunks will be down all day, crew will get as much sleep and rest as possible, no turn to. On completion of fueling and no later than 1400, all ships will be expected to have all boilers on line. Ships will continue with four boilers operating until further notice. 1900 commence run in during night of 15th and 16th to reach operating area, closest port of area eighty miles from Tokyo." Speed provided stealth for the daring mission.

Fueling at sea while underway was always a risky proposition. The USS *Wallace L. Lind* suffered a broken davit and damage to one of her 40mm mounts when waves brought the tin can and her fuel source, the heavy battleship USS *New Jersey*, together. Damage was light enough to allow the *Lind* to remain with the fleet. The big battleship sailored on without noticing.

Threats from the enemy found the fleet early in the expedition. The USS *Charles S. Sperry* destroyed a mine while serving picket duty, preventing the explosive from connecting with a carrier or other member of the vanguard.

Before the weather deteriorated on the 15th, a small fishing boat and a raiding Mitsubishi G4M *Betty* bomber were destroyed by the CAP. As the weather turned poor, the low visibility worked to the advantage of the American fleet by limiting its exposure to raiding enemy planes. The *Haynsworth* fueled early from the *Bunker Hill* before returning to its lonely picket duty twelve miles ahead of the task force. DD-700's role as watchman for the task group would yield dividends the next day.

The morning of 16 February followed a chilly 52 degree night. As the carriers prepared to launch their planes at first light, visibility was initially poor. The temperature had dropped to 42 degrees. Despite the conditions, seven strikes were launched starting at 0645. "That Friday morning was cold, terribly cold, and the dampness of the early winter morning continued into a sunless day. Only once did the sun try to break through the low misty cloud cover, but there was no warmth in the sunlight that reached topside of the *Sperry*. Her men heard reports on the strikes; men topside rubbed their hands and cheeks and ear, dried off the mist and spray, drank soup and coffee, had a candy bar at three, and watched the overcast sky. But the enemy was apparently stymied by the weather and the tactical surprise."

Announcing the attacks on Tokyo to Task Force 58, Admiral Nimitz reflected on the significance of the raids: "This operation has been long planned, and the opportunity to accomplish it, fulfills the deeply cherished desire of every officer and man in the Pacific Fleet." With more colorful prose, Task Group 58.4's Commander, Admiral Arthur Radford, praised the abilities of naval aviation against the enemy. "If the opportunity permits, kill the bastards scientifically." The *Haynsworth's* crew found Radford's urging in the day's posted Morning Orders. In a simpler note, Lothrop wished the crew good luck. As it turned, February 16, 1945 would be a historic day for the USS *Haynsworth*.

Frank Studenski S1c of the heavy cruiser *Boston* wrote, "Several Jap planes made attacks on our ships. We are about ninety miles from Tokyo. It has been quiet all day, except for a few bogies reported

Fighters and torpedo bombers warm up on the deck of the Bunker Hill 16 February 1945. (NARA 80-G-303988)

around the task force. We caught them by surprise. This is the coldest weather we have been in a long time. A *Zeke* was shot down fifteen miles away. The day's bag was 225 planes shot down, 125 on the ground, aircraft plants hit. Tonight was quiet, there were no reported bogies in the area."

Three years earlier, DesRon 62 Commander, Captain John Higgins was part of the Doolittle Raid against Japan. The morning of 18 April 1942 found Higgin's USS *Gwin* DD 433 as part of Task Force 18. Vice Admiral Halsey's war train encountered two Japanese picket ships. Cruiser gunfire and attacks from scout planes of the USS *Enterprise* led to the demise of the patrol boats but the Doolittle Raiders had lost the advantage of surprise. Now, in 1945, as the U.S. carriers approached Japan for just the second time in the war, the scenario was repeated but by this point, the picket ships no longer stood watch hundreds of miles from the homelands. Long range U.S. Navy patrol bombers and submarines had steadily forced them back closer to their native shores.

THE SOUND OF THE GUNS AND THE SIGHT OF BLACK SMOKE greeted the blue jackets in 58: "Early this morning ships on the horizon opened fire," wrote Studenski. "What it turned out to

"Smoke rises from destroyed picket ships ahead of Task Group 58.2." (NARA 80-G-308577)

be was destroyers were firing at several sampans, of which three were sunk."

During morning watch, the *Haynsworth* had secured for chow when a small fishing vessel was spotted by a lookout 7000 yards off the port bow. Marion Parker continued the tale: "1030. One of the carriers picked up a message in which the Japs gave the order for all planes to follow ours. So, we should see action soon."

Sinking the enemy pickets was paramount. The *Haynsworth* first bracketed a seventy-five foot fishing style boat with accurate 5" fire from 6000 yards. The forty 5" rounds were not enough to sink the wooden ship so Tackney ordered the *Haynsworth* in closer, bringing his destroyer within 700 yards. Nearly three dozen fifty gallon drums were stored on the forecastle. "For a good while there were no signs of life until we saw one survivor clinging to a piece of wood. Everyone started waving and motioning him to cover to the ship but he didn't seem to trust us and made no effort to come aboard. Once a wave flipped his board over and we thought he was done for, but he finally came up and just to make sure we didn't think he had drowned, he grinned and waved," recounted Bill Morton. With a severe leg wound,

Japanese picket ship attacked by the Haynsworth. (Courtesy of USS Haynsworth Association)

the prisoner was taken aboard the *Haynsworth* but two other enemy sailors refused to be picked up.

Of the Japanese sailors who would not board the *Haynsworth*, "we trained our 5" guns on the wooden ship and blasted them. We didn't have time to stop and try to convince them to come aboard," remembered Signalman John Vasquez. Morton recalled Cdr. Tackney's words, "'To Hell with them. We have to rejoin the formation.' It was a damned hard thing to do but the safety of the fleet comes before two enemy lives."

Three years earlier, as captain of the USS *Gamble*, then Lt. Cdr. Tackney was tasked with delivering a Japanese prisoner to Pearl Harbor. In late June of 1942, IJN Commander Kunizo Aiso, Chief Engineer of the carrier *Hiryu*, was rescued along with thirty three sailors adrift in a lifeboat 255 miles from Midway. After leading his crewmen out of a below decks engineering space in the sinking *Hiryu* during the Battle of Midway, Aiso set course for Japanese held Wake Island. They drifted for twelve days at sea before the USS *Ballard* rescued them. He was shamed that it was enemy forces that saved his ragged group rather than his Emperor's navy. Aiso was transferred to the *Gamble* for a trip to the POW camp on Hawaii. "It is a rare event today when a sailor can see his enemy eye to eye," recalled Water Tender First Class Dick Russell.

Tackney's cabin was turned into a temporary brig for the voyage. "The ship fitters had closed the battle ports in the Captain's cabin and had tightened the dogs with pipe wrenches, and then sawed the wings off the wing nuts." Tackney had unadorned officers khakis issued to his enemy peer but during the first day of the trip, Aiso complained about his food and refused to eat, instead ordering the stewards bring

Japanese picket ship attacked by the Haynsworth. (Courtesy of USS Haynsworth Association)

Note Japanese sailor holding onto debris on right. (Courtesy of USS Haynsworth Association)

him more traditional Japanese fare. As he was educated in an American university, there was no language barrier but the cultural barrier loomed large. When word of Aiso's actions reached Lt. Cdr. Tackney on the bridge, he passed word through the communications officer to Aiso, "that he would eat the food that was served him or not eat at all!" Problem solved. From then on the rival enemy commanders saw eye to eye.

After the *Haynsworth* secured from General Quarters, Seaman Bill Morton wrote "fifteen minutes later two of our planes circled us at an extremely low altitude and as they went by us a second time they signaled and waved for us to follow them. It was then that we noticed some planes on our starboard side bombing and strafing some target below the horizon...Immediately all engines went ahead flank to twenty-five knots and we headed out there...We made out two small craft...and they were burning fiercely amidships. As our planes swooped in on dive bombing runs, the ship on the left was returning fire from what appeared to be a .50 caliber machine gun."

With the arrival of *Haynsworth* on station, the *Hellcats* ceased their attacks so that the destroyer could commence fire with its 5" guns. At 3500 yards distance, Lt. Army Dennett unleashed the guns again. "Hits were obtained on first salvo and tremendous fireballs and smoked poured out of the target, apparently a fully equipped picket ship about

PHALANX AGAINST THE DIVINE WIND

110 foot long with four visible radio antennas, mounting a machine gun forward."

Dennett, the fire control gang, and the gunners turned their attention to the second vessel which was desperately trying to flee the situation. The guns opened again at a range of 600 yards towards the second burning ship, similar in appearance to the picket ship sunk earlier in the morning. Observing from the gun director high on the USS Astoria, Jim Thomson wrote, "The black oily smoke billows high in the sky, flames visible at its base...Terrific explosions as the can gets a direct hit on one ship."

After the brief attack, the *Haynsworth* came alongside to pick up survivors. Several of the Japanese officers and seaman deskside were committing *Seppuku*, the ritual act of disembowelment, to prevent falling into American hands. Some of the enemy sailors were dying, some were dead while others pretended to be dead. "When she floated down our starboard side, you could see two or three Japanese in the very forward part of the bow that had either committed hari-kari or caught some shrapnel because you could see their guts hanging out and blood running down the deck. One was thrashing his arms about in the last throes of death and it reminded me of the times we butchered hogs and cut their throats while they were still kicking," observed Morton. "It was really a sickening mess."

A sailor clutching some floating debris would only shake his head 'no' when motioned to come towards the destroyer. "A 5" gun was trained on him. One shot, all gone," stated Harold Bly RM3c.

"We saw there was nothing we could do so we backed off and blasted again and again. The second and third salvoes hit her oil tank so we left her all ablaze and turned to the other one. We shot into the second one that sent smoke and flames skyward and then moved in for prisoners."

One of the *Haynsworth's* crew sought revenge for the aerial attacks against the task force. Opening fire with a Thompson machine gun at the enemy in the water, he was quickly ordered to cease fire. Most of the foreign sailors finally boarded the destroyer but one refused to let go of his perch on the rudder.

The destroyer targeted the final picket boat. Several salvos from the forward 5" guns set the vessel on fire. "She began to sink rapidly, her stern going under first from the weight of the engines and then her nose slid under and all kinds of debris [emerged] including charts, half burned books, life preservers, a flag, and lots of wood. Then as the bow went under and had already disappeared, a large piece of the side came up and on it was four Japs. Then out the wreckage and debris came up more bobbing up and grabbing wood to help them [stay] afloat. The total count was ten. Where they or how they lived through the firing, I don't know, but they were in the water and we began the job of pulling them out."

"Some of the sailors came to us on their own," recalled Bill Vassey S1c who went into the Pacific that day, "but others wouldn't. I swam out with a lifeline and pulled them in to the ship and others pulled them aboard. They didn't pin any medals on our chest. Our efforts earned us a 'job well done.'"

Aboard the cruiser *Astoria*, Fred Lind saw the action. "I derived some sinister pleasure in watching the destroyer's guns cause severe explosions and dense smoke from their targets. "After the sinking, nine survivors were picked up. One was a seventeen year old kid who didn't know that all those ships were American until we started firing. Apparently the Japanese public isn't getting much news on what is happening. Well, we are happy to inform them."

Of the Japanese sailors who would not come aboard the *Haynsworth*, "we trained our 5" guns on them and blasted them. We didn't have time to stop and try to convince them to come aboard," recalled Signalman John Vasquez.

The medical team of Dr. Ley and his pharmacist mates were able to save most of the enemy seamen though James K. Jones, Jr. PhM2c, was "torn between anger at the POW's and his compassion as a medic." The images of *Hara*-Kiri would haunt Jones for the rest of his life.

The final count was twelve survivors from the guard boat *Nanshin Maru* #36, Patrol Craft *Wafu Maru* and an unidentified vessel. After they were brought aboard, Clay Lutz WT3c noticed that a Thompson machine gun was left unsecured against a passageway bulkhead near the prisoners. Lutz ran for the weapon before the prisoners noticed it: "They could have had quite a day! I didn't want any problems!"

Of the prisoners, one was a father with his twelve year old son. The fatal wounds to the face of the one sailor were beyond the healing powers of the doctor, Lt. Ley. "Two of them had pretty severe injuries. One had half his face shot away and the other had a bit of his side and rump well shot up. We transferred the three most seriously wounded to the carrier *Bunker Hill* this evening for better medical [care]...we still have seven aboard with minor wounds," recalled Bill Morton.

The prisoners were held in the forward diesel room down below since there was no brig big enough on the destroyer to hold them. U.S.

Upper left: Bill Morton SoM3c
(Courtesy of
Lynn Morton Lindenmann)

Upper right: Angelo Lizzari S1c
(Courtesy of Robert Lizzari);

Left: Edward Kelly TM3c
(Courtesy of Ed Kelly)

Navy dungarees from the ship's store replaced the prisoner's torn clothing.

Having a foreign enemy aboard the *Haynsworth* was a new experience for the young crew. Radarman Aakhus described the prisoners as being ravenously hungry. Seaman First Class Bill Morton observed, "It is funny to watch them eat because they do not know some of our foods but they really get it down in a hurry. Every time you hand them food, or refill their cups with coffee, they give you two or three half bows from a sitting position...We had cigarettes on the table for them...The youngest one really likes coffee. He drank four cups."

As none of the *Haynsworth* crew spoke Japanese, communication was tenuous at best. Gesturing was the means of communication that was universally understood as the rapid speech of the prisoners was difficult to comprehend. "They go by your sign language and everything they say is in Japanese which is more like chattering than anything else when they talk fast."

"The twelve year old received lots of attention from the crew. He was trained to repeat orders coming from the squawk box," remembered Harold Bly RM3c. "'Now here this: The smoking light is out on the main deck,' dead panned the youngster to his captors."

And, to the victors go the spoils. Angelo Lizzari S1c was one of the sailors aboard who kept some of the prisoners' money as a souvenir of the day.

Many of the bluejackets were not happy to have the enemy aboard their ship. "I warned the crew about the prisoners," recalled Gus Scutari. "Some night they'll go through the ship and shoot everyone."

But, Morton reflected on the war and what it meant to be an enemy combatant: "When they brought them aboard, all the fellows were standing around and pulling that *hero* stuff-'Kill the bastards!,' 'Throw them back in the water.,' 'What are you carrying him for? If he can't walk, to Hell with him!'

"Even though they are our enemies they are human, wounded and thoroughly beaten. I cannot feel enmity toward them that some of the other fellows show or, at least, they put on a show of it. What they need is rest, medical attention, food and clothing and I think we should give it to them now even though we might not have been so fortunate as they have been had we been in the same position. I can understand why we would have had to shoot them if they would have refused to come aboard. It would have endangered our fleet if we hadn't and a (Japanese) plane might rescue them with the information. After all this is still total war and will be until the day the last Jap and German have surrendered."

Three seriously wounded prisoners and two others, who were considered to be the most intelligent of the group, were transferred to the *Bunker Hill* during the afternoon. A line was shot across from the carrier to the can. It was made fast under the carrier deck overhang. A breeches buoy and alternately a litter basket were rigged to a traveling block that was pulled back and forth by sailors manning the line between the queen and her attendant.

But, the POWs were not the only thing transferred. Ed Kelly TM3c had left his heavy weather jacket unsecured on his bunk. The gear was confiscated and held in lieu of a fine to be paid. Topside for the transfer, dismay stained the torpedoman's face as other sailors pointed out that one of prisoners wore foul weather gear with 'KELLY' adorning the back: "We were all looking up and there goes *my* jacket on some Jap!"

Wounded prisoner transfer to USS Bunker Hill (NARA 80-G-303975)

One of three prisoners transferred to the USS Bunker Hill
(NARA 80-G-303977)

Two days later, the other seven POWs were highlined to the *Essex* where they were placed in the brig under Marine guard. No actionable intelligence was gained during interrogation but the *Haynsworth* received a message of congratulations from the Admiral Marc Mitscher. The messages from the other DesRon 62 crews weren't as positive as

Transfer of Japanese prisoners to USS Essex (CV-9) February 16, 1945. (NARA 80-G-308451-2)

the task force commander's praise. The *Haynsworth* was teased as being 'Jap lovers' for saving any of the enemy sailors.

Executive Officer Lt. Cdr. Scott Lothrop reminded the crew to limit the information sent home regarding the attack against the picket ships: "For letter writers, you may say only we had an opportunity to take and capture JAP prisoners aboard. No mention of how, where or from what shall be included in your letters. A description of the POWs may be given. Nothing more will be said about them."

The significance of taking prisoners on the high seas was not lost on Captain John Higgins, Commander of DesRon 62. With his endorsement, the warrior seaman, Cdr. Stephen Tackney was awarded the Bronze Star. For Tackney, the medal was a plus for his career but surviving the action without loss of American life was good for his soul.

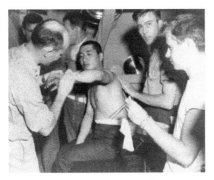 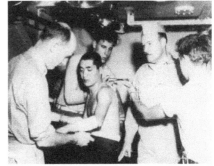

POW receiving treatment. (NARA G-80-308291)

Left: Japanese prisoners on board the USS Essex after transfer. (NARA 80-G-308465) Right: Task Group 58.3 Commander RADM Frederic Sherman in the USS Essex brig during the interrogation of the prisoners. A prisoner can be seen in the rear behind the bars. (NARA 80-G-308298)

"The prisoners became objects of considerable interest to the carrier's crew, who clustered around the cell doors, plied the prisoners with candy bars and cigarettes, and gave them their first lessons in Navy English. Thus, when Admiral Sherman came below to take a look at them, he was startled by the Japanese politely folding arms across stomach, bowing from the waist, and remarking what they had been told was the proper greeting to a flag officer, 'F--- you, Joe!'"

THE *DIVINE WIND* HAD BLOWN LIGHTLY since the attack against the *Ticonderoga* and the *Maddox* but returned to the Philippines on the 17th when a pack of suicide boats targeted landing craft ships in Subic Bay. Four LCS were struck, three were sunk, and more than fifty bluejackets perished.

*Damage to bow of the
USS Waldron.
(NARA 80-G-308773)*

ENCOUNTERS WITH ENEMY PATROL BOATS continued on
February 17-18. The USS *Dortch* DD-670 was hit by 3" cannon
fire from one of the enemy craft. Due to darkness and close proximity
to the other destroyers, the *Waldron* intervened: "0415 Sighted automatic weapon fire exchanged between destroyer and picket boat. 0459
Made radar contact on same picket boat bearing 214 degrees True, 6700
yards. Course was changed in order that the formation could avoid
Japanese craft. 0505-Sighted picket boat ahead and went to General
Quarters. 0509-Intentionally rammed and cut Japanese picket boat in
half, since it had turned into formation and there was no other means
to destroy it. 0518-Rejoined formation having sustained only minor
damage to bow. Two compartments forward are flooded."

The navigator of the 'Bloody W' witnessed the attack from the
bridge:

> *We were so close that we could hear the Japanese sailors on
> board the two halves screaming. Two depth charges exploded as
> the sections sank, raising our bow precipitously. The following
> morning we were able to clean our decks and found Japanese
> ammo cases and bits of the Japanese ship that had been thrown
> aboard...we were asked by ComDesRon if we needed anything.
> Captain Peckham picked up the TBS and replied, 'Affirmative:
> 6000 rolls of toilet paper!'*

The *Waldron* was detached from the task group to steam to Saipan
for repairs, her bow smashed in almost to the first twin 5" mount and
the ship's allotment of beer destroyed in a forward compartment.

OVER 1000 ALLIED PLANES TOOK TO THE AIR as strikes against Tokyo continued on February 17th. Resistance over the target was stiff: Seventy-two enemy planes were shot down. Another forty-four planes were destroyed on the ground against sixty American planes lost in combat. An additional twenty eight planes were lost due to water landings or other problems.

But, expected air opposition did not materialize over the task force. "Don't know what to think of this, our fliers are pounding Tokyo and the area around but as yet very little opposition," was Seaman Parker's reflection from the deck. The absolute control of the air for the Americans would not last. "From then on we were subject to constant enemy plane attacks, however most of the aircraft kept out of gun range."

MARINE RESCUE

1ˢᵗ Lt. Philip Wilmot, USMCR.
Mrs. Wilmot's garter is attached to
his left ear phone.
(Courtesy of Philip S. Wilmot)

HANG IN THERE, POTS," his squadron commander reassured the young marine flyer. "We'll make it back." 1st Lt. Philip Wilmot, flying in just his second mission of the war, nervously eyed the fuel gauge of his F4U-1D *Corsair* fighter. The VMF-451 Blue Devils had just finished a 'dog fight' with Japanese fighters who were fiercely protecting the Empire. Flying at full throttle during the battle had brought Wilmot's fuel levels dangerously low. Just the day before, twenty-one year old Wilmot and 1ˢᵗ Lt. James Anderson, Jr. shared in the inaugural aerial victory for the squadron after the two plane section combined to shoot down an Aichi E13A1 *Jake* floatplane off Tokyo's coast.

Leaving the Tokyo area, Wilmot's remaining fuel load of fifty gallons dwindled to just ten gallons as they approached their carrier, the USS *Bunker Hill*. The carrier couldn't land Wilmot right away so he was directed to the light carrier USS *Cowpens*. Lining up on the mast of the destroyer serving as the plane guard, Wilmot used it as a guide to get back on deck. Ahead was a carrier deck much narrower and shorter than the *Bunker Hill*. Coming in too fast to land safely, the Marine pilot was given the 'wave off' by the Landing Signal Officer. Throttling up, Wilmot pulled the long nosed fighter back up to clear the ship.

With the evasive maneuver, Wilmot used up the last of his fuel. As the engine cut out, he retracted the landing gear and leveled off the *Corsair's* nose. With heavy seas running, the Chance Vought fighter bounced off the first swell and then plowed through the next. Though Wilmot had pulled the canopy back and loosened his leg straps in preparation for the water landing, he left his rescue raft behind as he scrambled to clear the sinking *Corsair*. Wilmot had barely enough time to disconnect both his microphone and 'G' flying suit before the plane started the long dive to the ocean floor ten thousand feet below. After inflating his Mae West life vest, he opened a dye pack to mark his position in the ocean. Soon he was treading water in yellowish green waves. With his life in jeopardy, Wilmot discarded his helmet and the expensive goggles his wife had purchased for him. Also gone was her garter infused with Chanel No. 5 that he brought with him on missions.

As the carrier passed by him, a sailor near the LSO threw a smoke canister to mark Wilmot's position. As he bobbed up and down in the swells, the young pilot was spotted by the destroyer plane guard, the USS *Charles S. Sperry*. The destroyer came along with a cargo net hanging over its side. Two sailors were holding onto the net with one hand and ready to grab Wilmot with their free hands. A big blond sailor, tied to the ship by a rope, grabbed Wilmot and the two were quickly recovered.

Though Wilmot was accustomed to ocean swimming after growing up in southern California, treading water in the strong Pacific swells was a different situation. "I swallowed a lot of seawater which was full of dye. It made me very sick and caused me to vomit," recalled Wilmot. He was taken to sick bay along with his rescuer. The doctor offered both the U.S. Marine aviator and the sailor small bottles of 'medicinal' whiskey to help them warm up after exposure in the cold Pacific Ocean. "Lieutenant, are you going to drink your whiskey?" asked the sailor. Wilmot said 'no.' He passed it to his rescuer. The sailor revealed he would later retire to a private part of the destroyer to get drunk with his booty.

Wilmot was given the Captain's stateroom to rest as the *Sperry's* captain, Cdr. Harry McIlhenny, was using his sea cabin aft of the bridge. When Lt. Wilmot awoke, his uniform was cleaned and pressed. His flightsuit had also been cleaned but was faded by the process. His dog tags had not changed but his freshly cleaned shoes were now chartreuse from the dye in the water.

As a combat pilot who had been out bringing the fight to the Japanese, Wilmot was a celebrated guest of DD-697. As was custom, he was invited to dine with the other officers. When the destroyer rolled, Wilmot took a tumble from his chair but the navy officers never looked up or commented on their guest sprawled on the deck. Later the ship's doctor gave him a tour of the ship including the rarely seen spaces of the engine rooms.

After two days, Wilmot was reunited with the *Bunker Hill.* A line was shot across to the carrier and a bosun's chair was rigged up to transfer the pilot back to the aircraft carrier. As he was transferred from ship to ship, Wilmot was honored by the waves and salutes of the topside sailors of the *Sperry.* In exchange for their twenty-one year old pilot, the carrier sent over a barrel of ice cream to the rescue destroyer.

Wilmot would later admit he was always scared when he flew in combat but the Marine aviator was awarded the Distinguished Flying Cross for, "heroism and extraordinary achievement while participating in aerial flight, in actions against enemy forces in the Pacific Theater of Operations during World War II."

The actions of Wilmot and the hundreds of other American pilots accomplished the task force's goals of weakening Tokyo's aerial protection while creating a diversion to the upcoming Iwo Jima invasion. Despite battling the wintry seas, squally weather and high winds, the Tokyo raids were a stunning success for the aerial sledgehammer of Task Force 58. Admiral Nimitz announced that 509 enemy planes had been shot down or destroyed on the ground. An enemy escort carrier was left burning and sinking in the harbor of Yokohama while three destroyers and destroyer escorts had been sunk. Airplane engine factories had been bombed and maintenance facilities at several Japanese airfields had been destroyed.

The price for Admiral Mitscher's carriers was the loss of seventy-two aircraft in less than forty eight hours due to operations, combat, or mechanical problems. Of the planes that were lost due to combat, only half of the crews and the pilots, like Wilmot, were saved.

At day's end, the task force retired to the southeast as it steered towards Iwo Jima. Awaiting them would be the *Divine Wind*s swirling over the island of black sand.

CLOSE ENCOUNTERS AGAINST ENEMY PATROL BOATS CONTINUED in the early morning hours a few day later. With its surface search radar broken, the *English* was notified by the *Sperry* that a picket ship had closed between the *English* and the *USS Porter-*

field. Due to the *English's* proximity to the *Porterfield,* she was unable to fire. Once the enemy picket ship cleared the *Porterfield,* both the *Porterfield* and the USS *Callaghan* DD-792 turned their guns against the intruder. Score one more victory for the tin cans. But, the *Callaghan's* valiant crew could not know it then but their destroyer would not survive the war.

IWO JIMA

Iwo Jima as seen from the USS Haynsworth.
(Courtesy USS Haynsworth Association)

THE ALLIES ISLAND HOPPING CAMPAIGN CONTINUED
with its next jump at Iwo Jima on February 19, 1945. Thirty thousand U.S. Marines of the 3rd, 4th, and 5th divisions invaded the tiny island. Iwo Jima, just eight square miles in size, had over 22,000 Japanese soldiers and sailors garrisoned there. The flat island was noted for both its black volcanic sand and Mount Suribachi that dominated the southwest corner of the island.

Starting in June of 1944, the U.S. Navy and Army Air Force commenced with periodic bombardment of the island in advance of the coming invasion. In response to the heavy shelling, the Japanese defenders countered by building bunkers, digging elaborate tunnel systems, and constructing hidden artillery positions across the island.

The Battle for Iwo Jima was a brutal campaign of attrition. The invasion that American planners expected to last a week instead dragged on for five weeks from February 19th to March 26th of 1945. . The savage battle ended with the marines finally capturing the island but at a cost of 6,821 killed and 19,217 wounded. The Japanese fought to the last man and all but 219 of their 22,000 men force were killed.

Task Force 58 moved from its position off the east coast of Japan to the seas surrounding Iwo Jima on the 18th of February. Its mission:

to own the skies and to participate in the bombardment of the island. The invasion of Iwo Jima by U.S. Marines jumped off at 0845. Bombardment and airstrikes in support of the invasion continued on February 19.

Aboard the *Haynsworth*, the Morning Orders gave some background for the crew: "0645 First launch of VF [fighter] and VT [torpedo bomber] strikes against Iwo Jima. Approximately forty-five miles from Iwo Jima. Our mission is to provide air cover and strikes against Iwo Jima in preparation and support of the invasion landings there." *Haynsworth's* Parker noted, "0930. We are off the Bonins and our planes are going in to help with the landing. As yet we have had no action but can expect it at any time. Our forces are having a lot of trouble on landing but everything is going according to plan."

The morning's actions brought the *Haynsworth* and DesRon 62 close enough to Iwo Jima that Radioman Myreholt noted, "saw Mountain [Suribachi] on Iwo Jima twice during day." Recalled John Vasquez, "Because you could see Mount Suribachi, Iwo wasn't like most of the islands where you couldn't see land from the ship." Shipmate Marion Parker noted, "We could see the beach bombardment off in the distance of Iwo Jima."

During the day the USS *John W. Weeks* came under attack by air while at #3 picket station. During dusk General Quarters, her radar picked up the signal of enemy planes. "The first raid, approaching from the north, reversed course upon being fired upon by this vessel at 1908. At 1947 commenced firing in full radar control on raid approaching from the NE. A two engine plane, believed to be a [Mitsubishi bomber] *Betty*, passed close aboard while under fire by this vessel, strafing as it passed astern. Plane headed directly for TG 58.2, but was reported to have crashed in water short of formations. Minor damage was sustained by No. 2 torpedo mount when hit by what appeared to be a 12mm AP bullet. No personnel casualties." The intensity of the *Weeks'* counter barrage was reflected by the expenditure of 196 rounds of 5"/38. Her 20mm guns were able to get some rounds off while the *Betty* strafed the destroyer.

Frank Stout, a U.S. Navy correspondent, reported the tale of a second attack:

> *Japanese planes attacked a big U.S. carrier task force one night off Iwo Jima, as the enemy dropped flares. The U.S. destroyers were ordered to lay down smoke screens. To the consternation of every man aboard this ship, the USS John W. Weeks'*

smoke generator bloomed into bright, dancing flames that illu-
minated virtually the entire task group. It was a full minute be-
fore the flames were extinguished. But even with the help of illu-
mination the Japs failed to damage a single ship. Nevertheless, the
next day "Tokyo Rose" gleefully chortled over the radio: "Japa-
nese planes courageously attacked an American Task Force and
left one destroyer burning."

The climax came several weeks later, however, when task
force leaders—No doubt with tongues in their cheeks, assigned
code names to the ships of the fleet. With belated, but pointed
humor, they named the USS John W. Weeks, "Afterglow."

The *Haynsworth* was in the hot seat that evening. "1920 GQ was
sound and Jap planes were picked up by radar but none came in close.
We had four torpedoes fired at us but were fired from long distance
and passed in front of us. We were on picket duty twelve to fifteen
miles in front of task force," wrote Marion Parker. "The Jap planes
were after the carriers and several were knocked down by the ships
around them. We didn't get a chance to shoot. " The picket ships often
found themselves within the tempest when they were isolated from the
task group. The mutual fire support of the phalanx offered by the carrier group was of little use when a ship was alone on picket duty.

THE VETERAN MINSESWEEPER USS *GAMBLE* ABSORBED
TWO JAPANESE BOMBS while working with the bombardment group the day before the invasion. The old gal was eventually
towed to Guam. Her contribution to the war effort was ended after
earning seven battle stars during her twenty-six years of service. Cdr.
Tackney's previous command was scuttled by gunfire, a salute to her
during burial at sea. Newer destroyer minesweepers were coming on
line.

SERVICE FLAGS ADORNED WITH BLUE STARS for each family member in uniform hung in windows of American soldiers, marines, and sailors' homes. With thousands of sailors and marines
packed aboard hundreds of ships and landing craft, it wasn't uncommon for family members to serve in the same vicinity. While Robert
Matschat S1c was manning his 40mm gun position aboard the
Haynsworth, his brother Paul Matschat GM3c was doing the same
aboard the USS LCS 36. Mother Matschat kept the two blue star ban-
ner hanging in the front window of their Long Island home.

THE JAPANESE CAME CALLING. February 20ᵗʰ was used as a day for Task Group 58.3 to meet the fleet oilers. For the enemy, it was an opportunity to probe the phalanx on the seas and in the air. The *Haynsworth* received its vital fuel from the oiler USS *Monongahela* AO-42. "Refueling today and as yet everything is quiet. 0630 General Quarters sound and we went to our stations. The Jap planes came after us but our anti-aircraft fire kept them away out of range. They stayed around until 1000 but could not find an opening to get to us," reported Marion Parker. As in ancient Greece, penetrating the shields of the phalanx could be a deadly proposition.

A floating mine was reported by the cruiser *Pasadena* during the morning. The *Callaghan* destroyed it with gunfire. Saved this day, the *Callaghan's* destiny would be fatefully changed in just five months' time by the *Divine Wind*s.

A Japanese mine is destroyed by a destroyer.
(NARA 80-G series)

CARRIER AIRSTRIKES CONTINUED in support of the invasion for the next several days. Numerous enemy planes alternately closed and opened against the Task Force 58 during the evening of the 21ˢᵗ of February. While at General Quarters, the *Lind* fired at two raiders with her 5" guns. This was the inaugural use of her guns against the enemy. *Weeks* also reported five separate air attacks that evening over a seventy-five minute period. With the expenditure of 195 rounds, the 5" guns again drove away the aggressors. The *Haynsworth's* Ed Mital noted that "Jap planes attacked us twice tonight. We didn't get them and they didn't get us."

Though Task Force 58 was not targeted by kamikazes, the landing forces were. By day's end five ships had been hit by kamikazes including two tank landing ships (LST), two escort carriers (CVEs *Bismarck Sea* and *Lunga Point*) and the fleet carrier USS *Saratoga* CV-3. The 'Sara' was the oldest of the three remaining pre-World War II carriers.

After eighteen years of fleet service and three years of war, the carrier finally met the end of her days in combat. During the attack six kamikazes came at her. Despite being strafed, bombed, and rammed by the enemy attackers, the old girl survived. She lost 123 of her crew and another 192 were wounded. Her wounds were severe enough that she was dispatched to Eniwetok for initial repairs before heading back to the west coast of America for larger repairs. Though she had withstood the *Divine Wind* storm, age had caught up with her. Fleet Admiral Bill Halsey's old command would fight no more.

USS Saratoga. (NARA 80-G-273764)

Missions against the island continued throughout the day. "This morning we are with the rest of the cruiser bombardment force, we are nearing the island," wrote the *Boston's* Frank Studenski S1c. "Destroyers can be seen in close, firing star shells at the island. This morning is an overcast sky and planes were making strafing and rocket firing runs. Our targets were gun emplacements, block houses, shelters and ammo dumps. We were very close to shore of approximately 6500 yards on the north end of the island. We continued firing all day and late into the night. Fighters and bombers were over the island all day. Fighter planes were dropping napalm bombs on Mt. Suribachi and strafing as they made their runs. We were at General Quarters all day, till we secured from firing. The only hot food we had was coffee to go with the sandwiches. We retired from the area and will return in the morning."

While an evening movie boosted morale for the *Haynsworth's* crew, problems in the mess led to discontent. "A miscount in inventory in the Commissary Department which counted beans for flour puts us very low of flour for bread, having now only a week to ten days more supply." Radarman Ralph Aakhus commented negatively on his chow: "Dehydrated potatoes, beans of some sort, two slices of bread and some peanut butter."

A N AMERICAN FLAG ROSE OVER MOUNT SURIBACHI four days after the invasion commenced. A small group of marines had scrambled up the island's dominant peak with the mission to raise the American stars and stripes. Though they succeeded in their efforts, Command felt the flag was too small to be visible. A second detachment of marines scaled Suribachi to raise a larger flag. The symbol of freedom could be seen by the marines on land and the sailors at sea.

Bombardment and airstrikes continued as the weather turned and socked in the fleet on February 22nd. Rain squalls with visibility less than 2000 yards coupled with a ceiling of zero to 1500 feet were poor conditions for flying. The stormy weather also caused a change of plans for Task Group 58.3. Noted Marion Parker, "We were supposed to refuel but our tankers did not get to us so we just cruised around and planes went in again."

Attempted rescues at sea were the theme for the morning of February 23rd for DesRon 62. While at dawn General Quarters, the *Weeks'* crew spotted the life raft of Lt. Cdr. Robert G. Barnes. No one was aboard the raft, only some personnel effects of Ensign Daniel Valpey, USNR were found. Normally after a pilot was rescued, their raft would be recovered or destroyed so as not to appear to another vessel as a raft in distress.

Fate shone brightly on Valpey. In January, he was launched into low clouds before sunrise for a mission over Iwo Jima. Separated from the group, Valpey spent the day looking for his ships but winds with speeds of up to 100 knots kept him off course. He eventually had a successful water landing. Two and a half days later a search team aboard an *Avenger* found the missing VC-81 pilot. The young ensign was successfully returned to the USS *Natoma Bay* CVE-62.

Déjà vu. Four weeks later found Ensign Valpey in almost the same predicament. Three days prior to the invasion of Iwo Jima, Valpey was launched at 0530 as part of the CAP. Light rain and very low clouds caused the *Wildcat* pilot to lose his way again. At 1302 he put his FM-2 Grumman down in the ocean. His squadron commander, Lt. Cdr. Barnes, dropped his life raft to the downed pilot. After two days floating on the stormy Pacific, Valpey was finally picked up by a destroyer. For Valpey-who had pre-flight training with baseball pros Ted Williams and Johnny Pesky at Amherst, Massachusetts-the days spent in the raft were not cause to show anxiety. An outgoing and friendly gentleman, the twenty-one year old Valpey was noted for also being very a relaxed, even keeled pilot. Though Valpey was recovered, his raft was left to bob up and down on the swells. As it was a hazard to operations, *Weeks* destroyed the yellow inflatable boat.

Ensign Daniel Valpey.
(Courtesy of Ann Valpey)

M*AN OVERBOARD!* Weather influenced all aspects of operations on the 24th. The *English* was serving as plane guard for the *Cowpens* when she was hailed to be a lifeguard. "Sea is rough and this morning a boy fell from an aircraft carrier. We searched for him and also the planes helped but he must not have had on a life jacket, for we did not find him," recorded Marion Parker. Despite being nearby, neither the *English* nor the *Haynsworth* were able to affect a rescue after two hours of searching. Three other bluejackets from various ships were swept overboard. The bluejackets were not recovered. In the mounting waves, only one destroyer had success as a savior: At 0755 the *New* Jersey reported a sailor overboard. The *Irwin*, steaming in a standby position astern of the battleship, was able to rescue the sailor in just a few minutes.

Admiral Spruance wanted to take another crack at Japan. In preparation for a run at Tokyo in forty-eight hours, Vice Admiral Mitscher's Task Force 58 spent the day attempting to feed the hungry destroyers. "Refueled today and the sea is very rough so we all got wet. We took fuel from the *South Dakota*," wrote Marion Parker. Though skies were clear, the waves were building. By mid-afternoon the destroyers were taking green water over their bridges while absorbing the avalanches of forty to fifty foot waves. By mid-afternoon, further attempts at underway replenishment were halted.

Despite the seas, the destroyers were kept busy tending to the needs of the force. Mail from home and internal task force messages were delivered to the ships of 58.3 and the other task groups while supplies were ferried to the larger warships.

With the rushed tempo of operations, major repairs and overhauls to tired aircraft were not possible aboard the carriers. Salt water, hard deck landings, concussion from the guns, and damage from action wore down the metal birds. Those that couldn't be repaired easily were jettisoned over the side. Those that were marginally airworthy were traded off to the CVEs for replacement. *Cowpens* flew one of their 'flyable duds' to the USS *Windham Bay* CVE-92. In exchange the jeep carrier sent a *Hellcat* and *Helldiver* to the carrier while the *Lind* served as a livery service, transporting the taxi pilot came back to the *Cowpens*.

As the fleet turned north for strikes against Tokyo, speed had to be reduced to sixteen knots as many of the smaller ships had difficulty maintaining twenty knots in the heavy seas. Cdr. Robert Theobald's *John W. Weeks* found itself without its bloomers again when strong gusts ripped them from the forward 5" mounts. Mother Nature proved herself to be the day's enemy.

TOKYO WAS DEALT A THIRD STRIKE from Task Force 58. Overnight the carriers had moved within 180 miles of Emperor Hirohito. By the morning of the 25th, "the force was in the extremely rough, extremely cold weather off Tokyo, striking the homeland, saying in the most forceful manner possible, 'Your time has run out. The reign of Japanese brutality will soon be over; the rape of Nanking, the Death March on Bataan, your crimes against the helpless in the Indies, a thousand trite barbarisms, and more, like those, are soon to cease.'"

"We were spotted around 0230 by a Jap picket ship so our planes got a hot reception when they went in," recorded Parker in his log. In preparation for a long day at GQ, *Haynsworth* exec Lothrop ordered oversized portions served at breakfast and noon chow. Dinner would not be a question of when but if.

Despite the fact that the later airstrikes were cancelled due to weather, American airmen were still able to claim seventy-five Japanese planes destroyed versus the loss of six American planes. Radioman Third Class Keith Myreholt's log noted the score also included, "several small vessels damaged; two trains, one radar station, two hangars destroyed, other air installations damaged." In the months to come, allied planes would spend considerable time in the Emperor's airspace.

USS English DD-696 in rough seas, 1945.

In the seas around the task group, the *Haynsworth* saved another pilot: "We picked up a fighter pilot whose plane was shot up so he could not land on the carrier," noted Marion Parker. Ensign Edward Jindra of the Fighting Squadron Twelve flying from the USS *Randolph* was forced to ditch his ack-ack riddled Grumman *Hellcat*. On plane guard duty, the *Haynsworth* was ready. Despite the heavy seas and high winds that day, Second Class Seaman Bill Vassey jumped from the bow into the Pacific with nothing more than a lifeline attached to his waist. Swimming out to the young carrier pilot, Vassey embraced him. The deck crew pulled the pair back to the destroyer and helped them up the cargo net to safety. The *Haynsworth* had the twenty-four year old pilot aboard in time for noon chow.

With the task force battling heavy weather near Tokyo, the decision was made to take the fight south and launch attacks against the city of Nagoya. Once again, Spruance's ships battled the strong waves of the western Pacific. "Heading south to refuel with tankers and nothing going on," was Parker's sparse note... Rough seas and wind velocities as high as forty knots forced the next day's airstrikes to be scrubbed.

D ANGER LURKED IN THE NIGHT SEAS. A surface contact was spotted by radar at 0030. On the bows of the *English* and the *Porterfield*, a foreign vessel emerged ahead of them before penetrating the outer ranks of the phalanx. From the bridge of the *English*, John O'Leary QM2c described the initial encounter:

> *A request was made of the Task Group commander to open fire and sink the vessel. Permission was granted and we commenced firing. However the destroyer next to us stated to the task force commander that he had a better view of the target and requested permission to open fire which was granted to them.*

To confirm identification visually before engaging, the *Porterfield* closed the skunk. The engagement got hot for the *English*:

> *The next thing we knew there were 40mm shells flying over the top of our pilot house. Captain Smith was standing out on the bridge calling over the TBS radio for the other ship to cease fire. Simultaneously he issued an order to turn on the identification light to indicate we were a friendly ship.... When this order was given, the Captain was the only member of the bridge force that was standing. I think the rest of us dug fox holes in the steel decks.*

Fire and tracers crisscrossed the darkness as the *Porterfield* and the intruder landed hits. The picket ship's cannon and automatic gun fire took out the destroyer's radios while killing an officer and twelve bluejackets. *Porterfield's* 5" guns were of little use as their shots were fouled by the other task group warships down range. Erratic 40mm and 20mm fire targeted the picket as the two ships passed through the phalanx while green seas washed over the gunners. After sixteen minutes, DD-682 won the battle.

After the colored identification lights were illuminated, *English's* Cdr. James Smith ordered a turn hard over in the bounding seas to evade the friendly fire. As the twin rudders dug in, the can rolled on its side in the maneuver. Richard Earl Stuart F1c popped from his rack, hit the deck, and broke his nose. Gauze, sodium amytal-a barbiturate, codeine, and two ounces of brandy were used when the doctor, Lt.

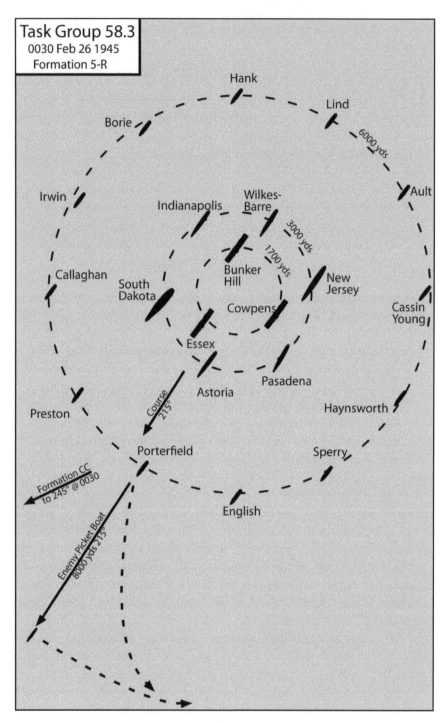

Task Group 58.3
0030 Feb 26 1945
Formation 5-R

Hank

Lind

6000 yds

Borie

Ault

Irwin

Indianapolis

Wilkes-
Barre

3000 yds

1700 yds

Bunker
Hill

New
Jersey

Callaghan

South
Dakota

Cowpens

Cassin
Young

Essex

Pasadena

Astoria

Haynsworth

Preston

Course 215°

Porterfield

Sperry

Formation CC
to 245° @ 0030

English

Enemy Picket Boat
8000 yds 215°

Diagram of the attack against the Japanese picket ship.
(USS Porterfield: Special Action Report of Surface Engagement of 26 February 1945)

Heyes Peterson, reset Stuart's nose. Later, the doctor returned to his normally scheduled medical rounds, the weekly inspection of the cooks and stewards for venereal disease and other afflictions.

ACTION FOR THE *ENGLISH* WAS NOT OVER. Topside, John O'Leary QM2c recalled the danger:

> We spotted a mine from the bridge and immediately raised the black signal flag to indicate that we had a mine in our view. The rule was that if you found it, it was your responsibility to destroy it. Being an outstanding destroyer, we sounded general quarters and started to circle the mine. We commenced to fire at it with the five inch guns but the roll and pitch were no match for the gunner mates. At a very slow rate of speed we circled ever closer and then called upon the 40 millimeters to take their turn but unfortunately with no better luck. Once again, Captain Smith tightened the circle even more so in order to let the 20 millimeters have a turn. I guess it just wasn't our day for they also were unsuccessful.
>
> Out of desperation, one of the gunner mates took a machine gun from the gun locker on the main deck and had a go at it. Normally what happens is the shell cracks the casing of the mine and it then sinks. Our trusty gunner, however, scored a direct hit on one of the horns of the mine and it let go. By this time, we were very close to our target and the concussion created a massive movement of air over the ship. Up on the bridge, Captain Smith was in his usual spot on the starboard wing when the movement passed over him. In doing so, it tore off his cap which went flying through the pilot house and over the port side never to be seen again!

Score two saves for the perimeter guards of the phalanx.

THE PACIFIC STORM RAGED IN ITS INTENSITY. The bounding seas caved in the starboard siding of the *Week's* Mount 51, the forward 5" gun turret, rendering it temporarily inoperative. In submission to the sea, speeds were reduced from twenty knots to eighteen knots and then again to fifteen knots for all of the ships.

FAIR WINDS AND FOLLOWING SEAS the next day allowed for the ships to refuel from the tankers. The *Haynsworth* took on fuel from the battleship *New Jersey* while other destroyers were busy delivering mail, photographs, parts, replacement pilots, and passengers to other vessels as well as their traditional duties of screening. Ensign Jindra was transferred from the *Haynsworth* over to the *Essex*.

As Task Force 58 with the *Haynsworth* steamed south post three weeks of combat, prisoner capture, and carrier strikes on what were truly high seas, Executive Officer Scott Lothrop cautioned the crew regarding, "the relaxation of censorship regulations, once again, it is stressed that personal experiences only may be revealed after the minimum thirty day period. This does not include such instances as the suicide dive attacks on the *Maddox*, the bombing of the *Ticonderoga*, *Langley*, and the like."

DesRon 62 was back up to full strength come Tuesday, February 27th when the *Waldron* returned from Saipan after repairs necessitated from her bow ramming the picket ship nine days earlier had been completed. When Task Group 58.4 was released to return to Ulithi, she sent Destroyer Division 99, another group of Federal Shipbuilding destroyers (*C.K. Bronson*, *Gatling*, *Healy*, *Dortch* and *Cotten*), to beef up Captain Higgin's destroyer screen.

Using its speed and stealth, the three remaining groups of the task force made a high speed run at thirty-two knots towards Okinawa on the First of March. The carriers launched strikes and photo reconnaissance missions against Okinawa and other islands in the Nansei Shoto group. The days were rapidly being crossed off the calendar. The final battle before the invasion of Japan was drawing close.

"THE DESTROYERS WERE LIFESAVERS"

1st Lt. Casimir Chop, USMCR, VMF-124. (Courtesy of The Flying Leatherneck Aviation Museum)

THE LAST DANCE, THEIR FINAL MISSION of World War II. After several months attached to Carrier Air Group 4 aboard the USS *Essex*, the VMF-124 "Deathheads" were flying their last combat missions. Their partners were the fifty-four *Hellcats* of VF-4, the fifteen *Avengers* of VT-4 and eighteen Marine *Corsairs* of VMF-213. They had flown together aboard the carrier since Task Force 38 embarked from Ulithi in December of 1944. For 1st Lt. Casimir Chop, it had been a good tour. He had nailed a *Zeke* fighter just four days earlier in the strikes against Tokyo.

For the pilots of the *Essex*, their targets were the airfields on Okinawa Gunto, Amami O Gunto and Minami Daito Shima. After morning strikes of forty fighters and fifteen torpedo bombers, a second group was sent back in the late afternoon to attack the Naha Airfield on Okinawa again. Sixteen VMF *Corsairs* loaded with 1000 lb. bombs formed the bulk of the attack group. Kazimah, as he was known, flew as part of the fighter-bomber sweep.

The Vought *Corsairs*, built in Connecticut, were not only exceptional fighter planes but also able to take on roles from other planes. The versatile birds from Stratford could function as bombers. With the increased risks to the carriers from kamikazes, the Fast Carrier Task Force carried fewer *Helldivers*. In their place were additional squadrons of *Corsairs*, most of them marine squadrons. The VMF squadrons were capably led by veteran pilots with several years of experience flying the big nosed bird in the aerial battles of the south Pacific.

After the strike was airborne, the twenty-three year old Chop armed his bomb by flipping a switch on the top right of the *Corsair's* dashboard. As they approached the airfield, he rolled the big fighter on its wing until it was almost on its back. As he eased the nose back up, he used the length of the engine cowl as a bomb sight to line up the Naha's runways. Screaming towards the island at over 400 knots, Chop hit the bomb release button on top of the stick as the ground began to rise up on the periphery of his vision. Despite the heavy gravitational pull trying to move the blood from his brain into his legs, his "G" suit kept the blood out his lower extremities. Failure of the suit could cause a pilot to black out and dive straight into the earth.

After hitting the release button, Chop's plane did not jump up as was usual when a bomb was released. Calling over to his wingman to take a look at his plane, Chop's fear was confirmed by his flying partner. The armed 1000 lb. bomb was hung up on its rack just below Chop in the cockpit. Trying again, he could not release the ordnance from its cradle. Minutes earlier, one of the *Avengers* was lost over the target by an explosion of its own bombs. Now Chop could not jettison his bomb.

The thirty *Avengers* and *Corsairs* turned southeast to return to their floating home. Twenty-nine planes would make landing approaches to reboard the carrier. Chop could not. Bringing armed bombs back aboard the carrier was forbidden, a prevention of the confluence of heaven and hell if ordnance and steel merged on the carrier deck. The *Essex* ordered him to bail out.

Just as he could not land his plane on his deck, the marine pilot could not ditch his plane in the seas either. His choices were limited as to how he would bail out: Climb out on the wing and dive to avoid the rear stabilizer or fall out. Neither method would guarantee that his parachute would open. The Deathhead pilots had heard tales of aviators whose chutes never opened when they 'hit the silk.'

The veteran pilot unbuckled his leg and shoulder harnesses, secured his canopy in the 'open' position and said goodbye to his wingman. The Greenwich Village native rolled the fighter on its back and then kicked the stick forward. He was ejected from the plane. While the *Corsair* met a fiery end when it impacted the Pacific, Chop floated down to the water near the task group. His wingman stayed overhead while watching his partner descend. Just as he was about to hit the water, Chop unbuckled the strap that kept him affixed to the parachute. With arms raised, the young lieutenant slipped free of the harness, entered the ocean, and waited for rescue.

In short order, the *Ault* left the circular destroyer screen and was headed to Chop's position. Using the orbiting *Corsair* as a guide, the tin can found the pilot and brought him back aboard quickly. Chop was in the water less than thirty minutes and transferred to the carrier, reunited with his buddies that same evening. 1ˢᵗ Lt. Chop had finished his last combat mission of the war. He was awarded the Distinguished Flying Cross for his efforts against the enemy.

IT WAS A DAY OF RESCUES for Destroyer Squadron 62. So many planes were aloft on missions (*Essex* alone launched 198 planes that day) that water landings were common. "Our planes went out at dawn for an attack. 0930 we are alongside the *Bunker Hill* topping off with fuel. The planes are coming off the raid, I saw one with a hole large enough to crawl through in its wing," recorded Marion Parker's journal as he reflected on the hazards of combat flying. Myreholt's journal noted that the *Haynsworth* rescued a pilot from the sea, "who crashed ahead of TG.58. Said our mission was very successful."

Left: 2nd Lt. Fred Briggs (Courtesy of Patty Matsukado)
Right: Lt. jg. Waller R. Puryear. (Courtesy airgroup4.com)

The *Ault* wasn't finished rescuing marine aviators. As *Corsairs* of VMF-221 strafed enemy planes along the edge of Yon Tan airfield, they flew through a harrowing barrage of anti-aircraft fire. Pulling up from their second run, 2ⁿᵈ Lt. Fred Briggs' right wing disintegrated rapidly. One flap was gone, the wing was shedding its fabric skin, an aileron was missing, and the .50 caliber ammunition was cooking off, sending shrapnel into the fuselage. The fighter was without hydraulics and most of its instruments had failed. By the time he approached the carriers, all that remained of his starboard wing was the leading edge, the metal under the ammo pans and guns, metal ribs, and the plastic wing tip.

Briggs was able to climb to 4500 feet before bailing out. His three division teammates circled the twenty-three year old pilot after he landed in the sea, each throwing dye markers to mark his position. The *Ault* arrived upon a confusing sea of color. As lookouts focused on the dyed colored areas, none noticed that the pilot was floating in his 'Mae West' life vest in an area without dye. With the destroyer bearing down on Briggs, he lifted his legs and pushed off the side of the tin can until he snagged the cargo net. Hauling himself aboard, the young marine was given a shot of whiskey and the captain's cabin to rest. Later Squadron Commander Capt. Higgins, "shook my hand and gave me a 'well done, my boy.'"

Another marine pilot, 1ˢᵗ Lt. Albert Simkunas whose plane was hit by AA while attacking targets on Okinawa, was forced to ditch his VMF-451 *Corsair* offshore after the engine lost oil pressure. A division of four *Corsairs* escorted the OS2U float plane piloted by Lt. Ted Hutchins. After Hutchins landed the *Kingfisher* to rescue Simkunas, the radioman yelled down to the marine to grab ahold. As enemy fire from the shore targeted the *Kingfisher*, the Pennsylvania native grasped the float strut while Hutchins taxied his plane away from beach. When they were out of small arms range, Simkunas was finally hoisted aboard. Offered water, Simkunas retorted, "That's the last thing I want."

After the flight returned to the task group, Simkunas was highlined from the *South Dakota* to the *Ault* and then back to home, the *Bunker Hill*, along with 2ⁿᵈ Lt. Briggs. Fresh ice cream was the dessert aboard the *Ault* during evening chow.

The *Sperry* rescued a pilot whose plane crashed off their port bow during the early afternoon about the same time that twenty-four year old Lt. jg. Waller R. Puryear from the *Essex* was recovered by Cdr. George Peckham's *Waldron*. Foul weather was a contributing factor for Puryear's failure to get airborne. After crashing into the ocean 2000 yards ahead of the carrier, the pilot from Fighting Squadron Four was rescued despite his suffering from exposure and shock. The auxiliary gas tank of his F6F *Hellcat* was sunk by 20mm machine gun fire. 1ˢᵗ Lt. Philip Wilmot of VMF-451, himself plucked from the unforgiving Pacific on February 17th, testified, "The destroyers were lifesavers. All the pilots knew it."

The *Lind* maneuvered to rescue two sailors who had fallen overboard from the carrier *Cowpens*. Despite being in the plane guard position, they were unable to recover the missing bluejackets. All that was found was a life ring floating in the water colored by a dyemarker.

After all the task force's planes were recovered, the groups began the return trip to Ulithi in the Caroline Islands. For the weary crews of the tin cans, the rest period could not come soon enough. Long days at General Quarters and hard sailing had taken a toll on the crews. "We were almost always tired," recalled Morris Gillett CRT. Pilot rescues at least were morale boosters. Radarman Ralph Aakhus highlighted his feelings in a letter home: "The chow isn't too good but we are getting ice cream nearly every day. This is to probably make us feel that they are doing us a favor. There are days of dissatisfaction, that is for sure."

A S THE SUN DAWNED on Task Group 58.3 on Friday, March 2nd, Cdr. James Smith's USS *English* was at the tip of the spear, steaming twelve miles ahead while on picket duty. Away from the protective shield of the phalanx, she was on her own to face the enemy which came in the form of another mine. The 40mm guns put an end to the threat. With a range of over two miles, the Bofors could neutralize a mine from a safe distance away from a tin can. Geysers traced a path to the menace as the gunners' aim was true: it took only took forty rounds of ammunition. Enroute from Iwo Jima to Okinawa, *Lind* also sank a floating mine with her 20mm Oerlikon machines guns.

The sailors' next targets would be the sands of Mog-Mog and some bottles of warm beer.

The Haynsworth comes alongside a tanker. (Courtesy of Gus Scutari)

EMERGENCY AT SEA

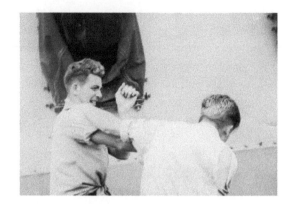

*Left: SoM1c Robert Chamberlin. Right: Phil Goldstein GM2c
and Jim Creedon FC2c (Courtesy of Phil Goldstein)*

THE RETURN TO ULITHI WAS FREE OF COMBAT BUT IT WASN'T DEVOID OF EXCITEMENT for the *Haynsworth's* young doctor. Caring for a crew of over three hundred men, Lt. Allyn Ley faced medical cases of various natures. Some were routine, some were not. And, not all medical treatment was duty related.

"We used to box on the fantail just for fun and one day I was boxing with a kid named O'Connor [Robert J. O'Connor S3c] from California," recalled sailor and pugilist Bill Morton. "I got the advantage and backed him up against the #3 five inch gun mount. I had my head to his shoulder delivering a series of body blows when he screamed. I backed off and we discovered a bolt welded to the mount for holding the movie projector had penetrated his back to the bone."

Later, the twenty-six year old doctor was faced with the possibility of having to perform surgery aboard a destroyer that was usually rolling or pitching when Sonarman First Class Robert Chamberlin reported to the medical department with severe pain in his abdomen. Diagnosis: Appendicitis. Commander Tackney, who spent most of his day on the bridge or in his sea cabin, gave up his stateroom so the stricken sailor could be treated. Ley administered the new miracle drug, penicillin, every four hours. Chamberlin was kept on an IV and nothing was given to him by mouth. Pharmacists Mate First Class Arthur Bland rotated four hour shifts with Ley. By that time, Ley had moved into the ship's wardroom next to Cdr. Tackney's stateroom. The wardroom couch served as his new sleeping berth. Surgery could be performed on the officers' mess table if Chamberlin's appendix ruptured. Additionally, the wardroom contained a folding treatment table and surgical lights were hung from the ceiling.

The Chicago native responded to the treatments, his temperature broke, and he was transferred to another ship at Ulithi that had both a surgeon (a medical school classmate of Dr. Ley) and a true surgical suite. Chamberlin survived and eventually returned to the *Haynsworth*.

The outcome could have been different as it was for another medical school classmate of Dr. Ley. "My friend had been confronted with a similar circumstance and, intimidated by his Commanding Officer, had tried to do the surgery on the ward room table. It was not a successful operation, and, by God, the sailor died," recalled Ley. The other doctor was transferred from his ship soon afterwards.

REPRIEVE

Drydocks in the Pacific.

A BATTLE STAR WAS AWARDED to all the destroyers of Commander Higgins' Squadron 62 for their participation in the 'Iwo Jima Operation' when Task Force 58 returned to Ulithi on March 4th. For the *Haynsworth*, it was their second award after two months of battle. The citation read:

> 10TH FEBRUARY 1945 – 3RD MARCH 1945. THIS VESSEL IN COMPANY WITH TASK FORCE #58 IN CARRIER RAIDS ON TOKYO AND IN SUPPORT OF LANDINGS ON IWO JIMA. TASK FORCE #58 CARRIED OUT STRIKES AGAINST TOKYO, THE ISLAND OF HONSHO AND OTHER ISLAND BASES OF THE JAPANESE EMPIRE, OKINAWA AND IWO JIMA. THIS VESSEL DESTROYED THREE JAPANESE PICKET BOATS AND TOOK TWELVE JAPANESE POW WHILE ABOUT 70 MILES SE OF TOKYO.

The ten days at the atoll were used for upkeep and repair after three weeks battling both the enemy and the stormy seas. The capabilities of the Ulithi repair crews were incredible. The Navy had ordered huge floating drydocks built for use in forward areas. Various sized drydocks could accommodate Mitscher's ships, from destroyers to fleet carriers. Sea going tugs brought the dock assemblies to the tiny atoll. Many ships in need of repair no longer had to return to Pearl Harbor or the United States as America's industrial might had reached across the mighty Pacific to keep its warships in the fight.

Seven of DesRon62's tin cans entered drydock during that period. Their time in the winter seas of the Western Pacific had taken a toll on the steel skinned warships. *Lind* entered drydock for twenty-four hours on March 5th while the *Ault* entered drydock on the 9th for a two day repair to her rudder. The *Weeks* entered floating drydock ARD-23 for three days to have her sound gear, rudders, and bilge keels fixed. After her work was complete, the *English* replaced her on March 10th to have her bottom scraped, repainted and repairs completed on her rudder. Finally, *Waldron* spent the 12th & 13th in drydock ARD-15. When not in drydock, the destroyers moored alongside the destroyer tender *Yosemite* for various repairs.

Radarman Third Class Nicholas Zeoli of the 673 foot long heavy cruiser USS *Boston* of TG 58.2 recalled, "We steered the ship between two rows of buildings on the water. Once secured, they refloated the drydock. Our ship was cradled between the two long buildings attached to the drydock. As soon as the water was pumped out, an army of workers, both men and women, poured out of the buildings. In three days our ship was repaired, welds were fixed, the underside scraped clean, and we were repainted!! After months of sea we were flirting with the female repair workers down on the drydock. You can bet that we were not allowed to step foot off the cruiser!"

ULITHI PROVIDED A CHANCE FOR THE SAILORS to stand on land again. *Mog-Mog*, one of the four largest islands of the atoll, was set aside for recreation. The *Haynsworth* sent its sailors ashore using either its own gig or one of the large motor launches sent from the battleships. Upon reaching the dock at the recreation island, the Navy Shore Patrol confiscated any knives found with the sailors. Each and every sailor on the island believed his ship was the best in the Navy. Better that the argument was settled with words or fists than cold steel.

On Mog-Mog, sailors could drink a bottle or two of warm beer, walk on the beach, swim in the warm waters, or play a friendly game of baseball or volleyball. "You could even gamble if you wanted to pay for it," was Gus Scutari's recollection. Despite the presence of hundreds of warships, the feeling of land beneath their feet, warm waters, and relaxation helped them forget the war for a brief time. "I was sitting on a log feeling sorry for myself, missing my brothers and my family," recalled Nick Zeoli. "Then I hear, 'Hey Nicky'! It was my buddy from home, John Vento. Can you imagine, a war as big as this and two friends run into each other on a little island?"

The daily impact of having thousands of sailors visit the small island had become noticeable. "When we visited Mog-Mog in February, there were coconuts four feet deep," recalled *Haynsworth's* A.C. Pickens. "A month later when we came back there were none! The sailors had eaten all the good ones and trampled the rest."

Cdr. Tackney and his officers did not maintain a strict clean shaven policy while at sea. "By the time we got to Mog-Mog, some guys looked like pirates because shaving wasn't enforced by the captain," remembered John Vasquez. "We had beards with beer."

Field expediency was found in the hundreds of yellow tubes planted at different spots on the island. For all the beer that was consumed by the sailors, the tubes represented a place to 'deposit' the remains.

Mog-Mog. (NARA 80-G-310177)

THE TIME SPENT AT ULITHI WASN'T WITHOUT RISK. For the enemy, a lagoon full of carriers presented a ripe target. "We were grimly reminded how desperately the Japs were determined to smash the Fast Carrier Task Force that had harassed their homeland from one end to the other and, together with American subs, had reduced their shipping to a precarious trickle."

On the evening of March 11th, two kamikazes, Yokosuka P1Y1 *Frances* long range bombers, dived from the skies. The small boat motor pool absorbed one attacker. The other twin engine hellion crashed through the stern of the USS *Randolph* CV-15 "Its bomb load, which possibly may have been released, penetrated the hull and interior bulkheads about several feet before exploding" within the Carbon Dioxide Transfer Shop. Twenty-seven men were killed and one hundred five wounded. Repairs were started straight away. With the entire repair facilities at its disposal, the *Randolph* would join the fleet again at Okinawa in early April but Admiral Mitscher had lost the use of one carrier before they had even sortied.

With the invasion of Okinawa looming, Cdr. Tackney and the other destroyer captains ordered extra drills for their gunnery, damage control, and medical departments. The encounters with kamikazes were to grow in intensity during the coming weeks.

USS Randolph receiving repairs from USS Jason AR-8

Damage at the aft end of the flight deck. (NARA 80-G-273790)

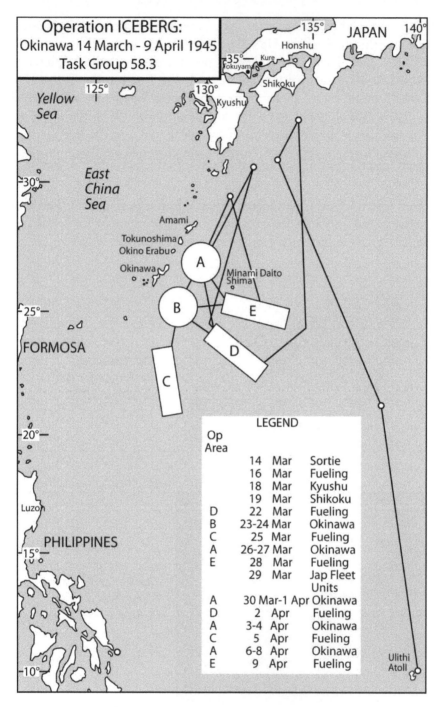

Operation ICEBERG:
Okinawa 14 March - 9 April 1945
Task Group 58.3

JAPAN

Honshu

Kure
Tokuyama

Shikoku

Yellow
Sea

Kyushu

East
China
Sea

Amami
Tokunoshima
Okino Erabu

Okinawa

A

Minami Daito
Shima

B

E

D

FORMOSA

C

Luzon

PHILIPPINES

Ulithi
Atoll

LEGEND			
Op Area			
	14	Mar	Sortie
	16	Mar	Fueling
	18	Mar	Kyushu
	19	Mar	Shikoku
D	22	Mar	Fueling
B	23-24	Mar	Okinawa
C	25	Mar	Fueling
A	26-27	Mar	Okinawa
E	28	Mar	Fueling
	29	Mar	Jap Fleet Units
A	30 Mar-1	Apr	Okinawa
D	2	Apr	Fueling
A	3-4	Apr	Okinawa
C	5	Apr	Fueling
A	6-8	Apr	Okinawa
E	9	Apr	Fueling

Task Group 58.3 Operations During ICEBERG
(Commander Task Group 58.3/38.3: Commander Carrier Division One:
Action Report 12 March -1 June, 1945)

PHALANX AGAINST THE DIVINE WIND

Part V

Okinawa

"These airborne attacks, far from turning aside the onset of heavily armored men, most likely served to incite their anger and to guarantee a furious collision of leveled spears. In short, for nearly three hundred years (650-350) no foreign army, despite any numerical superiority, withstood the charge of a Greek phalanx."

—*The Western Way of War* by Victor Davis Hanson

Operation ICEBERG

The fleet anchorage at Ulithi Atoll. (NARA 80-G-303950)

THE LAST STEPPING STONE TO JAPAN, Okinawa Jima, was the target in the advance north to the Japanese home islands. Lying less than 350 miles south of Japan, the Allies were continuing to tighten the noose around the Japanese empire. Operation ICEBERG, would be the last major attack before Operation DOWNFALL, the plan to invade Japan. For the destroyers, ICEBERG would be the toughest mission of the Pacific war. Their time in combat would be measured by burnt steel and bluejackets lying on palls shrouded in stars and stripes.

Task Force 58 broke from Ulithi on March 14 with the mission "to destroy enemy aircraft, aircraft facilities, naval forces, shipping and defenses in the Empire–Nansei Shoto– Formosa area, assist landing operations in Nansei Shoto by direct air support and surface bombardment, conduct photographic and air reconnaissance; in order to support the occupation of Okinawa Gunto." While the commanders had their orders, for the sailors aboard the destroyers, a reminder of what was to come was close at hand. "All hands looked at the damaged carrier [USS *Randolph*] as the *Ault* passed close aboard as it sortied three days later. If the Japs could inflict damage at that range, what

PHALANX AGAINST THE DIVINE WIND

Sailor on the Borie forecastle during attempts to refuel in heavy seas, March, 1945. (National Archives Photo)

would they do now when we moved in on them?" The answer would not be long in coming.

Four task groups stormed out of the atoll with fifteen aircraft carriers, ten battleships, seven cruisers, and nearly six dozen destroyers. The Screen Task Group, 58.3.4 was reconfigured so that in addition to DesRon 62, Destroyer Squadron 48 (DesDivs 95 & 96) was now a member. The seventeen destroyers served as the guards for the carriers *Bunker Hill, Essex* and *Cabot* with the express mission to "screen heavy ships against submarine, air and surface attack. Destroy enemy surface forces and submarines if opportunity occurs. Designated units form Destroyer Scouting Group when directed. Conduct bombardment of enemy shore installations, if directed." The number of destroyers under Capt. John Higgins' command would change frequently depending on the mission and ship availability.

While the *Divine Wind* had blown lightly against the Fast Carrier Task Force in February, it was expected that the suicidal winds would be growing in intensity as the Allies invaded islands closer to the Japanese home islands. But for the common seaman, the mission awaiting them was mostly conjecture rather than fact. Marion Parker penned in his journal: "Underway but have not found out where we will strike."

Strong seas greeted the fleet as it departed Ulithi. With the resultant pitching, numerous carrier planes made hard landings, blew tires, and stressed the fuselages.

The sailors took a pounding, too. Doc Ley and his pharmacist mates had patients right away. Three *Haynsworth* sailors were injured by heavy seas breaking over the *foc'sl* (forecastle) while they tried to secure the anchor. With a broken arm, leg and jaw, Bosun's Mate First Class Bill Nauck and Lt. Sidwell L. Smith were transferred to the battleship *South Dakota* the next day for further treatment of their injuries. Though the Chicago native Smith came back to the destroyer, much to the disappointment of his shipmates, Nauck never returned to the *Haynsworth*. After a long stay on the battlewagon, he was eventually transferred to the hospital ship USS *Bountiful* for additional medical treatment. Fate would have him reuniting with some of the *Haynsworth's* crew during their evacuation in April.

On the *Ides of March*, the *Haynsworth* served as the task group's bastion, far ahead on twelve mile picket duty. Several *Flash Red* messages brought the crew to General Quarters several times but no threats emerged. Sister cans were kept busy though with pilot rescues through the day. At 0729 a carrier reported one of their planes had made a water landing off its starboard beam. The *Weeks* collected the two airmen and then repeated the process again at 1540 when a marine flyer, 2nd Lt. Dewey Wambganss made a water landing. As he passed the *Bunker Hill* during the base leg of his landing approach, the VMF-451 flier stalled his *Corsair*, too intent on the *Corsair* ahead of him in its final approach. At mast level with the *Weeks*, he descended less than ninety feet to ditch in the ocean to terminate his flight.

The at sea salvation contrasted with *Week's* experience as plane guard the previous day. As the loss of the *Randolph* reminded the task force of the kamikaze threat, Admiral Mitscher's planes flew simulated coordinated attacks against the task groups after the fleet raised anchors at Ulithi for its race north to Tokyo.

Lt. jg. Frederick R. Horgan piloted a Grumman Avenger from the *Bunker Hill* as part of the tactical exercise. During his glide bombing run, the empennage tore loose from his plane. Topside on the *Weeks*, Morris Gillett CRT witnessed the tragedy unfold:

> *It was not uncommon for planes to make practice runs or dives in the general direction of the escort vessels. One morning during such drills a TBM, a torpedo bomber with a crew of three, was making a dummy dive with Weeks as the target. Just as it*

started to pull out of the dive both wings came off and the fuse-lage dove straight into the ocean. Both wings fell much slower, like feathers falling in a breeze. We immediately went to the spot but there was no sign of the plane's fuselage. It all happened in an instant and the men were gone.

Along with Horgan, crewmen Dewey Parker ARM2c and R. R. Gibbs ARM3c perished. DesDiv 124 Commander Richard W. Smith logged, "One plane crashed very close aboard, minus her wings. No survivors."

Their efforts were not in vain. The *Divine Wind* would arrive soon enough.

THE SAILOR'S FOCUS WAS NOT ALWAYS ON THE MISSION. During refueling south west of Iwo Jima on 16th, the *Weeks* and the *Lind* played the role of mailman and delivered welcomed correspondence across the task group. The *Haynsworth's* radarman Ralph Aakhus turned the calendar back to December: "Three packages arrived today. One contained a fruit cake and so me and my buddies had a party. Christmas at last!"

The next day: "At sea again. We had beans and rolls and coffee for breakfast. Sometimes there are pancakes and I really fill up then," wrote Aakhus to his family. "The sea is pretty smooth. Last evening we spotted a whale; he was really a monster. It is the first one I've ever seen. There are a lot of sharks in this area and you see them quite often."

DANGER LURKED IN THE SEAS ON SAINT PATRICK'S DAY. *Waldron's* captain, Cdr. Peckham, wrote: "Encountered several floating mines today. These are in the Japanese current, probably coming from the East China Sea." The horned saboteurs posed significant risk to ships. Mines were usually moored by chain but they could also be set loose to be carried by the waves after they were dropped by ships and planes, or launched by submarines. Japanese Type 93 mines were large, horned bombs packed with nearly 500 lbs. of explosives. Contact with a mine offered a journey to the depths of the sea for the destroyers.

The *Haynsworth's* captain, Cdr. Stephen Tackney was very familiar with the threat the mines posed to destroyers. As captain of the destroyer minesweeper USS *Gamble* on August 3, 1942, the DM-15 mined a channel near the South Pacific island of Espiritu Santo. The next day, without being given special instructions or a harbor pilot, the American destroyer USS *Tucker* entered the channel. One of the mines exploded against her hull. The survivor of the attack against Pearl Harbor settled quickly. Six of her bluejackets were lost.

Of the mines, the *Haynsworth's* Marion Parker GM3c noted, "There were ten or twelve of them." *Weeks*, *Ault*, *Lind* and *Walker* exploded enemy mines by gunfire while the *Haynsworth* accounted for two more with her 20mm machine guns. Some of the ordnance geysered as the tin can's skin shivered. Others slipped under the waves. For the young sailors, the action was nerve wracking, the tension palpable.

USS Tucker DD-374.

Japanese naval mine. (NARA 80-G-320304)

The hungry destroyers topped off their fuel bunkers from the heavy ships in preparation for the coming assault on Kyushu. Replenishment was not the only effort of the day aboard Tackney's ship. Training was a never ending part of the routine at sea. The *Haynsworth* held several airplane recognition 'schools' in the mess and in the wardroom. Later, *Fighter Director* films were shown in the wardroom. Lt. Cdr. Lothrop reminded the crew frequently that hostile planes were often detected first by the ship's lookouts rather than by radar. "Eternal vigilance is our only real protection against these attacks."

IN THE OPENING ROUNDS OF THE BATTLE OF MIDWAY, Lt. Cdr. John Waldron bravely led his squadron, Torpedo Squadron 8, against the Japanese carriers. Without the benefit of fighter cover, the slow obsolete TBD *Devastator* torpedo planes were slaughtered as they pressed their attacks home against Yamamoto's carriers. Only one pilot survived of the fifteen aircrews sent on the mission. But, their sacrifice helped to change the course of the battle thus leading to the American victory. Awarded the Navy Cross posthumously, Waldron was further honored when DD-699 was named for him. Eventually the USS *Waldron* saved more pilots and aircrew than any other destroyer in Squadron 62 during the battle for the Pacific.

1ˢᵗ Lt. James Anderson USMCR VMF-451 far left, first row standing. (Courtesy of Philip Wilmot)

The *Waldron* came to the rescue of 1st Lt. James Anderson, Jr., USMCR. The aviator's *Corsair* never gained flight after taking off from the *Bunker Hill* at 0841. Hitting the water on the destroyer's starboard side, Cdr. Peckham's crew recovered Anderson within fifteen minutes. The VMF-451 pilot was a guest of DD-699 until midafternoon when he was traded back to Task Force 58's flagship for a barrel of ice cream. Well heeled, handsome, intelligent, and confident, Anderson, a '42 graduate of Yale, was a pilot's pilot. His wingman, 1ˢᵗ

Lt. Philip Wilmot recalled, "You always knew you'd get home if you flew with Andy."

Saint Patrick's Day was concluded by a return to General Quarters at 2157 when an enemy air raid seemed imminent. "Jap planes spotted us tonight and started dropping flares at 2300," reported Parker. The ships were finally allowed to secure from General Quarters at midnight when the planes failed to appear over the American ships. However, the next day would bring the start of continual air attacks against Admiral Mitscher's Fast Carrier Task Force, a preamble for the task force as it spent more time in the Japanese home waters.

18 MARCH 1945: DAY 1 AGAINST THE HOME ISLANDS

USS Bunker Hill, March 18, 1945. (US Navy Photo 80-G-373737)

STEAMING INTO DANGER'S DOORWAY, Vice Admiral Mitscher's forces started their strikes against the Japanese home islands of Kyushu, Honshu, and Shikoku early on March 18th. "On completion of fueling, Task Force 58 will commence run in for strikes against Kyushu. Kyushu is an island which forms SW tip of Honshu, island of Japan. The bulk of the Jap's air strength is believed concentrated in Kyushu now—that is the aim of the Task Force now—Destruction of these remnants." Cdr. Tackney's *Haynsworth* and the other ships of Task Force 58 would be tangling with Kyushu's airpower for the next several months. Kamikazes would abbreviate the stay of many of the ships in these waters.

The hammer was sent to the anvil when the first fighter sweeps and CAP launched early from the carriers. A large fighter sweep targeted the island to neutralize Kyushu's many airfields. These attacks were followed by a second even larger raid of fighters, bombers, and torpedo planes. In a show of force, the Fast Carrier Task Force launched over five hundred planes against the enemy installations.

Moving within 100 miles of Kyushu's coast, the Navy's big stick stirred the imperial hornet nest. The hornets retaliated against the American raiders. Though the enemy planes were few in number, the "attacks were conducted in an aggressive and determined manner."

The morning of the 18th started with Captain Higgins' destroyers going to General Quarters at 0305. "Enemy aircraft reported near the force. It is evident we will not achieve the complete surprise we have had on former strikes." With foes in the air, the phalanx closed in on the carriers at 0532. Maximum anti-aircraft fire was ready as the eleven destroyers in the circular screen positioned themselves in defensive formation 5-V with the cruisers and the battleships.

At General Quarters all day, Captain Higgins' tin cans were immersed in the action. Raiding aircraft dropped flares over TG 58.3 at 0505. Targets were plentiful for the gun captains and their crews. Near dawn, the *Haynsworth* let loose with her 20mm and 40mm machine guns at enemy planes but splashed none while the *Hank* took on an enemy long range reconnaissance Mitsubishi Ki-46 *Dinah*. At 0605 both her 5" and 40mm guns started firing from a distance of 4000 yards. Despite the *Hank's* efforts, the plane escaped into a layer of clouds. Both the *Lind* and *Sperry* gunners also opened up on planes that dared to venture near the phalanx's shields. Anti-aircraft fire from other ships splashed two of the three bogeys while the CAP disposed of a twin engine *Betty* bomber.

Once again, the carriers found themselves in the bullseye as targets of their airborne foes. A *Zeke* dove from the skies but missed the flattops as it entered its watery tomb nearby. The crew of the *English* witnessed a *Judy* dive bomber dive out of the sun, slip through the screen and drop a bomb near the *Bunker Hill*. The invader was shot down immediately but the *Bunker Hill* would not be so lucky on May 11th. Meanwhile the *Ault* fired at a twin engine *Frances* bomber with her 5" guns but the invader escaped. Another *Judy* dive bomber "made a dive attack on the group and was shot down by AA fire. Bomb missed ahead and astern of USS *Essex*," recorded *Ault's* captain, Cdr. Joseph C. Wylie, Jr. A *Betty* bomber also infiltrated the screen but was disposed of by the CAP. The action included a Japanese *Dinah* long range reconnaissance plane dropping a bomb that landed astern of the *Haynsworth*. True to her nickname, no damage was inflicted on the 'Lucky 700.'

The *English* was both savior and destroyer: Midafternoon she recovered a bluejacket that had fallen overboard from the *Bunker* Hill. Less than two hours later, a floating raider tried to penetrate the phalanx. The *English* destroyed the naval mine bobbing in the swells. Danger to the task force lurked not just in the air but also on the seas.

Admiral Arthur Radford's Task Group 58.4 carriers were also in the crosshairs: A twin engine *Betty* bomber tangled with USS *Intrepid* CV-11. The plane almost made it but the gunners aboard the flattop took their vengeance on the Mitsubishi G4M. Crashing close aboard the flattop, the resulting explosion caused fires on the hangar deck. The blaze was quickly extinguished by the damage control parties before it got out of hand.

USS Intrepid.
(NARA 80-G-328545)

Stablemate USS *Enterprise* CV-6 found itself in the pipper's sight. The 'Gray Ghost,' a veteran of three years of battles against the Japanese, was struck by a dud Japanese bomb. Though it didn't explode, it did cause damage to the carrier. A bluejacket was lost in the action. The day's attacks were a harbinger of the battles that lay ahead in the hours to come for the phalanx.

"Six Planes Are Down"

*Left: USS Haynsworth rescue swimmer Henry Michalak S1c rescues a pilot.
(Courtesy of Capt. Hank Domeracki USN);
Right: Lt. jg. James Horan. (Courtesy of Tim Horan)*

DESPITE THE ATTACKS, the destroyers were active rescuing pilots and crews from numerous ditched planes. During the early plane launches, the *Waldron* recovered an *Essex* pilot who ended up in the drink due to problems during takeoff. A few hours later she pulled in another *Essex* flyboy who was forced to make a water landing inside the phalanx.

A flight of eleven SB2C/SBW *Helldivers* from the *Hancock* found that the range of the mission was greater than the capabilities of their fuel tanks. Each plane was loaded with two 500 pound bombs in the bomb bay and a pair of 250 pound bombs on the wings. After striking the airfield and hangars of the Kagoshima airfield, Kyushu, with *Avengers* and *Corsairs* squadrons, the big VB-6 Curtiss bombers turned back towards the carriers. "Due to excessive power settings, rapid climbs with full power and undue time in the rendezvous and a circuitous return route, all eleven planes were running low on gas." With the realization that the carriers were at the far range of their fuel, the pilots turned the fuel mixture control to 'auto-lean,' lowered engine rpms, increased the manifold pressure of the Wright R-2600 engine, and settled in for a flight relying on skill and prayer to get back. To cut the flight time back, they headed straight towards the long range picket destroyers. The Tomcat CAP, controlled by the pickets, would 'delouse' the squadron if any enemy planes tried to sneak into the carrier force with the bombers.

Six VB-6 birds were forced to make water landings short of the carrier deck as their engines sputtered from fuel starvation. Lt. Robert Eggleston Gardner was the first to put his plane down. Lt. jg. Douglas Helmer descended to sea level so that his backseat man, Thomas W. Schneider ARM2c, could drop a two man raft to Gardner and his backseater, David Jensen ARM1c. Both men were seen to safely escape the *Helldiver* and enter the raft. Twenty-three year old Minnesota native Lt. jg. James Horan also circled his plane around the raft. Both Gardner and Jensen waved back to indicate they were okay.

The *Helldivers* continued to drop from the sky and ditch in the East China Sea. Helmer put his bird down around the same time as the planes of Lt. jg. Ronald Somerville, Ensign Robert D. Moore, and Ensign John W. Dragoo hit the waves.

When Horan's fuel drained desperately low, he turned his big bird towards the task group and the safety of the phalanx. Horan instructed his radioman, Leroy Cox ARM2c, to lighten the plane as much as possible. Over the side from the gunner's position went the twin .30 machine gun mount, heavy ammunition cases, miscellaneous gear, and Cox's shoes. In preparation for ditching, the radioman held the two man raft and the ration pack.

When the engine began to cough, Horan turned his bird into the wind and nursed it down to the ocean's surface. Lowering his flaps to 45 degrees, he made a power stall landing at seventy knots, the *Helldiver* skidding across the waves until its nose dropped and it was turned around.

After escaping the cockpit, Horan couldn't find Cox. He dove repeatedly to the sinking plane in vain. When he finally surfaced, he saw the radioman swimming after their raft. They eventually both climbed aboard, a small yellow dot on a sea of dark blue.

The prow of a destroyer could be seen headed in their direction as the *Haynsworth* was again in its role as rescuer. A cargo net was hoisted over the side while Bill Vassey S1c and Harrison Beasley RT1c stood at the ready. Seaman Henry "Hank" Michalak, the rescue swimmer, instinctively dove into the water and recovered Horan and Cox. The salty sailor earned a medal for his heroic act, but at the same time was formally admonished for diving into the water instead of jumping in feet first. The difference between a reprimand and a medal for bravery was often measured in shades of gray. Michalak's impulsive act to save the pilot did not surprise the sailors of the *Haynsworth*.

After a quick examination of Horan and Cox by Doctor Ley, Cdr. Tackney logged, "Pilot and radioman were rescued, both in good condition."

For the task group, a combat pilot saved was a combat pilot earned. In just a few months' time, Lt. jg. Horan would earn the Navy's second highest award for combat valor, the Navy Cross, for sinking a destroyer despite strong enemy opposition.

Other destroyers came to the rescue of the VB-6 aircrews. The USS *Marshall* plucked Lt. jg. Helmer and his radioman from the sea while the USS *Hickox* saved Ensign Moore and Robert Mallon ARM2c. The final rescue was the USS *Wedderburn* coming to the aid of Lt. Somerville and his backseater, Louis F. Jakubec ARM2c. The plane of Ensign John Dragoo was seen to make a hard landing. Dragoo and his radioman, Duane Cole, ARM3c, were lost to the waves.

The average fuel load remaining in the tanks of the dive bombers from Bombing Squadron 6 that managed to return to the carriers was just five gallons, just enough for no more than five minutes flight time. The Commander of Carrier Air Group 6 wrote in his summary report of the raid, "Average of Fuel Consumed: ALL." Underwing, expendable fuel tanks would become a fixture for future raids of targets in excess of 200 miles distance.

Last seen by Lt. Horan in their raft, Lt. Gardner and his radioman were not found by the destroyers. Patrol planes from Iwo Jima and the Philippines were notified while surface craft were given the position where Gardner ditched his plane. Despite the intense search by the U.S. Navy, Gardner and Schneider, listed as missing in action, were never recovered from the unforgiving Pacific.

THE BIG BLUE BLANKET ACHIEVED SPECTACULAR DIVIDENDS from the day's attacks: 102 enemy aircraft shot down while another 275 were destroyed or damaged on the ground. Photo reconnaissance showed the airfields were heavily punished. Intelligence brought back reports of large numbers of enemy vessels in the Japanese Inland Sea.

With the phalanxes of the task groups drawn in around the carriers, the result of their efforts was telling. The CAP brought down twelve aircraft but the shipboard gunner's fusillade accounted for twenty-one hostile planes blown from the sky. Task Force Commander Vice Admiral Mitscher noted that, "The anti-aircraft gunnery was excellent. Perhaps gun crews were inclined to open fire well out of range but no one attempted to stop them as their fire was most comforting." Mitscher additionally praised the efforts of the tin cans: "It was a trying period, as little, if any, warning was being given by the radars in the force, and at times the first indication of an aircraft approaching was visual sighting by the close screen. The picket destroyers were invaluable with their visual sightings." The phalanx proved its mettle again that day.

Finally, at dusk, the destroyer screen opened ranks to its normal 5-R cruising disposition after the phalanx had been closed tightly all day.

For the crews of the *Haynsworth* and the band of destroyers, the day was spent at General Quarters. The fifteen long hours at the heightened fighting condition strained the crew. It was important to remain vigilant but despite the efforts, it was exhausting. Radarman Aakhus noted he "had about four hours sleep in the previous forty-eight hours. Chow was whenever you had the chance. Yesterday chow was brought up to us as we haven't been able to leave our posts. It's pretty cold so while topside we're wearing heavy weather gear. My face is sore from the salt spray coming over the bridge in a strong wind."

One sailor tried to keep his buddies relaxed. "All over the ship, guys had their sound powered phones on waiting for instructions. It was boring when nothing was happening," recalled Fire Controlman Gus Scutari. "I had my father mail me the needle from our old Victrola at home. By hooking it up to a turntable and taping it to the transmitter, I was able to play music through the whole ship. The guys loved it! But then a voice came over the phones, 'Who's playing that music? Turn it off!'" Scutari's disc jockey career met a quick demise.

Operation ICEBERG would not get easier in the weeks to come for the sailors of the phalanx.

19 MARCH: DAY 2 AGAINST THE HOME ISLANDS

USS Franklin CV-17, March 19, 1945. (NARA 80-G-273848)

FOR THE OFFICERS AND BLUEJACKETS OF TASK FORCE 58, Monday March 19th would be a day of battle forever seared into their memories. Steaming east of Kyushu, the battle groups sent strikes aloft against military targets at Kure, Kobe and Hiroshima. Rear Admiral Sherman's Task Group 58.3's planes targeted the Imperial Japanese Navy warships anchored at Kure. "Task force is gunning for CA's, CL's, DD's, and CVE's discovered and possibly damaged in yesterday's afternoon strikes," posted Lt. Cdr. Lothrop. Sherman's fliers would be joined by the aviators from Rear Admiral Joseph "Jocko" Clark's Task Group 58.1. Rear Admiral Ralph Davison's TG 58.2 carriers would launch planes to attack targets and installations in the Kure Naval Air Depot while Rear Admiral A. Radford's TG 58.4 would send attacks against targets at Kobe. Mortal aerial duels were about to commence.

Destroyer Division 96 was released from the protective screen to steam northeast and form a five ship picket line. While their forward

PHALANX AGAINST THE DIVINE WIND

position provided the task group with early radar warnings of incoming raiders, the movement resulted in the loss of nearly a third of the destroyers in the outer screen. Only eleven destroyers of Divisions 123, 124, and 95 were available to guard the carriers' flanks. The loss would be felt as the battle was waged.

As this day promised to be as long as the previous day, Lt. Cdr. Scott Lothrop made adjustments to the most basic but important of schedules for the sailors of the *Haynsworth*. Nineteen sailors from various divisions were pressed into service as supplemental mess cooks. It was critical that all sailors had a chance to eat and that sailors could be moved through the mess as quickly as possible. General Quarters required all aboard must be ready to fight without hesitation. The sailor's focus had to be to his duty, not his needs.

THE ACTION STARTED EARLY: The *English* sank another mine found floating close aboard. A couple hundred rounds from the 20mm guns put an end to the water borne menace. The next threats came from the air.

Japanese mine detonated by USS Ingersoll. (NARA 80-G photo)

Judy dive bomber targets the USS Enterprise. (NARA 80-G photo)

Flying south from Shikoku and east from Kyushu, the intersection point for the Japanese pilots became the center of the storm. A strong *Divine Wind* blew against the task groups at the aerial crossroads throughout the day as Task Force 58 moved within sixty-five miles of the coast of Honshu, the doorstep of Japan.

The USS *Stembel* DD-644 took down the first raider against the task force. On picket duty, its search and control radars tracked the plane at 0325 as it closed on the American force. Adjusting its course in response, Cdr. Matthew Schmidling's destroyer opened fire with its main battery at 0335 from a range of 5700 yards. It took just thirty-six 5" shells to bring the raider to a fiery end, a flaming comet diving across the darkened Pacific skies.

Before sunrise, enemy snoopers dropping flares began orbiting the group. "We were lit up all night," wrote the *Haynsworth's* Bill McKeen SM3c. The falling magnesium stars were released until dawn, illuminating parts of the task force as a prelude to attack.

Task group air operations commenced on schedule. The CAP and attack Sweep #1 started launches from Sherman's carriers at 0540. The *Waldron* took the sentry's role as plane guard for the day. With warnings of incoming malevolent planes, the destroyers closed the phalanx after first light with all anti-aircraft batteries alerted.

PHALANX AGAINST THE DIVINE WIND

Judy dive bomber targets the USS Wasp. (NARA 80-G-310026)

Minutes later the first enemy plane made an appearance over Task Group 58.3. The initial raider would be followed by several more small swarms of enemy planes all day. At 0744 a *Zeke* was reported by the *Ault* to the task group's officer of tactical control. As the group began evasive turns, the ships of the screen opened fire. Radioman Keith Myreholt of the *Haynsworth* reported, "Suicide diver bombers attacked carriers. First one attacked USS *Bunker Hill* and was shot down. Bursting into flames in mid-air and dropping like a hot potato." *Bunker Hill* and *Essex* escaped unharmed again at 0814. A *Judy* dive bomber was spotted diving out of the sun. Accurate AA fire from the group brought her demise near the carrier. Myreholt continued in his journal, "Second suicider tried for USS *Essex*. Missed by fifty feet hitting the water. Took two hits on way down." On fire, the raider hit the ocean close to the bow of the USS *Bunker Hill*. A twin engine enemy plane took heed of the warnings from the gunners and stayed out of range about the same time. The CAP disposed of three more enemy planes during the raids.

Though 58.3's carriers had survived the round of attacks, two columns of black smoke could be seen burning in the distance with accompanying explosions. Myreholt continued, "Two carriers of another TG hit by bombs. USS *Franklin* and USS *Wasp*."

In Adm. Jocko Clark's Task Group 58.1 the carrier USS *Wasp* CV-18 was hit by attackers at 0710 while just 52 miles from Shikoku. A *Judy* dive bomber burst out of the low clouds just 2000 feet above the carrier. Its 540 pound bomb penetrated the wooden flight deck and passed through two more decks before exploding. Despite the conflagration on the flight deck and ensuing damage below, *Wasp* stayed on station. Within thirty minutes the fire in the hangar deck was contained. Less than an hour after the attack, she was able to resume flight missions. Her losses were 102 sailors dead or missing with another 200 wounded. There was no time to mourn.

The aerial melee intensified. The radarmen on the *Haynsworth* and the other ships of the phalanx all saw the same thing: "Bogies on screen in all directions." The *Wasp* was targeted again by an enemy Nakajima B6N *Jill* torpedo bomber at 0832. Despite numerous hits by anti-aircraft fire, the mortally wounded plane continued on its path towards the carrier. As Captain Oscar Weller ordered course changes, the burning plane crashed close by. Fortunately, no additional casualties were suffered.

The action continued as one of *Wasp's* screening destroyers exploded a mine nearby at 0938. Having escaped further harm, the damaged carrier would stay with the task force until April before she was released to return to America for repairs.

In Task Group 58.2, the USS *Franklin* CV-13 had already launched twenty fighters for the attack against Itami Jima and an additional eight fighters for the CAP by 0657. She was beginning to launch planes for another strike against shipping in Kobe Harbor when a Japanese plane dived from the clouds. With accuracy the raider dropped two semi-armor piercing bombs against the *Franklin.* "Fires and continuous heavy explosions of our bombs, rockets and other ordnance reduced flight deck, hangar deck and after second deck to gutted and torn wreckage." She burned intensely while listing 13°. Captain Gehres' carrier was without both radio communications and power from her boilers. The scuttlebutt among the destroyers' bluejackets was that, "rumor has it that it will have to be sunk."

The carnage was horrific aboard the 'Big Ben.' Losses totaled 724 sailors killed and hundreds more wounded. Another 795 sailors were evacuated to the light cruiser USS *Santa Fe.* The attending destroyers *Hickox, Miller, Hunt, Tingey,* and *Marshall* recovered sailors trapped on the fantail, blown overboard or who had jumped to escape the confla-

USS Miller DD-535 comes to the rescue of the USS Franklin.
(NARA 80-G-273862)

gration. The tally for the small boys was 850 of the *Franklin's* muster saved.

Retribution was small but swift: The *Bataan* had just launched Lt. jg. Locke Trigg for a strike against Kobe. Despite the concentrated blooms of anti-aircraft fire erupting from the entire task group, his *Hellcat* chased the suspected bomber, a twin engine *Myrt*, twenty miles before sending the enemy plane to a watery grave.

THE BATTLE PLANS WERE REDRAWN ONCE ADMIRAL SPRUANCE GAVE THE ORDER to save 'Big Ben' rather than scuttle her. Her rescue would be a team effort. Dead in the water, *Franklin* was taken under tow by the heavy cruiser USS *Pittsburgh* CA-72. The tandem warships could only achieve five knots thereby forcing changes in formation speed for all of the task groups so as not to be too spread out. 'Fast' had been removed from the moniker 'Fast Carrier Task Force.'

DesRon 62 contributed two of her stable, *English* and *Waldron*, along with the cruiser *Astoria* to join *Franklin's* beefed up Praetorian Guard, Task Unit 58.2.9. They were joined by the five destroyers of Destroyer Division 96. To cover the skies over the *Franklin*, *Enterprise* was transferred from its task group to 58.2 while the Blue Devil squadron of the *Bunker* Hill provided top cover in the skies.

Still close to Japan's shores, Captain Leslie Gehres' ravaged carrier remained an enticing target for the enemy. At 1254 another enemy plane, a *Judy* divebomber, slipped past the CAP and through the ring of anti-aircraft fire with the wounded carrier in its sights. Its bomb missed *Franklin's* starboard quarter by a scant 200 yards.

Haynsworth's Ed Mital summed up the sight simply: "One of our ships is towing *Franklin*. She's in bad shape."

A RESPITE IN THE ATTACKS OCCURRED mid-morning allowing the carriers to recover the early CAP and planes from the first sweep. The second sweep was launched at 1010. Reports from the initial strike confirmed the presence of IJN carriers, cruisers, battleships, and destroyers at Kure. The fliers brought another wave of bombs and rockets to the duel against the Emperor's ships.

But, the Bushido boys were not done. Early afternoon, another wave of attacks were launched against the American warships. At 1318 two *Zekes* closed on 58.3. While the CAP disposed of one hostile flier, the *Haynsworth* took care of the other. Positioned between the cruiser *Pasadena* and the battleship *New Jersey*, *Haynsworth's* Gunnery officer Lt. Armistead "Army" Dennett tracked the plane from his position in the Mk 37 Gun Fire Control System above the bridge. On his command, the 5" guns opened fire on the plane diving from the clouds. In just ten seconds of firing, the main batteries picked off their target at 5000 yards. Cdr. Tackney logged, "We opened fire with 5" batteries while the plane was in her dive and shot 18 rounds of 5"/38 AAC [anti-aircraft common ammunition] before she was hit and crashed on our port bow. Although several of the other ships were firing, too, we believe it was our gunfire which destroyed this plane. She was definitely a suicide, but it is difficult to judge who her target was since the formation was making radical emergency course changes at high speed." Gunners Mate Third Class Marion Parker, serving in the aft 5" gun battery, declared: "We hit our stride today and brought down a dive bomber in six shots." Executive Officer Scott Lothrop offered praise to the gunners and firecontrolmen, "That was a wonderful shot that brought the *Zeke* down and I'm proud of every man who had a hand in it."

DesRon 62 mate DD-697 also scored a kill. The USS *Charles S. Sperry* was led by Cdr. Harry McIlhenny. No stranger to combat, the forty year old officer had been awarded a Navy Cross for his actions against an IJN submarine while commanding the USS *Reid* DD-369 in 1942. After attacks with depth charges forced the aggressor submarine to the surface, gunfire from the destroyer finished it off. A year later he won a Silver Star for protecting a convoy of landing craft when the

Reid fought off a raid of ten Japanese torpedo bombers near New Guinea.

Quad 40mm USS Haynsworth, 1945. (Courtesy USS Haynsworth Association)

Enemy plane passes near the USS San Jacinto. (NARA 80-G-328690)

McIlhenny logged, "1429 One type *Zero* enemy fighter made diving bomb run on us from 7000 yards after passing near Task Group 58.3. 1430 commenced firing, plane dropped bomb about 300 yards on starboard quarter bearing 200°T." Despite excellent shooting from *Sperry's* guns, "he came straight in. He grew closer and closer and the men topside kept firing, kept wondering when he'd blow up or when he'd strafe. His bomb dropped on her starboard quarter as the *Sperry's* stern kicked over in a turn. Pulling up his nose, he rode over number two torpedo mount as pieces of the plane tore loose. The port machine guns opened up; the pilot could no longer control his plane; the nose pulled up, the left wing lowered, and he circled into the sea. As the *Sperry* closed it, the debris sank."

"This was our first enemy plane," recorded McIlhenny. The plane's proximity was reflected in the expenditure of fifteen 5" shells, 360 40mm rounds and 550 20mm rounds. "By sunset a Japanese flag had been proudly painted on each side of the main battery director. Quiet elation was everywhere throughout the ship."

Another DesRon 62 member scored during the action. "USS *Lind* was given credit for shooting down one Jap plane by 5" guns which are controlled and fired by the computer," logged her Fire Controlman Bob Plum.

Soon after, another enemy bomber nosed over from 8000-10000 feet. The *Haynsworth* radioman Myreholt noted that at "1440 dive bomber came in at high altitude. All ships opened up laying pattern of AA fire under him." Within seconds, a black ring of fire bloomed in the sky. DesRon 62's *Weeks, Haynsworth, Borie, Hank, Waldron,* and *English* all attempted to shoot down the plane. "Could not come down. CAP splashed him at edge of force. Total of six planes for 58.3," summarized Myreholt. Crewmate Marion Parker noted, "Boy, the planes have been falling so fast I have lost count of the number." Admiral Mitscher agreed. Anti-aircraft drills for the following day were cancelled after the skies over the task force were streaked by fiery plumes of fallen bandits.

S ERVING ON PLANE GUARD DUTY, the *Waldron* had become a guardian angel for those that had lost their 'wings.' After a pilot rescue on the 17th, DD-699 was in action retrieving wayward aviators as she saved pilots from the *Essex*. At 0852 Ensign William 'Jimmy' Morton, USNR, of VF-83, crashed astern of the carrier in his *Hellcat* after running out of gas in the landing pattern. The twenty-one year old tar heel was aboard dry steel in just eight minutes time. Less than two hours later, Ensign Dennis Gray, USNR, also a victim of dwindling fuel supplies while stuck in the landing pattern, water landed his VBF-83 FG-1D *Corsair* near the *Essex*. Once again it took Cdr. George Peckham's *Waldron* eight minutes to affect the rescue. Salvation by the destroyer on this day was no guarantee for the future. Just three weeks later off Okinawa, the twenty-one year old Montana pilot's time ran out when he failed to return from a mission.

In the midst of the day's action, the USS *Walker* DD-517 saved a pilot and radioman from a *Bunker Hill* plane *Helldiver*. It ditched in the ocean 8000 yards from the tin can. Proceeding at high speed, the destroyer was able to affect the rescue thus allowing the aircrew to get back in the hunt with Bombing Squadron 84.

Post recovery of the third fighter sweep, the task group commenced its southerly retirement at 1500. The phalanx returned to its expanded cruising pattern 5-Roger at 1815. After eighty-six enemy air raids had emerged against the task force over the previous fifty-one hours, the armada was beyond the reach of the Emperor's raptors.

Finally, after long hours at General Quarters, the crew of the *Haynsworth* was relieved at 1845. "We had four hours sleep last night and Japs were after us again at 5 this a.m. 0120 up until 1700," reflected Marion Parker GM3c after a day spent in the aft 5" battery. Sleep was becoming a precious luxury for the crews of the tin can. "I am tired and sleepy and hope to get a few hours tonight. We have the mid watch so won't get over four hours [sleep]."

TARGET: KURE

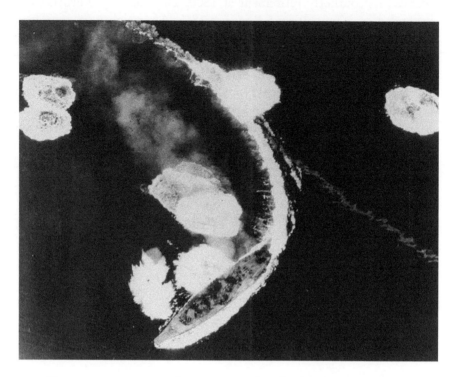

Yamato manuevers against American bombs. (NARA 80-G Photo)

THE PORT OF KURE SHELTERED THE SHATTERED RE-
MAINS of the Imperial Japanese Navy. Many of its largest warships were now anchored there. But, having lost three battleships, ten
cruisers, four carriers, and nine destroyers at the Battle of Leyte Gulf,
the few surviving warships were limited to home water operations.
The base was heavily defended by ack-ack and airfields. The Fast Carrier Task Force sent strikes against the anchorage and the shipyard
with its repair facilities, dock, and fuel depots.

The keel of the mighty *Yamato* was laid down at Kure in 1937.
Originally five *Yamato* class battleships were to be built. Her sister
Musashi was built at Nagasaki while a third battleship, *Shinano*, was
started at Yokosuka. As Japan began to rapidly lose her carriers, the
two unbuilt remaining battleships were cancelled. The need for battleships had already faded so it was decided the *Shinano* would be converted into an aircraft carrier. The American submarine *Archerfish* torpedoed that dream on November 28, 1944.

PHALANX AGAINST THE DIVINE WIND

While the U.S. Navy was not prepared for an attack on the sleepy Sunday morning at Pearl Harbor in 1941, the IJN knew it was just a matter of time before attacks on the home islands would come. By 1945 the *Yamato* bristled with anti-aircraft weapons. In addition to her six 6.1 inch guns and the twenty four 5.0 inch guns, she mounted 166 smaller anti-aircraft weapons. The time was approaching soon when the leviathan would have to use even her massive 18.1" cannon in her own defense.

As dawn broke, the American attack group crossed over to the island of Honshu. A large wave of planes from the carriers *Enterprise*, *Yorktown*, and *Intrepid* targeted the port of Kure. The *Yamato*, the most powerful ship in the world, could do little but maneuver and fire her anti-aircraft guns at the attackers. But like a bull trapped in a pen, eventually the battleship would break out.

The attack was fended off by a group of experienced Japanese pilots flying the advanced Kawanishi N1K1 *Shiden* fighters. Few veteran pilots remained in the either the IJN or IJA after the attrition of three plus years of war against the Allies. But, some of these surviving veterans were being used as flight instructors at a nearby airfield. Still, the combination of skills, superior aircraft and greater numbers allowed the American pilots to prevail. American pilots claimed more than two hundred planes shot down and a comparable number destroyed on the ground. Though the victory claims were slightly optimistic, the Fast Carrier Task Force's planes dominated the skies. Of 193 Japanese planes that took to the air, 161 eventually fell back to earth.

Vice Admiral Marc Mitscher stated that, "the attack was only moderately successful, mainly because of the extremely heavy and accurate AA fire encountered, one group alone losing thirteen aircraft at Kure."

The *Yamato* narrowly escaped. Just one bomb struck its bridge. Damage was also inflicted on two other battleships, several aircraft carriers, a cruiser, and several smaller vessels. In a few weeks' time, *Yamato* would sortie without the benefit of air cover. Her next wounds would be mortal.

20 MARCH: TASK FORCE 58

USS Franklin towed by USS Pittsburgh. (NARA 80-G-273919)

ADMIRAL MITSCHER'S FORCES SLOWLY DEPARTED THE TEMPEST after two days of air attacks by the enemy. Still under tow, the tandem *Pittsburgh* and *Franklin* managed just a few knots. To protect her, the task group added extra planes to augment the CAP flying overhead. Covering the retirement of the 'Big Ben,' DesDiv 96 remained with TG 58.2.

The plan for March 20th was to refuel the hungry destroyers from the heavy ships while safeguarding the wounded carriers. The task force's course and speed changed throughout the day as the warships maneuvered to protect the wounded *Franklin*. Reports were received mid-morning that enemy snoopers had discovered the task group's position. With the presence of raiding planes, refueling was started and halted numerous times. It proved to be another long day for the tin can sailors. But, by day's end, the phalanx's perimeter guards proved again their value safeguarding the task groups.

After filling her tanks, the *Haynsworth* was sent to replace the *Sperry* on picket duty. Steaming twelve miles ahead of the carriers, the *Haynsworth* observed an enemy dive bomber drop two bombs near TG 58.4 ten miles to the northwest. As the enemy plane fled the scene, she headed in the direction of the Cdr. Tackney's ship. At 1450, after tracking the raider for thirty seconds on the Mk.1 radar, Gunnery Of-

*Above: Kamikaze strikes
Halsey Powell alongside the
Hancock.
(U.S. Navy National Museum
of Naval Aviation photo)*

*Left: USS Halsey Powell fights
the fire on its stern.
(NARA 80-G-315259)*

ficer Lt. Dennett's opened fire with the main batteries. The 5" shells
and resulting explosions were enough to change the mind of the Japanese pilot. Turning his plane away from the destroyer, the raider escaped to fight another day.

At the same time, the USS *Halsey Powell* DD-686 of DesRon 53
was refueling from the carrier *Hancock*. When an enemy plane was
discovered making a run against TG 58.2, refueling operations were
halted while the klaxons called the sailors to their battlestations. As the
destroyer attempted to maneuver free of the carrier, both ships spread
a shield of lethal defensive fire. As it dove into the fusillade, the attacker took numerous hits. Breaking up directly over the carrier and the
can, the engine and large parts of the plane hit the aft end of *Halsey
Powell.* The thin skin of the destroyer was not enough to slow down
the enemy's bomb. The ordnance passed completely through the aft
deck and exited the hull near the keel without exploding. The butch-

er's bill: twelve sailors of her young crew were killed along with twenty-nine wounded.

The strike against *Halsey Powell* marked a turning point for kamikaze attacks. While the main targets continued to be the carriers, destroyers became the recipients of an increasing number of attacks, absorbing the brunt of kamikaze incursions rather than the flattops. By 1945 the U.S. Navy had greater shielding of capital ships by destroyers, deadly proximity fuzes mounted to 5" shells, and an overwhelming Combat Air Patrol covering the fleet. Picket destroyers extended the range of the task group's radar. For their enemy, it was becoming increasingly harder for marginal Japanese pilots in marginal planes to make it past the outer shields of defense to strike the carriers.

USS Enterprise surrounded by anti-aircraft fire while under attack.
(NARA 80-G-315272)

THE RAIDS CONTINUED. At 1615 the *Hancock's* stablemate, *Enterprise*, faced her own attacker. Diving on the Mighty E', the enemy plane faced fire from both carriers as it released its bomb. The explosive iron missed by the scantest of margins, just 50 feet off the port side of the veteran flattop. The next raider managed to close on the *Hancock* but its ordnance hit the water thirty yards from the port beam. Anti-aircraft fire from the phalanx sped the pilot's meeting with the afterlife.

USS Enterprise burns as seen from USS San Jacinto. (NARA 80-G-328526)

In the efforts to bring down the numerous bandits over TG 58.2, friendly 5" fire detonated over the *Enterprise*. Fuel from planes spotted forward sparked fires while ammunition in some of the 40mm mounts burned. At the same time, a Japanese bomb exploded close aboard. The conflagration was brought under control but the efforts resulted in the loss of radio and communication capabilities.

At 1644, the destroyers moved to cruising disposition 5-V. Closing their ranks to protect the carriers against incoming raids, the destroyers commenced emergency maneuvers at twenty-five knots. When the attack failed to emerge against TG 58.3, the screen returned to the expanded cruising screen of disposition 5-R at 1900. It was a short lived respite from attack.

Danger had not left the arena: An eight plane torpedo attack group careened toward Task Groups 58.1 and 58.3 while using the night's dark skies as cover. The *John W. Weeks* expended rounds but was unable to bring down a raider while *Charles S. Sperry* knocked one down at 2335. Opening fire from 7000 yards, a combination of early 5" fire and late 40mm rounds found their mark. At 2336 the *Ault* showed its gunnery skills by destroying an aerial invader with its 5" guns. Three minutes later it splashed a second plane. During the continued course of confusing night firing, the *Waldron* also claimed a raider it took under fire at 2336 after a *Betty* bomber crashed close aboard, her fiery descent absorbed by the seas. The last crack shots came from Cdr. Jim 'Snuffy' Smith's *English*. Her gunners took down a torpedo plane approaching the destroyer on its starboard bow. Out on its lonely picket sentry post, those sailors topside on the *Haynsworth* watched the flashes from the muzzles of the 5" guns light up the night while the resultant thunder reverberated across the water. It was a scene reminiscent of men-o-war firing broadsides at night centuries earlier.

Exhaustion dogged the tin can sailors but the results were telling. Captain Higgins' destroyers went to General Quarters four times as six raids were tracked. The final GQ lasted into the next day, finally ending at 0030. But the months of anti-aircraft practice and drilling had paid dividends as DesRon 62 claimed five kills in three minutes. Like on the plains of ancient Greece, penetrating the phalanx was tried at considerable risk to the attacker.

21 MARCH: A NEW THREAT EMERGES

Yokosuka Ohka rocket-powered kamikaze plane. (NARA 80-G photo)

STAGGERED. WITHIN A SHORT PERIOD AFTER LEAVING ULITHI, Admiral Mitscher had lost the services of the carriers *Randolph, Franklin, Wasp* and *Enterprise* along with their air groups. The invasion of Okinawa was just ten days away. With the loss of so much airpower, the decision was made to reorganize Task Force 58. Task Group 58.2 was returned to Ulithi for repairs to the carriers. Task Force 58 was reduced to just three task groups. Until early April, two task groups were made available daily for missions against the enemy while the third group replenished.

The reorganization of the groups strengthened the potent 58.3. Rear Admiral Sherman's armada had grown to thirty-one warships with a stable of three fleet carriers and two light carriers (Flagship *Bunker Hill, Essex, Hancock, Cabot* and *Bataan*). Destroyer Division 96 rejoined the group to bring the total of destroyers available for picket, plane guard, and screening duty up to seventeen. TG 58.3's size nearly rivaled that of the entire 1936 U.S. Navy Battle Force.

The *Enterprise* had been operating as a night attack carrier since the beginning of 1945. Her departure caused the number of night fighters on the remaining carriers to be increased to six planes as compensation. The change allowed the task force to maintain continual night CAP flights over Okinawa from March 25 through the April 7. Round the clock flying also kept Captain Higgins' destroyers providing plane guard duties full time. The small dogs were working hard to keep the big dogs safe.

The attacks continue unabated. Three hours past the conclusion of the previous evening's GQ, an American F6F-5N *Hellcat* nightfighter brought down a Betty twin engine bomber just thirty-five miles from Task Group 58.3. Japanese planes continued to track the slow retirement of the Fast Carrier Task Force.

Though the wounded carrier *Franklin* had shed its tow line and begun to steam slowly under her own power, it was necessary for Task Force 58 to correspondingly reduce its speed to keep the carrier from harm's way. Like the previous day, fueling was often interrupted as reports of enemy planes in the air came to the group. As early as 1040, the phalanx was formed as the CAP brought down three *Betty* bombers followed in short succession by another *Betty* and then a Nakajima J1N *Irving* twin engine reconnaissance plane.

Then, a new threat emerged. The Japanese had not abandoned their efforts to sink the American caravans. Eighteen *Betty* twin engine bombers came hunting for the force. Slung under sixteen of them were a new form of kamikaze, the *Ohka* aerial bomb. Packing over a ton of high explosives, these rocket powered human missiles were designed to be released at a range distant to the enemy and driven into Allied ships by their kamikaze pilots. *Ohka* translated into 'cherry blossom' but the Americans called them 'baka' bombs or 'fool's bomb.'

The overweight gaggle of Betty bombers was detected by radar long before they arrived over the slow moving caravan. The debut of this new kamikaze threat was doomed. The reinforced CAP destroyed each mother plane long before the rockets could be launched against Vice Admiral Mitscher's carriers. Again, the Japanese wantonly sacrificed men and material for no gain.

By the end of the day the CAP had downed twenty-one bombers and twelve fighters in the skies near or over the phalanx. Waldron's captain, Cdr. George Peckham, summed up the events: "At 1541 formed cruising disposition 5-R. This was the last gasp of the enemy. We had no further attacks or alerts. We have successfully countered or avoided every attack he could make." As TF 58 departed the Japanese home waters, Peckham wrote, "We are continuing southward toward our rendezvous with the logistics group tomorrow morning."

The Fast Replenishment Group merged with the ships of Task Force 58 three hundred miles south of Kyushu and out of the reach of most of the Japanese's planes. Thursday, March 22nd was the first day in a week where no attacks emerged from the skies above Vice Admiral Mitscher's forces. Aboard the *Haynsworth*, GM3c Marion Parker played the sightseer: "We met the tankers and took on fuel, which took all day for the 5ᵗʰ fleet to complete for we really have the ships around, 140 in all. What a sight! The Japs put out the dope that they had chased us south but they will be seeing more of us in a few days."

USS English approaches USS Ault to transfer guard mail.
(NARA 80-G-470607)

Capt. Higgins' players were in action all day. Filling the ravenous tin can's empty oil tanks was the first priority but other chores had to be completed as well. Just days away from the invasion of Okinawa Jima, the destroyers under Higgins' command were completing "an unusual number of mail, passenger, pilot replacement and freight transfer trips. At one time twelve out of the thirteen destroyers were making trips simultaneously."

The *John W. Weeks* swallowed the black gold from the oiler USS *Chipola* AO-63 and then set off to rendezvous with USS *Windham Bay*

Belly tank transfer to
USS Bunker Hill.
(NARA 80-G-315394)

of Task Unit 50.8.4 (CVE Plane Transport Unit) to accept aviation supplies, completely carpeting her topside decks with oval aluminum drop tanks. From there she delivered the airplane belly tanks to the *Bunker Hill.* Twice during the afternoon her gunners detonated Japanese Type 93 mines that reached where enemy airpower could not.

The *Haynsworth* acted as a ferry service bringing replacement pilots to the carriers and mail to ships in the various task groups. Destinations for pilot transfers included *Essex, Wasp, Yorktown, Hornet,* and *Hancock.* Cdr. Tackney's ship finally rejoined the group at 1600. Its reward for spending the day galloping across formations was to speed ahead of the group and serve again as one of the two picket destroyers twelve miles in the lead.

The high tempo of air operations over the enemy's home was not without pain or penalty. In Task Group 58.3 the three fleet carriers had written off over sixty planes in the week since they left Ulithi. Planes were lost during the air attacks. Some returned damaged while others never returned. Others had hard landings or were forced to ditch in the seas while some were just lost to mechanical problems while in the air. Worn out planes became classified as 'flyable duds.' The roster of serviceable planes decreased daily.

The USS *Bougainville* CVE-100 of the CVE Plane Transport Unit helped to replace some of the losses. She catapulted dozens of planes to needy carriers. 58.3 accepted thirteen pilots, fifteen F6F *Hellcats* and two SB2C-4 *Helldivers* to supplement those on hand. Twenty-two replacement pilots were distributed to the task force. Phil Wilmot of VMF-451 on the *Bunker Hill* recalled that, "our unit had flown together for a long time. The replacement pilots didn't have the time or the experience flying together that we original pilots had. We ended up losing four out of five replacement pilots. Their life expectancy was not very long as new guys."

The crews of the Fast Carrier Task Force received confirmation of their efforts over the past several days by way of a communiqué from Admiral Nimitz. During the attacks against Japan, 281 enemy aircraft were shot out of the air while another 275 aircraft were destroyed on the ground. An additional 175 aircraft were noted as "probably destroyed or damaged on the ground." In a message to his bluejackets, pilots, and officers serving in Task Force 58, the Commander in Chief of the Pacific praised their team efforts: "The reports reaching CinCPac show that the fighting on the 18, 19, 20, and 21 of March was hard and that the damage inflicted on the enemy required courage and endurance of the highest order together with all the skill and teamwork which has been developed in a many a hard fought engagement. You have shown that you can strike the enemy fleet in its home ports and can take his counterattacks with your chins up. Your country is proud of you and has complete confidence in your dauntless fighting spirit."

Task Force Commander Admiral Marc Mitscher added: "All hands in the task force fought magnificently as only veterans can. Damaged ships continued to battle while repairing their damage. Our courageous air men attacked targets through a blanket of anti-aircraft [fire]. The fine shooting by ships brought down many enemy planes which were on their way for a kill. Your country and your families will be proud of the battle you have just fought against Hirohito's poor best."

Task Force 58 commenced a high speed run towards Okinawa for the next day's operations. The increased pace and cover of darkness limited the enemy's ability to find Vice Admiral Marc Mitscher's carrier groups. In the months to come, enemy aircraft would spend much time over and in the steel ships of the Fast Carrier Task Force.

*SB2C of VB-84
prepares for launch
from USS Bunker Hill.
(NARA 80-G-303994)*

*U.S. Marine Corsair.
(NARA 80-G-315378)*

THE FAST CARRIER TASK FORCES FINAL CHAPTERS WERE ABOUT TO BEGIN. After two years of daring raids, sea battles, and support of invasions, Admiral Nimitz unleashed his carrier armada against the Ryukyu and Japanese home islands. Okinawa was the starting point of a five month battle to force the surrender of the Japanese. It was a show of force that hardly could have been imagined in the smoke following the attack at Pearl Harbor.

Starting on Friday, March 23rd, 1945, Task Force 58 sent daily airstrikes against Okinawa and the surrounding islands in preparation for the impending U.S. invasion. The armada spent several months sixty to eighty miles off the eastern shores of Okinawa. Strikes targeted enemy aircraft, airfields, AA sites, and other Japanese military installations on the large island and the islands that hopscotched north to Kyushu. Except during times of replenishment, they would be confined to this small parcel of ocean. It was also an area that would bring them in deadly contact with the enemy in the weeks to come.

With the anticipation of an extended day in combat, the *Haynsworth's* Executive Officer, Scott Lothrop, laid out the day's plan: "Today is a day of heavy strikes against Okinawa Jima. At time of launch we are about 135 miles SE of Okinawa Jima and will run in towards Okinawa Jima at maximum practical speed while our planes are proceeding towards target. We expect to have two days of continued heavy strikes made against Okinawa while the task force maneuvers along a NE-SW line SE of Okinawa. Every effort must be made to speed up feeding of crew during GQ. Gun crews sent down should rate head of mess line privileges."

The weather threatened operations as rain, strong winds and heavy seas put extra burdens on the pilots flying off the carriers. At 0600, the task group began to launch planes for the first fighter sweep of the day against airfields and beach defenses on Okinawa. Ten minutes into launching flights, *Bunker Hill* reported one of her *Corsairs* in the water. Within twelve minutes Lt. jg. Clifford S. Carter of VF-84 had been recovered by *Sperry*. Again, *Bunker Hill* reported another plane in the water an hour later. A VB-84 *Helldiver* "did not develop enough power for take-off and dribbled off the bow." The USS *Kidd* DD-661, in her service as plane guard, was able to recover Lt. John Barrows, a twenty seven year old South Dakota native, and his twenty two year old radioman, LaRoy Sell ARM1c.

Later that morning, lookouts aboard the *Waldron* reported an explosion on the water about eight miles distant. Parachutes were seen above the ocean at 0738. The pilot and crew of a TBM-3 *Avenger* from the *Cabot* were rescued after their plane had experienced engine failure. At Angels 5, flames burst from the engine nacelle enroute to their mission. Too far from their carrier to chance a return, the pilot and crew bailed out. By 0817 twenty-three year old Ensign Herbert A. Gidney, radioman Norman Sokolow ARM3c, and Wilfred Bond AMM3c were on the *Waldron's* deck.

The VT-29 aircrew remained as guests of Cdr. Peckham's destroyer for the next three days. The ship's doctor, a gynecologist in civilian life, Lt. Joseph Perry, described his role in the rescues:

The swimmer, with a small nylon line hooked to a harness type of arrangement, would swim out to the man in the water. Then the crew on deck would pull both men back to the ship where several men clinging to a cargo net over the side, would pass the man up to the deck. Then he would be taken to sick bay and I would check him over. The swimmer and those on the car-

go net who had gotten wet during the procedure were always given a shot of medical brandy, according to Navy custom to prevent pneumonia from being exposed to the elements. This procedure would involve one aviator, one swimmer and at most three men on the cargo net. I never understood why, when brandy time came, there were ten or more soaking wet in line for the brandy.

THE TRIPLE AXIS THREATS from the air, land, and sea continued. Action was close aboard as *English's* 20mm gunners sank another Japanese mine while opposition to the American planes over Okinawa was light. The phalanx was closed at 1310 when the first reports of enemy places were made though none closed on the armada. After the carrier planes had been recovered, the task group retired eastward for refueling. The crews were kept at GQ until securing at 2000. Okinawa would erupt soon enough.

HEAVY THUNDER AND EXPLOSIVE ERUPTIONS OF EARTH WERE THE CALLING CARDS of Task Unit 58.7. Formed on March 24th, the fast battleships of Task Force 58 merged forces for a pre-invasion bombardment of Okinawa. They were joined by some of the cruisers and Destroyer Division 96. *Wisconsin, Missouri, New Jersey, Washington, Indiana, Massachusetts, North Carolina,* and *South Dakota* raised the barrels of their 16" guns in a defiant salute of the Empire. For nearly five and half hours, the seventy-two cannon rained hell on the island. A few minutes after ceasing fire, the crews secured from GQ as the heavies made their way back to their home task groups.

The *Haynsworth* started the day still on picket duty twelve miles in advance of its task group but just sixty miles east of the island. "We were notified at 0800 Jap suicide planes will attempt dives on us this morning," noted Seaman Bill Morton. With the big guns away, the screen provided by the destroyers took on an extra importance. Marion Parker wrote, "We stayed out with the carriers but the Japs were too busy to come after us."

With the dawn sun the carriers launched airstrikes against Okinawa from south and east of the island. The targets for the day included airfields, midget sub bases and beach defenses.

Marine Major Emerson Dedrick of VMF-451 was part of the day's first aerial offensive mission. Attacking the Yontan airfield, his *Corsair* was damaged by anti-aircraft fire. The shrapnel sliced through hydraulic and electrical lines. Dedrick was unable to release his belly tank or fire off the eight rockets attached to the wings. The *Blue Devils* division leader was an experienced combat pilot with two kills already to his credit from a previous tour in the South Pacific but his greatest flying challenge emerged that day.

Dedrick, his *Corsair* barely airworthy, called over to his wingman that they were breaking off their attack. 1st. Lt. Wambsganss escorted Dedrick as the division leader turned his plane away from the action and back towards the task group. As they approached the carriers, it became apparent that the wheels were locked up in the wings. The senior pilot didn't have faith that his parachute would open. He preferred to keep control of his destiny: "I'm gonna land it in the water, Dewey."

En route, the two pilots reviewed the steps necessary to make a safe water landing. Working down the checklist, Wambsganss talked Dedrick all the way down to just above the ocean's surface. "God be with you, fella," offered the wingman to Dedrick. The most popular of the squadron's four majors waved goodbye to Wambsganss and started the process of putting the *Corsair* with the big white arrow on the tail down in the Pacific. He landed forward of the *Waldron* so that she would not have to back down or turn in order to effect his rescue.

Just as Dedrick's *Corsair* flew low over the seas, the powerful Pratt & Whitney radial engine stalled. The embrace with the sea became a violent collision that ripped the tail from Dedrick's bird. As the plane submarined down into the swells, Dedrick's wingman circled overhead for several minutes. The pilot did not escape the sinking plane

"We were in contact with him and told him how and where to land so he'd be close to us when he landed. Unfortunately, he was in pretty bad shape and made the mistake of landing in the water downwind. The plane went into the water and disappeared with him on board. We had to stay there for some twelve hours combing the water back and forth, hoping against hope we would find him," recalled the *Waldron's* navigator, Lt. Richard Bullis. Despite the proximity of the destroyer, just 300 yards away as the tragedy unfolded, no trace of the gangly twenty-seven year old pilot was ever found.

Cdr. George Peckham's *Waldron* noted, "There was no enemy activity near our task force today. It has been the most quiet strike-day we have had. Even though all air opposition on Okinawa appears eliminated, it would seem the enemy could launch attacks from their bases in Kyushu, 300 miles to the northeast." The same impression was left on *Haynsworth's* Bill Morton: "Still on picket [duty] 1500. Notified

Maj. Emerson Dedrick, VMF-451, Mojave Desert, 1944. (Courtesy of Philip Wilmot)

Cdr. George Ottinger. (Courtesy of Hank Ottinger)

that our fighters intercepted Japs." Further confirmation came from Vice Admiral Mitscher: "It became increasingly apparent that our initial strike on Kyushu facilities had interfered with enemy air group operations to a greater extent than had been hoped for."

The flyboys had done their job but at an equipment cost of nine planes and a human price of several pilots lost by 58.3 that day. Another senior airman, Cdr. George 'Bucky' Ottinger, commander of the *Bunker Hill's* Air Group 84, was lost, too. Leading a strike against an antiaircraft site protecting an enemy airfield, Ottinger's *Corsair* absorbed violent flak. He ditched offshore but with strong seas that day, he could not reach his raft. Other rafts were dropped by brother *Corsair*s circling overhead. A pair of *Kingfishers* was launched from the USS *Astoria* with four VMF-451 *Corsairs* flying topcover. By the time they arrived on station, Ottinger had expired. With no way to bring his corpse aboard the small rescue planes, he was left to the seas, the Pacific to become his grave.

MORALE HAD FLAGGED following the high speed tempo of operations since leaving Ulithi. Long days at GQ, rushed meals,

Anti-aircraft gun practice aboard USS Ault. (NARA 80-G-470603)

lost sleep and numerous air attacks against DesRon 62 and TG 58.3 had fatigued Tackney's crew. *Haynsworth's* exec, Lt. Cdr. Scott Lothrop addressed some of the crew's request for some entertainment beyond reading, playing cards, and shooting the bull. "Some questions have been asked concerning every night movies at sea. It is not considered advisable to have such a large portion of the crew crowded together in the mess hall when the ship is in these forward areas. Until a change in situation occurs, movies will be saved for days when ship is in tanker replenishment and fueling area." Instead of John Wayne, the *Haynsworth* was sent forward on picket duty again.

SUNDAY, MARCH 25TH, PROVIDED BREATHING ROOM for the task group. Other than the CAP, no missions were flown. Despite the day's slower tempo of operations, the destroyers were kept busy as the group moved south of Okinawa to converge with Rear Admiral Beary's Logistics Support Group 50.8. While bellying up to the oilers for fuel, six of the destroyers brought aboard mail for the group as well as other personnel. Mailman *Haynsworth* narrowly avoided collision with the larger *Wilkes Barre* during its appointed rounds with the *Essex*.

The *Sperry* delivered replacement pilots to the carriers while the *Ault* received forty-one replacement enlisted personnel from the oiler

Destroyers come alongside a carrier of TG 58.3 to refuel March 25, 1945.

USS *Cowanesque*. The can subsequently transferred the group by breeches buoy over to the *Essex*. Lifeguard duty was also in store for the *Sperry* as its crew recovered a sailor lost overboard from the cruiser *Astoria*.

Late afternoon, with their tanks full, Admiral Sherman's ships turned northward for their return to Okinawa, Captain Higgins' charges conducted anti-aircraft practice against a sleeve towed by a group plane. The ability of the ships to accurately nail enemy planes from a distance with their 5" guns would become ever more essential in the weeks to come.

During the journey, *Hank* picked up a sonar contact. Believed to possibly be a submarine, nine depth charges were fired from her 'K' guns without results. After it was determined to be a false alarm, *Hank* rejoined the destroyer screen protecting the carriers.

THE CARRIERS WERE BACK ON ACTION THE MORNING OF THE 26TH. Missions were sent against the islands of Sakashima, Amami, and Hinami to suppress enemy fighter planes. "Our planes made strikes all day and the radio shack hooked up the TBS [Talk Between Ships radio network]," recalled the *Haynsworth's*

Marion Parker. "I listened to the pilots talking back to the carriers, also between themselves. One fighter was over a town giving an account of what damage the bombers were doing."

The cans were in action, too. For DesRon 62, the entire day was spent at battle stations. Lookouts aboard the *Sperry* spotted a mine floating in the waters nearby. Her gunners were able to pick it off. Some mines sank but others were detonated as was the case this day. "As it burst, the spray skyrocketed a hundred feet into the air and as the sound wave hit, the ship quivered."

Pilot rescues proved to be the highlight of the *Waldron*'s morning. As the first airstrikes were launched seventy miles east of Okinawa, Ensign George Rawley of Fighting Squadron 6 crashed astern of the carrier USS *Hancock* at 0533. His F6F(N) *Hellcat* nightfighter hit the water following a spin as it tried to clear the flight deck. The destroyer had the VF-6 pilot aboard in just a few minutes.

At 0914 the *Hancock* signaled that another of her planes had gone over her side. Two minutes earlier, Ensign Wesley Midyett of Fighting Squadron Six brought his *Hellcat* in for a landing aboard the carrier. As the plane came down, it "bounced out of arresting gear while landing, applied throttle in an attempt to clear planes forward, crashed into deck 50 feet short of bow and went overboard taking F6F pilot, Lt. Richard M. Buck and FG1D pilot Lt. Frederick W. Bowen into the water with him." The *Waldron* was on the scene in minutes. The twenty-five year old Bowen was the only survivor of the three pilots whose planes plummeted into the Pacific. The Spokane native's luck would run out in 1952 while flying a *Corsair* over North Korea.

In the early afternoon, the USS *Walker* was able to recover Ensign Randolph Meyers after he ditched his *Corsair* in the drink. An hour later, Lt. jg. W. Keller put his *Hellcat* fighter down within the screen. The USS *Stembel* was on hand to affect the rescue.

The battle day ended with a brilliant sunset. Those aboard the ships took little comfort in the scenery. Sunrise and sunset were always opportune times for the enemy to attack. Day began and ended with required General Quarters alarms at dawn and dusk. For the sailors in the protective destroyer screen, "when on GQ the only thing we look for on the horizon is the enemy planes," recalled GM2c Phil Goldstein of the *Haynsworth*. A postcard finish to the day during wartime was not as important as self-preservation.

THE GLOWING IMAGE OF A BOGIE ON THE RADAR SCREEEN was reported at 2129. With a full moon, clear sky, and phosphorescent wakes trailing the warships, visibility was excellent for enemy fighters. As a countermove, all ships were ordered to make smoke to the mask the task group while at the same time bringing the tin cans into the phalanx. A few minutes later a Mitsubishi G4M *Betty* tangled with the night CAP. The twin engine bomber did not survive the encounter with the F6F-5(N) *Hellcats*.

Making smoke near the Depth Charge Racks. (Courtesy USS Haynsworth Association)

T WO LONG WEEKS SINCE THEIR DEPARTURE FROM ULITHI, and with no return date in sight, morale had already begun to decline. While the *Wallace L. Lind* was the 'Can with a Band,' the *Haynsworth* debuted W-H-I-Z. Operating from the diesel generator room, DD-700 became the first destroyer off Okinawa to have its own radio station. It offered a talent show for crew members. From Gus Scutari's harmonica to a quiz show held by the executive officer, it gave the bluejackets of the *Haynsworth* a distraction from the war. Cartons of cigarettes, paid for by the Federal Shipbuilding and Drydock Company, were the prizes for the winners.

While the *Divine Wind* had blown lightly against the 5th and 7th fleets at Iwo Jima, Okinawa would be an entirely different playing field. Iwo Jima was important to the Americans for establishing long range bombing bases to strike the Japanese home islands. Okinawa was also an important stepping stone in the advance to visit the Emperor's throne in Tokyo. But, Okinawa was part of a chain of islands, all containing Japanese held airfields. To the south, islands stretched to Formosa while to the north, islands hopscotched all the way to Kyushu. The winds of the Floating Chrysanthemums blew fiercely across the Ryukyus.

March 25, 1945 marked the beginning of a period of three months where destroyers and their step brothers, destroyer minesweepers, would absorb the brutality of the kamikazes. These steel warships became mangled wind breaks for pilots intent on sacrificing their lives for the empire. The USS *Kimberly* DD-521, serving on radar picket duty, was bracketed by a pair of dive bombers while at dawn General Quarters. One of the duo was expertly piloted as it jinked and jumped to keep in the destroyer's wake, keeping American guns ability to draw a bead on him to a minimum. Despite absorbing numerous hits, the raider kept coming. Crashing amidships, the attacker was consumed by the demolition of its own bomb. The following day, the USS *Robert H. Smith* DM-23 barely escaped its own attacker. Its chrysanthemum was swallowed by the ocean just yards from the steel skin of the destroyer minesweeper.

A IRSTRIKES CONTINUED AGAINST OKINAWA ON TUESDAY, THE 27TH, as the task group operated fifty miles offshore four days ahead of the invasion. Enemy strikes were sent against American forces: In Task Group 58.3, the USS *Chauncey* DD-667 shot down a Mitsubishi G3M *Nell* bomber at 0644 while an hour later another *Betty* bomber was disposed of by the CAP.

The *Waldron*, in its familiar role as life guard came to the rescue of a pilot whose plane failed to gain air as he left the carrier deck. Within four minutes the unidentified pilot was rescued and on the steel deck of the destroyer. Within ninety minutes, the group of pilots rescued over the previous two days were highlined back aboard the carrier USS *Hancock*.

T HE USS *O'BRIEN* DD-725 GOT IT THE NEXT DAY. After two earlier periods of GQ overnight, the destroyer was struck during dawn GQ. The first raider was blown out of the sky but the second hit aft of the superstructure. Fifty sailors were killed and nearly one hundred wounded. The USS *Callaghan* DD-792 got a haircut as another raider struck her mast before tumbling into the sea. The USS *Nevada* BB-36 was wounded, too. The old gal had survived major damage during the attack on Pearl Harbor. She had returned to the fight with three of the *Arizona's* 14" guns remounted in her #1 turret. *Nevada* was bloodied about the same time as the destroyers when the kamikaze struck its aft 14" gun turret. She buried ten of her own at sea that afternoon. The Japanese pilot was given a separate funeral.

RAID!

Left: Gus Scutari FC2c. (Courtesy Gus Scutari)
Right: Fire Control System. (Courtesy of NavSource)

HELL WAS UNLEASHED. On March 28th, Task Group 58.3 moved to attack the airfields on the tiny island of Minami Daito Shima, 180 miles east of Okinawa. The enemy raiders from Minami's airfields would remain a thorn in Mitscher's Task Force's backside until they were neutralized.

In what was a very quick attack, the four cruisers of Cruiser Division 17 and nine destroyers of DesRon 62 brought their main batteries to bear. Primary targets were both the north and south runways with secondary targets of ammunition storage areas, administration buildings and personnel barracks. "The intensive training in shore bombardment tactics both at Bermuda and at Pearl Harbor proved their value." For the *Haynsworth*, the target would be one of the three runways.

Down in the Plotting Room, Fire Controlman Gus Scutari gripped the twin handles of the Stable Element Mk. 6. Linked to the Mark 25 Fire Control Radar, the system computed the needed firing solution and then sent electronic signals to the three batteries of 5" guns. A gyroscope inside system automatically kept the guns stabilized as the ship pitched and rolled.

As the ships sailed parallel to Minami Daito Shima, targets were acquired. Watching a clock mounted to the bulkhead, Scutari pulled the left handle at the nineteen second mark. A tone was rung in the 5" batteries. A second later, Scutari pulled the right handle. A salvo of six shells was released against the island. Every twenty seconds for ten minutes, Scutari's pull released another deadly salvo of six shells against the target.

A deadly steel rain pummeled the little coral island with a ferocious intensity. The earth shook and exploded before the first sounds were heard. No place was truly safe on this small patch of rock. In thirty minutes, nearly three thousand rounds of 5"/38 caliber and seven hundred rounds of 6" shells struck the airfield. The fire exiting the ships guns was illuminated by the 110 starshells put up by the destroyers for illumination over the target. The shore bombardment from the fleet deafened Signalman John Vasquez and other shipmates standing watch topside on the *Haynsworth*. The damage control teams were kept busy by the blasts: "The burning wadding from the powder canister would blow back onto the ship. Small fires would be ignited." Morris Gillett CRT explained, "Most of this burning cork was swept harmlessly over the side but occasionally a small fire would start that required a little water."

And, as quickly as it started, it also ceased all at once. Commander Tackney recorded that "At 0201 Item shore bombardment against Minami Daito Shima was fired this date in company with ships of DesRon 62 and CruDiv 17. Expended were 181 rounds of 5"/38 shells. Target of this was Airstrip 'A.' At 0232 the Officer in Tactical Command [O.T.C.] ordered cease firing and Task Unit 58.3.9 retired to the southeast to rejoin the task force. Results were not known, but a red glow covered the sky over the island, visible for miles after leaving the target area." The carriers and battleships of 58.3 could clearly see the flashes from the guns of their junior partners many miles away. The attacking force withdrew in the night to return to Task Group 58.3 after accomplishing its mission. Aboard the *Haynsworth*, Ed Mital CM2c observed, "We left the island ablaze."

The reprieve for the Japanese on Minami Daito was short lived. After the return of DesRon 62 and Cruiser Division 17 to its task group, the carriers sent multiple aerial bombing sweeps against the island. Wave after wave of *Avengers*, *Helldivers*, *Hellcats* and *Corsairs* dropped explosive iron against targets while the fighters took strafing runs as well. By daylight, the Japanese gunners were ready for the flyers: "AA was intense, of all kinds, and accurate."

Underway replenishment from the oilers began almost as soon at the Task Group was reformed. While the *Haynsworth* brought transfer pilots to the *Essex* from the USS *Attu* CVE-102, the *Waldron* was again serving as the Johnny Weissmuller of the squadron. At 0826 *Waldron* raced to rescue a plane crew after an errant *Helldiver* crashed 1000 yards off the port bow. Anti-aircraft fire from the island had found its mark against the VB-84 dive bomber. Despite the damage, Lt. William T. Jacks, Jr. USNR was able to nurse his wounded plane back to the task group. Within a few minutes, the pilot and his radioman, Howard S. Pedersen ARM1c, were pulled from the ocean. Before being transferred back to the *Bunker* Hill, the guest aviators witnessed their host sink a Japanese naval mine by automatic weapons fire. The Japanese continued to prove themselves a dangerous foe from the land, sea, and the air.

EASTER WEEK

BREAKOUT! On Holy Thursday, Task Force 58 received a report that the Japanese fleet was enroute to the Sasebo Naval Base on western Kyushu. Task Force Commander Marc Mitscher was not going to await their arrival. His task groups turned north in hopes of engaging the last remnants of the enemy fleet. Reconnaissance planes were sent out, the CAP was launched, and airstrikes were sent against targets on the Japanese island of Kyushu. The cans of DesDiv 96 were released from the destroyer screen. Steaming ahead of the task group, destroyers *Kidd*, *Black*, *Bullard* and *Chauncey* formed a scouting line four across to intercept enemy threats on the sea and in the air.

Attacks came from the skies rather than by broadsides as several Japanese planes penetrated the phalanx's flanks. With reports of raiding planes rapidly approaching, the phalanx closed into its tight defensive formation while commencing evasive maneuvers. Cdr. Tackney of the *Haynsworth* wrote of the infiltration, "Several enemy aircraft raids were intercepted before they could reach our formation, but two planes came in undetected until thirty miles, and closed fast after that." Cdr. George DeMetropolis of the *Lind* picked up the tale from there: "At 1400, one enemy torpedo plane commenced closing the task group and was taken under fire." On the flank of the phalanx, *Haynsworth* also tried to take down the raider: "After dropping his bomb, he headed right toward us coming in from the starboard beam, low and fast. We opened fire with all our starboard batteries as soon as he came within range. Our firing made him alter course to starboard and he passed ahead of our bow and continued on." Tackney's gunners gave it their all with 20mm, 40mm and the 5" cannons all expending rounds at a furious rate.

Opportunity was fleeting. From the navigation deck of the *Haynsworth*, Bill Morton's view was from a different perspective: "Jap *Tojo* dove on *Cabot* CVL-28 and dropped its bomb in front of CVL-28 - just came through formation about thirty feet over water. We all missed our golden opportunity as another group shot him down."

Morton's shipmate Keith Myreholt also weighed in on the attack: "Dropped bomb astern of her and was coming in on us low over water making a very bad shot. Two men were hurt, [Gilbert] Mooney and [Manson] Morrill. Concussion from MT-2 [the second 5"/38]. Plane circled us and headed back over force. Pilot bailed out and plane crashed. *Mohawk* [Admiral Mitscher] refused to pick him up."

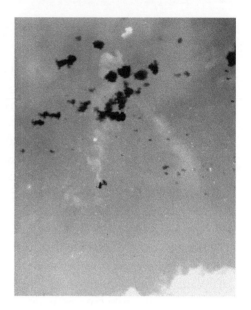

Left: Manson Morrill S1c. (Courtesy of Marti Kulpin)
Right: Enemy pilot in parachute while plane begins its descent.
(NARA 80-G-322422)

Other cans of DesRon 62 took a crack at the fleeing torpedo plane. The *Sperry* fired off 120 rounds from her 20mm guns. Unleashing her 5" guns, the *Lind* sent seventy-seven rounds against the invader. "Although direct hits were not observed, the plane was reported to have crashed shortly afterward," recorded Cdr. DeMetropolis. Aboard the *Haynsworth* Lt. Cdr. Lothrop chided the gunners, "48 rounds expended, no casualties and no plane shot down. Let's dope out what went wrong and get the next one. The *Ault* expended 304 rounds and didn't get him, either."

Aerial attacks were not the only threat on March 29th. The task group had entered an area sown with mines. The *Haynsworth* destroyed one by small caliber gunfire before *Weeks* sunk another. On the thin skinned destroyer, Morris Gillett CRT witnessed the destruction: "Another very important function of picket duty was to maintain an alert watch for floating mines the Japanese planted in action areas. When they were spotted by a ship, they would be exploded. This was usually done by 20mm gunfire while the mine was some distance from the ship. On occasions, however, we used a Springfield rifle to clear away the mine." Shrapnel rained on the *Week's* deck post the detonation.

PHALANX AGAINST THE DIVINE WIND

The *Waldron* capped the day by destroying another mine late in the afternoon thus escaping the fate of the USS *Halligan* DD-584. Just a few days prior, *Halligan* was on routine patrol when she passed over a mine. The explosion passed into the destroyer's magazines, multiplying its intensity. Half of the crew perished, the bow was obliterated and torn off at the forward stack, and her efforts in the war ended abruptly. She was abandoned, her steel carcass left to wash up on shore.

Left: Baxter, Elings, Hiveley. Right: Halloway, Georgius, Mudd.
(Courtesy of the USS Bunker Hill Association)

DEATH DIDN'T REQUIRE AN INVITATION. Often it appeared suddenly. Violence was frequently its calling card. After three months of combat, this was no longer a surprise for the tin can sailors. The *English*, while out on picket duty, witnessed three TBM-3s of VT-84 collide in mid-air with dive bombers from VB-84. Flying in overcast weather, the *Helldivers* accidentally turned into the path of *Avengers*. Lt. jg. Melvin Georgius' *Avenger* exploded killing the veteran pilot and his crewmen, James Mudd ARM2c and J. A. Holloway AOM1c, while another *Avenger* spun into the Pacific. An OS2U *Kingfisher* was able to rescue Ensign William Elings. Though the *Ault* retraced the *Bunker Hill*'s path, the effort was in vain. Homer 'Roger' Hiveley ARM3c and the turret gunner, Frank Lowell Baxter AOM3c, did not survive the collision. The *English* brought aboard Lt. Bernard

F. Berry, C. Johnson ARM1c, and Charles E. Metler AOM1c from their *Avenger* when it ditched nearby.

Combat was a fickle mistress. The tested and proven pilots did not always survive. By late March DesRon62 had already rescued dozens of pilots and aircrews. These recoveries returned combat experienced pilots to the American air squadrons. However, nothing could be done to save Navy Cross recipient Georgius. Flying from the USS *Lexington* almost three years, earlier Georgius had slammed his ordnance into an IJN carrier at the Battle of the Coral Sea, receiving his valor award post the pivotal battle. Lt. Berry had already finished one combat tour with VT-17 and was in the midst of his tour with VT-84. In the weeks to come, the *Divine Wind* would snuff out his life.

When it became evident there would be no engagement with the Japanese Navy, the task force retired south towards Okinawa late afternoon in support of operations there.

TOWARDS THE END OF MARCH, THE THIRD REICH WAS NEARLY DEFEATED as American forces poured into the Germany. In the Pacific, vast fleets were gathering near Okinawa for the largest invasion of World War II. 'Lucky' Day would commence within 48 hours. Task Force 58 continued with airstrikes and sweeps on March 30th. After the battles of battles of March 18-21, came a week of calm. "This last week has been completely devoid of enemy air attacks. Numerous bogies were reported but none came within sight of the formation." Nothing is forever.

Released from TF 58 to join a group of cruisers providing bombardment against targets on Okinawa, Fifth Fleet Commander Admiral Raymond Spruance's flagship, the USS *Indianapolis* CA-35, absorbed a hell bound kamikaze's plane and its bomb. Despite losing nine of her crew, the heavy cruiser remained in the fight. Admiral Spruance transferred his flag to the USS *New Mexico* BB-40 when the *Indy* left Okinawa for further repair. It would be five weeks before a kamikaze was able to penetrate the phalanx to strike another cruiser. However, the tin cans, unlike their bigger cruiser brothers, suffered dearly in Okinawa's waters during the spring of 1945.

THREE SOULS WERE SAVED ON GOOD FRIDAY. Flying a new replacement TBM-3, Lt. jg. Edward Laster launched from the USS *Intrepid* for an airstrike against targets on Okinawa. Before he could complete his mission, the engine began to sputter. Turning back, the Wright R-2600 cyclone engine froze as he neared Task Group 58.3.

After ditching, rescue swimmers helped bring the VT-10 pilot and his aircrew back to the *English.* They would remain as guests of Cdr. Smith for the next ten days.

Two rescue swimmers with lifelines surround raft. (NARA 80-G-315404)

Right: John Fuentes AMM1c, Lt. jg. Edward W. Laster, Lawrence M. Hebach ARM3c. (NARA 80-G-315401-2)

The destroyers took the opportunity when available to refuel from the larger vessels in the task group. The crews enjoyed a bit of rest as the

Fueling from USS Essex, 29 March 1945. (NARA 80-G photo)

only General Quarters of the two days were the routine dawn and sunset.

O N THE EVE OF THE INVASION, Saturday, March 31st, the *Essex* was indebted to her phalanx guards. The destroyers under Capt. Higgins' command remained busy on Lucky Day minus one, Holy Saturday. The *Haynsworth*, 'ever the pony express, received a division of four marine replacement pilots by highline. At this point the Tackney's bluejackets were well skilled in the maneuver, rigging a line to their superstructure while another was held by rolling block on a CVE. The flight division's leader, Capt. Tommy Tomlinson commented on his transfer: "The chief standing on a capstan attempted to maintain the highline in a desirable configuration by bellowing at his troops, 'Take 'er in, lads' or 'Let 'er out' to keep the line from sagging into the sea." One by one the pilots were transferred across. The senior pilot cursed afterwards, "The jolly destroyer men congratulated them for being so dry and suggested that had they known that their guests were to be marines that might have not been the case. A pox on them."

PHALANX AGAINST THE DIVINE WIND

The marine fliers were transferred in short order to the *Essex* in exchange for a load of plane belly tanks bound for the *Bunker Hill*.

The *Essex* gained four pilots but almost lost another during the first launch of the day. Ensign Richard Langdon's *Hellcat* careened off the carrier's deck and tore through the portside catwalk before landing in the seas. The *English* swooped in for the rescue. The VF-83 pilot would go on to shoot down three enemy planes and win the Navy Cross plus a DFC within a week's time.

An OS2U *Kingfisher* completed the next rescue. While attacking a midget submarine base, Lt. jg. Nils 'Red' Carlson's *Helldiver* collided with another *Helldiver*. His backseater, combat photographer W. R. Sander S2c, attempted to bail out at low altitude. He did not survive. The VB-83 pilot was able to ditch his bird 400 yards off the coast before the observation plane settled nearby for the rescue. The *English* retrieved Carlson from the base cruiser before highlining the twenty-one year old pilot to the USS *Essex*. Carlson would later go on to win the Navy Cross for flight actions during an attack against Japanese naval vessels.

Witnessed by Bill Morton of the *Haynsworth*, another airman wasn't as lucky. His plane went straight into the ocean. No one was saved.

Yet, the Fast Carrier Task Force was achieving its mission. Striking boldly against Kyushu, Tokyo and the airfields of Okinawa, TF 58's "big blue blanket" had cleared the skies over the fleet. The commander of DesDiv 96's *Bullard* noted that, "The task group was under light air attack this afternoon, one bogey being shot down by the CAP. We wonder why it is that the enemy continues to accept plane losses resulting from these sporadic attacks by single planes or very small groups of them. Our fighters seem to enjoy it, and, so far at least, we have not seen any degree of success resulting from this half-hearted policy."

Though the aerial opposition was light at the end of March, things were about to get hotter in the skies over Okinawa.

LEAVING PEARL

Two Johns,
Magliocchetti and
McAllister
at Pearl Harbor.
(McAllister Family
Collection)

FOUR MONTHS IS AN ETERNITY FOR YOUNG MEN, especially in times of war when life is often measured in days. For that period the *Haynsworth's* two seaman radio strikers, friends John McAllister and John Magliocchetti, had been training in Pearl Harbor to become rated radiomen. On Saint Patrick's Day, the Irish-American McAllister and his buddy earned their certificates of completion for both the Radioman Third Class training and the Fox Schedule courses.

During their time training at the radio school at Camp Catlin on Oahu, these young sailors were aware of the battles, triumphs and losses of the Fast Carrier Task Force. Navy communiques reported the attacks against targets in the South China Sea, Formosa, Iwo Jima, and Tokyo. At Pearl Harbor new ships of the line were continually arriving from America before they joined the fight to the west. The final push before the invasion of the Japanese home islands was about to begin. It was time for these teenage radiomen to return to their ship.

Magliocchetti and McAllister boarded the heavy cruiser USS *Quincy* CA-71 on March 31st. Their trip from Pearl Harbor would bring them to Ulithi. From there, other transportation would take the two radiomen to Task Force 58 off the coast of Okinawa. They would soon return to work with their friends in the *Haynsworth's* radio shack...Holcombe, Holiman, Goyer, Bly, Peres, Dyer, Davis, Myreholt, Ward, Wilkerson and Chief Campbell. They would reunite with their friends from the deck force like Ernie Satterly and Hobart MacLaughlan. Mag & Mac expected to rejoin the *Haynsworth* in the waters of the big island. Instead fate's malevolent intervention caused them not make to it any further than Ulithi.

THE JAPANESE COMMAND COUNTERED the Allied invasion forces surrounding Okinawa Jima by moving air groups. Among the numerous reassignments, *Air Group 210's* fighters and dive bombers were transferred to the Kokubo No. 1 Air Base and the Kushiro Airbase in the Kagoshima Prefecture of Kyushu. Seven Suisei *Judy* dive bombers would take to the air on April 6th.

LUCKY DAY: INVASION OF OKINAWA

Landing craft heading ashore. (NARA 80-G-315447)

A S DAWN BROKE ON EASTER, 1945, THE LARGEST AR-
MADA EVER TAKE TO THE SEAS converged on the biggest
island in the Ryukyu chain. Gathered around Okinawa were Task
Force 54-The Gunfire & Covering Force; Task Force 52-The Amphibious Support Force; Task Force 53-The Northern Attack Force; Task
Force 55-The Southern Attack Force; Task Force 57-The British Pacific Fleet; Task Force 56-Expeditionary Force; Task Force 51-
Amphibious Force; and Task Force 58-The Fast Carrier Task Force.
Thirteen hundred ships were poised to support the landing and operations of 182,000 U.S. Army and Marine troops. Ships of all kinds, from
small infantry landing craft to the colossal *Iowa* class battleships, from
oilers to cruisers, from minesweepers to carriers, steamed in the waters
surrounding the island. It would be a temptation too great for the enemy to pass up.

For Vice Admiral Marc Mitscher's Task Force 58, the mission was
to, "destroy enemy aircraft, aircraft facilities, naval forces, shipping and
defenses in the Empire-Nansei Shoto- Formosa area, assisting landing
operations in the Nansei Shoto by direct air support and surface bombardment, conducting photographic and air reconnaissance; in order to
support the capture and occupation of Okinawa Gunto." The previous
two weeks' operations had laid the path for the invasion by suppressing Japanese aerial incursions with strikes against Kyushu, Amami
Gunto, Okinawa Gunto, Sakishima Retto and Minami Daito.

PHALANX AGAINST THE DIVINE WIND

While Admiral Halsey thought the Japanese Empire was on the ropes, Admiral Spruance had a different view. It was apparent to all following the war that it was just a matter of time before the Allies invaded the Japanese home islands. After comparatively light aerial responses to the attacks on Japan, Spruance was of the opinion that the Empire was saving its strength for when it was needed most. With America landing on the Emperor's doorstep at Okinawa, the enemy response was sure to be strong. Unfortunately for the destroyers, Spruance was correct.

With the earlier withdrawal of three carriers and Task Group 58.2, the other carrier groups had been beefed up in preparation for the invasion. On Lucky Day, Rear Admiral Sherman's Task Group 58.3 was composed of five carriers, three battleships, four cruisers and twenty-one destroyers. Its missions were airstrikes in support of the amphibious landings at Okinawa. The roster of April 1st would change frequently in the weeks of protracted battle to come.

PRESIDENT ROOSEVELT HAD ACCEPTED the British solicitation in 1944 at Quebec to send a carrier group to the Pacific to fight with the American Fast Carrier Task Force. One of the main topics at the September "Octagon Conference" came to fruition in March of 1945. Shortly after the Task Force 58 steamed from the safe protection of Ulithi, the British Pacific Fleet (BPF) staged at the atoll and then sailed northward to join Mitscher's crusades at Okinawa.

Vice-Admiral Sir Bernard Rawlings led the new battle caravan. Designated as Task Force 57, the BPF was similar in size to an American task group. Her arsenal was composed of four state of the art fleet carriers (*Indomitable*, *Victorious*, *Indefatigable*, and *Illustrious*). TF 57 was augmented by two battleships, seven cruisers, and several destroyer flotillas. She brought an additional 260 planes to the task to supplement the nearly thousand planes in Task Force 58. Her pilots flew *Hellcats/ Gannets*, *Corsairs, Avengers, Wildcats/ Marlets*, Fairey *Firefly* fighters plus the Royal Navy version of the *Spitfire* known as the *Seafire*. The Supermarine *Walrus*, an amphibious biplane, was carried to effect rescues of pilots and crew left to the seas.

As a prelude to their joining Task Force 58, the British Pacific Fleet struck at the fuel jugular of the Imperial Japanese Army's air forces. In late January of 1945, the inaugural Pacific debut of Britain's own Fast Carrier Task Force was against refineries in Sumatra. Attacking the well defended aviation fuel refineries twice in a six day period, the Brits successfully crippled Japan's ability to put gas in the tanks of their suffering air forces. The Japanese exacted a toll on the BPF: sixteen air crews were lost in the raids.

Admiral Spruance's plan was to utilize the Brits in a reserve capacity to his TF 58. With the rapid succession of U.S. carrier damage in the third week of March and the subsequent withdrawal of TG 58.2, the BPF were called off the bench and entered on the player's roster. They got into the game in the early innings of ICEBERG.

While two of the Task Force 58 Groups would be on station daily northeast of Okinawa (with a third group rotating to the south for replenishment every third day), Vice Admiral Sir Philip Vian's Task Force 57 was positioned to the southwest of Okinawa. The Union Jack's aerial blanket was charged with suppressing the staging of Japanese planes flying from Formosa to airfields in the southernmost Ryukyu Islands.

For Task Force 58, "by a strange twist, Easter Sunday- was the day selected for the invasion of the strong enemy bastion of Okinawa, only three hundred and fifty miles from the home island of Kyushu and but four hundred miles from the China coast. The task of the carrier air forces on that day was to concentrate the heaviest strikes possible on the beaches selected for landing and then to give our troops necessary air support as they made their way inland."

As a precursor to the day's events, DesDiv 96 was released from the screen during the predawn hours to again form a radar picket line thirty miles north of Task Group 58.4. Captain Higgins also had sent *Borie* and *Hank* out the day prior as Task Group 58.3's radar pickets. Steaming twelve miles ahead, the two destroyers were the eyes of the group. The initial enemy approach came at 0148 when *Borie's* radars picked up a raider. A Mitsubishi *Betty* bomber was brought down in flames by an *Intrepid* night fighter from Admiral Radford's Task Group 58.4.

With the *English* as the plane guard for most of the day, Capt. Higgins was left with just ten destroyers to screen the five flattops. Two partial screens of five cans each were deployed to protect the launching and downwind courses of the group. This formation left the flanks of the screen covered only by the battleships and the cruisers. Both Higgins and Mitscher would have accepted more destroyers had they been available.

By dawn's early light, the fast carriers turned their bows into the wind. The full might of the task force was launched against Okinawa Gunto and Nansei Shoto. Unlike DesRon 62's forays in the South China Sea in January, the weather cooperated with the mission, a day

En route to Philippines USS English, unidentified destroyer, USS Hancock. (LT Cdr. Charles Jacobs 80-G-470288)

of fair winds and following seas. The big blue blanket controlled the skies over the islands. The first launch had been at 0545. The last plane would not be recovered until 1850 that evening.

As the sun's first rays warmed the steel of the warships, the heavies from Task Force 54, The Gunfire & Covering Force, turned their main and secondary batteries east towards Okinawa. Targets ashore were pounded by salvo after salvo. Two hours later, the landing crafts packed with marines and soldiers hit the beaches. Hundreds of landing craft ferried troops with the support of hundreds more warships and ancillary ships.

The biggest amphibious invasion in history had begun. And soon would follow the greatest series of kamikaze attacks in World War II.

THE BRITISH TASK FORCE 57 WAS NO MORE IMMUNE TO KAMIKAZE ATTACKS than their American cousins. While no enemy planes visited 58.3 on 'Lucky Day,' HMS *Indefatigable* absorbed a blow from the *Divine Wind*. A *Zero*, that had avoided the CAP, charged the ship to strike the flight deck and command island. The Royal Navy had sacrificed ship size for the benefit of armored flight decks, unlike the American carriers with their wooden decks. Despite the enemy plane striking the bullseye, damage was slight and the ship stayed in the game while remaining on station. "The USN liaison officer on *Indefatigable* commented: 'When a kamikaze hits a US carrier it means six months of repair at Pearl. When a kamikaze hits a Limey carrier it's just a case of *Sweepers, man your brooms.*'

British destroyers also found themselves in the crosshairs of Imperial pilots. The HMS *Ulster* narrowly missed swallowing a bomb. The nearby underwater explosion buckled in side plates of her thin skin. With a loss of propulsion and a severe list from flooding, the British can was lost to the battle, towed from the theater of operations for repair.

Damage was greater for several other vessels as the pilots of the *Tokko-tai* bracketed the invasion ships. Four became victims. The battleship USS *West Virginia* BB-48 was seriously damaged during the Pearl Harbor attack but repairs and modernization brought her back to service in the fleet. She survived this next attack when a 551 lb. bomb failed to detonate after passing through her metal skin near the second 14" gun turret. Despite the damage to the galley and laundry, the old gal never skipped a beat. She buried four of her own at sea but sailored on.

After a successful day in the air, Rear Admiral Sherman turned his task group south for its appointment with the oilers of the replenishment train. As the sun withdrew from the sky, the *Haynsworth's* log showed she had traveled 53,450 miles in just the nine months since her commissioning. Her time in combat would soon come to a violent close.

"WE'RE HAVING A TYPHOON! ALL RAIDS CANCELLED," wrote Ed Mital CM2c of April 2nd. Though the task group had no contact with opposing planes, it did find an enemy in the weather. Heavy seas and rain dictated the squadron's actions as a typhoon passed east of the group.

The *Borie* became a victim of the stormy seas. Cdr. Noah Adair recorded, "We were transferring pilots and mail to the *Essex* by breeches buoy when the heavy seas smashed us together twice, demolishing our after [smoke] stack, one of the forward 40mm mounts, and bending the mast at a crazy angle. Three days later we were detached to proceed to Ulithi for repairs." *Borie* would return to the hunt with Task Group 58.3 at the beginning of May. The day's luck wasn't all bad for DD-704. Earlier in the morning, *Borie* was able to rescue an F6F pilot forced to ditch in the churning seas.

Planned ferrying trips of pilots, passengers and mail were cancelled later in the morning as was rearming and provisioning. Sailors didn't

USS Borie attempting to refuel from carrier, early 1945.
(Official US Navy Photos)

venture topside unless it was an 'all hands' job, recalled Radarman Third Class Ralph Aakhus. *Haynsworth* fueled early in the day from the USS *Patuxent* AO-44 despite the rain and heavy swells. But, later in the day, the top heavy destroyer survived a comber that caught the crew's attention. "We heard it was a 50 degree roll, remembered Phil Goldstein. "Destroyers are lost with rolls like that."

With all of the hungry cans partly fed to at least 85% of fuel capacity, a high speed run north to Okinawa commenced in the late afternoon. The *Haynsworth* and the *Waldron* took the lead reins as the group's twin picket ships.

However, the strong winds of the storm did not prevent the *Divine Wind* from swirling over the invasion forces. Several troop ships were struck as was the former destroyer USS *Dickerson* APD-21. Converted to a high speed transport, the old WWI era warship swallowed a pair of kamikazes. The resultant explosions and fires devastated the ship. She lost a significant portion of her crew and was scuttled the next day with damage so extensive, repair was not an option.

BEFORE DAWN'S FIRST LIGHT FLICKERED ON THE HORIZON, air operations were underway on Sunday, April 3rd. The CAP was launched while DesDiv 96 raced thirty miles ahead again

Damaged aft stack, twin 40mm mount damage, on the USS Borie, 1 April 1945. (NARA 80-G-373755)

to form a radar picket line at 0400. Before 0700, airstrikes against multiple targets were launched from the flattops in support of the invasion forces. "Though little ground and small air opposition has been met, it is felt that any punch the Japs may throw should come soon," Lt. Cdr. Scott Lothrop warned the *Haynsworth* crew. "Be on the alert constantly,"

The light carrier *Bataan* sent a fighter sweep composed of twelve VF-47 *Hellcats*. Their target: the airfield at Kikai north of Okinawa Gunto. As the Grumman pilots prepared to launch their rockets against the airfield, they were jumped by a large group of enemy fighters. The battle was lopsided. The Americans claimed seven enemy fighters against light wounds of their own. Dominance of the air was the providence of the carrier pilots.

There was plenty of business for the lifeguards. Ensign Oliver Swisher's plane suffered damage from flak over the target and machine gun rounds stitched his plane during a dogfight. The twenty-seven year old Virginia native won the air battle bringing down a 'meatball' before heading back to the group. Circumstances required the Fighting

PHALANX AGAINST THE DIVINE WIND

USS English. (NARA 80-G-470613)

Squadron 47 pilot to ditch his plane in the drink but the *Ault* was on hand for the rescue. The young Navy Reserve officer would finish the war as an 'ace' with six kills to his credit plus nominations for two Distinguished Flying Crosses and eight Air Medals.

The *John W. Weeks* also rescued an aviator during the day's actions. VF-83's Lt. Darrell E. Way's *Hellcat* crashed as he attempted to land on the *Essex*. The deck of a tin can was more comforting than the heavy seas of the Pacific. While the destroyers often exchanged pilots for ice cream, sometime the rescuers were given something by the pilots. Way rewarded the rescue swimmer, Morris Gillett CRT, with his flight helmet.

Air opposition over the entire battlefield was light but midday GQ was sounded as radar picked up incoming bandits. The threat was quickly handled in a terminal manner by fighters from the *Bunker Hill*. This was repeated again near the end of the afternoon. Final score: American fighters 5, Japanese 0.

Destroyer chores that weren't completed the previous day were finished the next morning. After delivering mail to several ships, the *Sperry* received a war correspondent, AJ Crockett, from the *Essex*. His destination: the battles ashore on Okinawa.

When DesDiv96 rejoined the screen for the night, both the *Haynsworth* and *English* returned to the picket positions. Task Group 58.3 did not venture far during the night as flight operations were to begin again early the next day.

As the tin can settled in for a night of radar picket duty, the *Haynsworth*'s new morale booster, W-H-I-Z, was still finding its sea legs. Some of the material proffered was of the colorful 'sailor stories' variety. The exec offered some guidance in his morning order: "A radio program need not be all blood, smut, and tears. Perhaps there is a goodly percent of Ship's Company that enjoys the way of color story, but I'll bet a good number just shook their head and groaned last night. Asco Beans, yes- but garage doors, no. Do you want to be known the rest of your life by the foul quality of the stories you know? Be a little discreet in your W-H-I-Z stories – was it Shakespeare who stated the fact that a woman is a lot more beautiful with a few clothes on than none at all? Use the same attitude in your program material. Keep a *few* clothes on."

SUPPRESION OF ENEMY AIR ATTACKS FROM THE NORTH was 58.3's mission on April 4th and 5th. Carrier planes were dispatched 150 miles north to attack airfields on the tiny island of Amami Gunto. Lt. Cdr. Scott Lothrop appraised the officers and bluejackets of the days planned events: "Today our task group operates in support of the Northern landing forces on Okinawa Jima. Our position is from sixty to seventy-five miles east of the island. Reports indicate that [construction of] our landing strips are proceeding well, that we already have two airstrips in operation on the island from which our reconnaissance planes are operating." Marine *Corsair* squadrons, preloaded on escort carriers, were on their way from Ulithi to join the fight from these new airbases.

"No enemy attacks were made on our group today and some of the destroyers fueled from heavy ships," recorded the *Haynsworth's* yeoman in her war diary. Three destroyers at a time left the screen to approach the battleships. The *North Carolina*, *Washington* and *South Dakota* were on station five miles east of the carriers to receive the destroyers.

When they weren't feeding, the destroyers completed other task group chores. Cdr. McIlhenny's *Charles S. Sperry* was released from the screen to head south of Okinawa to Kerama Retto. Upon arrival, the war correspondent Crockett was transferred to the seaplane tender USS *Chandeleur* AV-10. In exchange, the *Sperry* received mail and four rescued pilots with four crewman. The tin can was in the dual roles of ferry service and mailman to the group for the rest of the day.

The *English* saved an ensign when Edward Wendt and his crewman were plucked from the tepid seas after they were forced to ditch their *Helldiver*. Fragments from their own bomb had struck the *Hancock's* Bombing Squadron 6 Curtiss bird. The dividend from the rescue would be realized in weeks to come when the young flier would win

USS Ault fuels from USS Essex. (NARA 80-G-470610)

the Navy Cross for his actions in an attack on the Yokosuka Naval Base.

After DesDiv 96 had been recovered from its daily radar picket line duty and flights completed for the day, the task group retired to the south to meet the service train, Task Group 50.8.

On the 5th of April, TG 58.3's ships refueled and provisioned from the oilers despite rough seas and high winds. The ravenous *Sumners* and *Fletcher* class destroyers drank til they had their fill. Once again, the destroyers under Captain Higgins crisscrossed the group as they refueled, laid provisions aboard and restocked the magazines. "As crew members we, of course, participated in all crew activities like loading supplies (apples and oranges lasted, at most, one day) and helping with fuel," recalled Fire Controlman Third Class Tom Scott.

After the basic necessities had been completed, the cans were further tasked with transferring personnel, ferrying pilots, freight and mail to other ships within the group. Commander Tackney's

Haynsworth logged the morning events: "0634 Fueling, ten knots off starboard side USS *Lackawanna* AO-40, completed 0818 21,813 gallons." *Charles S. Sperry* maneuvered close to another Federal Shipbuilding & Drydock Co. vessel: "1227-1507 Received twenty tons of fresh, dry and frozen provisions from USS *Mercury* [AK-42]."

After *Borie* had completed her transfers, she was detached from TG 58.3. Joining Task Unit 50.8.5, her next stop would be Ulithi for replacement of her starboard 40mm mount and smokestack. For *Borie* to return to the hunt, she would need a steel organ donor. The unknowing future donor was still in battle with Task Group 58.3.

THOUGH THE TIN CANS WERE ALWAYS IN MOTION with much to be done, there were times for quiet reflection. John Vasquez of the *Haynsworth* recalled the words of his friend and fellow signalman Cliff Heob: "I remember one night when the both of us were on the bridge and on lookout for any enemy action. As the ship swayed from side-to-side, up and down, a rocking motion enough to put anyone to sleep, the ocean breezes moved the halyards that hold the flags. We began to talk about things and I remember one thing he told me, 'that after the war was over, he would return to the South and buy some land.'" Unfortunately Lady Luck would not shine on Heob's dream.

On the eve of battle, Ralph Aakhus, in a letter to his mother, mentioned how he had nearly $300 saved for when he got home. He cautioned, "Don't get the idea I'm coming now." That evening Ernie Satterly had his hair cut by the ship's barber. "Make it good," he told the barber, "I've got a big date tomorrow."

Tom Scott recalled, "I had many talks with Ernie Satterly on the *Haynsworth*. I do not remember a first meeting but we frequently sat on deck--usually at his watch station, the twin 40mm gun mount. He told me that his twin brother and he agreed to go their separate ways in the service, avoiding the Sullivans' tragedy. Ernie went into the Navy in the Pacific and his brother joined the Navy in the Atlantic." Both Satterlys manned guns on ships half a world apart.

Ernie Satterly had a premonition he would not be coming home. He wrote to his twin brother, Charlie, "I have been reading the Easter story as you probably have been reading it, also." Just as his Lord knew his time was short as he prayed amongst the olive trees in the garden at Gethsemane two thousand years earlier, Ernie continued, "I don't think I will be home to see another Easter." His words were prophetic.

THE TASK FORCE'S MISSION PLANNER HAD SCHED-ULED STRIKES against Okinawa, Tokuno Shima, and Kikai Ji-ma for April 6th. The mission of the latter two raids was continued suppression of Japanese air activity against the fleet. But, April 5th had been a rare day for Vice Admiral Mitscher. No planes in the group were lost for any reason. During the previous four days, thirty planes were written off. Some pilots and aircrew had been recovered but just as many were killed or missing.

As evening set on Wednesday, April 5th, the task group set course to return to its hunting grounds in an area northeast of Okinawa. A strong wind would arrive over the next two days. The wind would be sent not as a force of nature, but rather as nature of the force of man. The *Waldron* warned in its war diary: "1700 *Walker*, *Weeks*, *Haynsworth* assigned picket stations. We have been informed that the enemy plans to attack in force tomorrow."

Aboard the *Haynsworth*, Commander Stephen Tackney's warship carried out its orders as it headed out on picket duty:

1743 on station, 24000 yards from center task force; CAPs maintained, no enemy contact. 1842 darkened ship, 17 knots 1935 commenced zig zagging on plan 6 USF 10-A, staying at 17 knots.

Far from the phalanx on the eve of the war's biggest kamikaze attack, the USS *Haynsworth* was in its lonely role as a task group sentry forward of the task group. Signalman Third Class John Vasquez's interpretation: "We were bait."

OPERATION TEN-GO: *KIKUSUI No.1*

THE ARRIVAL OF THE AMERICAN AND BRITISH FLEETS off Okinawa surprised the Japanese command. They had guessed wrong as to the date of the Allied invasion. Plans for attacking the Allied fleets had to be sped up. The IJN and the IJA adjusted its timetable for the ultimate aerial attacks that were designed to force the Allies to the negotiating table.

Conceived as a way to defeat the landings and destroy the air power of the allies, Operation Ten-Go or *'Floating Chrysanthemum,'* was a plan for a series of massive air and kamikaze attacks. Attrition had reduced the number of veteran pilots with airworthy planes available for service. Mechanics were scarce, new pilots had limited flight hours and a lack of spare parts and fuel hampered both the IJA and the IJN. Confronting them were fleets with more carriers, newer planes, better trained pilots and a system of coordinated radar-fighter plane operations. The Japanese response was both simple but incomprehensible to the Allies.

The kamikaze program had changed in concept since its inception the previous summer before the attacks in the Philippines. No longer were all of the pilots volunteers. Many were coerced into joining the *Tokubetsu Kōgeki tai* Special Attack Units. The new pilots were taught just rudimentary flying skills. The IJA pilots came right from flight school and were often teenagers with meager hours in the air.

Rather than send a few planes at a time on kamikaze attacks, the ten planned attacks or *Kikusui* would send massed kamikaze attacks against the fleet to overwhelm the CAP and the radar system. The IJA and IJN would both contribute planes to the plan. The IJN pilots would target the carriers while the IJA planes would attack troop, convoy, and supply ships.

Though the American fleet had sent large raids against airfields to suppress the threat from Formosa, Japan and Okinawa, the Japanese still had dozens of airfields and thousands of planes stationed on smaller islands of the Ryukyu chain, like Minami Daito Shima, as well as at fields in Korea. When it was apparent the American raids were coming, often many Japanese aircraft were flown to airfields distant to keep them from harm's way. The protection of their remaining airplanes was paramount to the Japanese's plan to fight back against the Allied invasion of the home islands.

Admiral Soemu Toyoda had accumulated 1800 planes for the *Ten-Go* attacks. Some initial raids were sent against Task Force 58 during the March raids on the Empire. Small raids were sent after the 5th Fleet surrounded Okinawa. But on April 6, 1945, Toyoda initiated what would be the largest kamikaze raid of World War II: *Kikusui No.1.* Nearly four hundred kamikazes would join almost as many non-kamikaze fliers in an attempt to overwhelm the Allie's defenses. By the end of April 7, 1945, dozens of American warships would know the impact of Japanese metal on American steel.

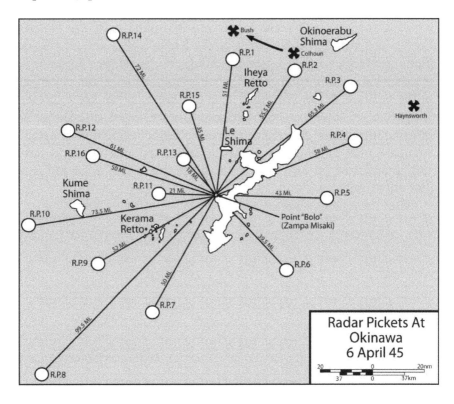

There was no doubt amongst the Allied leaders that the kamikazes would be coming in force. American cryptologists' efforts breaking Japanese codes confirmed the hunches of the admirals. Every effort was made to counter the *Divine Wind*.

In preparation of the invasion, a series of sixteen radar picket stations was established in a loose wagon wheel formation. Each station at the end of the spoke was twenty to sixty miles from the hub 'point bolo' on the western shores of central Okinawa. Destroyers served as pickets, steaming in a radius of 5000 yards from their station. Their radar extended the electrical eyes of the U.S. Navy forces. Specially trained fighter director officers manned the CICs. Each team controlled their own fighters known as 'Tiger CAPS.' But, their deployment made them targets of incoming raiders.

Each of Mitscher's task groups also had destroyers deployed as forward pickets, north and west of the groups. These sentries were joined by picket screens of several destroyers sent even further north to detect and intercept raiders. They also had their own Tiger CAPS.

From the viewpoint of the USS *Haynsworth*: "We were ready. And we were conscious of the many, many other parts of the fleet that were working together as a team to succeed in rolling back the Japanese Forces in order to restore peace in the Pacific. We knew of the amphibious forces, themselves, busy landing troops ashore. We knew of the preparatory bombardments by battleships, cruisers, and destroyers of the Japanese defenses on the island of Okinawa. We knew of other destroyers on distant picket stations in other threat directions. We knew of the close-in picket line of our destroyers off Kerama Rhetto, a landmark port of Okinawa. We had studied the enormously detailed and complicated operation orders that set this whole huge and complex effort underway.

"But the Japanese were ready, too."

PHALANX AGAINST THE DIVINE WIND

Part VI

Divine Wind Storm

Courage is the quality which enables one to meet danger and difficulties with firmness and with ability unimpaired. It is the opposite of cowardice. It does not mean absence of fear. Fear is a paralysis of the senses to which all normal human beings are subject to a degree. A courageous man has mastered fear. The true value of courage is lessened when it is combined with recklessness, foolhardiness or rashness. Courage is most admirable when it is daring, dauntless or intrepid. Cool courage implies ability to exercise sound judgment in the face of danger.

—*Bluejackets' Manual 1943*

6 APRIL 1945

USS *Haynsworth* 0350 6 April 1945

T*ADPOLE.* As a child, someone decided that the nickname best described Scott Lothrop for both his size and love of the water. The amphibian tag stuck. Family and friends shortened the moniker to 'Tad.' But, like a tadpole, given time, the young man matured into something more.

Young Lothrop had grown up in Massachusetts, sailing at a very young age. As a fourteen year old in the summer of 1933, he and his brother, Cummings, had saved their father's boat after it sunk in Hingham Harbor, Massachusetts. Lincoln Lothrop's sons used their ingenuity, ropes, and some barrels to slowly refloat their father's boat.

Scott Lothrop earned an appointment to Annapolis. "Tad chose wisely in selecting the Navy as his future profession. His close and life-long association with boats and salt water has given him a knowledge and love of the sea seldom found in others. In his native state of Massachusetts, Tad early became versed in the finer points of small boat racing and is now one of the finest sailors (sic) at the Naval Academy." Recognizing the leadership skills of their fellow midshipman, Lothrop's peers elected him Company Sub-commander. Five years later, the days spent at Annapolis, on the Eastern and Chesapeake Bays seemed like a dream, a distant memory.

Lt. Cdr. Scott Lothrop. (Courtesy of Peter Lothrop)

PHALANX AGAINST THE DIVINE WIND

Lothrop ducked out his stateroom, glancing down the red-lit passageway. Stepping out of the aft deckhouse, the sea breeze was light, the air not too cool. A waning half-moon was hidden in the sky. The storm clouds that had covered the fleet a few days before had been blown away but were replaced by an overcast sky. The seas were choppy. He didn't need to look past the lifelines to know. After a lifetime on the water, his feet sent a signal to his subconscious that the sea was in transition, the waves confused.

The word had already come down from above, Mitscher to Higgins to Tackney to Lothrop to bluejackets. The Task Force Commander had said that "today may be a busy day that the enemy was expected to launch large air attacks, and enemy surface ships were expected to sortie soon." Captain Higgins also alerted his destroyers to be ready to use their torpedoes in a surface action.

Lothrop walked down to the wardroom to grab a cup of coffee before heading up to the bridge. The Silex was nearly empty of the hot brew, evidence of the mid-watch also struggling to keep their eyes open. It had been twenty-three days since Task Force 58 had emerged from Ulithi on its crusade to conquer Okinawa. The crew was tired but none so much as probably the Captain and his Executive Officer. Cdr. Tackney was a ghost to most of the bluejackets. The ship's captain had the operational command while the exec handled the administrative end. Lothrop served as the more visible symbol of the ship's command. If the crew felt tired, they realized Lothrop must be exhausted. It seemed that the young exec never slept.

His watch showed 0355, a few minutes before the change of watch. He fumbled in his shirt pocket for his pack of cigarettes. Last chance to grab a smoke before heading topside in the darkened warship. He laid his freshly penned Morning Orders on the wardroom dining table. A yeoman would type it up and soon have it posted all over the destroyer.

The USS *Haynsworth* was in Condition of Readiness II. With a high expectation of hostilities, kamikaze watches were set on both port and starboard. Already half of the crew was on watch or manning their battle stations. Watch time had increased to six hours from the standard four hour shift. The captain was keeping the ship at Material Condition Baker. Most hatches were secured but a few were open to allow a freer flow of air to the crew. When "bogies" were detected, the squawk box would announce 'Set Condition Able.' At that point all the hatches would be secured. The bluejackets' pulses would increase correspondingly.

Lothrop returned to the deck by the starboard door from the wardroom. Avoiding the internal passageways, he set course for the pilot house. He hurdled up the stairs between the forward stack and the 40mm clipping room. As his feet hit the bridge deck, voices greeted him. "Morning, sir."; "Morning, Commander." A skeleton crew was on duty at the starboard twin 40mm guns. Lothrop, like the Captain and the Chief Petty Officers, worked the crew hard but the bluejackets respected both the man and the rank. "Morning, boys" he responded. The twenty-five year old officer smiled to himself. They were boys doing the job of men. Lenihan probably wasn't eighteen and Matschat couldn't have been much older than his peer. Lothrop often found it hard to believe he was just twenty-five.

The Executive Officer entered the pilot house through a hatch in the starboard bulkhead. The Captain emerged from his sea cabin onto the bridge as well. "Morning, sir," greeted the Officer of the Deck. "Morning, Army. What's the situation?" With his relief, Lt. Eshelman, joining them, Lt. Armistead Dennett covered their position, speed, bearing, and boiler status. The alert received an hour prior of enemy planes in the vicinity of the task group ended twenty minutes later when no planes closed the formation. The *Kidd*, *Bullard*, *and Black* from Division 96 were on their way north to form their daily radar picket line thirty miles in advance of the group. The *John W.* Weeks and *Waldron* were also out there on picket duty but the *Walker* was on the way up to replace the *Waldron* at picket station 12. The *Haynsworth* would remain at station 1 for the time being. As Dennett provided his summary, the destroyer turned a few degrees to port. It would continue to zig zag until dawn.

After the report Lothrop left the bridge by the portside ladder bringing him to a passageway outside the CIC and Radio Central. While it may have been sixty-seven degrees topside, he found it significantly warmer when he entered the CIC. The tubes of the radios and radar in the cramped compartment generated enough heat that the CIC was rarely cold. The ambient temperature was not lowered any by all the radarmen on duty despite the Buffalo Forge fans bolted to the bulkheads circulating air.

Looking at the plotting table and then at a radar set, Lothrop confirmed DDs 699-701 were in position, 24000 yards from the center of the task group. The radar showed the night CAP. A pair of F6F-5(N) *Hellcats* were overhead nearby. The rainy skies hid the warship's phosphorescent wake which was normally a trail marker for enemy planes.

CIC aboard USS Albert W. Grant. (NARA 80-G Photo)

The *Haynsworth* is already turning nineteen knots in advance of the dawn General Quarters. In preparation for what the task force has been warned would be a tough day, Lt. Eshelman orders Main (Engine Control) to "light off Boilers #1 and 3 and bring on line, expect speed to increase to twenty knots by 0530." With expected aerial attacks, it will be crucial to have all four boilers operating before daylight touches the destroyer.

At 0510 word comes down from the group. Enemy planes are in the area. Eshelman alerts all his batteries as dawn General Quarters is sounded. Across the ship, sleepy sailors man the guns, watching the darkness for the telltale flicker of a plane's exhaust in the sky, ears straining for the sound of an engine. The bluejackets know that an improvement in weather will bring a return of the Bushido boys.

Task Force 58

The *Divine Wind* had been blown out to sea by the storms of the previous days. By the morning of April 6, the "weather improved. Visibility was good. Winds were 20 knots...two distinct swells overriding one another. Waves were not high but the swells built up periods of pitching for the ship which were not uniform and as such hampered landing operations at times."

After a day of replenishment at sea, Task Group 58.3 was on the move. Leaving the oilers south of Okinawa the previous evening, the group steamed northeast on a track sixty miles parallel to the Ryukyu Islands.

In anticipation of the arrival of *Ten-Go* attackers, many bomber ground support missions from the fast attack fleet carriers are cancelled for the day. For the fleet carriers, this day will be all about the fighters. Vice Admiral Mitscher orders Task Groups 58.1 and 58.3 to work as a tandem unit. Rear Admiral Jocko Clark's TG 58.1 is charged with providing air support at Okinawa, while Rear Admiral Frederic Sherman's TG 58.3 has the mission of blocking Okinawa's northern approaches to enemy planes. Raids will be sent north against Amami O Shima while sweeps and searches from Amami O Shima to the southern tip of Kyushu will be carried out. The *Bunker Hill's* air group will strike Tokuno Airfield and vicinity, conducting sweeps and searches there. Task Force 58 had been stretched thin. Mitscher is still short one task group but the Brits in Task Force 57 are guarding the southern approaches from Formosa.

The mighty Fast Carrier Task Force which has relied on speed, power projection, and stealth finds itself essentially steaming in a nautical box. For two weeks it has been tethered to a sixty mile square area east of Okinawa. With the invasion fleet to the west side of Okinawa along with its attending radar picket stations, Task Force 58 has little choice but to operate in a limited area. For kamikazes flying from the Ryukyu Islands chain or Kyushu, it is not hard to find the US ships.

As the groups stop zig-sagging at 0530, Admiral Sherman orders his carriers slowly brought about into the wind to accommodate the day's first launches. Ten minutes later the first sweep, search, and CAP rise from the decks of his five carriers. Before the sun has warmed the metal skin of the ships, *Essex'* CAP makes the day's inaugural kill. A Mitsubishi *Betty* is sent flaming into the Pacific, just eighteen miles from the formation. Metal birds of prey will clash violently on April 6.

USS *Haynsworth* 0610

Sunrise but the sun stays hidden for the most part behind rain clouds. Eshelman calls an end to GQ a few minutes later. With all the boilers now on line, he orders the speed increased to twenty knots. Two sections of *Corsairs,* the Tiger CAP, have arrived overhead. The fighter director officers will keep them "under our radar and communications control, to vector out and destroy any detected incoming Japanese raids."

At 0800 Lt. Sidwell L. Smith relieves Eshelman. The *Haynsworth* is just thirty miles east of Okino Erabu Island as the task group steams south. After Smith completes the daily inspection of the ship's magazines and smokeless powder samples, he enters 'conditions normal' in the deck log. Minutes later the word comes from the CIC: "unidentified planes in area, twenty miles distant, closing." Smith orders the crew back to battle stations again. The bandit closes to within nine miles of the group before turning south. Flying at 20,000, feet the raider decides against testing the phalanx.

Finally, at 0846 Smith allows the crew to secure from General Quarters. For Gunners Mate Second Class Walter DeLoach, he and his crew on the starboard twin 40mm mount have a sense of what the day will hold for them. Today is just a few weeks past the long days at General Quarters during the Tokyo attacks. Already they had been called to the guns twice and the day is just starting. The scuttlebutt is that the Japanese were going to send raids in force. For now at least, all the planes above them wore white stars.

USS *Essex*

The pilots' ready room was quiet, tense, as it only was when the mission would be tough. Several pilots had trouble sleeping the night before. The usual joking and laughing has been replaced by an air of seriousness. The word had already come down that the Japanese were going to launch something big that day, something really big. Details of the day's missions are given to the *Corsair* pilots of VBF-83. The senior officers of the squadron never provided enough details of the plan to fully satisfy the junior fighter jockeys.

Each pilot had his own philosophy of what could happen to them. The squadron leaders considered themselves invincible. Aggressive with several tours of combat behind them, they feared no enemy. '*There isn't a Jap pilot that can shoot me down.*' Others held the belief of *fait accompli-'if your name is on a Japanese bullet, there's nothing you can do about that.*' While the aces were always looking to increase their score, some of the less senior fliers simply wondered if they would re-

Carrier Air Group 83 planes.

turn from the mission or ever get home. Wingman 1st Lt. Wilmot of the *Bunker Hill's* VMF-451 admitted, "I was scared a lot of the time."

The Japanese brought planes down at night to islands near Okinawa. The cover of darkness allowed the raiders to avoid the aviation blanket that the fleet kept in the skies during daylight. As the day progressed, the fighter planes from Task Force 58 would face their greatest aerial challenge to date. With one task group relieved from battle and another replenishing far to the south, Task Groups 58.1 and 58.3 are stretched thin.

When the signal is given, the F4U fighter pilots exit the ready room, leaving the smell of food and diesel oil behind. Headed out to the deck, each scans for his bent wing bird amongst the group situated on the aft end of the flight deck. After climbing aboard, the plane captain assists the pilot hooking him to his flight harness and then cinches him in. The Vought planes are fitted with 'pee' tubes. With the pressure of difficult missions ahead, some pilots felt the need to find relief before take-off. It was never a popular decision with the deck crew.

A white flag waving on the bridge is the signal to start the engines. The sweet smell of aviation fuel greets them in response. With the igni-

Lt. jg. Schiess VBF-83 lands on USS Essex.

tion switches flipped to START, The large radial engines belch to life, coughing up blue-black smoke as the pilots watch their bird's oil pressure rise. An eye is kept on the Fuel Pressure gauge, awaiting the desired 14 lbs./sq. inch. Cowl flaps were opened to cool the powerful engine, its vibrations rippling through the skin of the *Corsair*. With brakes set, the pilots wait for the yellow shirted plane directors to signal them to move forward on the deck. They turn the latch that spreads their bent wings.

At the designated spot, the engines are brought close to full power. The two thousand horsepower Pratt & Whitney radials turning the thirteen foot propeller cause the tails of the planes to rise from the deck. But, with a full load of fuel, ammunition and auxiliary tanks or external bombs, the *Corsairs* need every foot of the remaining flight deck to get airborne. The final plane director gives the signal, the brakes are released and the *Corsair* accelerates down the wooden flight deck. The first twin 5" mount was seen from the corner of the pilot's eyes. By the time they passed the 5" mounts forward of the 'island,' pilots are silently urging their birds airborne. "Sometimes your wheels were still on the deck as you left the carrier. That meant you would sink as you sought to gain speed," Wilmot recalled. "You instantly prayed your plane wouldn't settle so low it couldn't gain altitude."

Shortly after 0900, the carriers *Essex* and *Bunker Hills* launch their second Tiger Cap flights of the morning. Immediately after, the earlier *Sweep* and *Search* flights return. The carriers will be in a constant dance of launch and recovery all day.

Kokubu No. 1 Airbase, Kyushu 0930-1030

Seven D4Y3 Yokosuka Suisei "Comet" dive bombers of the 210th Naval Air Group, *Suisei Unit* (*Kamikaze Tokubetsu Kōgeki tai, Dai Futa-Hito-Maru Butai, Suisei-tai*) take off in small groups. They fly from the Kokubu No. 1 Air Base in the Kagoshima Prefecture on the island of Kyushu. While the Imperial Japanese Navy has named the D4Y as '*Comet*,' the American military has designated it by the codename of *Judy*. Thirteen men in seven *Judy* dive bombers of the 210th will not live to see the end of the day. The flight of 375 miles will take two hours to reach Okinawa.

USS *Haynsworth* 1050

Word comes up from the CIC, from the Executive Officer to the Captain, that ten to fifteen unidentified planes have been reported ten miles north of radar picket line, closing fast. The alarms scream General Quarters again. Across the ship, helmets are grabbed, life jackets are donned, flash cream applied, hatches sealed, doors dogged, and ammunition broken out of its lockers in preparation of impending attackers. The eyes of the sailors turn skyward in anticipation of attack.

A *Bunker Hill* pilot shoots down a *Dinah* long range reconnaissance plane thirty miles from the formation, between the destroyer picket line and Admiral Sherman's task group. After forty-two minutes, the bluejackets on the *Lucky 700* are allowed to secure from the morning's third period of General Quarters.

The repeated calls to man battle stations lose their urgency for some of the young sailors. The strain from waiting for attacks that often did not appear dampened the enthusiasm for the efforts involved. Seasoned veterans like Charles Lechner S1c caution their younger peers not to lose focus but to maintain their vigilance against attack. The New Yorker was aboard the USS *Bristol* DD-453 in 1943 when a German U-boat put a torpedo in her side, sinking the tin can and causing the loss of fifty-two of the ship's compliment.

PHALANX AGAINST THE DIVINE WIND

Task Group 58.3 1140

Missions against the airfields on Kikai Jima and Amami O Shima continue throughout the morning as the five carriers launch several strikes. Opposition from enemy planes and guns are light. Most of the blips glowing on the radarmen's screens are the planes of the big blue blanket. As midday approaches, so does the appearance of the enemy. Two *Judy* dive bombers attract the attention of several Fighting Squadron 83 *Hellcats* flying the CAP near Tokuno Shima. They are quickly disposed by the *Essex* pilots. Moments later the CAP from the *Bunker Hill* bring down a *Zeke* interloper.

As the morning concludes, the task groups are steaming due south. By 1200 Task Group 58.3 is sixty miles due east of northern Okinawa. Ready to emerge from their hornet's nest are nearly four hundred kamikazes.

USS *Haynsworth* 1200

As eight bells ring to indicate 1200 and the start of the afternoon watch, Lt. Smith is relieved by the destroyer's navigator, Lt. Leon Berk who takes charge as the Officer of the Deck. Berk orders flank speed with the reports of enemy planes in the area of the Task Force.

Down in the mess deck, two sailors reached for the last piece of pie. Fireman A.C. Pickens comes away with the slice. The sailor in line behind A.C. needles him for taking the final piece. It is a piece of pie that A.C. will never forget but not for its taste. This will be the last time the two sailors will see each other alive.

As the forenoon watch ends, sailors swap positions as some come off watch and others come on. Bernice Holiman RM2c replaces Isaac Peres RM3c in the radio shack. Peres, after a previous disagreement with Chief Barton Campbell, moves to his new GQ station in one of the 40mm clipping shacks. Keith Myreholt RM3c, who is supposed to have been on duty for the afternoon watch, traded his shift at John Dyer RM3c's request. Myreholt leaves and heads to the emergency radio shack for the afternoon watch. Chief Campbell and Arthur Goyer RM2c are on duty in the shack with Dyer, Carroll Davis RM3c, Holiman and Warner Holcombe RM1c.

Chief Campbell is in charge of the six souls crowded into the windowless compartment. The radiomen sit at the ready to capture messages from the fleet and the task group. Despite the background noise of fans, the hum of the radios, and messages coming over their headphones, the radiomen can still sense the battle going on around them. The metal skin of the ship acts like a nervous system as it transmits the movements and sounds of the destroyer.

Left: A. C. Pickens FC3c. (Courtesy of A. C. Pickens)
Right: Warner Holcombe RM1c in Radio Central. (Bill Morton Collection)

Task Group 58.3 1201-1226

Groups of bogies are filling the radar screens in Admiral Mitscher's ships. In rapid succession, the CAP from the *Essex* engages a group of olive and mottle brown colored *Zeke* fighters twenty to thirty miles from the task group. For the VF-83 *Hellcat* pilots, it is a field day:

The section of HELLCATS turned into the group of four ZEKES, picking the last two in formations. The ZEKES immediately made a diving 180 degree turn and Lt. jg. Clark got in a 45 degree deflection burst in the right wing root, flaming the ZEKE whose pilot bailed out. Ens. TARLTON followed his ZEKE, which was now maneuvering violently, and heading for a cloud at 7000 feet, and got several bursts into its starboard wing root...causing the ZEKE to smoke, then flame and splash. The other ZEKES were engaged momentarily but used cloud cover to advantage to escape...proceeded to make a run on the "tail-end-Charlie" of the enemy formation which, after receiving several bursts in the starboard wing and tail, dove for the water, but its wing fell off and it splashed...Riding the tails of two more ZEKES, one of which smoked and dove out of sight, and the other exploding when hit by bursts in the right wing. Seeing one more ZEKE in the vicinity, Lt. jg. Comella started a tail chase,

PHALANX AGAINST THE DIVINE WIND

The phalanx shoots down an enemy plane. (NARA 80-G photo)

getting in bursts wherever possible, and the ZEKE burst into flames. He followed this down until it was seen to splash.

The signal goes out in Task Group 58.3 to change to cruising formation 5-Victor, closing the phalanx. The destroyer screen moves from 6000 yards from the center to just 3000 yards in response to the approach of bandits. The firepower is maximized as the gunships hug the carriers. At the same time, the flattops are launching their charges. *Essex* launches its next strike: Twelve F6F, eight F4U, twelve SB2C, and fourteen TBM to attack the Wan airfield on Kikai Jima. They are accompanied by two F6F-5(P) photo-reconnaissance *Hellcats*.

At 1221 an enemy plane is detected diving at the task group. In response, Admiral Sherman orders high speed evasive maneuvers to evade the bandit. While a *Zeke* is picked off by the *Essex'* CAP, the phalanx of TG 58.3 opens fire on the diving *Judy*. It is eventually shot down by the *Cabot* at a range of 5000 yards.

Serving as a guard on the flank of the phalanx, *Charles S. Sperry*, "fired on one *Zeke* to starboard with everything she had, then as he hit the sea she opened with her port machine guns on a second *Zeke* who was close aboard, creeping-in under cover of the first. He got by her and had headed for the heavy ships, when still unhit, he misdived into the sea astern of his target."

During the attack, the *Bunker Hill* is in the midst of launching forty-three planes for its strike 'B.' A *Corsair* of VF-84 fails to grab enough air to achieve flight. The plane spins and lands in the water.

The *Stembel* retrieves Lt. jg. Harvey Matthews using a cargo net hanging over the starboard side. The Fighting Squadron 84 aviator is rescued after clinging to his belly tank for ten minutes, not expecting to be picked up until after the air attacks were completed.

USS *Haynsworth* 1220

Word is received that the *Haynsworth* should return from sentry duty to rejoin Task Group 58.3. Upon her arrival, she is to assume a plane guard station with the carriers. Previously turning nineteen knots, she increases her speed to twenty-three knots to close the 22000 yards between her picket station and the phalanx.

As the CAP over the task group engages bandits, the *Haynsworth's* alarms call the sailors back to General Quarters at 1227. With the General Quarters alarms ringing, all souls aboard the *Haynsworth* automatically move to their individual battle station. The action is reflexive, an almost unconscious act after months of combat. Each officer and bluejacket aboard knows their specific place and role when the threat of attack is imminent, the potential date with heaven moved forward.

Lt. Berk, as the officer of the deck, has been responsible for both the 'conn' and the 'deck.' As the conning officer, Berk is giving orders directly to the helmsman and lee helmsman. Cdr. Tackney announces he will "take the deck." This order relieves Berk of the responsibility of leading the fighting so that he can concentrate on engine and rudder orders. After three plus years of war, submarine chases, pilot rescues, bombardments, mine laying, and other actions to protect the carriers of the phalanx, the lean thirty-nine year old commander is ready to captain his ship safely through this next threat.

They are crowded in by the helmsman, the quartermaster of the watch, the bridge messenger, several sailors and radiomen that serve as bridge talkers as well as a yeoman and quartermaster striker serving as the air defense talkers.

Twenty-two year old Radio striker Harold Bly and Joseph Wilkerson RM3c man the sound phones of the JA command circuit. "Ugh," utters Wilkerson, testing the circuit. "Aye, ugh," acknowledges Bly.

Lt. Cdr. Scott Lothrop, the twenty-five year old executive officer, is already in the Combat Information Center. Located beneath the bridge, the CIC is adjacent to the radio shack. The compartment rapidly fills with radarmen including Mariano Saia, Milton Studley, Don Karos and a yeoman, Harold Moss Y3c. Radio Technicians Claude Reeder and Paul Layden report to the battle station. The fighter director officers are ready to coordinate plane response. Tracking planes, both enemy and friendly, will be up to these officers based on the readings of the air and surface radars. Before the hatches are closed, sixteen souls are crowded into the dimly lit room. There they will plot a course of action and assist Cdr. Tackney and weapon control in execution of that plan as the incoming raiders, closing fast, are tracked.

Paul Layden RT2c. (McAllister Collection)

Robert Chamberlin and two other sonarmen man the 'sound hut.' They send out electronic greetings in the form of pings to enemies who might be lurking beneath the waves. Harrison Beasley RT1c returns to the electronic counter measures booth in the deckhouse passageway.

Out on the wings of the bridge, bluejackets take their positions. Six lookouts, two responsible for the sea and four for the heavens stand ready at their positions. Bill Morton is among the group while Signalman Third Class John Vasquez, Signalman striker Ernie Satterly and two other signalmen take their positions around the bridge. Bill Morton dons his headset and helmet.

Seaman Oscar Jefferson Callahan climbs the mast to take position in the twentieth century version of a crow's nest. He dons a headset, an electronic tether that ties him into the JP gun control circuit.

The brain controls the movement but muscle memory is represented on the destroyer by the quartermaster ready to take the 'secondary conn,' an electrician's mate with a helmsman in 'after steering' and Keith Myreholt RM3c in the emergency radio shack. If the bridge is incapacitated or destroyed, these emergency sections will replace those lost in the superstructure.

In the few seconds post the alarm, three Damage Control Repair Parties move to their standby positions. Each team of eight or nine bluejackets is a palate of talents: mechanical, electrical, nautical. They are trained to fight fires, initiate salvage and repair, ensure recovery and provide relief. The teams serve as the can-do adrenaline aboard Tackney's warship.

Pearl Harbor survivor Jack Vaessen Electrician Mate First Class stands by the ready at the main generator switchboard in Repair Party No. II. Like December 7th, 1941 at Pearl Harbor, he will be called into action again as his ship is attacked by Japanese planes.

Down below, the full complement of water tenders and firemen fill the forward and after firerooms while machinist and electrician mates ensure propulsion in both engine rooms. The black gang stands at the ready for requests for speed from the bridge. Two motor machinist mates along with two electrician mates station themselves in the two emergency diesel rooms. Henry Bichon Electrician Mate Third Class hopes that no more Japanese prisoners will be captured this day and then held in the forward emergency diesel room. Fate will have it that the only Japanese citizen aboard the destroyer this day will not be counted amongst the living.

Sleep and rest are precious commodities on a warship, especially during periods of combat. As the alarm battles summon the sailors to their battle stations, Lt. Armistead Dennett, the twenty-four year old gunnery officer, scrambles up to the highest seat aboard. Just hours after getting off the middle watch at 0400, Dennett settles into his seat in the Gun Director above the bridge. He and four fire controlmen squeeze into the metal booth to scan the skies and direct the main 5" guns against raiders who tempt them. Below the sea deck, their systems are tied into the Main Battery Plot. Chief Robert Hall, Gus Scutari FC2c, and five other fire controlmen prepare to bring the guns to bear against the enemy.

Thirteen sailors crowd into each of three dual 5" batteries. Unless the fire control systems fail, these bluejackets will load the guns while Army Dennett and his charges stationed in the gun director move and fire the guns remotely. Speed is of the essence. While the proximity fuses attached to 5" shells are merciless at effective ranges, they are not capable of readily responding to close in attacks.

As the alarm screams, a cross section of the crew, including A. C. Pickens F1c, scrambles down several decks into the three 5" upper and lower handling rooms. Powder and 54 lb. shells are sent up from the bowels of the ship by bakers, gunner's mates, mess stewards, machinist mates, water tenders, and other ratings.

The four 40mm positions are manned by full crews, seven sailors on the twin 40's, thirteen on both of the quads. Each position is captained by a gunners mate with crews of seamen, cooks, strikers. The weapons crews are supplemented by ammunition passers. The Bofors devour rounds at a rate of 120 per minute in their attempts to bring fiery conclusions to attempted raids.

On the starboard twin 40mm mount, the '41,' Gunners Mate Second Class Walter DeLoach confirms with the bridge that the crew is ready after Lonnie Lee Aulbert S1c, Robert Matschat S1c, Hobart MacLaughlan S1c, Joseph Lenihan S1c, Ernie Satterly S1c, and William Kubena S1c report to the weapon station. Most of this band of brothers has spent long hours at the gun position since the *Haynsworth* left Pearl Harbor in December. Through their time in the South China Sea, raids on Tokyo, the invasion of Iwo Jima, destroying enemy picket ships, storms, and for two weeks off Okinawa, they have joined in a communal bond in defense of their ship. Satterly is a new addition to the gun crew after a recent reassignment from one of the enclosed forward 5" mounts. The transfer to the exposed weapon figures in his premonition of not returning to the United States.

Hours spent at General Quarters usually brought time for conversation: Oral testimony was given about the food awaiting them when they returned to the states. Each sailor's mother was the best cook. The taste of fresh lobster from Maine's MacLaughlan was countered with the flavor of Long Island oysters by Matschat. Lenihan spun tales of life in the Big Apple, a contrast from Kubena's life in a big family from western Pennsylvania and MacLaughlan playing clarinet on Sunday nights in the gazebo in his little hometown. MacLaughlan and Satterly, both serving on the twin mount, have twin siblings. Movie stars, chow, the war were always fodder for conversation. The St. Louis Cardinals beat the crosstown Browns in the '44 World Series but a new season was about to start. The Yankee Clipper, Joe DiMaggio was an enlisted man in the Army Air Force while the Splendid Splinter, Lt. Ted Williams, had taken to the air as a marine pilot. After the war, some had plans, some did not. Today there will be no time for conversation, enemy planes are in the vicinity.

Dozens of four round clips hang in the ready racks of the circular bulwark surrounding the weapons. Below the 40mm mount, Cliff Heob and Harold Dempsey have reported to their battle station in the ammunition clipping room. If things get hot in the air, they will be relied upon to keep the 40's fed with fresh clips.

Fire controlman Third Class Tom Scott and Weldon Powell Seaman First Class run across the deck towards the starboard Mark 51 director. They hurriedly ascend the ladder, eyes wide scanning the skies as they climb into the tub that directs fire from the starboard

Twin 40mm mount and Mark 51 Fire Control Director. (NARA 80-G Photo)

quad 40mm guns. They will have a ringside view of the action this fateful afternoon.

Eleven 20mm guns. The last defense. With an effective range of less than a mile, when the 'twenties' opened up, it was time to take stock of your situation. A plane hurtling towards a tin can only encounters 20mm fire in the last few seconds before it closes on the ship. For as surely as they announced their presence, they also announce that the situation is dire. The 20mm guns, unlike their big 5" and 40mm brothers, can be manhandled by one sailor. Their reaction time is quicker. Though not always capable of bringing down a plane, well sighted shots could kill an airborne warrior bent on destruction. With the offense on the one yard line, the twenties were the defense struggling to keep the opposition out of the end zone. They could have been called the "game and goal to go guns."

Bill Breckenridge TM3c, Robert Clarke TM2c and the other torpedomen move to their stations atop the tubes, along the K-guns, while Donald Messecar torpedoman striker stands at the ready along the depth charge racks.

PHALANX AGAINST THE DIVINE WIND

Lt. jg. Ley's small medical department hustles to their battle dressing stations. The doctor and James Jones PhM3c enter the ward room, just below the radio shack and the CIC, and prepare the area for potential victims. Arthur Bland PhM1c and Norton Kessler PhM3c report to their posts at the emergency dressing stations, located in the crew washroom at the aft end of the deckhouse and the general mess. Medical supplies are prepositioned at the stations. The next thirty hours will become a nightmare, one that cannot be relieved by awakening.

Every officer and sailor, three hundred thirty-six souls in all, has reported to his battle station. Throughout the steel ship, reports come back to the bridge that the guns are manned, doors are dogged, latches turned. The warship is an interconnected collection of steel boxes, electronics, communication lines, and weapons. The decks overflow with gunners, loaders, fire controllers, torpedomen, signalmen and lookouts. The destroyer is ready to live up to its name.

The morning's rainy skies have been replaced by skies with high alto-stratus layer and low patches of cumulus clouds about 1500 feet. On deck, the bluejackets scan the skies for the first sign of the *Tokkotai*. *Kikusui No. 1* is about to strike its first victim.

Six minutes after the call to General Quarters, the 'sugar charlie' radar detects a medium size incoming raid of bogeys. Their distance is just twenty-two miles from the tin can. The raid is reported to the Fighter Director Officer (FDO) on the Inter Fighter Director (IFD) circuit who then assigns a 'raid' designation.

After several hours on station, low fuel levels force the Tiger CAP that had been guarding the airspace above the picket destroyers back to the task group. Four *Hellcats* and seven *Corsairs* escorting an *Essex* bombing mission against the airfield at Kikai Jima are diverted by the Fighter Director Officer to intercept the incoming bogeys. He directs them to an altitude above the raiders while keeping them between enemy and the destroyer. The "fighters vectored out from the task group merged with bogey on scope until raid passed close aboard port beam. Although director was on target from 24000 yards in, fire could not be opened because of VF [fighters] close to bogey and because visual discrimination between VF and bogey could not be made."

"Spotting a medium sized incoming raid of bogeys, we vectored our CAP onto them. ...Our firecontrol radar was locked on throughout the dogfights, but we held our fire lest we shoot down our own people. Soon the 'tallyhos' from sighting the enemy aircraft came pouring in. The Secondary Battery officer had rigged himself a crow's-nest up on the mast for better visibility to control the 40mm and 20mm batteries. From him on the sound-powered phones came a running visual commentary as the CAP splashed first one, then another of the incoming raid, and their wreckage fell into the sea from the dogfights roaring overhead."

In the skies around Okinawa, the CAP had a dominant presence against their Japanese foes. Several *Corsairs* flying from the USS *Bennington* had close encounters:

Shortly after 1200 2nd Lts. James M. Hamilton and George G. Murray had added two more Jap planes to the bag while Major Herman Hanson Jr. had obtained a good view of a kamikaze in flight. Hanson, Murray, Hamilton and 2nd Lt. R. W. Koons, all of VMF-112, were on radar picket CAP north of Okinawa.

Hamilton and Koons sighted the first Jap. They swept down through the clouds after the enemy. Hamilton climbed on his tail. Moving better than 350 knots in a screaming dive he chased the Zeke right into the water. Hamilton pulled out just in time. The Jap plane hit and exploded. Almost the same instant the Jap jumped. The chute blossomed, but there was no trace of the Nip. A while later Hanson and Murray spotted a Jap plane darting in and out of the clouds. When the Jap pilot tried to split S away, Hanson climbed on this tail, opened fire. However, in putting negative Gs on his plane he jammed the machine gun link ammunition and put five guns temporarily out of commission.

Suddenly Hanson realized he was going to fly directly into the Jap. 'It looked like a certain collision,' he recalled. 'I pulled back on the stick. I barely cleared the tail and fuselage with my prop. I figure I wasn't more than 12 inches above him. I could see the rivets in the plane. There were two yellow stripes on his wings, where patches had evidently been placed. I saw the pilot clearly. Lashed beneath the plane was a big bomb. It was suspended by a makeshift arrangement of wires or ropes. The wires or ropes flapped in the wind.

The battle over the USS *Haynsworth* rages in the skies above. Vectored to intercept the raiding bogies, two F4U Corsairs pilots push up the rpm and throttle of the 2,000 horsepower Pratt & Whitney R2800 Double Wasp engines. By using emergency power settings the planes are able to close with a *Zero*. For a few moments the *Corsairs* are within 400 feet of the bandit thus allowing at least one of the American pi-

PHALANX AGAINST THE DIVINE WIND

lots to open fire. The roar of the weapons firing and attending vibrations though is music to the pursuer's ears. Brass rain falls to the Pacific from the *Corsairs* gun exhaust ports as the expended bullet casings fall away. The rounds find their mark as the *Zero* falls from the sky consumed in flame.

The pilots turn their attention to a nearby Yokosuka D4Y *Judy* dive bomber, the fastest dive bomber in the Pacific, Allied or Japanese. Not designed to match the speeds of fighters, it nonetheless outclasses the older *Vals*. The *Judy* was built for diving but the *Corsair's* rugged construction and excellent diving capabilities allow the American pilots to match the enemy's descent. All the planes emerge from the clouds in a steep dive. The F4U jockeys and their potential prey find the seas rushing to greet them. Though aware of what their approximate height was in the clouds, they have to pull up as the ocean is just seconds away. It is also likely that in a few seconds the destroyer's anti-aircraft guns will erupt at the kamikaze. Pulling out of the dive as soon as possible and regaining altitude allows the *Corsairs* to get back in the hunt safely. This enemy raider had gotten away but the hunting is good this day for the fighter pilots of the Essex.

At 1245 aboard the *Haynsworth*, "the sound of dog-fight and MG [machine gun] fire was heard and could be tracked from port bow to beam. A Judy or Zeke was then seen splashed 1500 yards on our port quarter. The sound of [machine gun] fire shifted on to starboard bow, almost overhead, and suddenly a *Judy* appeared in a very steep dive, out of the clouds, with two friendly *Corsairs*, one on each side. All pulled up sharply; the two Corsairs entered the clouds, the *Judy* flattened out short of the clouds and headed away from the ship, the ship's speed was increased to twenty-five knots and ship swung left to bring guns to bear."

The destroyer captains were of either one of two schools of thought when faced with kamikazes: Turn the bow towards the plane and maneuver radically at high speed or turn the ship perpendicular to the plane's path (crossing the 'T'), maintain a steady speed, and bring as many guns to bear on the raider as possible. Tackney was of the latter group of captains, a "go slow and shoot at them" tactician. A full broadside fusillade could include six 20mm guns, six 40mm guns, and all six 5" guns, all this firepower being hurled from an area not much longer than a football field.

"Her three twin 5-inch mounts were well aligned, her 40mm and 20mm crews well trained, her CIC and air controller crew with many hours of fighter direction under their belts. They all swung into combat like the professionals they were." The Executive Officer continued, "Finally, all the raid[s] save one aircraft were downed. The last dogfight brought a Japanese kamikaze out of the low overcast directly ahead of the ship just a few hundred yards away, trailed by two of our *Corsairs* on his tail. They pulled up sharply, just feet above the sea, and climbed back towards the overcast. In the overcast, the Jap winged over and threw the *Corsairs* off, reappearing plainly on our bow, clearly to make a kamikaze attack on us."

In March, while off Japan, some of the guns opened up against a 'bogey.' The crew was reminded by Lt. Cdr. Lothrop that, "some confusion has been caused by the indiscriminate use of the word 'bogey.' 'Bogey' is a code word to mean unidentified aircraft...It may be enemy. When definitely identified as enemy, the 'bogey' is classified as a 'bandit.' Thus there is a about a 30-70% chance a bogey may be friendly, Visual recognition is the only positive check."

Friendly fire had taken down numerous Navy and Marine planes as nervous gunners opened up against threats real and imagined. When a destroyer shot down his distinctly shaped gull winged *Corsair*, Maj. 'Trigger' Long of VMF-451 was so incensed, he ordered the ship's captain to have a *Corsair* image painted on all gun mounts aboard. Outranked, the young captain complied with the senior marine's order.

Eyes of all those topside strained skyward as the sounds of battle raged overhead. "We were ordered to hold fire with our two fighter planes in the air," recalled Bill Vassey. One of the ship's crew who had saved downed pilots, the eighteen year old South Carolina native stood by as ordered, a 40mm clip of shells in his hand ready to drop in the gun.

Stationed in their starboard quad 40mm fire director are Tom Scott and Weldon Powell. In their battlement they are, "on station to operate the fire control mechanism that pointed the 40mm gun. There were no impediments to our seeing to starboard. It was a low ceiling; we heard the planes above us as if they were having a dogfight—Zoom! Zoom! Zoom! Then 'the' plane came out of the clouds heading away. We were on picket so not close to other ships as potential targets. He still had his bomb so I assume his mission had been thwarted. I did see the Japanese plane drop its bomb as it flew away from us before reversing course. The impact of that did not register until later. I think he was thinking more of speed. Then he saw us."

Lt. Berk orders the lee helmsman to "signal all engines ahead flank-speed-emergency, make turns for thirty knots." As the Engine Order

Telegraph's handles are thrown forward, back, and forward again, bells begin to ring urgently in the fire and engine rooms. As the sound of the guns begins, the pressing need for increased speed is felt below as the boilermen begin pulling out burners and changing nozzles while valves were further opened to increase fuel pressure. The sailors of the top watch shift from the cruising turbines to the Main Ahead Turbines while the throttlemen simultaneously open fully the main feed water valves. As more feed water is being sent to the boilers, electrician mates on watch in the Engine Rooms light off the idle turbo-generator as means to split the electrical load between the two generators. The whine of the second turbine adds to the cacophony of bells, alarms and gunfire. The adrenaline levels of the bluejackets in the lower platforms increase correspondingly. On the bridge, the engine room pointers acknowledge the response for increased speed on the pilothouse's Bendix engine order telegraph. Even in the bowels of the ship, the recoil of the 20mm guns can be felt as the ship leans in its turns. The black gang instinctively knows the enemy is close, too close.

Crammed in the gun director compartment above the bridge, Lt. Dennett is ready to unleash the cannonade: "Main battery and starboard 20mm and 40mm fire was commenced. The Judy immediately turned to starboard, winging over in a sharp turn into the ship releasing or having his bomb knocked off as he did so."

"Our five inch opened up. It was a difficult traverse shot, and our bursts were behind. Finally as he turned towards us, one of our bursts blew his exterior bomb loose into the sea," according to the Executive Officer. The Pacific absorbs the bomb, most likely saving dozens of souls on Cdr. Tackney's ship.

"Main battery shifting from port to starboard, following the sound track while starboard 20mm and 40mm fire was commenced while the Judy was 1500 yards distant at an altitude of 150ft." Though the first rounds are in the ballpark, the kamikaze continues its hunt for the destroyer. On the bridge, stands Captain's Talker Harold Bly: "Above us was shooting, shooting, shooting. As our guns opened up, it felt like the whole damn thing was gonna come down on us."

The attacker holds the advantage at a low altitude, the enemy plane responding to its controls faster than the Federal Shipyard's warship. Lt. Berk orders his helmsman, "Shift your rudder." The ship begins its swing as it changes from left full to right full rudder. A sailor down in the after steering compartment sees the change in the rudder angle indicator on a repeater. He stands by as a precaution should the bridge be destroyed during the attack and he is ordered to take steering control. The redundancy of the controls is more than a caution. To a kamikaze, the deck below the bridge is the bullseye.

"As the *Judy* turned right, the left swing was checked and the ship swung right to keep all guns bearing. The bomb fell harmlessly into the water about 1000 yards abeam." Cdr. Tackney continued, the "*Judy* continued banking turn apparently intent on pulling up into bridge structure." Though the bomb was intended to pierce the destroyer's superstructure, the pilot may have dropped the ordnance as a defensive measure. Unsure if the two *Corsairs* and their twelve guns were still on his tail, the rising geyser would force the marine aviators to change their direction lest they fly through the wall of water rising from the Pacific. Other *Judy* pilots had been reported using this tactic to shake pursuers on their tails.

Oscar Jefferson Callahan S1c positioned in the makeshift crow's nest and other lookouts above decks, spot three or four Corsairs low and some distance beyond the bandit. The Judy is flying over 300 knots while just 100 feet above the seas. The fusillade from Commander Tackney's gunners are hitting their mark: "The 40s and the 20s tore into him, but he came on in relentlessly."

"The Captain has turned the ship very quickly and had saved the bridge from being hit square on," testified Ralph Aakhus. The aluminum skinned enemy attacker, looked "like a ball of fire."

On the bridge's wings, Bill Morton is serving as a phone talker. The attack is surreal. Time slows as Morton is hypnotized by the kamikaze targeting the ship's superstructure. "The spinner on the prop kept getting larger and larger." At the last moment, Morton steps around the edge of the pilot house, "accepting the fact I was about to die. I wasn't scared. Just resigned to what seemed to be inevitable."

While the Yokosuka D4Y has become a funeral pyre for the pilot, he is intent on completing his mission. His focus is on the superstructure, the heart of the destroyer. Needing just seconds to fulfill the duty his empire has asked of him, he hugs the sea for defense, just feet above the waves until pulling up at the last moment. The anathema does not waste effort pressing the button to fire his machine guns. His steed is moving at top speed.

"We couldn't stop him."

CATACLYSM. An apocalyptic scene manifests as the raider steers his plane into the tin can. A fireball rises above the massacre. Black smoke envelopes the destroyer's superstructure. The Executive Officer Lothrop reports, "He came on in, crashing abaft the bridge into one our 40mm mounts, destroying our Main Radio compartment with part of the plane coming into CIC, my battle station."

"The motor went through the side of the ship cutting a six foot square hole and ended up in the galley. The rest of the plane came across the deck and exploded," witnessed Ralph Aakhus RdM3c. Topside with headgear and telephones to the gunners, Aakhus' battle station is to the right and behind the starboard 40mm gun mount.

Signalman John Vasquez is nearby. As the plane approaches, Aakhus dives behind the bulkhead but Vasquez cannot find cover. The starboard twin 40mm gunners are hit while fire and shrapnel explode over the exposed decks.

The fireball created by the plane's high octane gasoline settles on top of the aft part of the bridge. Both 40mm mounts, port and starboard, are engulfed in flame. Near the burning signal flag box on the port side, radarman Ralph Aakhus finds signalman John Vasquez bleeding from his head, choking and collapsed on the deck. Aakhus picks up his wounded friend to aid his breathing. Bill Morton comes across Vasquez, too. "A piece of metal from the plane continued on to strike John Vasquez, completely taking out one fourth of his skull leaving his brain exposed." Vasquez requests Bill Morton prop him up against the bulkhead to help his breathing. "Aakhus was cradling him in his arms and I was talking to him to keep him from knowing how bad his injury was. He wanted us to keep him sitting up as when he lay down he said he couldn't breathe. It was difficult to keep him from feeling his head with his hand."

With the bandit targeting the superstructure, Seaman First Class Frank Lembo makes a snap decision that saves his life. As he turns to the ladder that descends from the starboard 40mm mount to the deck below, he finds another sailor, Hobart MacLaughlan S1c, is already at the top of the staircase. The twenty-six year old Paterson, New Jersey native instead runs in the opposite direction towards the port 40mm mount. Though the descending ball of flame engulfs Lembo, his sweater and wool cap prevent more serious burns. He escapes with burns to his hands and head. The fire robs Lembo of his vision. MacLaughlan, who reached the ladder, is not so lucky. The Maine native perishes instantly in the destruction.

The sound of the gunfire from both the planes above and the angry staccato firing of the *Haynsworth's* guns in response reverberates throughout the ship. Archie McGee EM2c sends Jack Vaessen EM1c topside from the forward engine switchboard. Having survived the onslaught of Japanese planes attacking his ship at Pearl Harbor,

Left: Frank Lembo S1c. (Courtesy Francine Lembo)
Right: Jack Vaessen EM1c.

Vaessen heads up. His concern for his buddies topside on duty over-rides his respect for the orders to have all hatches closed as part of Condition I General Quarters. As he enters the passage way between the engine room and the top deck, the dive bomber impacts the *Haynsworth*. The resulting blast is deafening. The pressure wave from the ignition of the aviation fuel causes Vaessen to lose the hearing in his right ear. Stunned momentarily by the injury, Vaessen hurries back to his watch station, the engine room's main switchboard. Finding no paper, he writes the time of the attack on the switchboard itself. Like during the attack at Pearl Harbor, the Navy Cross recipient puts the ship's safety above his own as he checks the electrical switches to see which are still in operation and where repairs will have to be made. The impact of the plane has caused lights to be lost in some compart-ments while all radio, sonar, and radar capabilities are obliterated for the destroyer.

Ignited aviation fuel has become the dragon's breath, both envelop-ing the starboard side and exhaled into the vents: "Tremendous gaso-line fireball flashed instantly, searing through the Main Radio, across the 40mm gun platform, igniting the flag bags and pyrotechnic lockers, gutting the transmitter room and Radio Central sending a fireball through the CIC and into the plot and starting roaring persistent fires in Main Radio, Radio, and Radar Transmitter Room as well as lesser fires on 40mm platforms, after end of bridge, and in the galley. Com-plete destruction of radio equipment is apparent."

Chuck Lechner S1c, loader on the boat deck 40mm gun, cradles his friend Bob Matschat, 40mm first loader, as he lies mortally wounded

Engine Switchboard.
(Courtesy of Navsource)

along his position at the bridge starboard 40mm gun. "Bob had just gone up for duty when the Jap suicide plane came for us. We were ordered on deck and then it hit. Bob got out of his turret and walked around and called to his friend 'see what they did to my eyes.' He became dizzy and fell. He was carried below and later transferred for further treatment."

The stench of burning flesh, the sweet odor of high octane aviation fuel, the acrid smell of the black smoke replaces the familiar smells of the 40mm gun mount of lubricating oils, spent powder and sweat. Five of the seven crew members of the starboard 40mm gun nearest the bridge die as a result of the impact and subsequent damage inflicted by the Japanese plane. Fireman A. C. Pickens will never again hear the voice of the sailor who just thirty minutes before had needled him for taking the last piece of pie.

Sharing a common bulkhead with Radio Central, the Combat Information Center is impacted by the raider. A fireball trailing acrid smoke bursts through an air vent. The red lights normally lighting the compartment fail. Through the smoke, desperate hands search for battle lanterns. The fireball's tentacles wrap around several of the sailors and officers in the CIC. Mariano Saia, an easy going and popular plank owner, is burned across his face and hands. Though his wounds are not fatal, the New York native will need more medical care than can be provided by the destroyer's medical department.

*Top row (left to right): Hobart MacLaughlan S1c (Courtesy of Hobart
MacLaughlan); Joseph P. Lenihan S1c (Courtesy of John Murphy); John
Francis Knott S1c (Courtesy of Judy Knott)*

*Middle row (left to right): Lonnie L. Aulbert S2c (Courtesy of Rodney
Aulbert); William Kubena S1c (Courtesy of Louis Kubena); Robert Daniel
Matschat S1c (Courtesy of Matschat family).*

*Bottom row (left to right): Ernest Satterly S1c (Courtesy of Satterly family);
John Vasquez SM3c (Courtesy of John Vasquez).*

Left to right:
Arthur Kidd S1c,
Paul Layden RT1c,
Donald Ward RM3c
(McAllister Family
Collection)

Airborne, radarman Don Karos crashes head first into another bulkhead. Stunned, he finds himself on the deck of the CIC struggling to see in the now darkened and smoke filled compartment. Like his injury in January while refueling during a typhoon, Karos is again struck across the face. Warm blood drips from the wounds on his forehead into his eyes. Despite the injuries, Karos is able to extricate himself from the shambles by feeling his way to the compartment's hatchway. He'll be awarded the Purple Heart medal later for his injuries.

Both Radio Transmitter Mates, Paul Layden RT1c and Claude Reeder RT1c, suddenly are battling both fire and smoke. Though wounded, both men escape the compartment with burns to the face and hands along with the many radarmen, fighter director officers, and the Executive Officer. The CIC, the nerve center of the warship, is now a broken, burning compartment.

Months of training and drilling, rehearsals for disaster start the victims in motion. This is a time of action rather than contemplation. "Standing in my CIC spot at the Air Plot table, where as Executive Officer my job was to keep the Captain on the bridge informed of the overall picture, the fireball rushed at me from the starboard bulkhead. It blew me and others through the port joiner door into the passageway outside. From there we picked ourselves up, beat out the flames from our clothing and set about doing what had to be done to save the ship. Afraid, then? Curiously, no. Not then. Too much to do."

Having abandoned the CIC, the Executive Officer rushes to open the hatch to Radio Central. The door is hot to the touch. As he crosses its threshold, Lt. Cdr. Lothrop is greeted by an inferno of burning men and material. All six radiomen are alive but on fire. One is tangled in the wires, tethered and trapped. The rescue begins immediately as the wounded radiomen are evacuated from the choking, blinding smoke and fire. Lothrop will be awarded the Purple Heart, "for tearing

*Left: Milton Studley RdM3c with his son on leave.
(Courtesy of Milton Studley)
Right: Donald Karos RdM3c. (Courtesy of Cory Nokelby)*

off burning clothing from sailors on fire, and receiving, himself, burns on his own hands."

Charged with the safety of the ship and his crew, Cdr. Tackney calls for Stop Engines and orders the *Haynsworth* swung out of the wind to determine the extent of damage. Smoke engulfs the pilothouse while the deck underneath the Captain's feet begins to warm from the fire burning in the compartments below. Thousands of pounds of explosives are to be found in the ship's magazines, torpedoes and dozens of depth charges staged on the sea deck. It is imperative for the survival of the *Haynsworth* that the fire be contained before consuming these weapons. Every second that the acrid black cloud rises from the destroyer, the longer it serves as a beacon to the kettle of Japanese vultures that thrive on the wounded steel skinned ships of the 5th Fleet.

The forward engine room cuts power to radio and radar rooms as ordered. Commander Tackney vacates the pilothouse to investigate aft end of bridge as explosions are heard. As he crisscrosses the navigation bridge deckways, several sailors jump into the seas to rescue Lonnie Aulbert. Burned and wounded, Aulbert struggles to survive in the Pacific.

Adrenaline. It is the hormone that creates heroes. Doctor Ley could have explained when a man is facing his own mortality, a syndrome known as 'fight or flight' takes over. The brain singularly focuses on the action needed for survival. The neurologic messages to the mesentery are shut down. Blood is pulled away from the digestive organs and pumped to the muscles. Pain is ignored because it is not felt.

PHALANX AGAINST THE DIVINE WIND

George Morrisey RdM3c and Mariano Saia RdM3c.
(Courtesy of Loren Morrissey)

Some 40mm rounds are cooking off as are rounds from the kamikaze's machine guns. Despite the fact there are dozens of four shell 40mm clips covered in gasoline and fire, very few detonate. But, from the port side, one of the signalmen instinctively reacts to the fire around the gun emplacement. Oblivious to his own personal safely, he climbs into the charred 40mm mount and begins to throw loaded 40mm clips over the side of the ship. When asked about it later, he has no recollection of his actions.

Fire rages near the forward quintuple torpedo mount. Each of the five torpedoes contains 800 lbs. of TNT. Yards away are Tom Scott and Gus Weldon still at general quarters in the 40mm fire control station. "I was wondering if the fire could impact the torpedoes," recalled Scott. Just having one torpedo blow up could magnify the devastation.

Below the #41 mount, Harold Dempsey TM1c and Clifford Heob S1c are in harm's way in the 40mm ammunition clipping room: "The Jap plane cleared our ship and making a short left turn came in our starboard beam, crashing into the Radio...The impact was terrific, destroying all our Radio [and] Radar equipment, one 40mm gun, its mount and crew." With the roar of the Judy's engine getting closer,

Clifford Heob S1c.
(Courtesy of Kim Seibert)

the guns surrounding their battle station suddenly firing furiously, the clipping room shaking and vibrating, and with a warning arriving over the telephone is received by Heob about the track of the Japanese plane, the men try to escape their tomb. "Neither Cliff nor Harold knew what had happened until they opened the door to face boiling smoke and leaping flames. I believe it was that complete selflessness of Clifford's that caused him to fumble with the earphones just the second it took to give Harold his chance to leap out. Hands over his face, he ducked under the torpedo tubes, and dashing through flames, reached safety, receiving face and hand burns. I believe Clifford would have made it, too, but the dense smoke blinded him causing him to stumble over the phone wires at his feet and pitch head first from the upper deck, through the flames to the main deck, breaking his neck and dying instantly."

For Bill Morton crouching near the pilothouse, time went into slow motion as the kamikaze "hit low on the #41 mount on the starboard side and low enough his engine plowed into the radio room. One man [Lonnie Lee Aulbert S2c] was blown out of the 40mm tub and survived. When I found I had not been killed I picked myself off the deck to survey the damage. I looked over to the flying bridge and it seemed there was fire everywhere. I walked back to the signal bridge and I happened to look into the 'flag bag' and staring up at me was the severed head of Ernie Satterly, a signalman striker."

While the radio room has absorbed the impact of the engine, the starboard twin 40mm mount is impacted by the left wing of the dive bomber. Lonnie Lee Aulbert S2c is struck and knocked overboard. Aulbert surfaces in a pool of burning fuel and oil. Fire has burned off his ears and caused severe burns by the time he brought back aboard. The bandit's plane has crushed his left side, shattered his left femur,

Oscar Jefferson Callahan S1c.
(Courtesy of Dianne Callahan Jones)

and taken a finger from his right hand. Aulbert is one of the most seriously wounded patients that Doctor Ley must attempt to save. The doctor records his prognosis as "probably fatal."

Annihilation. While Aulbert is blown clear of the devastation, his shipmates on the 40mm gun do not survive the attack. Ammunition passer Joseph Lenihan S1c of New York City has breathed his last breath at age seventeen. The mount captain, Gunners Mate Second Class Walter DeLoach is killed instantly along with John F. Knott S1c, the thirty year old father of two sons. The Thurmont, Maryland native has been in the Navy just thirteen months. William Kubena S1c suffers the same fate as DeLoach and Lenihan: the carnage makes survival impossible for the nineteen year old native of Pennsylvania. He leaves behind his parents, six brothers and three sisters. Blue stars hanging in windows back home will be exchanged for gold.

Trapped in the crow's nest, lookout Oscar Jefferson Callahan S1c, stares in horror as the kamikaze turns around and returns to strike the ship forward of his post. He tries to jump clear. The phone cords tether him. He is swung back to the deck. Though Callahan escapes the fiery reach of the burning aviation gas cloud, the twenty-three year Georgia native is struck across the face by debris. His back and face injured, Callahan scrambles across the signal deck through choking black smoke and fire to escape.

Down in the plotting room which holds all interior shipboard communication and public address systems, the six sailors and their chief hear the roar of the engines of the planes, the sound of the machine guns, and the return fire of their ship. The *Haynsworth* shudders from the impact. The plotting room quickly fills with smoke which comes in faster than the exhaust fans can initially remove it. After receiving permission to abandon their compartment, they flee through a hatch into the galley. After a quick headcount they realize that only six of them are gathered. Gus Scutari FC1c and the five others return to the plotting room to find Chief Robert Hall on his knees testing the various circuits for the Captains Command controls, the switchboards and the sound powered phone system. The machinery and gyrocompass in the compartment are integral for gun fire control and navigational related instrumentation. Since the ship is still at GQ, they stay in the compartment as the fans eventually clear the smoke.

Perplexed by the ship coming to a halt, A.C. Pickens stands by at his battle station, located in the ship's bowels on the third platform deck. He had been loading the fifty-four pound 5" shells onto the hoist that brings them to the #52 mount. The sound of the 20mm guns opening fire had carried all the way down the three levels of the ship to the magazine. "We knew we were in trouble when we heard the 20's open fire." In less than twenty seconds the firing of all the ship's guns are met by the sound and vibration of the collision. The guns fall silent. "There was lots of confusion below decks, people were scared to death. We were ordered to evacuate the magazine and went topside. When we came through the hatch, there was fire all around which we hadn't expected to see. We didn't know what had just happened. One guy was so scared he was shaking. He couldn't connect the fire hose to the nozzle so I grabbed the hose from him and connected it in a single spin." With fire enveloping the superstructure, the crew from the magazine was stranded on the forward part of the ship.

The *Battle, Watch, and Routine Bill* for the *Haynsworth* specifies that the three pharmacist mates will move to separate areas in the ship so that no single attack can exterminate the destroyer's Medical Department. As battle station alarms are sounded, Pharmacist Mate Second Class James Jones, Jr., attempts to exit from a compartment in the superstructure to his battle station in the Officer's Ward Room. The shockwave and ensuing rocking of the *Haynsworth* sends Jones flying backwards. A table stops his momentum but fractures several of his vertebrae. Staggering and injured, Jones is out of the fight. Refusing Dr. Ley's offer of morphine for his wounds, the twenty-one year old stays with the doctor. "In spite of his injury, he carried on his responsibilities assisting me in the wardroom-operating room as we cared for the several badly burned and otherwise wounded shipmates," recalled Dr. Ley. Jones will be awarded the Purple Heart for his wounds but the accommodation will not prevent a lifetime of nightmares generated by the sights of the burned and dying sailors

Left: James Kenneth Jones, Jr. PhM2c.
(Courtesy of 1SG Lynne Jones, U.S. Army Ret.)
Right: Lt. Allyn Ley, MD. (With permission of the Archives & Special
Collections, Columbia University Health Sciences Library)

Task Group 58.1 1257

The destroyer picket line from 58.1 has been tracking a group of bogies since 1208. By 1257 the group has closed the distance to the USS *Sigsbee*, USS *Dashiell*, and the USS *Harrison* from fifteen to just eight miles. A pair of *Corsairs* from the Tiger CAP takes up the pursuit while the destroyers commence emergency turns. The CAP picks off a *Judy* dive bomber but a group of three *Zekes* turn towards the destroyers of the picket line. In succession, 5," 40mm, and 20mm batteries open up against the attackers. The hurricane of ordnance takes down one plane as it crashes close aboard the *Harrison*. "The second plane hit the water several hundred yards out, bounced into the air again, and crashed about twenty five yards off the beam of the ship." The *Dashiell's* guns find their mark and bring down the last bandit. All three destroyers survive the attack without casualties though a gun turret on the *Harrison* is hit by shrapnel.

USS *Haynsworth*

Preparation and rapid response: Though the ship is still at General Quarters, battling the conflagration across the superstructure is the first priority for the damage control parties. Providing first aid assistance to the casualties, if possible, is their next mission. Isolated from the task group, the focus of the gunners did not change. "We knew something had happened but we were too busy tracking planes in our vicinity," recalled Gunners Mate Phil Goldstein who was at his position within the aft 5" mount. "It wasn't until the ship started slowing and then stopped that we wondered exactly what had happened. Even then, we still had a job to do. There was a lot of happening above us in the skies."

Since the *Haynsworth*'s first cruise the summer before, her damage control parties have drilled regularly to respond to catastrophes. Her sailors were trained at boot camp to rid themselves of the fear of fire. Immediately after the divebomber impacts the side of the superstructure, damage control responds to the call. The fire is fought from two directions: Hoses are led aft from forward of CIC; from the opposite direction, hoses are led forward from aft of Radio Central. "The fire was of such intensity it was impossible reach [the] magazine sprinkling system to 40mm Ordnance Ready Service room B-0103M so a hose was played on the after bulkhead of this magazine for cooling. Additional hoses were led up to the bridge from forward, later from aft to combat fire on signal bridge and 40mm platform and to keep magazines cool from topside while water was sprayed on the port 40mm magazine."

Heroic efforts continue. His hands already burned from beating out the fire on his clothes and those of the radiomen, Lt. Cdr. Lothrop leads a damage control party from aft into the flaming area in Radio Central. Entry was made "by means of fog from all purpose nozzles. Thereafter, fire was fought by combination of solid stream and fog, solid stream being played on burnable materials other than electrical equipment and fog to act both as protection for men on the hoses and to cool down working area. Carbon dioxide was used extensively on electrical equipment, but flames in electrical equipment finally had to be beaten down with solid streams of salt water. Additional hoses had now been led to wrecked area from starboard 20mm platform and played into transmitter room and on wreckage on main deck."

Thick choking smoke in radio central confronts the firefighters. The conflagration necessitates the use of asbestos suits and Rescue Breathing Apparatus (RBA). The suits, used for fighting fires within the ship's compartments, are not only heavy and cumbersome but also conduct heat to the wearer. The RBAs fog up "so rapidly as only to be a hindrance to the firefighters. The black billowing smoke could only be penetrated by wet-cell floodlights and the heat produced by the conflagration so intense that firefighters had to be relieved after just 90 seconds."

Sailors respond to damage caused by the kamikaze.
Note the sailor at top wearing a Rescue Breathing Apparatus.
(Courtesy of USS Haynsworth Association)

Ralph Aakhus noted that "The Lieutenant Commander [Lothrop] was right in there fighting fire but there were some ensigns on the fantail waiting to jump in the water if the ship went down."

The forward fireroom is secured and temporarily abandoned due to the infiltration of the smoke. The galley, near the end of the fireball's deadly path, is brought under control with the use of just one hose. Impaled through both sides of one of the galley's large kettles is a machine gun from the attacking plane. A moment earlier one of the cooks, Walter Adolph Kania SC2c, had been stirring soup in the cauldron. The twenty-four year old Ohio native has been in the navy nearly five years. A year earlier, Kania had escaped injury during an air attack against his previous ship, the USS *Plunkett* DD-431. Off Anzio, German planes bombed the destroyer, killing fifty-three officers and sailors. Today, though the next meal is lost, Kania escapes with just wounds to his right arm.

Due to the large amounts of water being sprayed topside on the fires, it is imperative to remove the accumulating water. The extra topside weight decreases the stability of the already top heavy *Sumner* class destroyer. Damage control team members set up three portside

Enemy machine gun recovered from the galley. (NARA photo)

submersible pumps to remove water from the compartments. Damage control parties also set up two handy-billys. The portable pumps not only drain the accumulating water but are put it to use creating foam to fight the fires.

The combined efforts of the damage control teams bring the main fire under control in ten minutes but it takes an additional fifty-five minutes for complete extinguishment. Commander Tackney orders the *Haynsworth* to be swung slowly through the wind back and forth to allow repair parties the opportunity to attack the fire from all directions as well as allow the terrific smoke to clear from alternating sides. "An hour later we had the fires under control." Upon reflection, Lothrop thought, "it seemed almost as if he carried napalm somewhere in the aircraft, the fire was so difficult to overcome."

Amidst the carnage, emerges the wounded. Captivated by the sight of the kamikaze hurtling towards the destroyer, a sailor running along the deck had passed underneath the 5" guns as they erupted. Concussed from the blast, he staggers along the deck, bleeding from the eyes, ears, nose, and mouth. Torpedoman Ed Kelly is confused by the wet toilet

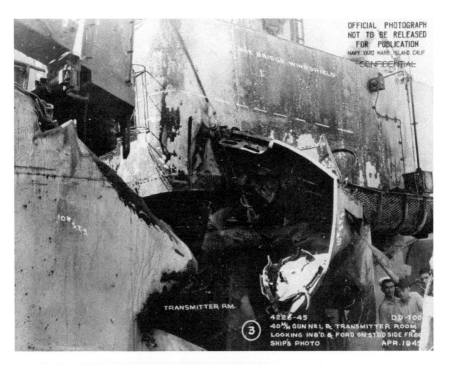

Damage from the kamikaze attack (National Archives Photos)

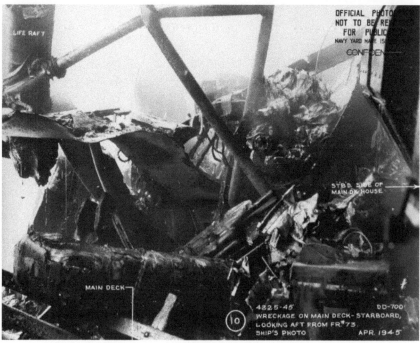

Damage from the kamikaze attack (National Archives Photos)

paper hanging off another sailor passing him. Repulsed, he realizes it is skin. The victims "had burns so bad, their flesh had an appearance similar to a cooked turkey."

Heroic deeds are performed by sailors who would be uncomfortable wearing that label. Louie Clark, Storekeeper 2nd Class recalled years later, "Our ship lay dead in the water and was on fire from mid-ship forward. The Japanese pilot was killed and thrown on the deck. Part of the plane that dived onto the bridge went on down to the galley. Everything on the bridge was gone including our flag. Even though we were on fire, these two un-remembered shipmates climbed up there and tied the remains of our flag with a small piece of line. They let the enemy know that our flag was still there. Did they receive medals for this historic act? To my knowledge, no."

Damage reports are brought to Captain Tackney:

> *The following material casualties were suffered as a result of the crash: Frames 65-88 main deck, deck house, and all surrounding areas scorched by fire. Radio transmitter room completely ruptured, and main radio outboard bulkhead buckled and ruptured. CIC heavily scorched by fire; All radio equipment, insulation, ducting, and electrical leads completely destroyed. Mount #41 destroyed - platform insides warped, buckled, ruptured, and heavily scorched. All radar equipment heavily damaged due to fire and fragmentation, area around the after part of the bridge damaged. No. 1 stack scorched. Galley scorched and various galley equipment rendered inoperative. Flag bags and all signal flags destroyed.*

The attack was brusque. The crew of the Haynsworth had but a few seconds to defend herself. Her gun crews expended 25 rounds 5"/38, 156 rounds 40mm, 240 rounds of 20mm; all six 5" guns fired, six of the 40mm, and five of the 20mm machine guns. The whole time period elapsed was twenty seconds: five seconds to time track first shots, ten seconds to first hits by 40mm, twenty seconds from first shot to last.

Second and third degree burns. Fractures. Smoke inhalation. The ship's doctor and pharmacist mates are overwhelmed with dozens of severely wounded and dying sailors. The sickbay is not nearly large enough to treat the wounded so the Wardroom is used as a Forward

Battle Dressing station. With the larger space, tables to support medical litters (stretchers), medical supplies, operating room lights and a folding surgical table, the wardroom quickly becomes the focal point of care on the *Haynsworth*. But with fire nearby and just a single emergency light trying to pierce the dark, battle lanterns are employed in the compartment. Overflow patients are treated in the ship's mess. Saving the greatest numbers of sailor's lives with the meager medical facilities of a tin can requires Lt. Ley and pharmacist mates Kessler and Bland triage the wounded. The triaging determines who will receive the highest priority for treatment. Pharmacist's mate James Jones tries to assist but he is also a victim, his vertebrae fractured.

His brain exposed, Signalman John Vasquez's head lays opened by a piece of shrapnel. Ley sprinkles sulfa powder after wiping cerebrospinal fluid and blood from the traumatic wound. After wrapping the signalman's head with dressings, the doctor annotates on Vasquez's medical card, "expectant." Ley's medical opinion is that Vasquez's death will be imminent. Ley doesn't have time to hold hands. He moves on to the next wounded bluejacket.

For the severely burned sailors, fluids and pain relief are critical. Intravenous solutions and plasma are initiated while morphine is injected to ease the excruciating burns. The radiomen have the most severe burns. When the kamikaze's plane punctured the sealed Radio Transmitter room, the pressure burst the hatchway into the Central Radio compartment. The implosion forced a dramatic change in pressure. Muscle tissue was forced against muscle tissue in the vital organs. The hollow spaces where fluids are normally found were violently compressed. Spleens and bladders are ruptured, the stomach and bowels injured. The lungs, like sponges, are rapidly deflated. The next breath draws in super-heated air tinged with fire and gasoline causing searing burns to the nose, larynx, and lungs. The rubber gaskets around the hatches burn as acidic smoke is released. After three or four breaths, the radiomen, Goyer, Holiman, Dyer, and Chief Campbell have sustained life threatening burns to their pulmonary system. Holcombe and Davis, slightly protected by their positions in the compartment but like the others, have sustained fragmentation wounds. All have suffered severe burns.

With the small medical department overwhelmed by the scores of casualties, Frank Lembo is brought for treatment, burned and unable to see. His gear spared his body from burns but his eyes, face, and hands are not as lucky. Ley bandages the wounds, praying silently that his patient will regain his sight.

With the fires extinguished and the destroyer underway to rejoin the task group, the Executive Officer calls for a muster on station. Petty officers submit their reports to the Chief Petty Officer. In the blink of an eye, the kamikaze has killed seven blue jackets. Another two dozen are wounded. Many of the burned are in need of medical care greater than the capabilities of Lt. Ley's medical department. Ley fully expects seven more of his patients to have limited time left on the earth. Lothrop scans the report before he submits it to Cdr. Tackney. The printed words are staggering and serve to punctuate the exhaustion of the twenty-five year old executive officer and the warrior captain.

Jack Vaessen EM1c, the hero at Pearl Harbor, decides against seeking medical attention for the deafness in his right ear. The decision costs him part of his hearing for the rest of his life. When Vaessen finally emerges from the engine room to the deck, victims of the attack are being stacked on the deck. The corpse of the raiding pilot lies nearby.

Down in the emergency radio shack, radio communication goes dead. Keith Myreholt RM3c vacates his station to investigate. As he moves forward, he discovers that the antennas on the mast have been severed. Flames billow from radio compartments. What the fire hasn't destroyed in the radio shack, salt water from the fire hoses has.

Myreholt moves back down the deck house passageway to Emergency Radio. His progress is blocked by officers rushing to the backup radio shack. As each one enters the area, Myreholt takes a step back deferring to rank. When the officers begin to ask where the radioman is, Myreholt leans forward and calls from the end of the passageway, "down here, sir."

Isaac Peres RM2c emerges from his battle station in the portside #42 40mm ammunition clipping room. With complete destruction to the radio rooms, it is essential that communication be regained with the task group. As it stands, the column of black smoke rising from the mute vessel serves as a beacon for other attackers. Peres moves through the deck house to the Emergency Radio compartment.

Perez explained, "It was the duty of a radio shack member to immediately go to the emergency radio shack and take over the duties of the regular radio shack. Which is what I did when I learned the radio shack was hit. I immediately contacted the bridge and gave them instructions about getting back to the fleet." Located on the portside sea deck outward of the aft smoke stack, the backup radio "shack" is a much smaller version of the radio transmitter and radio central rooms

Left: Joseph Wilkerson RM3c. (Courtesy Mariana Steele)
Right: Don Ward RM3c.

that were destroyed by kamikaze. Equipped with radio transmitters and receivers plus generators to provide power, the cramped compartment has the bare necessities needed for a skeleton crew to send and receive signals. With the majority of the *Haynsworth's* radiomen killed or wounded, it is up to Myreholt and Peres to relay messages back and forth to the bridge using sound powered phones while Bly and Wilkerson remain on duty in the pilothouse.

Task Force 58 1330

Destroyer Screen Commander John Higgins designates the *Waldron* to relieve the blind *Haynsworth* at #1 picket station. At the same time Rear Admiral 'Jocko' Clark's Task Group 58.1 is under aerial pressure. After shooting down two enemy planes in two minutes, the USS *San Jacinto* CVL-30 is in the sights of a third bandit. With one wheel down as though it were an American plane about to land, the plane is spotted by lookouts while it is still 4000 yards away. A lead wall is sent airborne by the carrier as sixteen 40mm and eleven 20mm guns bring the enemy into their gunsights. Forty seconds of firing find their mark as plane hits the water just ahead of the light carrier. The collision with the seas detonates the bomb aboard. The pilot, in pieces, is blown over the bow of the ship.

USS *Haynsworth* 1340

Blind. Hustling at 28 knots to rejoin Task Group 58.3, the *Haynsworth* relies on other ships to provide directional coaching since

PHALANX AGAINST THE DIVINE WIND

Left: Keith Myreholt RM3c. (Courtesy of Karen Shinn)
Center: Isaac Peres RM2c. (Courtesy of Isaac Peres);
Right: Emergency Radio Shack (Courtesy of Navsource)

her radar is out. Though wounded, her propulsion systems remain intact. But, in the battles of 1945, it is the coordinated radio-radar-fire control systems with the CAP overhead that protect the ships. The *Haynsworth* now has none of these capabilities. Its guns now must be manually operated since the radar fire control system has been taken out. The signal flags have been consumed by the fire. "It had taken us an hour to control the fires. By then the whole forward superstructure, Main Radio, CIC, radars, firecontrol director tower were a burnt-out shambles. We had limped back to the task force destroyer screen. About the most we were good for there was use as a rescue destroyer."

At 1412, the *H*aynsworth takes position 2000 yards outboard of the USS *Washington* BB-56, thus re-entering the protection of the phalanx. Her aerial flanks are covered by the partner destroyers in the outer screen and the cruisers and battleships in the inner screen. The CAP hunts above the group.

Fifth Fleet Surrounding Okinawa

Less than two and half hours after striking the *Haynsworth*, kamikazes return to target the destroyers. The USS *Bush* DD-529, serving on the radar picket line at Radar Picket No.1, is bracketed by a torpedo bomber. Despite intense and accurate fire, the kamikaze hurtles towards the tin can at sea level. It finds it mark between the two smokestacks. A terrific explosion from the bomb decimates the destroyer amidships, causes flooding, and destroys the deckhouse. The

USS Rodman.
(NARA 80-G photo)

ship loses its ability to use its sets of quad 40mm guns as well as three 5" guns. She is floating but at risk of breaking into two pieces.

Two minutes later at 1515 a destroyer minesweeper group off northern Okinawa finds itself in the bullseye when a swarm of bandits appears overhead. "Total of about 35 enemy planes, mostly *Vals*, attacked during the afternoon. About 12-15 expended themselves on or near *Rodman* and *Emmons*." One crashes into the forecastle of the USS *Rodman* DMS-21. With the aid of the USS *Emmons* DMS-22, the USS *Ransom* AM-283, and the CAP now on station, numerous other enemy planes are shot down. Despite the efforts, the destroyer minesweeper *Emmons* absorbs five bomb laden kamikazes. With a loss of power and steering, her senior officers killed, a third of her crew killed or wounded, and the potential for the magazines to explode, the minesweeper is abandoned. She is later sunk by the USS *Ellyson* DMS-19. Sixty of her crew are lost with the ship and remain forever on duty.

In the maelstrom, *Ransom* is damaged. With guns unleashed, the minesweeper brings down three suiciders close aboard. "One splashing 400 yards astern, one 40 feet off the bow, another 10 feet off the port beam. The last plane's bomb caused some damage," but she escapes with just two sailors having minor wounds. *Ransom* recovers fifty-two survivors from *Rodman* and *Emmons*.

At the same time *Rodman* was under attack, the USS *Taussig* DD-746, a *Sumner* serving with Task Group 58.1, is tasked with a recovering a Japanese pilot who has bailed out of his burning plane. While the rescue is being attempted, an enemy fighter dives on the DesRon 61 destroyer. "The *Oscar* dropped one bomb which hit the water about thirty feet on the port beam giving the ship a considerable shaking up but causing no operational damage or casualties." The pilot from the former plane was plucked from the sea "from a fancy red life raft wearing silk scarf with Nip inscription 'Kamikaze Special Attack Unit 3.' Says he flew from Kikai Jima. Graduated from Kisarazu late 1944 and is a flight instructor. Now matriculating in *Hornet*," signaled Admiral Mitscher.

Japanese pilot recovery.
(NARA 80-G-317332)

At 1530, while on station at Radar Picket Position No.2, the USS *Colhoun* DD-801, is witness to the tornado of enemy planes attacking the *Bush*. While the *Colhoun* steams at emergency speed to assist, numerous CAP divisions are sent to engage the bandits. At 1635, the rescuer arrives on station as enemy planes fall from the sky. She, too, will soon fall victim to the 'floating chrysanthemums.'

Breakout: Surface Special Attack Force 1520

As hundreds of Imperial planes begin take to the air from the islands around Okinawa, the Imperial Japanese Navy orders its largest kamikaze to sea. Sortieing from Tokuyama, the battleship *Yamato* is launched in a desperate final mission. With the meager accompaniment of a light cruiser and eight destroyers, the leviathan has been ordered to fight its way to the western Okinawa Gunto before beaching itself to become a steel castle on the shore. She is to fight until she is no longer able. Her crew will disembark and join their brothers fighting the Allies ashore. *Yamato* is loaded with a full complement of ammunition but her oil bunkers are just partially full. There will be no turning back.

In concert with *Yamato*'s mission, hundreds of kamikazes will be sent to destroy Vice Admiral Mitscher's carrier force. Though nearly seven hundred Imperial Army and Navy planes will be launched to

USS Colboun (top) steaming from USS Bush, obscured by smoke. (NARA 80-G 317258)

clear the seas of the mighty American and British carriers, none are sent to cover the Surface Special Attack Force. Vice Admiral Seiichi Ito's force is the last chance for the Imperial Japanese Navy to save face in the battle of the Pacific.

Special Escort Carrier Task Unit enroute Okinawa

Vice Admiral Marc Mitscher's planes are spread thin. With swarms of Japanese planes heading towards Okinawa, Mitscher is tasked with providing planes for numerous missions. The CAP must be maintained to protect the various task groups in the waters near Okinawa. Admirals Sherman and Clark's task groups have been assigned missions against airfields north of the big island. Additional CAPS are covering the task group's radar picket lines and the 5th Fleet radar picket stations surrounding Okinawa. The soldiers and marines on the ground require air support against fortified targets on the island. Admiral Spruance has sent four CVEs loaded with marine *Corsair* squadrons from Ulithi on April 2nd. They will fly from their steel mothers' nests to roost on newly captured airfields on the island. Their presence should take the pressure off Task Force 58 but the slower CVEs require six days to make the journey. They will not arrive until April 7th.

Fifth Fleet surrounding Okinawa

In rapid succession, Admiral Spruance's ships are targeted as multiple raids begin to emerge against the fleet. At 1618 the destroyer escort

USS Witter.
(Courtesy of NavSource)

USS *Witter* DE-636 comes under attack from two intruders, one coming from port, the other starboard. Pouring on the steam, the DE's guns splashes one kamikaze but the other penetrates her hull at the water line. Six sailors are killed but the *Buckley* class destroyer escort is eventually saved.

Without warning, the USS *Robin* YMS-311 finds itself surrounded by a swarm of attacking *Val* dive bombers. Three of the assailants target *Robin*. As bluejackets rush to their battlestations when the General Quarters alarms sound, a *Val* strikes the ship at the forecastle. While one sailor is killed, the minesweeper shoots down two other bandits. The action around Le Shima is non-stop: *Robin's* crew witness twenty-six kamikazes attempting suicide dives nearby.

Less than fifteen minutes later, the next kamikaze finds its victim. Having brought a bandit under fire, the USS *LST 447* is bracketed for destruction. Trailing a long black tail of smoke, the intruder hugs the water before crashing into the landing ship just above the waterline. Its bomb passes through the thin skin of the hull to detonate inside the ship. The explosion tears the deck from most of the ship. The devastation is so great that her captain gives the order to abandon ship within ten minutes of the kamikaze strike. The Navy loses five bluejackets in the raid.

Right behind the LST 447's attacker come more raiders to the anchorages at Kerama Retto. At 1647 a kamikaze impacts one of America's miracle ships, the SS *Logan Victory*. The cargo ship is loaded with ammunition for the troops ashore. The plum target reaches skyward when her load of eighteen million pounds of ordnance begins to explode. She is abandoned. Fifteen of her crew are lost.

Throughout the afternoon, enemy planes have closed the USS *Howorth* DD-592. The first five are splashed close aboard. "The machine gun batteries were expending ammunition so rapidly that it was

LST 447 explodes. (Richard L. Hamel MoMM2c, courtesy of NavSource)

difficult to keep them supplied, although all repair parties and torpedomen are engaged in breaking it out." At 1708 the *Howorth*'s luck runs out against the sixth raider. The *Zeke* crashes into the Mark 37 gun director atop the bridge. Fires erupt but are brought under control. Her luck returns when she splashes the seventh raider. Nine of her crew will not return to America.

Expert marksmanship is a constant theme for the day. Four minutes after the *Howorth*'s attack, the USS *Hyman* DD-732 shoots down three attackers before she is finally hit. The forth plane, wounded by *Hyman*'s gunners, crashes "amidships in vicinity of torpedo tubes. A subsequent explosion of a torpedo warhead or a delayed action bomb resulted in extensive topside damage, flooding of the forward engine room and numerous personal casualties." She manages to bring down three more raiders before a fourth breaks off its attack. She loses ten of her compliment in the attack.

Eleven minutes later, the USS *Facility* AM-233 has a close brush when a *Zero* shot down close aboard continues its attack underwater. The aerial corpse strikes the ocean just ahead of the bow. As the minesweeper passes over the plane, the screw is damaged from the contact. There are no casualties except to the pilot with the rising sun sewn on his flight suit.

PHALANX AGAINST THE DIVINE WIND

USS Mullany receiving temporary repairs.
(Lt. Frank H. White photo, courtesy of the USS Mullany Association)

Soon after, a second kamikaze strikes the *Bush* at Radar Picket Station No. 1. Another follows twenty minutes later. The weakened ship begins to collapse, eventually sinking. The three Tokkotai pilots take eighty-seven of *Bush's* crew with them to the hereafter. Guardian *Colhoun* suffers similarly. Despite shooting down several attackers, she is mortally wounded by kamikazes. The destroyer is abandoned. She is later sunk by the *Cassin Young* DD-793. Thirty-five souls perish aboard the *Colhoun*.

The destroyers continue to take it on the chin. The USS *Mullany* DD-528, after fighting off several bandits, loses the battle at 1746 when a kamikaze flies into the deck house aft. Communication and steering control are lost from the explosion. As the flames grow, the tin can jettisons its torpedoes but efforts to jettison the depth charges fail. The exploding ash cans buckle and twist the steel bulkheads causing further agony to the ship. The aft magazines cannot be flooded. With the risk of the magazines exploding, the captain orders the ship abandoned but not before they open fire again on enemy planes. To both port and starboard sides, bandits meet a watery grave. Later after the fire is extinguished, the captain returns with a salvage party. Cdr. Albert Momm loses thirty of his crew to the kamikaze attack.

A kamikaze strikes the Newcomb. (NARA 80-G-322419)

South of Okinawa, the British Fleet is not immune to the long reach of the kamikazes. The carrier HMS *Illustrious* escapes major damage when a *Judy* dive bomber clips the forward end of the superstructure. Flipped into the ocean, the bandit's bomb explodes beneath the waves. The pressure causes several frames to be cracked and flooding to occur from broken plates. She will eventually be forced to retreat from the battle scene for repair.

As the sun descends on the western horizon, the USS *Newcomb* DD-586 has been fending off attackers for over ninety minutes when a Japanese intruder strikes the destroyer. Right behind it, the forth attacker of the day is shot down but the fifth attacker also strikes amidships. Dead in the water, the *Newcomb* has lost propulsion, communications, and water pressure to fight the fires. Three minutes later the sixth attacker crashes in the same area amidships as the previous two attackers. The USS *Leutze* DD-481 comes to her aid, fire hoses spraying water between the ships. A seventh attacker joins the melee with the *Newcomb* in its sights. Despite absorbing hits from 5" guns, it passes over *Newcomb* and hits *Leutze* at the fantail. The punishment *Newcomb* has absorbed is incredible: "All decking and superstructure between frames 102 and 135 missing, including two torpedo mounts, two 40mm mounts and magazines, four 20mm mounts, after stack, supply office, sick bay, emergency radio, torpedo workshop, and loading machines." She is towed to safety by fellow destroyers. *Leutze*, despite bomb damage at the waterline, is able to exit the area for the safety of the Kerama Retto anchorage to the south. *Newcomb* suffers forty killed while *Leutze* has lost seven of her crew.

PHALANX AGAINST THE DIVINE WIND

Above:
USS Newcomb.
(NARA 80-G-330105)

Left:
USS Newcomb.
(NARA 80-G-330100)

During the afternoon's melees, the USS *Hutchins* DD-476 has been fending off attacks almost continually from 1652 when she spots three *Kate* torpedo planes making a run on nearby vessels. Intense anti-aircraft fire splashes all three with the *Hutchins* getting credit for the second bandit. Attacks continue as groups of enemy planes descend on the wounded *Newcomb* and *Leutze*. As the final kamikaze strikes the *Newcomb*, friendly fire from other ships in the area kills a *Hutchins* bluejacket while wounding three others, including the destroyer division commander. The *Hutchins* stays on station to rescue survivors of the *Newcomb* attack.

The Leutze is struck. (NARA 80-G-322422)

USS Leutze. (NARA 80-G photo)

After finishing its mine sweeping mission for the day, the USS *Defense* AM-317 is taken under attack by a group of bandits at 1805. Increasing speed while maneuvering, the ship absorbs two *Val* dive bombers. Minutes later two more *Vals* come after her. She bags one kamikaze but the fourth attacker escapes. Damage is light. No blue-jackets perish but nine are wounded. *Defense* lives up to her name as she manages to rescue fifty survivors from the *Newcomb*. She concludes her efforts by towing the crippled *Leutze* back to Kerama Retto.

The USS *Devastator* AM-318 also lives up to her name. At 1738 she splashes an enemy plane but thirty-six minutes later a *Val* dive bomber in a low angle dive brackets the minesweeper. "Turned ship left quickly, unmasking and firing all port machine guns at range of about 1500 yards. Plane crash 50 yards off port quarter." Plane parts are impaled in the ship as a result of the explosion. Casualties are limited to four blue-jackets struck by shrapnel. Material casualties include the 'movie' locker, "igniting films. Burning films jettisoned. No damage from fire. Hole in engine room plugged with mattress...parts of body of pilot strewn on deck."

Three minutes later, lookouts aboard the USS *Fieberling* alert the bridge that a *Zeke* carrying two bombs has sets it sights on her. The destroyer escort counters with evasive maneuvers and fire from its 20mm guns. The guns hit home as rounds impact the plane. In a last ditch effort to make something of its attack, the pilot releases his bombs which narrowly miss the after director. "He then winged over sharp right, broad on our starboard quarter and struck upside down on the SA radar antenna, cutting through his right wing, spinning and splashing forty yards on our port bow." By using its close in weapons and its ability to turn tightly, the warship escapes harm. The only casualty in the attack is a citizen of the Empire.

USS *Haynsworth* 1805

While the *Fieberling* is fending off its attacker, the *Haynsworth* comes alongside the starboard side of the battleship *South Dakota*. Within the protective screen of the phalanx, the damaged *Haynsworth* commences transfer of her most seriously wounded. Dr. Ley with his pharmacist mates have done all they can do with the meager medical facilities of a tin can. Physical and spiritual needs of the worst wounded will be tended by the staffs of their task group partner.

Fifth Fleet surrounding Okinawa

By 1816 the CIC aboard the USS *Morris* DD-417 has been tracking a raider for twenty minutes. Her captain has rung up thirty knots as her main batteries open up when the bandit commences its attack on

*Medical transfer
from the Haynsworth.
(Courtesy of the
USS Haynsworth Association)*

the tin can. Soon the 20mm and 40mm guns join in. Though their rounds are hitting their mark, the *Kate* bomber closes the distance rapidly. It plows into the ship between the two forward 5" guns. Fire erupts across the deck and into the wardroom and living spaces forward. Not enough water pressure is available to extinguish the blaze so the forward magazines are flooded to save the ship. The CIC, Squadron Commander's cabin, and radio shack begin to burn causing the bridge to become a dangerous place to serve. Damage control efforts by other ships save the destroyer. None the less, she will be eventually scrapped. Thirteen sailors succumb to the attack.

As the sun hangs low in the sky, a *Judy* dive bomber in a conventional attack comes after the USS *Harding* DMS-28. The destroyer minesweeper's captain rings up speed to keep the attacker on her beam, weapons firing from 11000 yards out. The attacker's bomb explodes underwater close astern, drenching the fantail in an ocean spray. The rudder and screws are damaged from the blast but no casualties are suffered. She will not be so lucky in ten days when a kamikaze will take the lives of twenty-two of her crew.

Within the protective destroyer screen of TG 58.3, the USS *Hale* DD-642 retrieves a *Bunker Hill* flyer, Lt. jg. Vernon P. Biddle. After a mission against the Tokuno Shima airfield, the VF-84 pilot was forced to water land his *Corsair* after mechanical troubles developed.

USS Morris. (NARA 80-G-330101)

The sun finishes its daily mission in the skies over Okinawa at 1840. There is no need to sound alarm for dusk General Quarters as the ships of the phalanx and its pickets have been at their battlestations for most of the day.

Ten minutes later the first day of *Kikusui No.1* concludes spectacularly: A kamikaze hits its mark when a second *Victory* ship falls victim as she seeks to clear the now dangerous anchorage at Kerama Retto. Just two months post launching, SS *Hobbs Victory* is struck amidships portside causing massive damage to the boat deck and the midship house. Burning brightly as the sun escapes Okinawa, *Hobbs* is abandoned. Other ships effort to combat the flames but it is too late. After losing eleven merchantmen and one sailor, *Hobbs* eventually explodes and sinks.

The USS Morris DD-417 (NARA 80-G-330109)

Task Group 58.3 1850

The phalanx finally relaxes its screen around the carriers as the group returns to cruising disposition 5-Roger. By day's end, Task Force 58's pilots and gunnery crews claimed 236 enemy planes shot down. The *Essex's* pilots alone claim sixty-five victories. Combat losses for the carrier groups are just two American planes. The harrowing attacks of the first day of *Kikusui No. 1* are completed.

USS *Haynsworth* 1850

Just before his transfer to the *South Dakota*, Bill McKeen asks Vasquez if he is Roman Catholic. "Yes, pray for me," replies the bandaged signalman, his brain exposed by shrapnel. The trauma to Vasquez's skull forces Dr. Ley to annotate in the medical record, "Prognosis: probably fatal." *...and blessed are thou amongst women. Holy Mary, mother of God, pray for us sinners now and at the hour of our death. Amen.*

Less than fifteen minutes later, the *Haynsworth* completes the transfer of its most seriously wounded bluejackets. Six of her eleven radiomen are in dire shape as they are accepted by the battleship's medical company.

Aulbert, Lonnie Lee S2c

Campbell, Barton M. CRM
Davis, Carroll L. RM3c
Dyer, John R. RM3c
Goyer, Arthur A. RM2c
Holcombe, Warner C. RM1c
Holiman, Bernice R. RM2c
Matschat, Robert D. S1c
Saia, Mariano RdM3c
Studley Milton H. RdM3c
Vasquez, John SM3c

Ley expects that seven of those transferred will likely die from their burns and wounds. Three more bluejackets are considered to be serious cases. Only a radarman, twenty-two year Buffalo native Saia, rates a 'favorable' prognosis.

Aboard the *South Dakota*, the *Haynsworth's* sailors have both their physical and spiritual wounds tended. The battleship's chaplains, Cdr. Reverend Harold Post and Cdr. Father James F. Cunningham, are on the scene as the injured are brought aboard. Morphine has eased the suffering from the burns. Like his peers, Radioman Third Class John Dyer, "was transferred to this ship several hours after the action took place suffering severely from burns, although in no pain. The doctors went to work on him and his companions immediately and did everything known to medical science. I talked to him in sick bay, he went to confession, was anointed and received the last sacraments on Friday night, April 6th. He was conscious at the time, found it fairly easy to talk and seemed to have a chance, a very slim one for recovery," wrote Father Cunningham to the Dyer family...*My cup runs over. Surely goodness and mercy shall follow me All the days of my life; And I will dwell in the house of the LORD Forever.*

Though the *Haynsworth* has been alongside the *South Dakota* numerous times throughout the war in the Pacific for fuel and mail transfers, today she is a welcome sight for the tired and injured sailors of the destroyer. For the previous five hours the crew of the *Haynsworth* has feared that they will be subject to further kamikaze attacks as the reports, sights, and sounds of the massive *Kikusui* raid envelope them. A.C. Pickens spots a comrade from the engineering school at the Great Lakes Naval Station aboard the massive battlewagon. "It was reassuring during this big battle to get a friendly wave and smile from an old friend. For the first time that day we felt safe."

Though dozens of wounded remain aboard the stricken destroyer, the transfer of the most seriously wounded relieves the young doctor of caring for the seven sailors he anticipates will die soon. For the twenty six year old destroyer's doctor, "it was a horrible day and the outcome was tragic, but we [Ley & the pharmacist mates] did everything we possibly could." Years later, Dr. Ley told Lt. Dennett, the ship's gunnery officer that, "it was the longest day of his medical career."

After barely escaping the crushing impact and conflagration of the kamikaze while serving at his battlestation outside the bridge, Sonarman Bill Morton reports to Sick Bay for care by Dr. Ley. The bluejacket explains to the exhausted doctor, "I went into the sound hut to make coffee. Just when I lifted the Silex off the burner to let it go down, a wave bounced off the battleship next to us and caused the coffee to spill down my arm." After the day's holocaust, the usually approachable Lt. Ley vents, "All the damage and fire we had today and you burn yourself with coffee." No Purple Heart will be awarded for these wounds.

WITH THE COVER OF DARKENING SKIES, the officers and crew of the *Haynsworth* finally are able to secure from GQ at 1910. Moving to condition Baker, readiness condition II, half the crew are able to leave their battle stations, The *Haynsworth* and Task Group 58.3 are again due east of Okino Erabu Island.

Sailors pick through the kamikaze wreckage for souvenirs. But, frustration turns to anger when it discovered that part of the plane was built in America. Found in the debris is a propeller part stamped *BUFFALO FORGE*.

Among the charred detritus of steel, weapons, and gear lie the pilot's mortal remains, prone on the deck. Black humor reigns. One sailor quips that perhaps the kamikaze dropped his bomb prematurely so that he would not be hurt in the crash.

The cadaver's uniform is adorned by bright red leather boots. When the footwear begins to attract the attention of the sailors, the bridge decides it is time to dispose of the kamikaze's remains. Initially, the corpse was not to be moved or touched for fear it was booby trapped. Carpenters Mate Second Class Eddie Mital is ordered to prepare the kamikaze pilot's body for burial. Instead he throws the corpse into the sea, unweighted. Mital ends up losing a stripe for his actions.

The kamikaze's engine after removal from the Radio Transmitter compartment. (National Archives)

U.S. Navy Handbook of Damage Control:

"25-14. The dead. Later, collection and identification of the dead may be undertaken. Work parties under proper supervision must be provided so that the dead may be collected and properly identified. A responsible officer (not necessarily a medical officer; the latter will be busy with the wounded) should be designated to carry on this work under the direction of the senior medical officer. Disposition of the dead will depend upon the circumstances, but if buried at sea care should be taken that the body is properly shrouded and weighted, and that a hole is cut in the top of the shroud to allow for the escape of air."

FIFTY-FOUR POUND 5" PROJECTILES WILL SERVE AS BALLAST FOR THE DEAD. A Boatswain's mate confers with the *Haynsworth's* gunnery officer, Lt. Armistead Dennett, about using brass practice 5" projectiles to weight the shrouds. With just twelve practice rounds on hand, the decision was made to use live rounds. Their heft will ensure would ensure that the victims descend to the depths of the ocean. *Haynsworth's* dead are sewn into canvas coffins, the 5" shells between their legs. The cold storage refrigerated compartment below decks is transformed into a temporary morgue.

THE WARRIOR SEAMAN, CDR. STEPHEN NOEL TACKNEY REPORTED TO HIS SUPERIORS that "as a unit of Task Force 58 operating offensively against the Japanese, on picket station about seventy-eight miles NE of Okinawa Jima, this vessel was attacked by a Japanese suicide dive bomber resulting in thirty four casualties and considerable damage to the vessel. In the defense of the *Haynsworth*, the fighting of the severe fire caused by the suicide crash, and the subsequent Ship's Force repairs and handling of the casualties, the conduct and performance of duty of every member of the ship's company was in all respects in accordance with the best traditions of the Navy. By means of their efforts, fire was brought under control in ten minutes and the ship was able to rejoin the task group."

The Captain went on to further praise his crew: "[The] performance of every man and officer on the ship was outstanding during the suicide attack, fighting the resulting fire, and in repairs accomplished by the Ship's Force subsequent to the attack. Order and discipline was evident throughout. Every man on the ship stood by his station until ordered to leave; every man on the ship obeyed orders unhesitatingly; man after man and officer after officer risked his life and limb in the rapid conquering of the raging fire. The manner in which lower ratings and strikers have fleeted up into the jobs vacated by their wounded seniors speaks very highly for their personal initiative and adaptability."

Fifth Fleet Surrounding Okinawa

THE BUTCHER'S BILL FOR APRIL 6 IS ENOURMOUS. Admiral Spruance's ships have lost 363 sailors, either killed or missing. Another 432 sailors are wounded. While still in the hunt, the *Haynsworth* will need extensive repairs to be restored to full fighting capabilities. Three ships will not be repaired until after the war is over. Three more ships will be eventually scrapped or decommissioned. Four warships and two *Victory* ships are already either sunk or scuttled. Another carrier has been injured in Task Force 57, the British Pacific Fleet. Admiral Spruance cannot afford to release her until more carriers can arrive to replace all those that have been damaged since Task Force 58 sortied from Ulithi in mid-March.

By the end of the day over three hundred Japanese planes are downed by the pilots and gunners of the Allied fleets. For those serving aboard the *Haynsworth*, from Cdr. Tackney and Lt. Cdr. Lothrop to the lowest enlisted ratings, nightmares of the day's actions will haunt most for the rest of their lives. Few are immune.

USS *Quincy* Underway From Pearl Harbor

THE *HAYNSWORTH'S* NEWEST RADIOMEN ARE EAGER TO REJOIN THEIR SHIP. As the cruiser heads east enroute to Ulithi, they, along with the entire Fifth Fleet, hear Admiral Nimitiz' message about the battle for Okinawa:

> *By late afternoon on April 6 (East Longitude Date), Hellcat and Corsair fighters from two fast carrier task groups of the U. S. Pacific Fleet commanded by Rear Admirals Frederick C. Sherman and J. J. Clark, USN, had shot down about 150 enemy aircraft which were attempting to attack fleet surface units in the area of the Ryukyus. This tally of damage is preliminary and incomplete. Some ships of our forces received minor damage but all remain fully operational.*

John McAllister and John Magliocchetti take pride in the knowledge that their task group has been so successful in the battle. Missing from the message is that twenty ships have been hit by kamikazes and five are sunk. Nimitz also does not forewarn of the second day of the battle yet to emerge.

7 April 1945: The Storm Continues

Task Force 58

K *IKUSUI NO.1* WAS NOT OVER. Though the massed attacks of April 6 have passed, the kamikazes are by no means finished. The next day brings a renewal of the Japanese efforts to combat the Allied invasion forces with devastating attacks from the air and the sea. The Allies are seeking retribution.

USS *Haynsworth*

E VERY DAY HAD A PLAN. Before the sun came up, the Exec had penned a summary of what was *supposed* to happen over the next twenty-four hours. A yeoman would type it up and then distribute or post the morning orders across the ship. As sailors staggered out of their racks to head to dawn GQ or morning chow, those that weren't already on watch, could see what the plan held for the day. After fifteen days at Okinawa, post hundreds of kamikaze attacks emerging from the skies to strike thirty U.S. Navy ships during that period, a sailor could hope the news would be posted that the task group was returning to Ulithi for rest and replenishment. Hope was replaced by reality. Seven comrades lay sewn in the canvas coffins crafted by the boatswain mates.

Lt. Cdr. Lothrop laid out the plan for their burial in the morning orders. The blueprint was just guidance. In war, like civilian life, things don't always go accordingly as designed. "In accordance with the provisions of the United States Navy Regulations, the dead from our action against the enemy will be buried at sea this date. It is unfortunate that our facilities do not permit the preservation of the remains for burial ashore, but decision has been made that we cannot do so." The national colors will be unmasted at 1400 before the dead are committed to the sea.

Within Task Group 58.3, the *Haynsworth* is sailing blind without radar. The destruction of the radio transmitter room and radio central turns the destroyer deaf to most radio communications from the fleet. "For light in CIC we had one bare bulb work light rigged up on an extension cord, hanging over the Air Plot table. The air search radar console lay capsized, a mangled wreck to starboard. Every transceiver had been burnt out by the fire. We had one receiver brought forward

The damaged Combat Information Center after cleaning.
(National Archives Photo)

from Secondary [Emergency] Radio, rigged to the telling circuit of incoming raids, and we plotted these in grease on the Air Plot. Nothing, absolutely nothing, else worked."

Relying on the limited capacity of the emergency radio shack, the few remaining radiomen and the skills of its signalmen, the "Lucky 700" steams within the protective screen of the group. She will not leave the safety of the screen's mutual fire protection for the rest of the time she fights with the Fast Carrier Task Force.

Surface Special Attack Force

LIKE A RODEO BULL LOCKED IN ITS PEN, the *Yamato* was fearsome but not dangerous. But if freed from the confines of a harbor and out in the open sea, the massive dreadnaught is a major threat to any ship. The Fast Carrier Task Force has been hunting for her since she had escaped relatively unscathed from the Battle off Samar Island in October of the previous year. She is the last jewel remaining in what had once been the Imperial Japanese Navy's crown.

At 0200 the Surface Special Attack Force passes the Miyazaki coast and reaches the entrance to Osumi Kaikyo Channel. Having sortied the day before at 1520, it isn't long before the mission is exposed. Lying in wait are the submarines USS *Hackleback* and USS *Threadfin* which spot Vice Admiral Seiichi Ito's convoy in the Inland Sea at 2020. Skirting around the coast of Kyushu, Ito plans to steam his ships away from the Fast Carrier Task Force. His goal is the invasion fleet operating off the west coast of Okinawa.

Task Force 58 0300

WITH EXPECTATION OF CONTINUING HOSTILITIES, NIGHT FIGHTERS ARE LAUNCHED as Task Groups 58.1 and 58.3 remain on station overnight. The flickering exhaust flames of the *Hellcats* are shrouded to avoid detection by prying eyes. Below decks, mechanics and armorers have been working furiously all night. This day's flights will be a maximum effort by Mitscher's carriers. Every plane that can fly, will fly. Navy planes will set out to seek and destroy the *Surface Special Attack Force*. Most of the marines and their *Corsairs* will be left to provide the CAP. 1 Lt. Wilmot of VMF-451 observes that, "the navy fliers really liked attacking enemy warships."

Coverage of the radar picket line will again be established as the destroyers *Bullard*, *Kidd*, *Black* and *Chauncey* of DesDiv 96 move north thirty miles at 0400. They are joined by the four destroyers of DesDiv 50 from Task Group 58.1. DesDiv 96's destroyers steam eight miles to the east of its partner. Each group will control its own four plane CAP. Each will be busy again this day.

With the *Charles S. Sperry* on plane guard duty plus the *Walker*, *Waldron* and *Lind* on picket duty, Captain Higgins is left with just eight destroyers for the circular screen guarding the five carriers. One, the *Haynsworth*, is of limited value with its radar guided fire control system destroyed. With the need to protect the flattops, Higgins recalls *Lind* back as the first flights are launched. Every boiler offline is brought back on line. The task group will be hustling at twenty-six knots all day for flight operations. Overcast early, the clouds will break later to open the sky.

On the western side of Okinawa, the Commander of Task Force 51 grants permission to the USS *Ellyson* DMS-19 to sink the burned out and drifting carcass of the destroyer USS *Emmons*. Commissioned as DD-457 two days before the Pearl Harbor attack, *Emmons* was converted to a destroyer mine sweeper in November, 1944. She was forged

PHALANX AGAINST THE DIVINE WIND

of tough steel by the Bath Iron Works. It takes ninety-six rounds of 5" shells to finish what the kamikazes started the day before.

At 0340 the USS *Wesson* DE-184 relieves the USS *Sterett* DD-407 north of Ie Shima. Its mission for the day is to protect two large landing craft. The *Wesson*, now near the northwest portion of the protective circle, fights off air attacks until dawn. *Sterett* will later be hit by a kamikaze on April 9th.

Day two of *Kikusui No.1* begins on the *Haynsworth*. Reveille is piped at 0515. Minutes later the crew answers the call of the alarms for the dawn GQ period. Despite the expected battles in the air, for the *Haynsworth*, April 7th will be a day of tending to its wounds and reflection of sailors lost to the *Divine Wind*.

Surface Special Attack Force 0600

THE RISING SUN GREETS THE *YAMATO* as she launches her Aichi E13A *Jake* reconnaissance floatplane. This will be her only air cover after fighters break away around 1000.

Task Force 58 0600

AT DAWN'S FIRST LIGHT, the USS *Bunker Hill* launches two dozen *Hellcat* fighters. In groups of four, they will fly six of the ten search vectors where the Japanese force might be found. Each group will fly as far as Kyushu, 325 miles northwest of the fleet. Poised in anticipation of a fight are the strike forces on the decks of the carriers. The word comes back at 0835 from an *Essex* search group: Vice Admiral Ito's Special Surface Attack Force has been discovered. *Yamato's* fate has been sealed.

Just minutes prior, DesDiv 50's CAP brought down a Mitsubishi A6M3 *Hamp* fighter. It is the start of a long day combating enemy fighters over Vice Admiral Mitscher's ships. Five minutes after American planes find the Japanese naval caravan, Japanese planes attack American ships in forward northern positions. The USS *Bennett* DD-487 fires her 5" guns against attacking *Val* dive bombers. The CAP takes down two of the raiders. A third escapes both the gunfire and the guardian planes. As the destroyer increases its speed to twenty-two knots, its captain takes evasive actions by turning to starboard. The *Val* passes astern of ship, turned to the left and crashes into starboard side of ship." The raider's bomb penetrates the tin can's thin skin, passing completely through before detonating against the #2 boiler. The destroyer is able to limp to the protective safety of the Kerama Retto harbor. Seven of her company are killed, eighteen are wounded.

Minutes later the destroyer escort *Wesson* opens fire on three Japanese fighters as they cross her bow. At the same time a fourth fighter dives down from the clouds and hits the ship between its smokestacks, directly on the torpedo racks. Despite the loss of seven men and significant damage, she is able to leave the area with the assistance of the destroyer USS *Lang* DD-339. The *Wesson* joins the ranks of the *Haynsworth* and the other twenty-one ships struck by the aerial force of *Operation Ten-Go*.

Ninety minutes after the *Yamato* alert has been received, the decks of nine carriers are awash in blue gray smoke as over two hundred planes are readied for launch. Today the *Avengers* will carry torpedoes while both the dive bombers and fighters will carry bombs. The fuel hungry fighters wear the recently delivered belly tanks for the 270 mile trek. Task Groups 58.1 and 58.3 launch their flights starting at 1006. Rear Admiral Radford's 58.4, still steaming north from its meeting with the replenishment group, launches its strikes forty-five minutes later. In a short period of time, nearly four hundred American planes are in the hunt. This will be nearly an all navy adventure. Most of the marine fliers are left behind to fly the CAP and provide local support. It is an incredible sight for the blue jackets as the groups took flight. From the *Lind*, Bob Plum reported that the, "sky is completely filled with our planes."

No sooner are the strikes away than the search planes are recovered. With reports of numerous raiders approaching the Task Force from multiple directions, the purple shirted fuel handlers feed aviation gas to the fighters. They are relaunched to reinforce the CAP.

At 1041 Admiral Sherman's task group comes under attack from an enemy plane in a suicide dive. The anti-aircraft gunners, with months of combat experience under their belts, find their mark. Scratch one bandit.

About this time, the first of the *Haynsworth's* wounded sailors dies aboard the *South Dakota*. With a Protestant chaplain at his side, eighteen year old Robert Matschat S1c, grandson himself of a German Lutheran pastor, succumbs to his wounds. Reverend Harold F. Post has spent the evening in the sick bay along with the Catholic chaplain, Cdr. James F. Cunningham. By Matschat's side, Lt. Post "is reading to him from the Scripture when he died." Matschat will become the first of the *Haynsworth's* casualties buried at sea, the first of a crew that had come together just ten months earlier. *...Yea, though I walk through the*

    PHALANX AGAINST THE DIVINE WIND

valley of the shadow of death, I will fear no evil; For You are with me; Your rod and Your staff, they comfort me. You prepare a table before me in the presence of my enemies...

Surface Special Attack Force 1014

The *YAMATO* AND HER CARAVAN HAVE BEEN PERIODI- CALLY UNDER SURVEILLANCE since the prior evening. Mid-morning two Martin PBM *Mariner*s, long range reconnaissance seaplanes from Patrol Bomber Squadron 21, discover the Attack Force. They have the ability and range, unlike the fighters, to follow the Surface Special Attack Force throughout the day.

The pesky horseflies are nearly swatted by the warships below. The leviathan's gunners load 'beehive' rounds into what have become the largest anti-aircraft guns, the main 18.1" surface cannon. The ordnance is like buckshot. Each shell contains thousands of 20mm shot timed to explode after one second in the air. After the first broadsides are sent against the Americans, the pilots duck into the clouds. Hide and seek with Ito's ships has begun. Weapons are fired in their direction for five hours.

A Japanese scout plane sends a message that Task Force 58 has been spotted 250 miles southeast. The Japanese are still confident that the previous days *Divine Wind*s have crippled the American carrier force.

USS *Haynsworth*

REPAIR DOMINATES THE EFFORTS ON THE *HAYNS-WORTH.* The warship constructed of a keel and thousands of steel plates, remains in the battle. But for the crew, the strain is tenable. Sonarman Bill Morton risks receiving a court martial. "I was ordered to take a crew into the radio room and begin cleaning up. I refused because I had been by there the day before when it looked like Frankenstein's laboratory with electrical sparks jumping all over it. I told him unless the electricians could assure us all the power was off, I wasn't taking a crew in there to get electrocuted after they survived the day before."

The mental images of his crewmates on fire leaves Sonarman Robert Chamberlin deeply troubled. The stench from the sick bay and the odor of burned flesh is repulsive to the sailors. Unfamiliar with having to face their own mortality, black humor reigns amongst the young

Radio Central after cleaning. Note the burned and torn cables in the top left. Four men from this compartment died from their burns. (National Archives)

crew. The scenes of the attack will spark nightmares for many blue-jackets and officers for decades to come.

Surface Special Attack Force 1107

G HOSTS? LARGE BLIPS APPEAR ON THE RADAR SCREENS. Despite the triumphant victory the day before, electronic images indicate that an immense mass of planes are just sixty-three miles southeast and closing fast. The Surface Special Attack Force increases speed in response. Moments later a delayed report indicates that an island lookout station has spotted a large force of 150 U.S. carrier planes. An additional eight F6F *Hellcats* appear and surveil the Attack Force. The sky remains overcast as *Yahagi* and *Yamato* open fire again while the ships begin radical turns.

REPORTS OF ENEMY PLANES APPROACHING, distance of seventeen miles, are received. DesDiv 50's CAP quickly disposes of four Kawanishi N1K-J fighters. Though the *George* fighters are equal to the *Hellcats* in performance, their pilots are no match for the American pilots in their *Corsairs*. The Tiger CAP from the *Cabot*, also controlled by DesDiv 96, brings down two Nakajima Ki-44 *Tojo* fighters.

The General Quarters alarm sounds across the task group's ships. The flattops move to *Torpedo Defense Stations*, the phalanx of destroyers closes in on the carriers, bluejackets man their battle stations. A minute later the kamikaze dives through the clouds, targeting the *Bunker Hill*. The frightening whine of the plane's dive is met by the cacophony of the guns as the screen opens fire with all guns that can bear. Golden tracer fire arcs across the water. Changing direction in response to the rapid blooms of anti-aircraft fire, the raider steers his flying weapon towards the *Hancock*.

During his fatal dive, the kamikaze releases his bomb as his last earthly act. His ordnance punctures the flight deck at the bow. The explosion sends its guide cartwheeling down the flight deck. The burning plane lands atop *Hancock*'s planes spotted on stern deck. The planes that weren't part of the *Yamato* strike force become burning symbols of *Kikusui No.1*. Ignited aviation fuel spreads across the aft end of the ship. Fires burn at both ends of Captain Robert Hickey's vessel.

"The explosion causes *Hancock* to maneuver blindly due to fires burning forward and aft along the hangar deck," reports Cdr. Joseph C. Wylie, Jr., Captain of the *Ault*. The phalanx guards change course and open the screen as Hickey attempts to bring the wind to his starboard side and clear the smoke enveloping the blazing carrier. To maintain the integrity of the phalanx and assist in rescue, Rear Admiral Sherman's group follows the lead of their wounded partner and maneuvers in kind.

As the attack metastasizes, the battle fatigued tin can sailors topside stand in shocked amazement of the explosions that rock the *Hancock's* deck. The burning aviation fuel adds to the intensifying conflagration. The wounded *Haynsworth*, sailing within the protected external flank of the phalanx, is close enough to witness the many carrier sailors blown over the side. "From my position in the fire control director," related Lt. Armistead Dennett, "I could sailors jumping into the water to escape from being trapped in the flames." Still making twenty-six

USS Hancock. (U.S. Navy Naval Aviation Museum Photo)

knots while executing sharp turns, *Hancock's* sailors are spread over a wide swath of ocean.

Twenty-three year old Phil Mulé AMM3c is in the *Hancock's* catapult crew compartment with eight other sailors when the bomb penetrates the flight deck and ignites planes on the hangar deck. Six bluejackets escape the compartment but three die of smoke inhalation. "I stumbled out and was leaning over the catwalk below the flight deck. The next thing I knew, I was awake in the water. I fell seventy-five feet but I have no memory of that. They told us not to buckle our helmets in case we ever hit the water. That advice might have saved my life."

Nearby screening destroyers, as well as the *Essex*, rush to the aide of the burning carrier. A caravan of destroyers- *Erben, English, Sperry, Haynsworth, Weeks* and *Ault*-start the rescues immediately. A Martin *Mariner* seaplane is launched from a support group in southern Okinawa as the battleship *Washington* puts her own OS2U *Kingfisher* scout plane up in the air. Aboard the *Hancock* and the nearby *John W. Weeks*, rafts, life jackets and other equipment that will float are tossed overboard in hopes the sailors in the water can be saved. While the rescue unfolds, the screen collapses in forming cruising disposition 5-V. The phalanx will be ready for the next round.

USS Hancock seen from the USS John W. Weeks.
(Chuck Guthrie photo. Courtesy of the USS John W. Weeks Association)

Controlling the fires quickly is the key to saving *Hancock*. Aboard 'Hannah,' damage control parties bring the fires under control in less than twenty minutes. Their experiences of January 20, when an armed *Avenger* blew up on her flight deck and later on March 20 when a kamikaze struck the USS *Halsey Powell* DD-686 aside of her, have taught the damage control parties well.

Cdr. Tackney's *Haynsworth* plays her part. The ship that was rescued is now the rescuer. Damaged by a kamikaze like her fleet partner *Hancock*, the Lucky 700 recovers eight sailors from the sea. Bill Breckenridge TM2c is the first to help bring a *Hancock* survivor aboard the *Haynsworth* unlike the previous day when Breckenridge was kept at his GQ station on the torpedoes, despite the proximity of the fire from the kamikaze attack. Doctor Ley and the pharmacist mates, exhausted from caring for dozens of wounded in the previous twenty-three hours, make room for several more burn victims.

Spontaneity, as much as courage and opportunity, creates heroes. At the sight of the fleet carrier burning at both ends of the flight deck, Cdr. McIlhenny orders *Charles S. Sperry* to leave the circular screen. Already at flank speed, the group is still firing at attacking planes while *Sperry* maneuvers to assist her charge.

As they close on the stricken carrier, many of the destroyer's men jump from the deck, swimming to save the sailors blown overboard from the attack. Radioman Second Class William Ballough is one of the many *Sperry* men who have taken to the water. "Without regard for his own safety and knowing the danger from his own ship's propellers and that the force was still under attack, he repeatedly went into the water and brought men to the ship's side where they were brought aboard." As the attack continued, *Sperry* temporarily has to abandon both the rescuers and victims. Ballough "promptly swam to a group of survivors and rendered assistance to two injured men and was later picked up by another rescue destroyer. His courage and disregard for his own safety were in keeping with the highest traditions of the United States Naval Service." Ballough will earn the Silver Star for his actions.

Ballough's recognition for his efforts was not unique. Seaman Second Class John L. Callahan had also entered the seas when a warning was shouted that two *Sally* bombers were, "low on the horizon, dead ahead!" Callahan is able to return to his destroyer just as it begins to lay fire against the raiders. When the firing ceases, Callahan resumes his role as rescuer as he assists in the recovery of several *Hancock* sailors. Like Ballough, Callahan has been a regular in saving pilots. For his actions, the U.S. Navy will also award Callahan the Silver Star.

Twelve other sailors from the *Sperry* earn the Bronze Star that afternoon for their rescue efforts. The recipients are a mixed group: torpedomen, electrician's mates, a water tender, a shipfitter, a metalsmith and several seamen. Their actions save nineteen of the *Hancock's* company. All the while the *Sperry* fires at enemy planes to keep them at bay, expending 144 rounds of 5"/38. Four planes are taken under fire throughout the day. The gunners claim two assists.

With burns to his face and hands, the *Hancock's* Phil Mulé has been in the water for nearly an hour. Just a few days prior, he had traded away his small life belt when a member of the flight deck crew offered him a Mae West vest in exchange. "I could have kissed him!" Though the vest only partially inflated, it keeps Mulé afloat before he spots a destroyer that has stopped dead in the water. He and other bluejackets do their best to swim towards DD-701.

Cdr. Robert Theobald's *John W. Weeks* is en route to the carrier when the tragedy unfolds. Spontaneously many of her sailors jump into the water without lifelines to aid the wounded while rafts are jettisoned from the destroyer. Her men rescue twenty-three sailors, twelve of whom are severely burned. Chief Radio Technician Morris F. Gillett moves from his battlestation to save the carrier's men:

> *Seeing the peril of the men, many wounded in the water, men from the Weeks, including me were in the water to assist getting the men, first to a raft then aboard our ship for attention. I could see several men in the vicinity of one raft and swam to it as fast as I was able. Two men needed immediate help. One had received flash burns and was clinging to the web lines of the raft. His hands were severely burned up to where his shirt sleeve had protected him. Although flash burns from guns or bombs are severe, they can be prevented by as little as the thickness of a piece of a cloth or the flash-burn ointment we normally wore during wore General Quarters or any action. At any rate, this man without ointment was in bad shape. As he clung to the lines, I could see them cutting through the burned flesh. I shouted to him, "I have you" as I grabbed both his sleeved arms. He relaxed completely and I was able to get him onto the raft. In addition to the hands, his neck, face and head were "burned white."*

Theobald receives an order to get underway again as enemy planes are still in the area. He tells the radioman to ignore the order so that his men can save more sailors. When the sickbay fills up, Theobald offers up his stateroom to Phil Mulé and other *Hancock* sailors.

Though the *Ault* retraces the *Hancock*'s path, the effort is in vain. The *English* recovers eight enlisted men from the ocean while *Erben* adds fourteen to the count. *Erben* also recovers one of *Sperry's* rescue swimmers. The actions of the small dogs pay dividends. Though thirty-five sailors are listed as missing in action—including three sailors from Phil Mulé's catapult crew—the cans save seventy-three of the *Hancock's* crew.

The latest kamikaze attack increases the strain of the boys on the *Haynsworth*. "Fear? Yes, believe it. As those crosses came in towards the center of the Air Plot, my mind just told me again and again that the bogeys were coming back to finish us off. Never mind that we were now in the shelter of the whole massive task force." Lt. Cdr. Lothrop continued, "What to do, in the face of such irrationality and

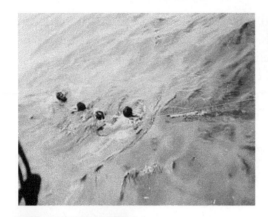

*Above left and center: USS Hancock survivors pulled from the water.
(Chuck Guthrie photos.
Courtesy of USS John W. Weeks Association)*

*Right: CRT Morris Gillett.
(Courtesy of Morris Gillett)*

fear? Make jokes. Talk. Anything to help the others and thereby help yourself. Hang onto the edge of the plotting table so hard that you later found you'd splintered away an edge just from the grip."

The *Bunker* Hill strengthens its CAP by launching three additional fighters as reports of enemy planes in the air continue to be received. Anti-aircraft fire destroys two *Zeke* fighters as they attempt to penetrate the phalanx. Twelve miles away on picket duty, the *Waldron* witnesses the angry black blooms of the main batteries opening up. Inside the ring of fire, the *Hancock* continues to belch fire and smoke.

Special Escort Carrier Task Unit 1204-1625

The jeep carriers USS *Breton* CVE-23, USS *Sitkoh Bay* CVE-86, USS *White Plains* CVE-66, and USS *Hollandia* CVE-97 are approaching Okinawa from the southeast, out of harm's way. The *Breton* and *Sitkoh Bay* launch their Marine Air Groups to their new home at Yontan Field. The four squadrons are the equivalent of a fleet carrier's fighter compliment. The marine *Corsairs* are too late to get in the game against the attacks over western and northwestern Okinawa though they do bring down a raider making a suicide run against the *Sitkoh Bay*.

Surface Special Attack Force 1232

THE FIRST ATTACK WAVE OF US PLANES IS SPOTTED by the *Yamato* less than three miles away. Closing fast are 280 fighters, bombers and torpedo planes from ten different carriers. For a brief moment, American fliers are amazed at the leviathan that dwarfs the U.S. Navy's battleships. The *Yamato's* massive pagoda superstructure stands eighty feet above her sea deck thus making her an easy target to spot. She is a few feet shorter than Admiral Spruance's largest battleships but, as she was never designed to enter the Panama Canal, *Yamato's* beam is twenty feet broader than the American navy's biggest battleships. She is a heavyweight at 71,000 tons versus the middleweight 52,000 ton *Iowa* class battleships.

The *Yamato* opens fire with her huge 18.1 inch guns in the forward two turrets along with other anti-aircraft weapons. The Americans drop both bombs and torpedoes, strafing with machine guns and rockets as they attack. As a portent of things to come for the Surface Special Attack Force one of the screening destroyers, *Asashimo*, is attacked and sunk.

As American planes come within range, the *Yamato* opens fire with her smaller weaponry: Twenty-four 127mm/5 inch cannons along with one hundred sixty-two 25mm anti-aircraft guns. The cacophony on deck from the guns is deafening. To the pilots on the receiving end, the anti-aircraft fire looks like 'golden golf balls' as it rockets towards the American planes.

Despite the withering fire from the *Yamato*, her time in World War II is end nearing its end. Two bombs explode near the mainmast marking the beginning of a savage attack from the carrier force planes. Soon she is hit by the first of many torpedoes. One of the exploding 'fish' is delivered by Torpedo Eighty Four pilot Ensign William Elings. Saved at sea after a mid-air collision on March 29th, Elings pays the Navy back as he presses home the attack. He later will be awarded the Navy Cross for this action.

The *Yamato's* guns shoot down a few of the attacking American force but not nearly enough to make a difference in the end. Her numerous anti-aircraft guns are clustered around the superstructure of the ship thus making inviting targets for strafing American fighter planes. By incapacitating these guns, the fighters have allowed the Grumman *Avenger* torpedo bombers and Curtiss *Helldiver* dive bombers to have some relief from anti-aircraft fire as they fly in coordinated attacks. After what seems an eternity to the Japanese sailors, the first wave retires. The *Asashimo* is sunk, the *Hamakaze* lies gravely wounded, the *Suzutsuki* is on fire, the *Yahagi* adrift, and the *Yamato* wounded. It is 1250 and the attack has been going on less than fifteen minutes.

Yamato under attack. (National Archives)

Task Force 58

THROUGHOUT THE MORNING, RUNNING ACCOUNTS OF THE BATTLE are broadcast aloud allowing the sailors of Task Force 58 to hear radio transmissions from the navy pilots attacking the *Yamato*. After a day and a half of intense aerial attacks against the Allies, audible proof of an American victory encourages Mitscher's team. Cheers erupt across the fleet.

But vigilance against attack is still critical as Lt. Cdr. Lothrop had reminded his watches numerous times. "An enemy plane bearing 131 degrees T, distant 10,000 yards, was shot down by anti-aircraft fire of heavy units. 1304 Second enemy plane shot down as it attempted to dive on the carriers of the formation."

Less than thirty minutes later, the *Hancock's* smoke and gaggle of attending destroyers make her an obvious target for Japanese planes.

USS Hancock, April 7, 1945. (NARA 80-G-328563)

"Two planes were sighted flying low on the water far out. These planes were identified as *Kates* [torpedo bombers] and the task group commander was so notified. By their manners, it is believed they were commencing an attack on the rescuing destroyers, some of which were dead in the water," recorded the *Ault's* Cdr. Joseph Riley, Jr. Under ComDesRon 48's Captain W. Marshall, who was given charge of the rescue efforts, "rescue destroyers commenced firing, increased speed and maneuvered to unmask battery but remaining in vicinity of *Hancock* men in water to cover them from strafing." Marshall recalls the destroyers as the phalanx fully reforms at 1400. Like many other 'floating chrysanthemums' during the battle, *Corsairs* from the CAP lead the enemy to their watery graves.

For the wounded and dying *Haynsworth* sailors aboard the *South Dakota*, the sounds of battle carry on down to the sick bay. As a *Kate* torpedo bomber passes near BB-57, her close range guns fire ferociously thus sending the attacker to a gravesite near the battleship's starboard beam. In the few seconds that the anti-aircraft guns are in use, 644 rounds are unleashed.

The *Bunker Hill* becomes a foster mother during the battle, accepting twelve of *Hancock's* returning planes as aerial orphans.

Surface Special Attack Force 1322

THE SECOND WAVE ARRIVES OVER THE WOUNDED CARAVAN. VB-83 *Helldivers* find their mark as they punish the

Hancock as viewed from USS Essex. (National Archives)

battleship. A 1000 lb. bomb dropped by a VBF-83 *Corsair* buries itself in the *Yamato's* superstructure. The respite between attacks is brief. Eleven minutes after the arrival of attackers from the *Essex* and the *Bataan*, the third wave, 110 planes from Admiral Radford's TG 58.4, arrives on station. Grumman *Avengers* flood the water with torpedoes while *Hellcats*, *Corsairs* and *Helldivers* drop a storm of bombs against the Surface Special Attack Force. Fifty caliber lead hail is sent against the gunners on the ship's decks.

Task Group 58.3 1347

THE RAMPARTS CONTINUED TO BE ATTACKED. Like the *Haynsworth* the day before, the USS *Walker* steams twelve miles ahead of the group on sentry duty as one of the two radar picket ships. Down in its CIC, an approaching plane is designated as a "bogey." The 'sugar charlie' radar tracks the path of the raider when it is still thirty-six miles away, closing on a northerly course. Traveling at 300 knots, the plane will arrive in short order.

When it does appear, the *Zeke* is duking it out with four *Corsairs* of the CAP. With the presence of the friendlies, fire from the main batteries is withheld. As the raider continues on its path towards the *Walker*, the can opens up with her machine guns from a range of 3500 yards. The group of five planes passes over the ship at 2000 feet. Realizing that his time on earth is short and there no carriers are in sight, the

An SB2C-3 Helldiver begins its dive against the Yamato.
(National Archives)

Zeke breaks away in a sharp left turn towards the *Walker*. Cdr. Philip Quirk turns his destroyer in a parallel movement to allow all guns to bear. DD-517 is turning twenty-six knots as the kamikaze dives astern of the ship. The four American pilots decide to live another day, unlike their rival, and break off the chase as 20mm and 40mm rounds begin to fill the air. The *Walker* is luckier than *Haynsworth* as the plane misses the bullseye. Banking hard in an attempt to hit the bridge, the kamikaze passes just forward of the pilot house. Its left wing cuts through the lifelines on the deck before the fighter hits the water just twenty-five feet ahead of the can.

USS *Haynsworth* 1400

BURIAL SERVICES ARE SCHEDULED FOR 1400 HOURS. Though the *Haynsworth* unmasks its colors as preparation for the funeral, the General Quarters alarm ends any thought of committing her sailors to the deep. Two hundred seventy miles away, over three thousand sailors of the *Yamato* and her caravan are about to be committed to the depths of the East China Sea against their will.

Surface Special Attack Force 1402

MORE EXPLOSIONS ROCK THE *YAMATO* as three bombs and a torpedo find their mark. Despite the blows, the battleship continues to absorb them. Her screening cruiser, *Yahagi*, finally succumbs after being hit by twelve bombs and seven torpedoes.

Several more American torpedoes catch the listing *Yamato's* exposed starboard underside. She is less heavily armored here and the final torpedoes deliver the coup de grace. The flooding from the torpedo strikes causes the mighty *Yamato* to list fifteen degrees. Bombs have decreased her speed to just twelve knots. She is afire amidships, her anti-aircraft batteries ineffective. Her attendants are wounded and cannot aid in the battleship's defense. As her list increases, *Yamato* begins its slow roll to port, its red underside becoming increasingly exposed.

Task Group 58.3 1420

AN ENEMY PLANE PUSHES OVER FROM 5000 YARDS AS IT BEGINS A DIVE over Admiral Sherman's task group. By the time it has reached 500 feet, the *Zeke* is a flaming wreck as 5" shells from the *Ault* and *English* find their mark. The aerial conflagration slams into the ocean close aboard the *Essex*. Cdr. James Smith's *English* claims credit for the downed kamikaze after observing hits from both her 5" and 40mm guns.

While that pilot died in his attempt another did not. The ships of Destroyer Squadron 62 have become adept at rescuing pilots and sailors from the Pacific over the past ninety-nine days on station with Task Force 38/58. Cdr. George Chamber's USS *Hank* is tasked with a new type of rescue: "1433 Left formation to search for Japanese pilot reported in water astern of formation. 1442 Sighted Japanese pilot. Commenced approach to pick up pilot, observed holding gun in hand. As ship approached, pilot concealed gun behind his head and lay back in the water, evidently attempting to appear dead. 1446. Abandoned enemy."

The *Hank* then maneuvers to retrieve Ensign John Gannon and Ralph Foulks ARM3c from their sinking VB-17 *Helldiver* from the USS *Hornet*. Pressing home their attack against the Imperial Japanese Navy, Gannon's bird absorbed numerous rounds of anti-aircraft fire while dropping a bomb on an enemy destroyer during the initial attack. He nurses it back to the task force but must put the plane down in the water short of his own task group. Of the 152 enemy planes shot down in the battle, the *Hornet*'s pilots will lay claim to over a third of the kills. Gannon earns a Silver Star while Foulks will be awarded a Distinguished Flying Cross for his part. From Gannon and Foulks' rescue, the *Hank* races back to the area of *Hancock*'s kamikaze strike to search for survivors and investigate debris in the water.

Closer to Okinawa, minor damage occurs when a kamikaze is splashed near the auxiliary minesweeper USS *YMS-81*. At just 136 feet long, she was one of the smallest fleet vessels at Okinawa and dwarfed in size by the 376 foot destroyers. But, her size works to her advantage. Despite pulling minesweeping gear, she maneuvers radically to avoid the attacking *Val* dive bomber. Nearby, the USS *YMS*-140 escapes a similar fate. No casualties are suffered by the bluejackets.

Surface Special Attack Force 1423

BEFORE SHE FINALLY CAPSIZES, the listing *Yamato* rolls heavily to port, her superstructure almost touching the waves. The No. 1 magazine, the home of much of *Yamato*'s cannon powder, explodes. The force rips the mighty ship into two pieces. It has taken less than two hours of plane to ship fighting, along with eleven torpedo strikes and six bomb hits, to destroy what was once the crown jewel of the Imperial Japanese Navy. Nearly the entire crew perishes.

From the time she was commissioned until she sank, the only time the *Yamato* fired her massive 18.1 inch cannon in battle against other ships was during the Battle of Samar Island the previous October. Her sinking confirms the change in naval battle tactics. Carriers had proven themselves to be the queen of the fleet while the coffin of the Japanese Imperial Navy was slammed shut when its leviathan *Yamato* explodes and sinks at 1423.

With the loss of the *Yamato*, the Imperial Japanese Navy surface fleet that once roamed the Pacific with impunity, is now defeated.

Task Group 58.3

VICTORY! The word spreads quickly that the big blue blanket has sunk the *Yamato*, two cruisers and three destroyers. Three more destroyers are severely damaged and lie dead in the water. An anonymous sailor aboard the USS *John W. Weeks* DD-701 wrote,

> *The drama in the reports of our fly-boys who were giving the*
> *Yamato and her escorts a fancy pasting. The squawk box kept us*

The Yamato explodes. (NARA 80-G-413914)

abreast of successive developments in the attack. First we heard that the Yamato had been slowed down by several hits. Then she was left dead in the water. Knowing the deadly efficiency of our fly-boys when it came to destroying anything sporting the Japanese 'meatball,' to us it was foregoing conclusion that the Yamato's watertight days were about over. Then down she went! Each of us extended from our hearts personal 'well done' to the Navy birdmen who never let them get back alive.

In the minutes after the *Yamato* succumbs to her wounds, the next group of attackers appears over Admiral Sherman's group. The Tiger CAP-furnished by the *Bunker Hill* and directed by the fighter director team aboard the USS *Chauncey* DD-667-reports shooting down a *Francis*. Just a few minutes later another raider tries to slip past the CAP. The Mitsubishi Ki-46 *Dinah* doesn't last long after attracting the attention of the *Corsairs*. Going for the hat-trick, the *Corsairs*, bring down a *Judy* dive bomber not long after the last score.

About the same time, *John W. Weeks* continues the destroyer's tradition of being a pilot's best friend. Lt. jg. Locke Trigg, Jr. is forced to ditch his *Hellcat* near the destroyer. During the mission against the *Surface Special Attack Force*, the twenty-three year old Tennessee native pressed home his attack against a Japanese destroyer. After dropping a 500 lb. bomb, enemy anti-aircraft rounds impacted Trigg's VF-47 fighter causing damage to the rudder and the aft part of the fuselage.

He is able to fly the wounded bird back to the task group but cannot bring it back aboard the *Bataan*. The destroyer is able to recover the pilot who enacted revenge for the attack on the *Franklin* back on March 19th. Trigg will finish the war as a highly decorated pilot having earned the Silver Star, two Distinguished Flying Crosses, and five Air Medals.

The threat to the group has not been eliminated. Just as the strike planes begin to return from the *Yamato* mission, the CAP controlled by DesDiv 96 pounces on two Mitsubishi G4M *Betty* bombers. The scorecard for the DesDiv 96 CAP stands at seven for the day.

Surface Special Attack Force 1500

AMIDST THE OIL SLICKED FLOTSAM AND JETSAM FROM THE MAELSTROM, a *Helldiver* pilot spots a Torpedo Squadron Thirty pilot clinging to his yellow Goodyear dinghy. Flak had set Lt jg. William Delaney's TBM-3 afire. Delaney pulled up to allow his crewmen height enough to parachute free. When he had no choice himself, Delaney took to the silk from the *Avenger*, coming down near the vestiges of the Attack Force. The two Patrol Bombing Patrol Squadron *Mariners*, which have been on station and under fire since the dawn of the attack, are alerted to Delaney's plight. Lt. Jim Young brings his PBM down for an open water landing while his partner's PBM circles nearby to draw off fire. Despite the proximity of the remaining vessels and hundreds of Japanese sailors in the waters, Delaney is pulled aboard the gull winged flying boat. The long hours on station force Lts. Young and Sims to finally abandon their search for William Tilley AMM2c and Edward Mawhinney ARM1c. They will be declared dead by the Navy postwar.

Task Group 58.3 1530

IN THE MIDST OF THE AERIAL MELEE around Task Group 58.3, the battleship *South Dakota* halfmasts it colors. Cdr. Tackney's destroyer also lowers its colors in respect for its dead. Buried at sea is the *Haynsworth*'s Seaman First Class Robert Matschat who has succumbed from the extensive burns inflicted the day prior. A few minutes later, Reverend Post and an honor guard also commit Radioman Second Class Bernice Holiman to the deep. As their bodies descend towards Davy Jones' locker, two more enemy planes are dispatched by anti-aircraft fire over Task Group 58.1.

The U.S. Navy had learned its lessons well from previous attacks on its carriers. A carrier's planes filled with high octane aviation gas when ready for battle. Aboard the carrier *Hancock*, bombs and torpedoes would have been brought up to the hangar deck in preparation for the hunt for the *Yamato*. It was a recipe for a deadly cocktail when fire erupted. Instead, the fuel lines were charged with inflammable gas. Fire teams managed to have the fire under control within forty minutes. The deck fire was out in just over an hour so that by 1630 the *Hancock* was able to recover its planes launched earlier in the day. The cost of the kamikaze's damage was high however. *Hancock* has lost seventy-two sailors and another eighty-two are injured. It is to be the second greatest single loss of life during the thirty hour attack. Only the destroyer USS *Bush* had returned more of her crew to God.

With a raging conflagration fed by 150,000 gallons of diesel fuel, the *LST 447* succumbs to fate at 1615. After capsizing, she finally sinks after twenty-four hours afire. The towering black cloud serves as a navigation aid for those determined to kill themselves from the air.

The destroyer divisions on the radar picket lines had been under attack throughout the day. As Destroyer Divisions 96 and 50 rejoin the Task Group at 1758, Halsey's trident tactics of defense receive further confirmation as successful methods of fleet defense. The fighter director teams working with the Tiger CAPs under their control take credit for fourteen enemy planes shot down before they could reach the phalanx.

Though the number of bogies on the radarmen's screens have nearly disappeared, *Kikusui No. 1* still has an encore in the wings. At 1846, the USS *Maryland* BB-46 is heading north to intercept the remnants of the Surface Special Attack Force. A single Japanese plane targets the *Fighting Mary*. Despite heavy anti-aircraft fire that damages the attacker, the kamikaze manages to hit its mark. With a 250 kg bomb attached, the wounded plane strikes the *Maryland*'s aft #3 sixteen inch gun turret. Atop the turret are several 20mm anti-aircraft weapons. The carnage is significant with casualties of thirty-one killed and thirty-eight wounded. The battleship is a tough veteran after serving twenty-five years with the fleet. She is a survivor of the Pearl Harbor attack and a kamikaze strike on November 16, 1944 during the invasion of the Philippines. Despite the damage and loss of crew, she absorbs the blow and stays in the hunt.

The *Divine Wind* of *Kikusui No. 1* has been blown out. The largest kamikaze attack in World War II is over. Twenty-six US ships are vic-

Lt. Cdr. Scott Lothrop.
(Courtesy of the
USS Haynsworth Association)

tims to the *Tokubetsu Kōgeki tai.* Six have been sunk. The winds have been calmed by the end of April 7 but they will stir again soon.

USS *Haynsworth* Burial at Sea 1816

THE NEXT FEW MINUTES WILL BE SOME OF THE MOST IMPORTANT OF HIS NAVY CAREER. Despite the attacks against the fleet, he slips from the remains of the CIC back into his cabin. Cold water splashed on his face helps him to prepare. Straightening his tie, he looks into the mirror and is provoked by the face he finds staring back at him. Sleep has been a precious friend for but a few minutes in the previous thirty-six hours. He ignores the pain from his burned hands. The battle for the land, sea, and air around Okinawa will not stop for any man, certainly not for a single ship's officer. It is 1800. All crew members not on duty have been ordered to muster amidships for the burial at sea of their dead comrades. Now it is time for the twenty-five year old officer to lead the crew in a new manner.

Lieutenant Commander Scott Lothrop has been the Executive Officer of the *Haynsworth* for its entire time in commission, at sea and often engaged in battle. For most of the ship's men, the *Haynsworth* was the only U.S. Navy vessel the crew has served. This collection of eighteen and nineteen year old sailors is a family, a congregation, a team. Service aboard a tin can was not the anonymous service of those on the capital ships. The freshness of their young faces, the eager grins of youth, has been replaced by the toughened expressions of men serving in combat. Lothrop knew that the ship may be powered by its boilers but it is the crew of the *Haynsworth* that move the ship, who brought the vessel to life. And now for the first time they will bury some of their own.

Promptly at 1816 hours the flag is lowered to half-mast. "Bow into the wind," commands Cdr. Tackney. With the battle still raging, Tackney feels he cannot leave the bridge to attend the services. His duty remains to protect the ship and his men. The engines are slowed just enough that the ship can maintain headway. All those aboard feel the vibration through the steel as the RPMs of the screws slowed. Lothrop departs his stateroom, emerging from the deckhouse amidships, onto the port side sea deck.

With the approach of the Executive Officer, the crew is called to attention. With a snap, all present bring heels together, arms straight to their sides, chins up with heads back. The honor guard bring their rifles to a vertical position directly in front of them. "Sir, ship and crew are ready for the burial ceremony to proceed." Lothrop's response to the report: "Crew, parade rest!"

Lothrop would have preferred that this burial be more traditional. On another day, on a day without battle, nearly the ship's entire crew would be gathered. Instead of the sailor's white uniforms and the officer's white dress uniforms, the uniform of the day is dungarees and chambray shirts for the sailors, khakis for the officers. Lothrop, like each crew member, feels exposed. The USS *Haynsworth* is still serving as part of the screen for the carriers, planes are still flying overhead, and the battle is still being waged. The greatest kamikaze attack of the war has continued into a second day. Though all eyes are on the ceremony, no one is relaxed enough not to strain for the sound of foreign planes. The nagging feeling is reinforced by the helmeted crews already on duty at all the weapons stations. The aft 5" gun mount is manned as are the 20mm machine guns on the fantail, the depth charge racks, and the depth charge K-guns. The quad 40mm tubs above the sea deck are manned as are both sets of torpedoes. Just a few dozen yards down the deck, the superstructure is scorched black. Steel bulkheads are broken open.

Assembled on the deck with the executive officer are part of the crew, a five man honor guard of gunner's mates, six pall bearers, and three body bearers. The remains of seven of their shipmates are lined along the deck. Each set of remains had been sewn into their individual hammock. The impromptu body bags are weighted with 54 pound 5" shells. The space amidships of the *Haynsworth* is tight. Shipmates crowd the deck, the battle stations, and the top of the deckhouse.

On this cool April Saturday, just one week after Holy Saturday, Lt. Cdr. Scott Lothrop fulfills the dual role of Exec and surrogate chaplain. With heads bowed, the assembled crew of teenagers and young men listen to the burial service. After reading from scripture, Tad Lothrop offers some thoughts and prayers for the loss of their shipmates. "Crew, Attention! Present arms!" orders Lothrop, his own hands still bandaged from burns. All render hand salutes as the body bearers-Olen Bonham S1c, Chief Fire Control Officer Robert Hall, and Chief Engineers Mate Robert Rome-lift the remains of Gunners Mate 2nd Class Walter DeLoach onto the pall. "Unto Almighty God we commend the soul of our brother departed, and we commit his body to the deep; in sure and certain hope of the resurrection unto eternal life, though our Lord, Jesus Christ, Amen." By an order from Lt. Cdr. Lothrop, the pall bearers -Robert Chamberlin SoM1c; George Humphrey, Jr. QM1c; Charles Gruber SoM2c; Scott Kirkpatrick, Coxswain; Herman Lakoff M1c; Albert Schlimbach RdM3c- raise the pall allowing DeLoach's remains to slide from underneath the flag into the sea. Bubbles trail the descent.

As DeLoach is committed to the deep, Chief Gunners Mate Eugene Fletcher orders, "Honor Guard! Attention!" No shots are fired as salutes, the *Haynsworth* is still in the midst of hostilities. Instead each of the Honor Guard brings his rifle to a vertical position as a salute, the right hand at the top of the stock, the left clenching the barrel. The prayer of committal and rifle salute are repeated for Seaman First Class Clifford Heob and Seaman First Class John Knott.

Post thirty hours of battle for the seas, Lothrop reads the Catholic Prayer of Committal for Seaman First Class William Kubena and Seaman First Class Joseph Lenihan: "Lord God, by the power of your Word, you stilled the chaos of the primeval seas, you made the raging waters of the Flood subside, and calmed the storm on the Sea of Galilee. As we commit the body of our brother to the deep, grant him peace and tranquility until that day that when he and all who believe in you will be raised to the glory of new life promised in the waters of baptism. We ask this through Christ our Lord, Amen."

Seaman First Class Hobart MacLaughlan and Seaman First Class Ernest Satterly were both Protestant. Lt. Cdr. Lothrop again reads the Protestant Prayer of Committal. The Honor Guard -Chief Gunners Mate Eugene Fletcher, Andrew Domarasky GM3c, Charles Chambers GM1c, Phillip Goldstein GM2c, and Marvin Lentz GM1c-again raise their Springfield rifles upon command for each sailor. Like the sailors who have succumbed to the wounds, all of the members of the Honor

Unknown ship's burial at sea. The officers and crew are at parade rest. The honor guard stands parallel to the deck past the pall. Note the bugler behind the honor squad who is ready to blow "Taps." The Pharmacists Mates have brought the corpse to the pall upon the litter (stretcher) seen on the deck between the honor guard and the floater net on the left.

Guard, Body Bearers, and Pall Bearers chosen by the Executive Officer, Scott Lothrop, are part of the original crew, the *Haynsworth's* plank owners.

After Satterly is committed to the deep, Lt. Cdr. Lothrop commands, "Order Arms!" All salutes are ended as right arms came back to the sides of the sailors.

Reflecting on the death of Satterly, "Ernie was younger than me, an easy-going, always pleasant guy. His death was quite a loss!" remembered Tom Scott. Tears spilled from eyes as the stress of the attack and long battle slipped from the restrained faces of the *Haynsworth* shipmates. Carpenter's Mate Ed Mital scrawled in his journal, "The crew held up nicely. Despite the sorrow. "

As *Taps* is blown, the flag is folded three times before being presented to the capable Executive Officer. "Ship's company! Dismissed!"

Cdr. Lothrop then departs for the CIC as the burial contingent scatters.

As the crew returns to their battle stations, they can again feel and hear the rpms of the screws rise as the *Haynsworth* changes direction. The entire service lasts but a sparse ten minutes. Nightmares of the attack will haunt the young executive officer and many of his charge for the rest of their lives.

USS *Haynsworth* and USS *South Dakota* 1829

WITH MORE WOUNDED SAILORS ABOARD, Captain Tackney maneuvers his destroyer back alongside the *South Dakota*. Three of the eight sailors recovered from the seas during the attack on the *Hancock* are sent first: Donald L. Johnson Coxswain, Frank Tallaiva F1c, and Thomas Neafcy AMM3c are highlined across. Each suffers either 2nd or 3rd degree burns.

Next, he sends two of his own: Frank Lembo S1c and Edward Malkiewicz S1c. Caught in the open the day before, their burns are beyond the medical capabilities offered by Dr. Ley and the pharmacist mates. Malkiewicz suffers from the 3rd degree burns of his legs, right hand and face. Lembo's eyes are bandaged. The *Haynsworth's* doctor is concerned the burns have caused permanent blindness.

Lt. Ley's stocks of medical supplies are replaced by the medical department of the battleship. While the destroyer is alongside, Radioman Second Class Arthur Goyer passes away in the battleship's medical facilities. The burn wounds and ensuing shock could not be overcome. The Catholic priest that brought them aboard, Father James Cunningham, performs the sacrament of Last Rites for Goyer. *...Corpus tuum custodiat et animam tuam salvet....*

As the *Haynsworth* casts off from the *South Dakota* at 1900, another of her sailors dies aboard the battleship. Radioman Third Class John Dyer succumbs to his wounds sustained the day before. Cdr. Cunningham is with Dyer. Like his radio shack partner Goyer, Dyer receives *Viaticum*, the Last Rites, from the Paulist priest. *...We give him Glory as we give you into his arms in everlasting peace...*

Minutes later the 'Lucky 700' secures from General Quarters. At the same time cruising disposition is changed to 5-Roger. The destroyer screen relaxes its protective grip around the precious carriers. At that moment, the officers and sailors of the *Haynsworth* leave the drawn screen of the phalanx. It is the last time during the war that

Left: Father James F. Cunningham, Cdr., USNR.
(Courtesy of the Paulist Archives)
Right: John R. Dyer RM3c. (Courtesy of Mrs. Helen Dyer Richmond)

Cdr. Stephen Tackney's ship will steam in the 5-Victor disposition, the secure screen of the steel phalanx.

USS *South Dakota* 2025

TWO HOURS AFTER *HAYNSWORTH* COMMITS ITS DEAD TO THE SEA, the *South Dakota* unmasts its colors again. The remains of the two *Haynsworth* radiomen from upstate New York, John Dyer of Plattsburgh and Arthur Goyer of Troy, are buried at sea. Short in stature but big in popularity amongst the *Haynsworth's* crew, Goyer had heeded his nations call for help when it was needed most. Just four weeks after the attack on Pearl Harbor, Arthur Alonzo Goyer volunteered for service in the navy. He and Dyer have given their lives in the service of their country.

USS *Quincy* En Route to Ulithi

ADMIRAL NIMITZ' CELEBRATORY COMMUNIQUÉ IS READ over the cruiser's loudspeaker for all the officers and crew to hear:

> *On April 6 and 7 (East Longitude Dates) the enemy attempt-*
> *ed strong counterattacks against our forces operating in the vicin-*
> *ity of Okinawa. During the late afternoon and evening of April*
> *6, a large force of enemy aircraft attacked our ships and shore in-*

stallations in the vicinity of Okinawa. One hundred sixteen of these enemy aircraft were destroyed-55 by our fighters and the remainder by our anti-aircraft fire. The attacking enemy aircraft pressed their attacks in with desperation and succeeded in sinking three of our destroyers and damaging several destroyers and smaller craft. No larger fleet units were hit.

The returning *Haynsworth* radiomen, McAllister and Magliocchetti, know that there are over a hundred destroyers in the waters off the Ryukyu Islands. The odds are slim that the Lucky 700 has been harmed.

USS *Haynsworth* 2348

AFTER THE SUN GOES DOWN ON TASK GROUP 58.3, the *Haynsworth* is making eighteen knots, 9200 yards ahead of the center of the group. She zig-zags in the night for protection. At days' end, she loses her senior radioman, Chief Barton Campbell when the twenty-four year old Ohio native dies aboard the *South Dakota*. Campbell, who had joined the Navy a year before Pearl Harbor, is the last radioman and the last soul to perish from the attack on the *Haynsworth*.

ADMIRAL NIMITZ COULD NOT PUBLICLY RELEASE THE COSTS OF THE BATTLE: Twenty-six ships have been damaged or sunk including twelve destroyers. Nearly 500 sailors have lost their lives. An additional 584 are wounded. The Empire has sent 355 kamikazes against the Fifth Fleet at Okinawa plus another 344 conventional aerial missions. Most of the kamikazes have been sacrificed to the guns of the American planes and ships. The *Yamato* has been sunk, leaving the Imperial Japanese Navy's surface fleet virtually destroyed. But, this is not the last gasp of the Rising Sun. The *Divine Wind* has not yet been extinguished as it smolders in the embers of the IJN and IJA. April 6-7 1945 is just the first of ten *Kikusuis*.

Yet, Armistead Dennett remembered that, "At the end of the day we were all depressed by loss of our shipmates and damage to the ship. But, we had news that the *Yamato* had been sunk and a feeling that the end of the war was near."

8 April 1945: Task Group 58.3

THOUGH THE GREATEST *DIVINE WIND* STORM IN WORLD WAR II WAS OVER, the battle continued for control of the air, land and sea of Okinawa. The second storm was just a few days away. For the moment, Admiral Sherman's task group remained on station east of Okinawa Jima.

Chief Radioman Barton Campbell, succumbing to the first and second degree burns that covered his body, was buried. At 0555, Capt. Charles Momsen of *South Dakota* ordered the flag set to half mast. A few minutes later a chaplain recited prayers over the Ohio native's corpse, the U.S. Marine honor guard fired three volleys over the seas as Campbell was committed to the deep. The colors were two blocked before raised to full mast as the service concluded. One minute later, the sun rose over the horizon to illuminate the skies over Okinawa.

For the destroyers of 58.3.4, the destroyer screen, the day started on a familiar note with DesDiv 96 steaming ahead early to form its radar picket line while *Waldron* and *Walker* held the picket sentry positions. The planes of the group were up early. Though some enemy planes attempted to reach the group in the afternoon, the CAP was positioned to pounce. None of the bogeys could penetrate the aerial blanket or the vicious anti-aircraft fire from the group.

Steaming at radar picket station No.3, just east of TG 58.3 and not far from the *Haynsworth's* picket station two days earlier, the USS *Gregory* DD-802 suffered the day's lone kamikaze strike. Targeted by three *Divine Wind* messengers, she shot down two after the first struck the tin can at the waterline. She survived but her fight in the Pacific was done.

Aboard the *Haynsworth*, Bill McKeen recorded in his journal, "No action, thank God!" The *Haynsworth* will hear no more shots in anger nor witness any other attacks from the *Divine Wind* during its days in the Pacific.

Relieved: Task Unit 53.3.10

REAR ADMIRAL SHERMAN TURNED HIS TASK GROUP SOUTH after all friendly planes were recovered the prior evening. The day would be spent with Rear Admiral Beary's support group. In the safety of the waters south of Okinawa, the group took its fill of oil, provisions and ammunition. For the small dogs, it was also a

USS Hancock burial services, April 9, 1945.
(Courtesy U.S. Navy BUMED Office of Medical History 09-7938-10

day of transferring mail, pilots, passengers and freight amongst the big dogs.

For the wounded *Hancock*, the morning of Sunday, April 9th was a day of reunification and preparation. The carrier sent twenty six of her airworthy planes to the *Essex* and the *Bunker Hill*. Twelve flyable duds are sent back to the 'Hanna' for transport out of the battle area. *Cabot* also sheds some of her better planes to the remaining carriers.

The eight destroyers that rescued sailors from the carrier come alongside to return the survivors to their ship. Efforts by the destroyers to protect the carriers and their crews do not go unnoticed. While underway, the *Hancock* "sent us a message telling of our guts and how much she appreciated us picking up her men under fire," noted *Haynsworth's* Bill McKeen.

Several ships requiring repair or overhaul were transferred to a new task unit, 53.3.10. For the men of the *Haynsworth*, they learned their time in battle was over. The damaged destroyer was ordered east for repair. Executive Officer Scott Lothrop officially broke the news to the crew: "Squadron Commander has recommended that we be returned to Ulithi for repairs. Don't ask me if that is where they will

Burial at sea on the Hancock, April 9, 1945. (NARA 80-G-328574)

all be done, but I think that those of you are breaking out your blues for pressing for stateside liberty are a little off the mark." He continued, "Our schedule beyond tomorrow is not known at present writing."

Excitement and elation about returning possibly to America is tempered with the bitter news of war. Lothrop informed the officers and crew, "It is with deep regret I announce the deaths of Holiman, Matschat, Campbell, Goyer, and Dyer after their transfer to the USS *South Dakota*."

The *Haynsworth*, along with sister destroyer USS *Stembel* DD-644, and the carriers *Hancock* and *Cabot* set a southeasterly course for Ulithi. *Cabot* is suffering from mechanical exhaustion, personnel shortages and in need of overhaul after seventeen months fighting in the Pacific. Her efforts have earned her nine battle stars. The *Stembel* has a fuel leak needing the skills of a destroyer tender. They expect to arrive at the atoll on April 11th. Despite their damage, the destroyers act as a screening ships for the carriers of the small task group. In a Y shaped caravan, the two destroyers lead the way south, each 30 degrees on either bow of the *Hancock*. *Cabot* trails her sister, 1500 yards behind the larger fleet carrier. *Haynsworth's* limited radio capability wanes as repairs are attempted. She relies on signals relayed by the *Stembel*.

For the *Hancock*, she must bury her dead. At 1300 she unmasts her colors while a large contingent of her crew gather in formation in the hangar deck. An honor guard stands watch over the remains of the casualties, the twenty nine sailors who perished aboard the ship during the attack of the seventh. *Taps* was sounded by a bugler from his position near the postside airplane elevator. Following prayers and a twenty one gun salute, the corpses, shrouded and covered by American flags, were brought to palls at the edge of the deck. In groups of five they were commited to the deep, leaving their surviving brothers behind. The departed will remain on duty in the waters east of Okinawa joining another thirty five *Hancock* men missing in action, never to be recovered, forever on duty. Twelve sailors from the *Haynsworth* remain on eternal watch in the same waters.

After basic repairs at Ulithi are completed, Cdr. Tackney's *Haynsworth* returned to America by way of Eniwetok and Pearl Harbor. For the officers and sailors of the *Haynsworth*, the long trip home to America had begun. *Haynsworth's* departure from the war mirrored its entrance as it steamed with a small caravan out of the combat zone. Though the guns were still manned during the journey, there were no more long hours at General Quarters nor did Japanese planes threaten their passage.

The USS *Haynsworth's* service with the phalanx had ended.

THE BATTLE AGAINST THE *DIVINE WIND* HAD TAKEN A TOLL from the *Haynsworth's* boys, both physically and spiritually. After 100 days of service in the war zone, Lt. Armistead Dennett pulled a pen and paper from the desk in his stateroom. In a letter to his father, the gunnery officer wrote, "Haven't heard from you in a long time...there's little I can say that would interest you. My adventures cover 370 feet from bow to stern and a million miles of water." A six cent air mail stamp is the toll to transport the correspondence back to America.

The tedium and lack of contact with civilization is a common theme in the outgoing mail. Bill McKeen penned in a note home, "It will sure be good to get away from it all." Ralph Aakhus' written thoughts to his family reflect those of the crew: "We have had very little mail on this trip out, hopefully it will catch up with us tomorrow. Things have been pretty tough lately and I'll never be able to tell you about it in my letters. I'm feeling fine and there's nothing to worry about. Just hope I'll be able to get home sometime before too long. Today I have been busy and am feeling tired."

Path of the kamikaze attack against USS Haynsworth. (National Archives photo)

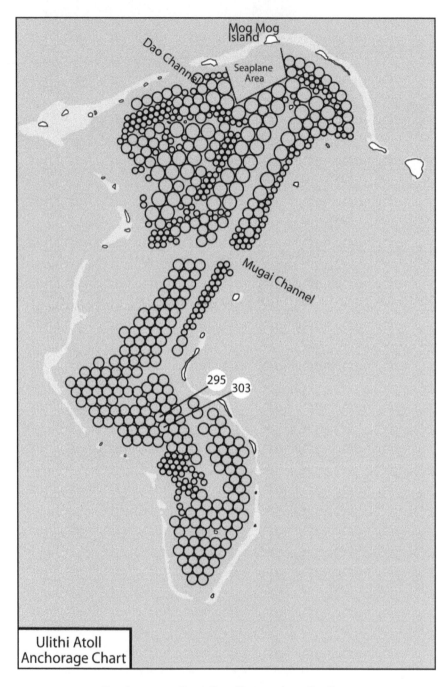

Berths 295 and 303 lie adjacent to each other.

PHALANX AGAINST THE DIVINE WIND

EN ROUTE TO ULITHI

AFTER ELEVEN DAYS AT SEA, the cruiser *Quincy* arrived at Ulithi on the morning of April 11ᵗʰ. Approaching the Mugai Channel from a westerly direction, the cruiser crossed into the atoll late morning and berthed initially at the north end where the heaviest vessels were moored.

Proceding independently on various courses and speeds, the *Haynsworth* entered the Ulithi Lagoon at 1342. By 1447 she had moored alongside the USS *Sepulga* AO-20. The oiler was moored at berth 303, west of the southern channel. Fueling for the wounded ship would last until 1604. A few minutes later the *Haynsworth* prepared to get underway to steam to another berth alongside a destroyer tender. Repairs of the ship's physical wounds would start here and finish stateside.

Also needing refueling, the cruiser *Quincy* left the northern anchorage of the atoll and headed south to refuel alongside the USS *Schuykill* AO-76. The oiler was moored at berth 295, west of the southern channel. The two radiomen passengers were notified to grab their seabags. McAllister and Magliocchetti were to begin the transfer that they thought would bring them to the battle at Okinawa. As the cruiser replenished, a motorboat came alongside to gather the two tin can radiomen aboard. Nearby in the berth directly south, a *Sumner* class destroyer was feeding from an oiler.

Scorched. Blackened, mangled gun tub. Bulkheads blown in where the radio transmitter room was located. The sight of the wounded ship filled their vision but their focus was on its wounds. The '700' on the bow confirmed their sense of dread as the destroyer's motor launch approached the tin can. There would be no further transportation needed to return the newly minted radiomen to their ship. McAllister and Magliochetti had returned to the *Haynsworth*.

THE TWO PLANKOWNERS STEPPED OFF THE GIG AND REACHED FOR THE DESTROYER'S GANGWAY. Mounting the steps to bring them aboard, the seabags on their backs suddenly became heavier with the realization of the extent of the devastation. Mac's hand clenched the lifeline tightly. Reaching the quarter deck, they turned aft to salute the National Ensign then individually requested permission from the Officer of the Deck to board their ship. With their salutes returned, they came aboard for the first time since Pearl Harbor in December of '44.

As they were led to admin for in processing, they gazed at the scorched and twisted metal topside. Normally it would have been Chief Radioman Campbell to escort them but another Chief took charge. "Hey, Mac." "Hello Mag." Old buddies they had known since Sampson, Norfolk, Brooklyn, and training days in the Atlantic greeted them. "Hey," managed Mac, a quiver in his voice, his easy smile nervously subdued. Uneasy feelings rose form the depths of their stomachs. "Who got it?" they queried. "Radio Central and the starboard twin 40 took most of it. Dyer, Campbell, Goyer, Holiman. Little Red Davis and Holcombe are burned pretty bad." Each name was a punch to the gut. The muster amongst the buddies continued with the roll call of the dead on the 40mm. Mac & Mag knew most of them from their first days at Sampson. Satterly was a neighbor at home for McAllister. He and Hobie MacLaughlan had made the most of their last day in the states while on liberty in Los Angeles the previous October. For Magliocchetti, the blackened, twisted steel of the starboard 40mm had been his battlestation. He realized another bluejacket had died in his place.

They were sent below to stow their gear before reporting to Commander Tackney. In the two berthing areas, there were twenty empty racks to choose from, each the bedding area of a buddy who was no longer able to serve the *Haynsworth*. Twelve belonged to souls who would remain on duty for all of time. There was no easy choice to make. "Grab a rack, drop your sack and get up to the bridge. After you meet with the Captain, get down to Emergency Radio. We need you."

AFTERMATH

AWEEK AFTER THE KAMIKAZE ATTACK, the USS Haynsworth was moored alongside a destroyer tender within the protective harbor of the Ulithi Atoll. Other ships damaged in the war against the Divine Wind were already there with more arriving daily. The destroyer was at Condition III. Her weapons were manned while sailors on the watch searched for enemy planes in the sky and kamikaze submarines in the waters. The deadly fingers of the kamikazes had reached the relative safety of Ulithi several times before. A moored ship cannot maneuver and thus becomes a larger target.

As preparation for more extensive repairs than could be completed at Ulithi, Lt. Robert Eshelman, the ship's communication officer, was dispatched to Hawaii bearing photos of the damage taken by the ship's photographer, Bill Morton SoM2c. A list of radio, radar, gunnery, mess, and other equipment needing repair or replacement filled several pages.

Sailors under scorched starboard twin 40mm mount. The plane's engine is secured to the Main Deck. (National Archives photo)

A BABY FACED RADIOMAN RAN DOWN THE PASSAGE-WAY from the emergency radio room up to officer country, the superstructure. After locating Cdr. Stephen Tackney, he hesitantly passed the ship's captain a decoded message. The destroyer's captain read the dispatch, frowned, and studied it again. The weight of command on his face reflected both his exhaustion and that of his crew after months of battle. Gripping the dispatch in his hand, Tackney asked the young radioman if he had taken the message in code. "Yes, sir," the bluejacket responded. "Sailor, didn't you just finish radio school?" The radioman again answered, "Yes, sir." Tackney eyed radioman John McAllister for another moment. "Go back and confirm that President Roosevelt has died." A third response of "Yes, sir" and the nineteen year old sailor hustled back to the emergency radio shack.

NEWS OF THE PRESIDENT'S DEATH was sent by Secretary of the Navy James Forrestal to all ships and stations of the United States Navy:

> *I have the sad duty of announcing to the naval service the death of Franklin Delano Roosevelt, the President of the United States, which occurred on twelve April.*
>
> *The world has lost a champion of democracy who can ill be spared by our country and the Allied cause. The Navy which he so dearly loved can pay no better tribute to his memory than to carry on in the tradition of which he was so proud.*
>
> *Colors shall be displayed at half-mast for thirty days beginning 0800 thirteen April West Longitude Date insofar as war operations permit. Memorial services shall be held on the day of the funeral to be announced later at all yards and stations and on board all vessels of the Navy, war operations permitting.*
>
> *Wearing of mourning badges and firing of salutes will be dispensed with in view of war conditions."*

For a generation that had known no other President than the long serving Roosevelt, the news of his death had a deep impact on the *Haynsworth's* crew. "Today we all heard the broadcast of the death of President Roosevelt. I feel badly and hope the new President will be able to carry the load and end this [war] as soon as possible. I'm not sure anyone will be able to do the job President Roosevelt did. All ships in the Navy will fly the flag at half-mast for thirty days," wrote radarman Ralph Aakhus. "I'm going to try to get to Sunday services as we haven't been able to go very often out here. I have to go now. In a few minutes there will be a five minute period of silence for the burial of the President."

WHILE THE STEMBEL RETURNED TO THE FIGHT OFF OKINAWA SEVERAL DAYS LATER, the Haynsworth spent six days at Ulithi for emergency repairs. Her wounds were ministered to by the destroyer tenders USS Sierra AD-18 and USS Yosemite AD-19. The shattered bulkheads and debris were torched away and she was made light tight, again, in preparation for the long passage to America. The scorched paint on her starboard side remained a battle tattoo.

Shattered bulkheads and equipment have been removed. A temporary patch covers Radio Central to the right of the Radio Transmitter compartment. The crow's nest can be seen on the mast to the left of the national colors. (National Archives photo)

She got and she gave: The *Haynsworth* became a steel organ donor for her squadron mate, *Borie*, which was badly damaged on April 2nd in its collision with the carrier *Essex*. The *Sierra* removed DD-700's after stack and her only remaining twin 40mm mount. These were grafted onto the *Borie* so she could return to the fight with DesRon 62 and Task Group 58.3.

The stress of combat escaped at Ulithi. With the two destroyers moored alongside each other, some of the *Haynsworth's* crew placed blame for the kamikaze attack and subsequent loss of friends on the *Borie*. With DD-704 out of the hunt due to its wounds, her sister ship, *Haynsworth*, had to pick up the slack so that the picket stations far from the protection of the phalanx were manned. Before she was struck by the kamikaze, DD-700 had spent four out of five days on picket duty. Easy access between the ships allowed tempers to flare between the crews of the two destroyers. Fists flew.

BY DAWN'S EARLY LIGHT ON MONDAY, APRIL 17TH, Cdr. Stephen Noel Tackney took the USS Haynsworth back to sea. Leaving the protective anchorage of Ulithi, she steamed east by herself. On April 21, DD-700 arrived at Eniwetok for replenishment. Her visit was brief as she refueled for the journey east to Hawaii. After eight hours, she was on the move again.

On the 18th, the *Haynsworth* crossed the 180th meredian for the second time during the war. Eddie Mital mused, "Today is Monday and tomorrow is, too."

THE SMELL OF FLOWERS AND TROPICAL PLANTS greeted the *Haynsworth* sailors as they neared Oahu. The sense of apprehension that marked their arrival at Pearl Harbor in October had been replaced by sense of relief as they returned on April 27th.

The U.S. Navy's focus at Pearl Harbor was centered on ships heading west toward the fight. The *Haynsworth* would have to continue to California for needed substantial repairs. With his ship temporarily moored in safe waters, Ed Mital CM2c wrote: "Arrived at Pearl Harbor. Seems like Heaven. Tonight they are giving us a party. Also, Navy Band is coming to the ship. The dope is that we will go to the states for repairs. Fingers crossed." A day later when his prayers were granted, Mital wrote his final wartime journal entry: "Wahoo! California, here we come! Also going to get some leave. I'm in heaven." Bill McKeen recorded similar thoughts: "Under weigh for Mare Island and seventeen days leave-very nice day!"

The final journey together for the war crew of the USS *Haynsworth* had begun.

Task Force 58 Okinawa

AS THE *HAYNSWORTH* WAS MAKING ITS TRIP STATE-SIDE, her wounded bluejackets aboard the *South Dakota* were finally leaving the battle, weeks after their ship had departed. The destroyer boys were attuned to the sounds and vibrations of battle. After their arrival aboard the *South Dakota* on April 6 & 7, the fast battleship engaged the Bushido boys in nearly daily battles. The emergency turns following General Quarters alarms confirmed the enemy was nearby. Air defense was offered by the same type of 5," 40mm, and 20mm guns as DD-700. The difference between the two types of ships armament was the quantity of weapons mounted. BB-57 carried sixty eight 40mm guns, seventy-six 20mm Oerlikons, and sixteen 5" guns. When the battleship shot down a *Kate* midday on April 7, 644 rounds were sent towards the torpedo bomber in just a few seconds. A few days later during *Kikusui No.2*, attackers presented themselves numerous times. By evening, the big ship had replied to their appearance with 683 5" shells, 5625 40mm rounds, and 7082 20mm shots. The ordnance expended stood as testament to the close in attacks still developing within the phalanx as the battle for the skies of Okinawa continued. The sounds and vibrations carried down to the Purple Heart sailors below deck in the sick bay. Morphine eased the pain of the fractures and the burns but could not completely mask the nightmares that erupted from their subconscious post the attacks.

Left to right: Mariano Saia RdM3c, Milton Studley RdM3c, Bill Nauck BM1c. Note: Purple Hearts on Saia and Studley's ribbons. (Courtesy of Milton Studley II)

The tin can boys were finally transferred at sea to the USS *Bountiful* AH-9 on May 1st. In a break between *Kikusui No. 4 & No. 5*, the hospital ship entered the battle formation to effect a first of its kind patient evacuation from a combatant ship. The eight kamikaze attack survivors and Bosuns Mate First Class William Nauck, wounded by

OFFICIAL PHOTOGRAPH
NOT TO BE RELEASED
FOR PUBLICATION
NAVY YARD MARE ISLAND, CALIF

RESTRICTED

USS Haynsworth at Mare Island, CA for repairs. (National Archives photo)

heavy seas back in early March, were headed for a navy hospital on Guam before an eventual return to the United States.

USS *Haynsworth*

S HE RETURNED TO AMERICA A WOUNDED SENTRY. Cdr. Tackney's destroyer set course for the shipyard at Mare Island, California. After over four months at sea, almost continually in combat, the *Haynsworth* finally returned to the welcome shores of the United States on May 3rd, 1945, seven months since they had sailed from Long Beach.

As she approached California, Cdr. Tackney's ship answered the challenge of a U.S. Navy blimp on coastal patrol. It was a radical departure from the radar blip of enemy planes.

"Man the Rails!" With her sailors lining the lifelines of the boat deck, the *Haynsworth* entered the ship channel to San Francisco Bay at mid morning. After an initial inspection by Horticultural and Yard inspectors, the Lucky 700 proceeded to the ammunition dock at Mare Island where her ordnance was off loaded.

If arrival on America's shores was not reason enough to celebrate, just several days later on May 7th the Germans surrendered to the Allies. The war in Europe had ended after six years.

There were various other reasons for the crew of the *Haynsworth* to celebrate. Almost all received leave to go visit family. Some got married while others were transferred to new assignments aboard ships or at military schools. For some it was simple as just being on dry land for an extended time. Marion Parker GM3c had endured nine months of seasickness. California represented an end to his problem at sea. Offered a transfer months earlier, Parker refused. He lived up to his promise to stay with the original crew, the plank owners of the *Haynsworth*, until its mission was completed. GM2c Phil Goldstein stated that it "shows you the caliber of men aboard ship. I was honored to serve with him."

SUBMARINE PURSUITS. REPELLING JAPANESE AIR ATTACKS. PILOT RESCUES. SHORE BOMBARDMENT. RADAR PICKET DUTY. KAMIKAZES. For one hundred days the USS *Haynsworth* had served with Destroyer Squadron 62 protecting the most potent naval weapon ever created, the Fast Carrier Task Force 38/58.

The crew had endured typhoons and bounding seas, long hours at General Quarters, accidents and injuries, maelstroms of aerial attacks and the death of comrades with the subsequent evacuation of the wounded while the victims were hastily buried at sea as the battle for the Pacific raged around them. The *Haynsworth's* role in combat had ended when she departed Okinawa. For her efforts, the phalanx guard earned her third battle star after just one hundred days in the war zone:

14 MARCH 1945 – 9 APRIL 1945: THIS VESSEL IN COMPANY WITH TASK FORCE 58 IN CARRIER STRIKES AGAINST KYUSHU, KURE AND OKINAWA JIMA AND IN SUPPORT OF LANDINGS ON OKINAWA JIMA, THIS VESSEL SHOT DOWN ONE JAPANESE "ZEKE" DIVING ON THE TASK GROUP ON 19 MARCH 1945. THIS VESSEL CARRIED OUT SOME SHORE BOMBARDMENT OF MINAMI DAITO JIMA ON 28 MARCH 1945. OPERATIONS WITH TASK FORCE 58 TEMPORARILY SUSPENDED FOR REPAIRS WHEN THIS VESSEL WAS STRUCK BY A JAPANESE SUICIDE DIVE BOMBER ON THE 6TH

APRIL 1945. DEPARTED TASK FORCE 58, 9 APRIL
1945.

FOUR REPLACEMENT RADIOMEN REPORTED ABOARD
Captain Tackney's warship on May 4th. With McAllister and
Magliocchetti already back aboard, DD-700 had a full complement of
radiomen again. Three additional radarmen reported aboard the following day.

The crew that brought her to life less than a year earlier began to
scatter. Goodbyes had been said at sea. Only a skeleton crew stayed
with the ship as her needs were tended to from the shore. One by one
the bluejackets approached the Officer of the Deck at the brow. Each
saluted then request permission to go ashore. With "permission granted," each did an about face before rendering a salute toward the National Ensign. With their seabags on their backs, they descended down
the brow to shore. Many would never return to the *Haynsworth*.

Their seabags contained copies of the daily Morning Orders posted
by Lt. Cdr. Scott Lothrop. These plans were popular souvenirs with
the crew during their time in battle. Copies of the Morning Orders for
April 7, the day after the kamikaze strike, were scattered to sailors'
homes across America. After their fateful day, Lt. Cdr. Lothrop had
added a postscript for the crew:

> *NOTE: It is hard to find words to express the feeling I have
> for the manner in which the crew acted in the emergency – or
> just the feeling I have for the crew after yesterday. I feel as if I had
> had the privilege of seeing inside you for a brief moment and
> finding inside something fine that comes out under stress such as
> yesterday. I am intensely proud of each one of you. –The Execu-
> tive Officer*

MOORED DOCKSIDE, THE MECHANICAL LIFE WAS
DRAINED FROM THE VESSEL. Electrical, steam and water
lines were brought across from shore, all utilities came from the pier.
The remaining two boilers, her evaporators, and generators were shut
down. The stacks were covered like the guns. As she once was at
Kearney and for a time in Brooklyn Naval Yard in 1944, the Lucky
700 transformed to cold iron again.

PHALANX AGAINST THE DIVINE WIND

EPILOGUE

Destroyer Squadron 62

THE JAPANESE KEPT COMING. The warships surrounding Okinawa remained in the crosshairs. The carriers were the ultimate prize but it was the destroyers that kept taking the brunt for the fleet. Picket duty became an even lonelier proposition as the role became more deadly.

Four days after the inaugural *Kikusui No. 1* rained down on ships of the Allies, Operation Ten-Go released its second raid. Though smaller than the 355 kamikaze planes of the first raid, the sequel sent another 185 planes towards Okinawa on April 11-12. During the attacks, twenty-four more ships were struck, eight of them destroyers.

As they had since the end of December, 1944, Destroyer Squadron 62 continued to sink mines, rescue pilots and sailors, and fend off enemy air attacks while guarding the carriers. Just a few weeks earlier, the squadron was at full strength with all nine sister *Sumners* operational. But in a matter of just one week's time, three were damaged and eventually detached from the task group for repair. Captain Higgins' original squadron was rapidly depleted by both combat and operations. At one point during the intense action of early April, six of the seventeen destroyers were detached from the Destroyer Screen TG 58.3.4. Out of action for periods of time were the *Hale, Stembel, Kidd, Haynsworth, Hank*, and *Borie*.

As the *Haynsworth* was moving into the channel at Ulithi, squadron mate DD-702 was heading into danger. *Wallace L. Lind* had reported to its radar picket post during late afternoon of April 10th. The next day, fourteen miles ahead of the task group, bogies were detected by radar. Cdr. George Chambers ordered evasive maneuvers at 1350 as the Japanese *Zekes* closed on the destroyer. The gun crews were ready when the kamikaze dove from the low clouds. As the plane turned towards the bridge, Chambers called for hard left rudder to counteract the assault. "Portside automatic weapons opened fire at a range of 1000 yards, at which range the plane commenced strafing." The guns were hitting their mark as the attacker's plane began to break apart. "Continued hits by the 40mm battery seemed to literally lift the plane in the air and it skimmed over the two after 40mm batteries and crashed in the water close aboard." Though there was no significant damage to the tin can, three sailors were killed in the action.

The kamikaze closes in on the USS Kidd.
(Courtesy of the USS Kidd Veterans Museum)

The USS *Kidd*, as part of the 58.3.4 destroyer screen, became a victim during its duty as a radar picket. At the same time the kamikaze missed *Lind*, *Kidd* began firing at a raider. The CAP finished the job but just a few minutes later another kamikaze came after *Bullard*. The two DesDiv 96 squadron mates combined fire to down the plane before it could crash aboard *Bullard*. The kamikaze came close enough to dent the ship, rip down cables and tear various gear from the bulkheads when its left wing impacted the deck.

Using speed as a defense, the division increased to twenty-five knots as another kamikaze appeared to target the *Black*. At the last moment it cleared the destroyer and hurtled towards the *Kidd*. Furious anti-aircraft fire was expended but despite numerous hits, the enemy plane crashed into the *Kidd*. The impact extended from starboard to port as the attacker's bomb exploded just off the port side. The destruction killed thirty-eight sailors including the ship's captain and her doctor. Fifty-five more were wounded.

The ordeal was not over. As the *Kidd* retired from the scene with a protective screen composed of *Black*, *Bullard* and *Chauncey*, the de-

Wreckage of USS Hazelwood.

stroyer came under attack again. A raider dropped a bomb between *Kidd* and *Hale* as the latter attempted to transfer her doctor to the former. Anti-aircraft fire found some purchase as the smoking attacker fled. Two hours later enemy planes came again towards *Kidd*. *Hale's* gun crews managed to keep the raiders at bay.

A NOTHER *62* CAN GOT IT. The *Hank* was relieved and returned to Ulithi on April 16th after damage was caused by a raiding aircraft. Assigned to picket duty on April 11th, "A *Zeke* fighter was sighted off the port bow heading directly for the bridge, and would have found his mark if it had not been for accurate fire of the 40mm and 20mm machine guns. Though he did not succeed in his mission, he flew low enough to knock one man overboard, decapitate another, and riddle a third with his machine gun fire. The *Zeke* crashed into the sea and exploded close aboard the starboard quarter." The concussion from the crash knocked out the ship's fire control system. The *Hank* returned to the task group with squadron mate *Borie* after repairs on May 1st. The sister destroyers would face the *Divine Wind* again together before the war ended.

Ed and John Magliocchetti. (Courtesy of Marianna Steele)

MORE RAIDS FOLLOWED. *Kikusui No.3* was released on April 15-16 followed by *No.4* almost two weeks later on April 27-28. Between the massed attacks, kamikazes also preyed on the ships singly or in small groups. The USS *Hazelwood* DD-531 was screening for Task Group 58.4 northeast of Okinawa when they were attacked on April 29th. Despite successfully fending off several kamikazes, one slipped through. The maneuverable *Zero* fighter, strafing as it came, hit the destroyer between the forward stack and the superstructure. The aviation fuel created an inferno as it splattered across the ship. The explosion from its bomb destroyed the superstructure. Ten officers and sixty-seven sailors were killed, including Radarman 2nd Class Ed Magliocchetti, brother of the *Haynsworth's* John. The latter had escaped the attack against the *Haynsworth* while in transit to the battle. The service flag in their parents' window changed from two blue stars to one blue star and one gold star, one living son and one son killed in defense of his country.

MAY PROVIDED LITTLE RELIEF FROM THE ATTACKS. Operation Ten-Go continued with further flights of Floating Chrysanthemums. *Kikusui No.6* bore in on Task Group 58.3 on the morning of May 11th. By early morning, bogies forced the destroyers to close the phalanx. Less than an hour later two kamikazes made 'landings' on the flight deck of the *Bunker Hill*. Task Force Commander Vice Admiral Mitscher escaped death as the second attacker crashed less than one hundred feet from his position on the carrier's command island. Nearby, thirty pilots were asphyxiated in the ready room near the flight deck. Among those lost was Ensign William

USS Charles S. Sperry comes alongside USS Bunker Hill.
(NARA 80-G-373392)

Elings, rescued at sea on March 29th and a hero in the attack against the *Yamato*. Lt. Berry and his aircrew also lost their lives in the dark, smoke filled passageways.

With fires raging amidships and at the stern of the carrier, the Destroyer Screen Commander released five of his destroyers from the phalanx to stay with the *Bunker Hill*. The *English*, *Sperry*, and *Stembel* came alongside to aid the stricken carrier to fight the fires aboard the larger warship. As the *English* was spraying the fire near the 500 lb. bomb stowage area, three sailors jumped from a 40mm gun platform to the deck of the destroyer. Others jumped into the ocean. Life jackets and other floating objects were tossed overboard while the *English's* damage control teams transferred rescue breathing apparatuses and sections of hose to CV-17. Both the *Ault* and *Waldron* trailed the carrier, rescuing sailors as they were found in the water.

During the rescues, three more bandits appeared in the skies. The CAP finished the flying careers of two of them but a third kamikaze dived towards the burning *Bunker Hill*. As the screening ships opened fire, the bandit switched targets, winged over and came after the *Ault*. The destroyer's main batteries had been tracking the raider since its first appearance on radar. The fire from the 20mm, 40mm, and 5" guns found their mark. The plane crashed close aboard.

DesRon 62 destroyer portside sprays water on the Bunker Hill.
(NARA 80-G-328618)

By midafternoon the fires aboard *Bunker Hill* were under control. The *English* transferred Task Force Commander Mitscher and his staff to the venerable and long serving USS *Enterprise* CV-6. Meanwhile, the *Bunker Hill* left the group with the *Ault* and *Waldron* as her escorts so she could be tended to by the Logistics Support Group 50.8. At day's end, 396 sailors perished but the tin cans from Destroyer Squadron 62 rescued fifty sailors from the seas.

DesDiv 124 had been sent out that morning with DesDiv 96 to form the radar picket line away from the phalanx. For the *Lind,* "today was almost THE day. A *Zeke* made a suicide run on us, came in high and strafed our deck. Our 20's and 40's exploded him in mid-air and pieces of plane littered our deck. The plane crashed just past our mast and stack, about 20 yards off our stern."

ADMIRAL SPRUANCE WAS A LIGHTNING ROD AGAIN. On May 12th, his flagship, the USS *New Mexico,* was attacked by two kamikazes that snuck upon by the battleship by tailing the CAP. One bomb hit the old gal while the second plane was able to bring

Admirals Halsey and Spruance meet in April 1945. (NARA 80-G-322429)

'honor' to his family by crashing into the ship. Fifty-four bluejackets were killed but Spruance and the *New Mexico* stayed in the hunt.

Two days later, the combat veteran of four years, the USS *Enterprise* was struck by a kamikaze. Fires were contained quickly. The *Waldron*, always the lifeguard, rescued eight sailors from CV-6. For the Fast Carrier Task Force, the *Gray Ghost* was to be the last flattop hit by a kamikaze during the war.

After seventy-nine days on station, Task Force 58 was finally relieved on June 10. It had been eighty-eight days since the squadron had sailed from Ulithi. The Fast Carrier Task Force turned west and headed to Leyte.

Operation ICEBERG finally came to an end when Okinawa was declared 'secure' on June 21, 1945. It was the United States Navy's costliest Pacific battle: 36 ships were sunk, 368 were damaged. Over 4900 sailors were killed and an almost equal amount wounded in attacks around the Ryukyu Islands.

WHILE AT ULITHI, 58 BECAME 38, again as Fifth Fleet metamorphosed into Third Fleet. Admirals Halsey and McCain retook the reins from Admirals Spruance and Mitscher.

After a month in the Philippines, Task Force 38, set its sights on Japan. The remaining lethal breezes of the *Divine Wind*s struck lightly across Okinawa through June. Eighteen attacks occurred while in July there were only five more successful aerial kamikaze attacks against the U.S. Navy. Remembered by some as 'sacrificial lambs,' the destroyers, their brothers, the destroyer mine sweepers, and their little brothers, the destroyer escorts, continued to absorb the blows from the air.

Though the *Divine Wind*s were dwindling, they were not fully extinguished. With the invasion of the home islands a near certainty, the Japanese military had begun to hoard its meager aerial resources for the time when the American invasion fleets ventured nearby. But, just as they had done before the Okinawan invasion, small numbers of kamikazes were sortied against the Allied warships. Serving at a radar picket station on July 29, the USS *Callaghan* DD-792 was taken under attack by an obsolete wood and fabric skinned biplane. Shells passed right through the attacker's cloth skin. The kamikaze's bomb punctured the tin can's aft engine room leading to explosions from munition stores. Forty-seven sailors perished. *Callaghan* was the last destroyer sunk by kamikazes in the World War II.

BEFORE THERE WAS THE USS *BORIE* DD-704, THERE WAS ANOTHER *BORIE*. Launched just after the first World War, the USS *Borie* DD-215 was finally able to pursue an enemy decades later when the world deemed it was time for the next World War. In an attack against a German submarine, U-405, she laid depth charges over her target. Forced to the surface, the sub was mounted by the destroyer as a large wave dropped *Borie's* bow atop U-405. The foes became entangled with the tin can atop the Kriegsmarine vessel for fifteen minutes. The two vessels exchanged shots at close range before they separated and the chase began again. The old destroyer won the shoot out after U-405 signaled surrender. The tactical victory was tempered by the severe damage to the hull of the destroyer. Eventually she had to be sunk by her peers. Less than two years later, her namesake, DD-704, would also close with the enemy in a deadly fight.

On August 9th the carrier force launched airstrikes against Northern Honshu and Hokkaido. Earlier that morning DesDiv 124, less the *Lind* but plus the USS *Brenner* DD-806, steamed fifty miles ahead of the task group. Deployed as a radar picket station southwest of TF 38, enemy planes were encountered throughout the day. By midafternoon, none of the enemy planes had ventured within gun range of the destroyers. That changed at 1450 when a raider was detected. The Gen-

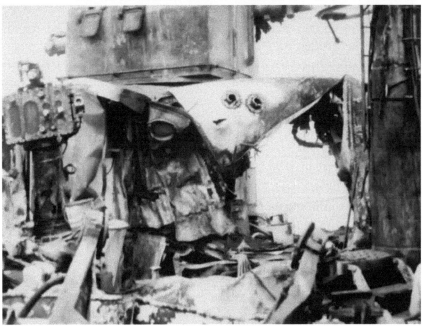

Damage to both forward 5" batteries and the superstructure (gun director top, mast right).

eral Quarters alarm sounded as the kamikaze circled the warships of the picket station. All the destroyers opened fire while at the same time increasing speeds to twenty-seven knots. As the plane pulled astern of the *Borie*, its captain, Cdr. Noah Adair, increased his ship's speed to thirty knots while calling for left full rudder. The *Val* dive bomber had the ship's bridge in his crosshairs when he struck DD-704 between the forward stack and the 5" gun director atop the superstructure. The kamikaze's bomb passed through the thin skin of the tin can, exploding outside of the ship.

The crews of both twin 40mm mounts on the starboard and port sides of the bridge, along with the crews of the 20mm guns nearby, were all wounded or killed. Sailors topside along the bridge suffered the same fate while the gun crews in both forward 5" gun mounts were riddled with shrapnel. Many in the enclosed guns were killed. The same port twin 40mm mount that had escaped damage as part of the *Haynsworth*, was destroyed as the starboard twin mount of the *Borie*.

Like the *Haynsworth* and many other brother destroyers before, *Borie's* superstructure was awash in flame. Steering was initially lost but damage control parties were able to bring the blaze under control in twenty minutes. In the gun tubs, 40mm ammunition cooked off for a period of time.

Raiders weren't done with the damaged destroyer. Commander Adair recorded that at, "1526 plane attacked ship using same general tactics. Plane turned to start run on this ship and was shot down by combined fire of No.3 5" and after 40mm mounts when 3000 yards from this ship." The maelstrom continued as three more kamikazes came at the band of destroyers. The triumvirate became victims of accurate anti-aircraft fire from their intended targets. Two of the three kamikazes, wings shot off, crashed close aboard Cdr. George's Chamber's *Hank*. The high speed impacts with the ocean showered the destroyer with debris and gasoline. Five of her sailors were killed while one missing sailor was never found.

The rest of the ninth and extending into the next day, the destroyers searched for survivors of the attacks. The cost to the *Borie* was thirteen missing, thirty-five sailors killed, and sixty-six wounded. The most severely wounded were transferred to the USS *Rescue AH-18* for care. Cdr. Adair led the burial at sea for her dead that afternoon. He would later be awarded the Silver Star for, "conspicuous gallantry and intrepidity as Commanding Officer of the Destroyer USS *Borie* in action against enemy Japanese forces near the shores of the Japanese Empire on 9 August 1945."

Flag being hung on the Haynsworth's former aft stack, transplanted on the Borie.

T HE SECOND ATOMIC BOMB WAS DROPPED on Nagasaki the same day that the *Borie* was attacked while the Soviets invaded Japanese held Manchuria. Just a few days later, the USS *Lagrange*, an attack transport ship, was struck by the last breath of the *Divine Wind* while anchored in Nakagusuku Bay. For the *Borie* and the *Hank*, their battles against kamikazes represented the final attacks by the *Tokubetsu Kōgeki tai* against warships in World War II. The phalanx would not close in response to attacks by the *Divine Wind* ever again.

For the Americans, no fleet carriers were sunk by the *Divine Wind* though many, like the *Bunker* Hill, were taken out of the hunt. The only ship lost larger than the destroyers were three "jeep" carriers. One of these, the *St. Lo*, was lost during the original kamikaze attack of October 25, 1944.

The six ships sunk during *Kikusui No.1* represented thirteen percent of the total number of ships lost to kamikazes in World War II.

READING BIBLE, LCDR DELLER & CHIEF BOSUN SALUTING.

USS Borie burial at sea.

Further, destroyers accounted for thirty percent of the losses for the entire war in the Pacific. Their roles in the phalanx or performing picket duty kept them steaming into harm's way. By war's end nearly one hundred destroyers had suffered from the *Divine Wind*s.

THE *HAYNSWORTH* REMAINED IN CALIFORNIA FOR THE REST OF THE WAR. Her wounds were tended, equipment replaced, repairs and overhauls completed. With the prospect of facing kamikazes again, the aft torpedo tubes were removed and an additional quad 40mm gun tub was added to beef up fire power. Radioman Third Class John McAllister proposed that a scuttle hatch be installed in the deck of the radio shack. With almost daily kamikaze strikes against destroyers off Okinawa, it was deemed a prudent suggestion. As a post mortem, the hatch was installed.

The long hulled *Sumners* that Cdr. Brodie had desired, the *Gearing* class, were being commissioned. Just as many of the *Haynsworth*'s sailors had gone through destroyer training in Norfolk, VA, the new crews to man the newly commissioned *Fletcher*, *Sumner*, and *Gearing* classes had to be trained. The 'Lucky 700' provided the education. Sev-

***Repairs and upgrades including new aft quad 40mm to USS Haynsworth.
(National Archives)***

eral months were spent as a training ship as crews prepared for the up-coming invasion of Japan.

While many of the original *Haynsworth* crew remained with the destroyer, there were changes in the ship's company. On July 18th, the destroyer's second captain, Cdr. Stephen Tackney, was relieved by Cdr. Jimmy Smith USN. Tackney was promoted to Command Destroyer Divison 124 (DD's 701-704) in late August. He returned to the Pacific to relieve Cdr. R. W. Smith. Japan would formally sign the peace agreement nine days later to end the war.

Changes were in store for the destroyer's Executive Officer, Lt. Cdr. Scott Lothrop. Following his tenure with the *Haynsworth*, Lothrop earned his first command, the USS *Nelson* DD-623. Lothrop was just twenty six years old. His actions on April 6 also earned the young officer both a Purple Heart and a Bronze Star with Valor attachment:

> *For meritorious service as Executive Officer of the U.S.S. HAYNSWORTH during operations against enemy Japanese forces in the Pacific War Area from December 30, 1944 to April 9, 1945. Serving with distinction in an assignment of vital importance, Lieutenant Commander Lothrop skillfully organized the inexperienced company of his ship into an effective fighting team and, in addition, rendered invaluable assistance to his commanding officer during the damaging of his ship by the enemy on April 6 and during additional combat operations. By his skill and devotion to duty, Lieutenant Commander Lothrop upheld the highest traditions of the United States Naval Service." Lieutenant Commander Lothrop is authorized to wear the Combat "V."*
>
> *For the President, James Forrestal, Secretary of the Navy.*

Lt. Harry A Cummings came aboard the *Haynsworth* to replace the plankowner executive officer while Lt. Armistead Dennett was transferred from the *Haynsworth* after its arrival at Mare Island. His next billet was at Annapolis for graduate school.

After months at sea, the sailors of the DD-700 took advantage of the leave they had earned. Some visited family, some visited girl friends, and some did both. After nearly three years at war in the Navy, Ed Mital hurried home to visit Orena, the receptionist for a local doctor. When they had first met, she had passed out at the sight of his blood from a procedure done in the office. Ed was convinced she fainted because she was taken with him. That evening he told his mother she would be the girl he would marry. On May 13, 1945 Mital's prediction came true.

The three pharmacist mates, Kessler, Bland and Jones, were temporarily transferred to a Navy post on Puerto Rico to treat casualties of non-combat encounters. While there, they operated a venereal disease clinic.

Post the repairs at Mare Island, a plaque was installed on the #41 40mm mount. The plaque honored the brave sailors who gave their

Left: Mr. and Mrs. John Magliocchetti in San Franciso, 1945.
(Courtesy of Marianna Steele)
Center: Plaque remembering the fallen from the attack of 6 April 1945.
(Courtesy of John Vasquez)
Right: Warner C. Holcombe RM1c, postwar.
(Courtesy of the Oakland Yacht Club)

life on April 6, 1945 including the six members of the 40mm gun crew and the four radiomen. Along with the names of those killed were the words, "They stuck to their guns."

For those that had survived the attack, recovery came in stages. Radioman Warner Crockett Holcombe was among a group of wounded *Haynsworth* blue jackets transferred from the *South Dakota* by way of the hospital ship, USS *Bountiful*, to a 1,000 bed Navy hospital on Guam. At the end of May, 1945, the lanky San Francisco native was evacuated to the United States aboard the USS *Bolivar* along with 451 other casualties from the battle of Okinawa. Numerous surgeries and skin grafts awaited him before he was finally discharged by the Navy after nearly four years of service. Friends remember Holcombe as a reserved gentleman who could rise to any social occasion.

Third Class Radioman Carroll Leo Davis, Jr., like Holcombe, was burned during the attack. On June 20, 1945, Davis was transferred to U.S. Navy Base Hospital 18 on Guam. Six days later the Hoopeston, Illinois native was transferred to the hospital ship, USS *Bountiful*. The plank owner radioman, with personality to match his fiery red hair, eventually made his way back to America. Despite his injuries, Davis recovered sufficiently that he returned to active duty.

Seaman Second Class Lonnie L. Aulbert endured twenty-eight months of hospital care ranging from the officer's ward room of the *Haynsworth* all the way to the burn unit at Bethesda Naval Hospital.

The short lean sailor lost two inches of height from his 5' 6" frame due to the shattered bone in his left femur. He never regained full use of his left hand. His ears were burned off while scars remained across his face and hands.

COVERED IN TARPS ACROSS HER AFT DECK, the heavy cruiser USS *Indianapolis* was in drydock near the *Haynsworth's* berth. In early July, the *Haynsworth's* A.C. Pickens visited a buddy assigned to the cruiser. Pickens asked why the tarps were in place. His friend responded, "We're going to carry a secret weapon to end the war."

Two weeks later, several large crates were brought aboard the thirteen-year old cruiser. Under strict security, the boxes were stored in the ship's hangars. The ship left Mare Island the same day. Traveling at high speed the heavy cruiser arrived at the island of Tinian in the northern Mariana Islands chain. Captain Charles McVay's vessel had steamed 5000 miles in just ten days. On July 26, uranium and the parts for the two atom bombs were delivered to the U.S. Army Air Force at Tinian. These weapons were used in the world's only two nuclear attacks, Hiroshima on August 6th and Nagasaki on August 9th, 1945.

TOKYO BAY'S ANCHORAGE WAS FILLED the morning of September 2nd, 1945. Allied ships of every description, except one, were moored there, from the smallest gunboats to the largest battleships. Pearl Harbor victim USS *West Virginia* was on hand to represent the span of the war. Destroyers were represented by fifty American, Australian, and British warships. From the phalanx, the *Ault* and the *Wallace L. Lind* moored within shouting distance of the 'Mighty Mo.' *Lind* transported Vice Admirals John S. McCain and John H. Towers to the ceremony while *Ault's* guests included Commodore John Higgins, the former Commander of DesRon 62. Military dignitaries from both sides were aboard the USS *Missouri* for the signing of the peace document.

The fleet carriers, targets throughout the war, stayed at sea. Their representatives were a flyover of 450 planes coming in low over the anchorage.

Topside on the *Missouri*, all spaces were filled by officers and sailors. As movie cameras rolled, signatures from both sides, Allied and Axis, were inked on the surrender treaty. After nearly four years, the Allied war in the Pacific against Japan had ended.

Tokyo Bay. (NARA 80-G-421130)

For Commander Stephen N. Tackney, the ceremony brought a conclusion to the warrior seaman's time in battle: From the first shots at Pearl Harbor, the desperate times in the Solomons, the phalanx missions with Task Force 38/58, and the final kamikaze attacks as the Japanese military smoldered in its embers.

As the war came to its conclusion, fourteen tin cans lay in the depths of the Pacific, victims of the *Divine Wind*s. Another two brother destroyer minesweepers would also remain on eternal duty. Over one hundred destroyers were hit or damaged by kamikazes during the ten month campaign. But, the phalanx held throughout the war. No fleet carriers, cruisers, or battleships were sunk by the aerial warriors of the Japanese Empire's *Tokubetsu Kōgeki tai.*

AT WAR'S END, all service members received a letter from their Commander in Chief, President Harry Truman

> *To you who answered the call of your country and served in its Armed Forces to bring about the total defeat of the enemy, I extend the heartfelt thanks of a grateful Nation. As one of the Na-*

Surrender Ceremony.
USS Wallace L. Lind at anchor in upper right of photo.

tion's finest, you undertook the most severe task one can be called upon to perform. Because you demonstrated the fortitude, resourcefulness and calm judgment necessary to carry out that task, we now look to you for leadership and example in further exalting our country in peace. *Harry Truman*

BEFORE THEY BECAME KNOWN AS THE *GREATEST GENERATION*, the USS *Haynsworth* comrades wrote of the bonds of brotherhood forged in battle. George Schneider S1c penned a letter postwar to the family of his friend, Clifford Heob S1c, killed in action during the April 6 attack:

PHALANX AGAINST THE DIVINE WIND

Our Countrymen would call Clifford Heob 'hero'; yet, were he to speak, he would tell you this: That each act called heroism is but the instinctive gesture of forgetting self when another stands in danger. We who served in action know it; you who served in silence know it. But let me tell you of Clifford Heob and you will see the millions of Cliffords. Clifford was a typical American boy, born and reared in a typical American family and home; a pleasant chap, liked by all who knew him. I don't say that Cliff knew no fear—no, he was too much an American for that. Like all of us, he knew fear but knew the remedy: Faith and Selflessness. Maybe Cliff was a 'hero'; maybe 'hero' is but a word. But the true act of selflessness remains and is our God given heritage.

Of his service aboard the *Haynsworth*, Storekeeper First Class Louie Clark wrote, "I was allowed to come back from the war through the Grace of God! You (each of you) were a great bunch of good men. Through a joint effort we helped each other. I was scared on many occasions. The hurricane in the Philippines and in the mine field were among the worst."

The Executive Officer, Lt. Cdr. Scott Lothrop, reflecting on his crew post the kamikaze attack said, "Admire the guts and will of your men who even under such gross conditions were doing the very best they could. Oh, Lordy, I admired those men that day...You wish you had told them then. And all the time, I thought I was helping them. Well, I was, sort of. Because...you do go on....We were one terrific team of shipmates."

THE SECRETARY OF THE NAVY
WASHINGTON

June 5, 1946

My dear Mr. McAllister:

I have addressed this letter to reach you after
all the formalities of your separation from active service
are completed. I have done so because, without formality but
as clearly as I know how to say it, I want the Navy's pride in
you, which it is my privilege to express, to reach into your
civil life and to remain with you always.

You have served in the greatest Navy in the world.

It crushed two enemy fleets at once, receiving their
surrenders only four months apart.

It brought our land-based airpower within bombing
range of the enemy, and set our ground armies on the beachheads
of final victory.

It performed the multitude of tasks necessary to
support these military operations.

No other Navy at any time has done so much. For
your part in these achievements you deserve to be proud as
long as you live. The Nation which you served at a time of
crisis will remember you with gratitude.

The best wishes of the Navy go with you into civilian
life. Good luck!

Sincerely yours,

James Forrestal

James Forrestal

Mr. John Albert McAllister
140 Renwick St.
Newburgh, New York

Appendices

THE CREW

Capt. John Martin Higgins, USN, eventually retired as a Rear Admiral. After his tour as ComDesRon 62, Higgins served as Commander of Destroyers, Task Flotilla 3. During World War II, he earned the Navy Cross and two Legions of Merit, both with Combat "V." During the Korean War he earned a Distinguished Service Medal and the Silver Star. Higgins passed away in 1973.

Cdr. Stephen Noel Tackney, USN, temporarily assumed command of DesRon 62 at the end of 1945. Post the war he studied at the Naval War College before serving on the staff of the Chief of Naval Operations. Later he served in the Bureau of Military Sea Transport. Unbeknownst to the fighting destroyer captains of Destroyer Squadron 62, most of them would be promoted to Rear Admiral by retirement. Tackney was no exception, retiring in 1958. He and his wife, Priscilla, raised seven children. At one point all three of his sons were officers serving in the United States Navy. Following his own thirty year naval career, Adm. Tackney earned a master's degree in math education then taught high school math. His Falls Church students not only were challenged to do their best in math, they also learned their building had 'decks,' 'walls,' and 'overheads.' He was known as 'The Admiral' within the corridors of the Virginia high school. Tackney and Japanese Cdr. Asio became friends post the war. Tackney passed in 1970. The warrior seaman and his wife are buried on the grounds of the United States Naval Academy at Annapolis.

Cdr. Robert Brodie, USN, would later go on to command DesRon 11 then captain the USS *Missouri* BB-63 from April 53 to April 54. He retired in 1957 as a Rear Admiral. Brodie passed away from cancer in 1977.

Lt. Cdr. Scott Lothrop, USN, the twenty-five year old executive officer, became a ship's captain at age twenty-six. His nickname as a CO was, "Hard Way Lothrop." Lothrop was Executive Officer of three ships and Commanding Officer of four other vessels. The navy sent him to Harvard where he earned a master's degree in Nuclear Physics. His son, Peter, also attended the USNA. Scott retired as a Rear Admiral. His motto was, "When properly led, a U.S. Naval sailor could accomplish anything!" Though invited to the reunions of many of his ships, Lothrop only attended reunions of the USS *Haynsworth* DD-700. Lothrop passed in 1998.

Lt. Armistead "Army" Dennett, USN, returned to Annapolis in 1946 where he met his future wife, Louise. They were married just a few months later. He captained the USS *Woodson* DE-359 in 1951 and the USS *Wallace L. Lind* DD-703 1958-1960. Dennett retired from the U.S. Navy in 1962 after 20 years of service. Army then worked for NASA in Houston as a projects engineer. He and Louise retired to his native Maine.

Lt. Robert Eshelman, USNR, an attorney before the war, returned to practice post the battle. His son, Robert, also served as both a naval officer and an attorney.

Lt. jg. Allyn B. Ley, USNR, the USS *Haynsworth's* doctor, left the U.S. Navy in 1946. He returned to New York to work at New York Hospital/Cornell Medical College for several years before completing a fellowship in Hematology at Harvard Medical School. He taught medicine at Cornell. Doctor Ley and his wife, Sidney, had six children. He was reunited with John Vasquez at a USS *Haynsworth* reunion over fifty years past the battle. Ley had no idea Vasquez had survived the carnage of April 6, 1945. He passed away in 2006.

Ralph Aakhus RdM3c was transferred to the USS *Vulcan* after the *Haynsworth* returned to Ulithi post the kamikaze attack. He later met up with his cousin, an army soldier, and they toured Hiroshima. He was discharged in 1946, eventually to return home and run the family farm and saw mill. Aakhus and his wife, Mickey, were married in 1948 and still live in Minnesota.

Lonnie Aulbert S1c endured 28 months of hospital care for his wounds before his final release. He rejoined his family in South Carolina. He and his wife, Doris, had three children. Aulbert worked for 21 years as a rural route postal carrier before health issues forced his retirement. He and Doris both passed away in 2012.

Harold Bly RM3c finished his time in the Navy, re-enlisted to serve three more years as a tin can sailor and then transferred to the Air Force. Polio ended his military career in 1957. He lives in Florida.

Oscar Jefferson Callahan S1c stayed with the *Haynsworth*, eventually becoming a Radio Man Third Class. He returned to Georgia after the war. He worked as a welder at Brunswick Pulp & Paper. He passed away in 1998.

Louie Clark SK1c met two of the Iwo Jima flag raisers including James Bradley after the *Haynsworth* returned to California. "These three are remembered [for raising the flag over Iwo Jima]. The two that raised the flag on the *Haynsworth* are un-remembered. They wanted the world to know what the true meaning of our flag stands for and were willing to die for it. I saw them go through smoke and fire and replace it." Clark passed away in 2012.

John Dyer RM3c was the oldest of six children when he enlisted in the navy. Memorial markers have been established at the Calvary Cemetery in Rutland, Vermont, home of his father, at the Saratoga National Cemetery at Schuylerville, New York and at the National Memorial Cemetery of the Pacific in Honolulu.

Phillip Goldstein GM2c of the Bronx, married his high school sweetheart in 1940. He worked for Brewster Aviation Corp building U.S. Navy planes until he joined the navy in 1943. After the war, Goldstein returned to New York where he became a sales rep in the garment industry. After 5 years as a salesman on the road, he became sales manager for a sweater firm selling to department stores. He is semi-retired and living in Florida. 'Goldie' works part-time for the Del-Ray Police Department.

Warner Crockett Holcombe RM1c returned to the San Francisco area. He eventually married and served as the Commodore of the Oakland Yacht Club. With friends, he sailed the world several times in his 45' *Stevens* sailboat before retiring to Mexico. He passed away in 1996 in Laguna Hills, California.

James K. Jones, Jr. PhM2c survived the battle against Japan, but his uncle was not as lucky. Held as a POW by the Japanese, he was killed when the transport *Maru* holding him was sunk by American planes. Jones was reassigned to the *Haynsworth* during the Korean War. After returning home from World War II, he married Lois Jean Wilson and they had two children both of whom served in the military. Jones worked as a power lineman with the Kentucky Utilities Company and held a private pilot's license. He died in 1986.

Edward R. Kelly TM3c returned to his native Philadelphia, got married, and ran a bread delivery route until he was called up for the Korean War. Ed was released from duty as soon as he reported. Eventually he became a father and finished his career working for the Post Office. He had many interests but his greatest delights were his family. He passed away suddenly in 1986.

Frank Lembo S1c survived with minor scars and his vision intact. He opened Lembo Machineworks in Paterson, New Jersey before he purchased the Greenwood Lake Airport in West Milford. A quiet, pleasant man, he enjoyed the company of his family. The successful business man and entrepreneur passed away in 1978 after suffering a stroke.

Angelo Joseph Lizzari S1c returned to his native Vermont and operated several gas stations after the war. Both his son and grandson were career U.S. Army soldiers.

Clay Lutz WT3c was regular Navy and so stayed on active duty postwar. After his service, he came home to his native Maryland and worked for the local phone company for thirty-six years before retiring as an engineer. Lutz currently lives in North Carolina.

John Magliocchetti RM3c returned to New Jersey and worked for Ford Motors. His daughter, Marianna, later worked for Ford in Michigan. Another Ford employee noticed her name and made the connection. Through Marianna, Bob Sink was reunited with his shipmate John.

Edwin E. Maugel SoM3c lost one of his brothers during the Battle of the Bulge. His younger brother fought in the Korean War as an U.S. Army soldier. Married to Marian, they reside in Ohio. He still has the miniature Christmas tree that he had on board the *Haynsworth* during 1944.

Bill McKeen SM3c played minor league baseball for the Giants. He married and had two children. A fixture at the USS *Haynsworth* reunions, he passed away in 2008.

Donald Messecar S1c worked several jobs postwar, mostly truck driving, before taking a parks department job for the Town of Amherst, NY. He retired from there in 1990. Messecar served as a volunteer fireman for over twenty-five years.

Henry 'Hank' Michalak S1c, originally of Depew, NY, worked construction after the war. He died in Sanford, Florida and to the end, he was proud of having been a sailor. His nephew and namesake, Henry 'Hank' Domeracki retired as a Captain in the United States Navy.

Edward Mital CM2 married his sweetheart from home, Orena, while on leave after the kamikaze attack. They eventually had four daughters. He had a successful career as a building contractor in Tennessee. He passed away in 1973.

Manson Morrill S1c returned from the war with partial hearing loss from the actions of March 29, 1945. He was awarded the Purple Heart. He worked as a carpenter in his native New Hampshire. Married with three children, Morrill passed away in November, 1978. He never spoke of his service aboard the *Haynsworth* to his family.

William Morton SoM3c worked as a photographer and a printer full time, part time as a writer and an actor. He married his beloved Mae during the war. They had two children. Bill was the organizer of the early USS *Haynsworth* reunions and served as an officer for USS *Haynsworth Association*. He passed away in 2013.

Tom Murphy S1c married his high school sweetheart, Pauline, in 1947. He completed his high school education postwar and later served as the postmaster in Belmont, New Hampshire. In 1960, Murphy helped thwart a plot to assassinate then presidential candidate JFK. He passed away in 2002 leaving behind "Polly," six daughters and numerous grand and great grandchildren.

Keith Myreholt, RM2c told his son post the war that he always felt he was living on borrowed time. He took that 'borrowed time' and made a great life. He married Agnes in 1947 and had four children followed by six grandchildren and seven great grandchildren. "So seventeen lives are on this planet as of today, because my Dad made it thru the war. He always seemed to be a happy person and I only found out about the *Haynsworth* when my grandmother gave me his diary in the 1970's.

She told me about the kamikaze attack," recalled daughter Karen Shinn. Myreholt worked as a printer in California before he and Agnes retired to South Dakota. He passed away in 1998.

Marion Parker GM3c was 36 years old and married with two daughters when he came aboard the *Haynsworth*. Before and after the war, he managed a men's clothing store in his hometown, of Wadesboro, NC. A former local star athlete and local hero, Marion was a popular man in town. He passed away in 1968 just days after his 60th birthday.

Isaac Peres RM3c returned to NYC postwar. He and his wife, Pearl, retired to Florida after 38 years of manufacturing desk supplies in New York. They had two children.

Arthus "A.C." Pickens F1c returned to construction after the war and then bought additional land to farm in the 1950's. His oldest son Steve became an aeronautical engineer. A.C., Jr. continues to work the farm that his father purchased in Jasper County, IL. Arthus passed away on June 26, 2014. His death left just eighteen surviving crew members of the Haynsworth.

Mariano Saia RdM3c returned to his native Buffalo, New York. He started a heating & cooling construction company which has remained in the family. He married and raised a family. Saia passed away in 2009.

Tom Scott FC3c returned to school after the war and graduated from the Univ. of Tennessee. "I messed around in graduate schools until my GI Bill expired, then worked three years in Chicago prior to returning to school at U. of Minn. majoring in psychology (counseling). I worked in the Counseling Centers at Univ. of Texas and the Univ. of Tennessee and wound up teaching at the Univ. of North Dakota where I retired in 1989."

Constantino 'Gus' Scutari FC2c returned to Long Island and married his wife, Fran. After joining the VFW, he quickly worked his way up to commander. For two decades he has organized the Syosset Memorial Day Parade. With his harmonica, he continues to entertain at USS *Haynsworth* reunions.

Milton Studley RdM3c returned to the grocery produce business after the war. He and his wife eventually had six children. He took life simply and enjoyed the moment. Eventually they moved to Florida. He passed away in 1971 at the age of 56.

Jack Vaessen EM1c was discharged from the Navy in September 1945 after seven and a half years of active service. He married Barbara post war. Jack still has the flashlight and wrench he used to save himself when the USS *Utah* capsized during the Pearl Harbor attack. Jack celebrated his 100th birthday in 2016 with two other survivors of the USS *Utah*. He lives in California.

John Vasquez SM3c married his wife Jennie in 1946. They had four children together, 10 grandchildren, and 15 great-grandchildren before Jennie passed in 2008. After the war, John worked for the Post Office and then later Kidder Peabody Investment Co. on Wall Street. He remains a very healthy and active senior citizen. John lives with his daughter in New Jersey.

THE SAVED

Lt. John E. Barrows survived the war but his radioman, twenty two year old **LaRoy Sell ARM1c** of Indiana, was killed when a kamikaze struck their ship, the USS *Bunker Hill*, during *Kikusui No.6*.

Lt. Bernard F. Berry and his crew, **C. T. Johnson ARM1c** USN, and **Charles Edgar Metler AOM1c USNR**, were among the casualties of the kamikaze strike against the USS *Bunker Hill*.

Lt. William Frederick Bowen, **USNR**, earned a Distinguished Flying Cross in World War II. He returned to combat flying *Corsairs* as the commander of VF-884 during the Korean War. He was lost over Pyongyang, North Korea in September, 1952. Bowen was officially declared dead the next year.

2ⁿᵈ Lt. Frederick Briggs, USMCR, was airborne when kamikazes hit the USS *Bunker Hill*. After his combat days, the Oregonian worked as a migratory bird biologist and in the pharmaceutical industry. He and his wife Clarabelle had two daughters. He passed away in August, 2013.

Lt. jg. Nils A. A. Carlson, USN, stayed in the Navy through the jet age. He retired as a Commander. Carlson married a ballroom dance instructor, Mary, and together they had three children. He passed away in 1974.

Ens. Royce Carruth survived World War II but did not survive action in Korea. He was thirty years old when he was shot down while flying a VF-821 *Corsair* over Sinpyeong, Korea on June 20, 1951. He was declared dead in May, 1954.

Lt. jg. Clifford S. Carter was the recipient of the Distinguished Flying Cross medal and the Air Medal with 3 Gold Stars. The Framingham Massachusetts native's luck ran out after twenty combat missions when a kamikaze struck the USS *Bunker Hill* on 11 May 1945.

1ˢᵗ Lt. Casimir 'Kazimah' Chop, USMCR, became a bartender in postwar California. He was recalled by the U.S. Marines for the Korean War to fly helicopters. After the war he flew helicopters in the LA area and served as a pilot on the 1950's television show "Whirlybirds."

As a flight instructor, his students included Frank Sinatra and Dean Martin. Post his military service, Chop served as president of the United States Bartenders Guild.

Ensign William Elings, USNR, was killed on May 11, 1945. During *Kikusui No.6*, a *Zero* slammed into the island of the USS *Bunker Hill*. Thirty pilots and crewman of Air Group 84 were killed instantly.

Ensign Dennis M. Gray, Jr., USNR, entered a rain squall with three other *Corsairs* on April 10, 1945 while flying a CAP mission. The other planes exited the clouds but the Stevensville, Montana native was never seen again and was later declared to be missing in action.

Lt. jg. James T. Horan, Jr., USNR, remained in the reserves for many years. He and his wife, Margaret, had five children. Horan worked as a pharmaceutical sales rep before purchasing and managing an indoor tennis club. He passed away in 1998.

Lt. William T. Jacks, Jr., USNR, and his radioman, **Howard S. Pedersen ARM1C, USN,** were awarded Distinguished Flying Crosses for the attacks on Tokyo. Both were killed on May 11, 1945 when a kamikaze impacted the USS *Bunker Hill*.

Ensign Edward Jindra, USNR, survived combat but was seriously burned when an Army P-38 *Lightning*, "flat-hatting" or flying low to show off, crashed his plane into the USS *Randolph*. The Navy pilot's time in the war ended as he evacuated to the USS *Refuge*. He returned to live in his native Illinois. Jindra passed away in 2009.

Ensign Richard Henry Langdon, USNR, had a week to remember after his rescue. He and his section leader ambushed a group of seven Japanese *Myrts* on 3 April 1945. Langdon claimed three kills, his partner got the other four. On 7 April, he scored a direct bomb hit on an IJN cruiser which won him the Navy Cross. At the end of his tour, he had earned two DFCs. Langdon passed away in 1995.

Ensign Knox Scott, USNR, and his radioman, **Eugene A. Wengler ARM3c**, survived the war. Scott completed eighty carrier takeoffs, eleven at night. When a kamikaze hit the USS *Enterprise* on May 14, 1945, the war ended for VT(N)-90. Wengler returned to NYC and earned a business degree. He worked for several companies as an accountant and later as a controller. Wengler passed in 2009 but not before reuniting with his pilot many years earlier.

Lt. jg. Donald F. Seiz, USNR, and his crew, **John Brady ARM3c and Clifford Gallant AMM3c,** flew their slow TBF bomber in a torpedo mission against Hong Kong's harbor on January 16, 1945. Caught in a hellish crossfire of anti-aircraft fire in their flight across the harbor, they did not survive the mission.

1ˢᵗ Lt. Albert C. Simkunas (later changed to Sims) USMC survived the kamikaze attack on the USS *Bunker* Hill. He was called back to duty five years later to fly *Corsairs* for ground attack missions in the Korean War. He retired from the U.S. Marines in 1963. Sims passed away shortly thereafter.

Ensign Daniel Valpey, **USNR**, survived the war. He remained a flyer until his retirement as a Commander in 1964. Valpey owned an HVAC company in Lawrence, Massachusetts. He passed away in November, 2004. Valpey is survived by his wife, Ann, and six children.

1ˢᵗ Lt. Philip 'Pots' Wilmot, USMCR, of VMF-451, finished the war with 66 carrier landings and credit for one plane shot down. After finishing his service in the Marine Corps Reserve, Wilmot entered dental school. He earned his civilian pilot's license in 1942 and continues to fly his personal plane. He was married for over 70 years to his bride, Mary Francis before she passed away in 2015. "The only thing I have done that is important was fighting in World War II." He can be seen in the DVD *Blue Devils Squadron*.

Philip Mulé AMM3c was eventually transferred to the USS *Bountiful* before being sent to a hospital on Guam. Post war he alternated between attending reunions of the USS *Hancock* and the USS *John W. Weeks*. Mulé was able to express his thanks for the efforts of Cdr. (later Adm.) Theobald to the *John W. Weeks* captain's widow postwar. He is retired and lives on Long Island.

Robert Plum FC2c, lost from the decks of the USS *Wallace L. Lind* but saved by the *Haynsworth*, was an only child. He considered his shipmates to be his brothers and attended the reunions of both DesRon 62 destroyers. Though he worked in the insurance industry after the war, his love was playing the clarinet in his band, The Bob

Kats. Plum passed away in 2012, just a few days shy of his 95th birthday.

(McAllister Family Collection)

John 'Jack' McAllister RM3c, USNR

Though World War II came to an end in September 1945, most of the crew had less than two years of military service. They would have to wait to be discharged.

On May 9th of 1946, Radioman Third Class John McAllister, like many of his peers from the spring class of 1944, was honorably discharged from the United States Naval Reserve at the USN Personnel Separation Center, Long Beach, Long Island, NY. During his time on active service during World War II he had earned the American Theater Medal, Victory Medal, and Asiatic Pacific Medal. His entire service during the war was either training or on board the *Haynsworth*. He was the last of the McAllister's three sons to finish his service to the country.

McAllister returned to Schoonmaker & Son's Department store in Newburgh, NY. He work repaired and sold refrigerators at the store before he was recalled back to active duty again by the navy after the communist invasion of Korea in 1950. He served as a radioman aboard the destroyer escort USS *Spangler* DE-696, the frigate USS *Glendale* PF-36, and the destroyer USS *Boyd* DD-544. Both the *Glendale* and the *Boyd* served the Pacific Fleet in support of the fight for Korea. After two years of service, Jack was again honorably discharged by the Navy.

After returning from the Korean War, Jack was accepted by the Fire Department of Newburgh, New York. Ironically one of the biggest fires he fought during his three decades in the department was the conflagration that erupted at Schoonmaker & Son's building in the early 1970's.

Cautious in revealing his deep emotions, Jack nonetheless was generally outgoing and friendly. "Mac was a quiet guy with a constant smile on his face," recalled fellow radioman Calvin Weiss. However, when family conversation became frivolous or misdirected, Jack would remind all that his ship was hit by a kamikaze and he could have been aboard when it happened. His statement was not an invitation to discuss the attack but rather an indirect message to realize what should be valued as important in life and what should be noted as trivial.

Later after he was married, Jack said many times to his wife and daughters that he always felt he had been given a second life. God, he felt, had rewarded him with life when many of those close to him were killed or injured on that fateful day in April of 1945. If the timing of his orders had been slightly different, Jack knew that most likely he would have been working in the radio shack that day northeast of Okinawa.

Like many of his generation, Jack held membership in the American Legion, VFW, and the Catholic War Veterans. He served as chaplain for the local American Legion. In 1984, he retired from the Newburgh, New York Fire Department after nearly thirty years of service as a fireman and lieutenant.

Jack was able to become reacquainted with many of his *Haynsworth* shipmates when he attended the ship's second reunion held in 1990 at Boston. The next year he joined them again when they gathered in Atlantic Beach, Florida.

Six months before the 1992 reunion, Jack was diagnosed with lung cancer. A lifetime of smoking and fighting fires had caught up with him. Despite the attack on his health, he planned to attend his final reunion with his shipmates in Biloxi, Mississippi. During his treatment for the tumor, he wore a new navy peacoat on colder mornings to daily mass at St. Patrick's R.C. He never complained about his diagnosis and his fate. Though the cancer ravaging his body caused him great pain, he did not talk about what he was enduring. A week before the reunion, Jack's health began to fail quickly. He passed away early on November 11th, Veteran's Day, 1992. The next day the *Haynsworth* crew gathered together in Biloxi for their reunion. Jack was a day ahead of them as he reunited in Heaven with Chief Campbell, Goyer,

Dyer, Holiman, Satterly, MacLaughlan and the other *Haynsworth* sailors that had left the world of the living before him.

McAllister's remains are interred on a hill overlooking the Hudson River.

USS *Haynsworth* DD-700

After repairs were completed at Mare Island, the *Haynsworth* had duty at Treasure Island, California, as a training ship from 17 July to 5 September, 1945. After several months of operations at Pearl Harbor, she sailed for the east coast. On 14 January, 1946, she reached Boston in April. Decommissioned, the *Haynsworth* spent a year in the Reserve Fleet. Many of her young crew who had joined the navy 1944 completed their enlistment and were discharged from active duty that spring.

Returning to active service in March 1947, the *Haynsworth* based her operations from Algiers, Louisiana, conducting reserve training cruises in the Gulf and in the Caribbean until the summer of 1949 before sailing with the 6th Fleet in the Mediterranean. She returned to Norfolk in February 1950. She arrived at Charleston 10 days later and was decommissioned there 19 May to rejoin the Reserve Fleet.

The Korean War brought the *Haynsworth* back to service when she was recommissioned at Charleston on 22 September 1950. Cdr. Herbert F. Rommel, nephew of the Desert Fox Irwin Rommel, captained her during training and operations along the East Coast and the Caribbean. She sailed 3 September 1951 for duty in the Mediterranean.

After more operations on the East Coast and in the Caribbean, and a Midshipman cruise to the North Atlantic, the *Haynsworth* sailed from Norfolk 2 November 1953 for a round-the-world cruise. While in the Pacific she was assigned duty for four months in the Far East with the 7th Fleet, a vital peace-keeping force in that part of the world. The *Haynsworth* returned to Norfolk in June, 1954 to resume her support of the 6th Fleet. In 1958 with the Suez crisis still unsettled, U.S. Navy units stood by in the eastern Mediterranean and evacuated U.S. nationals from Egypt.

The *Haynsworth* made five deployments to the Mediterranean, supporting the Navy's peacekeeping role and keeping a watchful eye on the troubled spots of the free world. In 1959, the *Haynsworth* took part in the historic "Operation Inland Seas," commemorating the opening of the mighty St. Lawrence Seaway, steaming up the St. Lawrence to Montreal.

Late in 1961 while in the Mediterranean, the *Haynsworth* delivered emergency food rations to flood-ravaged Africa; and on 3 October 1962, she stood by off Cape Canaveral as a rescue ship and witnessed the takeoff of astronaut Cdr. Walter Schirra on his historic six orbit flight of the earth. Later that month, under much more serious circumstances, she hastened to the Caribbean and participated in the naval blockade of Cuba, effectively checking the Communist threat to the security of the Western Hemisphere.

In February 1963, the *Haynsworth* deployed to the Mediterranean, the Red Sea, and the Gulf of Aden for operations with the 6th Fleet. After returning to Norfolk, she embarked midshipmen for an Atlantic cruise from 1 August to 10 September; then underwent overhaul at New Orleans, La., and Orange, Tex., before arriving Galveston in February, 1964 to begin duty as a Naval Reserve training ship.

Assigned to Reserve Destroyer Squadron 34, the *Haynsworth* operated out of Galveston while providing valuable on board training facilities for hundreds of Naval Reservists. Manned by a nucleus crew, she steamed to ports along the Gulf and Atlantic coasts, and numerous training cruises carried her into the Caribbean. Into mid-1967 she continued to bolster the strength of the Navy and the Nation through intense, skilled, and effective training which maintained the caliber and readiness of the Naval Reserve.

The *Haynsworth* was decommissioned in 1970 and sold to Taiwan soon after. DD-700 was rechristened as the DDG-905 *Yuen Yang*. She served the Taiwan Navy for several decades before ultimately being decommissioned in 2000. She was sunk as a target on October 13, 2001.

The USS *Haynsworth* now rests in the waters off Formosa where she served her first missions with the Fast Carrier Task Force 38 in January of 1945.

(Adapted from Naval Historical History & Heritage Command, Department of the Navy)

POST SCRIPT

The Sampson Naval Training Base was turned over to the Air Force after the war. It was used as an U.S. Air Force Base until 1956 and then closed. The U.S. Army Depot at Seneca is still active. Sailors continue to use *The Bluejacket's Manual*. The RMS *Queen Mary*, escorted by the USS *Haynsworth* during its inaugural mission in 1944, is permanently moored at the Port of Long Beach, CA. The *Haynsworth* left this port in October of 1944 as it headed west to the battles in the Pacific.

Post World War II, the *Iowa* class battleships were recommissioned in the 1980s. Their 20mm and 40mm guns were removed and replaced with the *Phalanx Close In Weapons System*. All four *Iowa* class battleships are now decommissioned. No ships in commission have guns that rival the 16" naval cannon that were forged at the Watervliet Arsenal for American battleships.

At Pearl Harbor, the former battleship USS *Utah* was never refloated or refitted. Partially submerged, her rusting remains still has some of its crew entombed and therefore, like the USS *Arizona*, is a war grave. A color guard stands watch over her. Across Ford Island, oil continues to leak from the USS *Arizona*. Some have likened the blackened bubbles to tears for her crew.

The *Yamato* and *Musashi* hold the distinction of being the largest battleships ever built. The *Yamato* rests in two pieces a quarter mile down in the ocean, 290 miles southeast of *Kyushu*. Just as in World War II, she is just several hours flight time from the USS *Haynsworth*.

CHAPTER NOTES

Boot

"Physically fit..." John A. McAllister Family Collection
"The Navy then gave him..." Author unknown

Destroyer Training: Norfolk Virginia

"The Brush is organized...," USS *Brush* DD-745: Welcome on Board, U.S. Navy, 1957

USS *Haynsworth*

"On one day alone in Mary 1942..." Cunningham, John, *Made in New Jersey: The Industrial Story of a State*, New Brunswick, New Jersey, Rutgers University Press, 1954
"A natural aptitude..." Heavilin, J.S., *The 1927 Lucky Bag*, Schilling Press, New York, 1927 P.360
"Army is a..." Baker, Jones, Hausnauer, Inc., *The 1942 Lucky Bag*, Buffalo, New York, 1941 P.94
"Destroyer Addition to Growing Sea Power..." Associated Press, New York, April 15, 1944
"The Brush is devoid..."USS *Brush* ibid

Sea Trials

"The pressure of hard shakedown..." USS *Charles. S. Sperry* DD-697 War History, 1945

Plankowners: First Mission

"We have agreed that the British Fleet..." Office, US Secretary of the Combined Chiefs of Staff (United States and Great Britain), *Octagon Conference, September 1944: Paper and Minutes of Meetings, Octagon Conference and Minutes of Combined Chiefs of Staff Meetings in London, June 1944*, Joint History Office, Washington DC, 1944

Kamikaze: *Divine Wind*

"While planes were expendable..." Halsey, William, J. Bryan III, *Admiral Halsey's Story*, McGraw-Hill Book Company, Inc., New York, 1947, P.232

Destination Pearl Harbor

"This morning the coast..." Studenski, Frank J. S1c, *War Diary of the U.S.S. Boston CA69*, self-published, 1989

"As reports were received..." *Charles S. Sperry* ibid

"Coordinated simultaneous approach by..." Naval message sent to Commander Task Force 38, 25 November 1944, website navalaviationmuseum.org/education/online-exhibits/kamikaze, Accessed September 28, 2014

Departure

"When the Ault went to sea..." USS *Ault* War History, 1945

Ulithi Bound

"When the minecraft..." Hansen, Richard; *The USS Gamble in the South Pacific World War II*, Solving Light Books; Annapolis, MD; 2014; P. 26 (With permission)

"The cooks did a tremendous..." Hansen ibid, P. 27

"Within a month of the occupation..." Spangler, George, *Ulithi*, website laffey.org/Ulithi/Page%201/Ulithi.htm, 1998, Accessed 6 July 2013

Joining the Pacific Fleet

"Halsey had shown that far..." Borneman, Walter R., *The Admirals: Nimitz, Halsey, Leahy, and King-The Five-Star Admirals Who Won the War At Sea,* - New York, Little, Brown and Company, 2012, P.233

"No one who has not..." Halsey ibid, P. 239

Task Force 38: Halsey's Hammer

"Leaving Ulithi, the destroyers..." Bullis, Richard, Jack Melnick, *The History of United States Ship Waldron: Destroyer 699*, Self Published, 1991, P.19

"If I had to give credit..." Halsey ibid, P. 69

"Entailed keeping a blanket of fighters..." Halsey, ibid, P.233

"Task Force #38 is underway..." USS *Haynsworth* Morning Orders, 31 December 1944

1945

"attempted to stop the plane..." VF-7 War History, ibid P.57

"a hunting knife..." VT(N)-90 Squadron History-Embarkation & January 1945, website: cv6.org.ship.logs/vtn90-4501.html, Accessed January 9, 2015

Rescue at Sea

"A cold front moved slowly across Formosa..." *Carrier Strikes on the China Coast, January 1945*, Aerology and Naval Warfare, CNO, Aerology Section, Washington, D.C., July 1945

"he had bagged three VT-8 *Avengers*...," Mrazek, Robert J., *A Dawn Like Thunder: The True Story of Torpedo Squadron Eight*, Back Bay Books, New York, 2008 P. 283

"Fayle had to ditch..." Lundstrom, John B., *The First Team and the Guadalcanal Campaign*, Naval Institute Press, Annapolis, 2005, P. 153-154

"These raids were made against the airfields..."USS *Haynsworth* War Diary, 1-31 January 1945

"Coming about to windward..." USS *Charles. S. Sperry* War Diary, 1-31 January, 1945

"The crew found..." USS *Haynsworth* Morning Orders, 7 January 1945

"wind and weather conditions..." *Charles. S. Sperry* ibid

"Were excellent indoctrination..." *Charles. S. Sperry* War Diary ibid

"Hard luck seemed to dog..." VF-7 War History, 1945, P. 61

"Admiral Halsey sent out a message..." "The crew found..." USS *Haynsworth* Morning Orders 9 January 1945

"As soon as it was sighted..." Hansen, Richard, ibid P. 47

"An air bubble six feet in diameter..." USS *Gamble*, War Diary, 1-31 August 1942

"You will not get out alive": The South China Sea

"It was a bold action..." USS *Ault* War History ibid

"While at precautionary General Quarters..." USS *Lind* War Diary, 1-31 January, 1945

"Just to strike a cheery note..." USS *Haynsworth* Morning Orders, 12 January 1945

Replenishment at Sea

"0320-Depth charge projector..." USS *Waldron* War Diary 1-31, January, 1945

"By that day..." *Charles. S. Sperry* War Diary ibid

"Five men, believed to be Japanese..." USS *Hank* War Diary, 1-31 January, 1945

Storm: Nature's Hammer

"Fear is a very personal thing..." Lothrop, Scott Lt. Cdr., Personal Letters, Postwar

"We don't know how you got in..." Morison, Samuel Eliot, *History of United States Naval Operations in World War II: The Liberation of the Philippines*

Luzon, Mindanao, the Visayas 1944-1945, Little, Brown, and Company, Boston, 1959, P. 172

"We were attacked by planes." Parker, Marion GM3c Personal War Diary

"The night promised to be rugged..." Halsey ibid, P. 247

"Today is another strike day..." USS *Haynsworth* Morning Orders, 22 January 1945

"Was attacked by enemy planes..." *USS Borie* War Diary, 1-31 January 1945

"Up all hammocks..." USS *Haynsworth* Morning Orders, 23 January 1945

"His hook caught on a wire..." VT(N)-90 War History, 1945

"Only Navy pilots could..." USS *Haynsworth* Morning Orders ibid

"I am so proud of you..." USS *Boston* War Diary, 1-31 January 1945

"The Third Fleet..." CINCPOA Press Release No. 1, 28 JANUARY 1945

"The Captain and the Executive Officer..." USS *Haynsworth* Morning Orders ibid

Operation JAMBOREE: Attacks Against Japan

"Destroy enemy aircraft..." USS *Haynsworth* War Diary, 1-28 February, 1945

Target: Tokyo

"Iwo Jima was about to be taken..." USS *Ault* War History ibid

"That Friday morning was cold..."USS *Charles. S. Sperry* War History ibid

"This operation has been long planned..." CINCPOA Communiqué No. 259, 15 February 1945

"Kill the bastards scientifically." USS *Haynsworth* Morning Orders, 16 February 1945

"Several Jap planes..." Studenski ibid

"What it turn out..." Studenski ibid

"It is a rare event today..." Hansen ibid P. 51

"The ship fitters had..." Hansen ibid P. 50

"that he would eat..." Hansen ibid P.55

"The black oily smoke billows..." Lind, Fred, Chapter Sixteen" Operation Jamboree, website: mighty90.com/OperationJamboree.html, Accessed 7 January 2014

"I derived some sinister pleasure..." Thomson, Jim, Chapter Sixteen" Operation Jamboree, website: mighty90.com/OperationJamboree.html, Accessed 7 January 2014

"We were all looking up..." Personal Account Edward R. Kelly TM3c

"For letter writers, you may say..." USS *Haynsworth* Morning Orders, 19 February 1945

"F--- you, Joe!" Morison, Samuel Eliot, *History of United States Naval Operations in World War II: Victory in the Pacific*, Little Brown and Company, Boston, 1960 P. 24

"0415 Sighted automatic weapon fire..." USS *Waldron* War Diary 1-28 February, 1945

"We were so close..." Bullis, Richard, Jack Melnick, *The History of United States Ship Waldron: Destroyer 699*, Self Published, 1991, with permission

"From then on we were subject..." USS *Borie* War History, 1945

Marine Rescue

"Nimitz announced that 509 enemy planes..." CINCPOA Communiqué No. 263, 19 February, 1945

Iwo Jima

"The first raid, approaching from the north..." USS *John W. Weeks* War Diary, 1-28 February, 1945

"Japanese planes attacked a big U.S. carrier..."Stout, Frank Navy Correspondent, *Japanese Plane Attack*, 1945, website: ussjwweeks701.org/pdf_files/newsletter_2013-03.pdf, Accessed 4 August 2013

"This morning we are with..." Studenski ibid

"A miscount in inventory..." USS *Haynsworth* Morning Orders, 21 February 1945

"The force was in the extremely rough..." USS *Charles S. Sperry* War History ibid

"A request was made..." O'Leary, John QM2c, "World War II Autobiography," p. 18, with permission

"We spotted a mine..." O'Leary, John QM2c, ibid p.21

"the relaxation of censorship..." USS *Haynsworth* Morning Orders, 28 February 1945

The Destroyers Were Lifesavers

"well done, my boy" Caswell, Dean Col., *Fighting Falcons: The Saga of Marine Fighter Squadron VMF 221*, VMF 221 Foundation, 2004, P. 112, with permission

"That's the last thing..." Stanny, Viola, Interview by phone with the author, 15 February 2015

"We were almost always tired." Gillett, Morris CRT, *My War*, p. 94, with permission

Reprieve

"We were grimly reminded..." USS *Ault* War History ibid

"Its bomb load..." USS *Randolph* War Damage, Report of 31 March 1945

Operation ICEBERG

"to destroy enemy aircraft..." ComDesRon 62 War Diary, 1-31 March 1945
"All hands looked at the damaged carrier..." USS *Ault* War History ibid
"screen heavy ships against submarine..." ComDesRon 62 War Diary ibid
"It was not uncommon for planes..." Gillett, Morris CRT, *My War*, ibid, p. 98
"One plane crashed..." ComDesDiv 124 War Diary 1-31 March 1945

18 March 1945: Day 1 Against the Homes Islands

"On completion of fueling..." USS *Haynsworth* Morning Orders, 18 March
    1945
"Attacks were conducted in an aggressive..." ComTaskFor 58, Report of Op-
    erations of Task Force Fifty-Eight in Support of Landings at Okinawa, 14
    March through 28 May (East Longitude Dates), including Actions against
    Kyushu, Nansei Shoto, Japanese Fleet at Kure, the *Yamato*, and Opera-
    tions in Direct Support of Landings at Okinawa; 18 June 1945
"Enemy aircraft reported..."USS *Waldron* War Diary, 1-31 March 1945
"Made a dive attack..." USS *Ault* War Diary, 1-31 March 1945

"Six Planes Are Down"

"Due to excessive power settings..." VB-6 War History, 1945
"Pilot and radioman..." USS *Haynsworth* War Diary, 1-31 March 1945
"The antiaircraft gunnery was excellent..." Report of Operations of Task
    Force Fifty-Eight in Support of Landings at Okinawa 14 March through
    28 May (East Longitude Dates), including Actions Against Kyushu,
    Nansei Shoto, Japanese Fleet at Kure, the *Yamato*, and Operations in Di-
    rect Support of Landings at Okinawa.

19 March: Day 2 Against the Home Islands

"Task Force is gunning for..." USS *Haynsworth* Morning Orders, 19 March
    1945
"Bogies on screen in all directions..." USS *Hancock*, Report of Air Operations
    Against Kyushu, Shikoku, & Honshu, Japan, Ryukyu Islands and Jap
    Task Force, 3/18/45- 5/11/45
"Rumor has it..." Plum, Robert F2c, Personal War Diary, 1945
"We opened fire with 5" batteries..." USS *Haynsworth,* Report of Operations
    During Strikes On Japan, Ryukyus and Jap Task Force, 3/18/45-4/9/45
"That was a wonderful shot..." USS *Haynsworth* Morning Orders, 22 March
    1945
"1429 One type *Zero*..." USS *Charles S. Sperry* War Diary, 1-31 March 1945
"Despite excellent shooting..." USS *Charles S. Sperry* War History ibid
"By sunset a Japanese flag..." USS *Charles S. Sperry* War History ibid

Target: Kure

"American pilots claimed more than... Morison, Samuel Eliot, *History of United States Naval Operations in World War II: Victory in the Pacific*, ibid, P. 100

"The attack was only moderately successful..." Report of Operations of Task Force Fifty-Eight in Support of Landings at Okinawa 14 March through 28 May (East Longitude Dates), including Actions Against Kyushu, Nansei Shoto, Japanese Fleet at Kure, the *Yamato*, and Operations in Direct Support of Landings at Okinawa, 1945

21 March: A New Threat Emerges

"At 1541 formed cruising disposition 5-R..." USS *Waldron* War Diary ibid

"We are continuing southward..." USS *Waldron* War Diary ibid

"An unusual number of mail..." ComDesRon 62 War Diary ibid

"Probably destroyed or damaged..." CINCPOA Communiqué No. 307, 23 March 1945

"The reports reaching CinCPac..." ComAirGroup 6, War History: April 10, 1944-October 15, 1945

"All hands in the task force..." ComDesRon 52 War Diary, 1-31 March 1945

Okinawa Gunto

"Today is a day of heavy strikes..." USS *Haynsworth* Morning Orders, 23 March 1945

"did not develop enough power..." VB-84 War History, 1945

"The swimmer..." Bullis ibid P.16

"We were in contact with him..." Bullis ibid, P.30

"There was no enemy activity..." USS *Waldron* War Diary ibid

"It became increasingly apparent..." Report of Operations of Task Force Fifty-Eight in Support of Landings at Okinawa 14 March through 28 May (East Longitude Dates), including Actions Against Kyushu, Nansei Shoto, Japanese Fleet at Kure, the *Yamato*, and Operations in Direct Support of Landings at Okinawa ibid

"Some questions have been asked..." USS *Haynsworth* Morning Orders, 24 March 1945

"As it burst..." USS *Charles S. Sperry* War History ibid

"bounced out of arresting gear..." ComAirGroup 6, ACA-1 Reports of Air Operations Against Japan, Ryukyu Islands and Jap Task Force, 3/18/45 – 5/24/45

Raid

"The intensive training..." USS *Hank* War History, 1945

"The burning wadding from..." Gillett, Morris, *My War*, Self-published, p.91, With Permission

"At 201 item shore bombardment..." USS *Haynsworth* Action Report 14 March to 9 April 1945

"AA was intense, of all kinds..." VB-84 War History, 1945

Easter

"Several enemy aircraft raids..." USS *Haynsworth* War Diary ibid

"At 1400, one enemy torpedo plane..." USS *Wallace L. Lind* War Diary, 1-31 March 1945

"After dropping his bomb..." USS *Haynsworth* War Diary ibid

"Although direct hits..." USS *Wallace L. Lind* War Diary ibid

"48 rounds expended..." USS *Haynsworth* Morning Orders, 30 March 1945

"Another very important function..." Gillett, Morris CRT, *Stories from the Forties*, website: ussjwweeks701.org/stories_from_our_members.htm#Picket_Duty_(late_March_1945)_By_Morris_Gillett, Accessed October 12, 2014. With permission of the author.

"This last week..." USS *English* War Diary, 1-31 March 1945

"The chief standing on a..." Tomlinson, Tommy, *The Threadbare Buzzard*, Zenith Press, 2004, pp 214-215, With permission.

"The Task Group was under..."ComDesDiv 96 War Diary, 1-30 April 1945

Leaving Pearl

"Seven Suisei *Judy*..." Gordon, Bill, *Meiji Air Base Monument*, website: kamikazeimages.net/monuments/meiji/index.htm#n1, Accessed 5 July 2013

Lucky Day: Invasion of Okinawa

"destroy enemy aircraft..."USS *Bunker Hill* Report of Air Operations Against Kyushu & Honshu, Japan, Ryukyu Islands and Jap Task Force, 3/18/45-5/11/45

"By a strange twist..." Commander Air Group 83 War History, 1945

"We were transferring pilots..." USS *Borie* War Diary, 1-30 April 1945

"Though little ground..." USS *Haynsworth* Morning Orders, 3 April 1945

"A radio program need not be..." USS *Haynsworth* Morning Orders ibid

"Today our task group..." USS *Haynsworth* Morning Orders, 4 April 1945

"0634 Fueling..." USS *Haynsworth* War Diary, 1-30 April 1945

"127-1507 Received 20 tons USS *Charles. S. Sperry* War Diary, 1-30 April 1945

Operation TEN-GO: *Kikusui No. 1*

"We were ready..." Lothrop ibid

6 April 1945

"Tad chose wisely..." Lanier, William D., *The 1940 Lucky Bag*, Baker, Jones, Hausauer, Inc., Buffalo, New York, 1940

"Today may be a busy day..." ComDesRon 62 War Diary, 1-30 April 1945

"weather improved..." USS *Bunker Hill* War Diary, 1-30 April 1945

"Under our radar..." Lothrop ibid

"The section of *Hellcats*..." ComAirGroup 83 ACA Reports of air operations against Japan, Ryukyu Islands and Jap Task Force, 3/18/45-5/24/45, P. 405

"Fired on one *Zeke*..." USS *Charles S. Sperry* War History

"Fighters vectored out..." USS *Haynsworth* War Diary ibid

"Spotting a medium sized incoming raid..." Lothrop ibid

"Shortly after 1200 2nd Lts..." VMF-112 War Diary, 1-30 April 1945

"Her three twin 5-inch mounts..." Lothrop ibid

"Finally, all the raid [s]..." Lothrop ibid

"Some confusion has been caused..." USS *Haynsworth* Morning Orders, 30 March 1945

"on station to operate the fire control..." Scott Thomas FC2c, interview with author, 2013

"Main battery and starboard 20mm..." USS *Haynsworth* War Diary ibid

"Our five inch opened up..." Lothrop ibid

"Main battery shifting..." USS *Haynsworth* War Diary ibid

"Above us was shooting..." Bly, Harold RM2c, interview with the author, 2014

"As the Judy turned right..." USS *Haynsworth* War Diary ibid

"The 40s and 20s tore into him..." Lothrop ibid

"The Captain has turned the ship..." Aakhus, Ralph RdM2c, Personal Letters, 1945

"We couldn't stop him..." Lothrop ibid

"He came on in..." Lothrop ibid

"The motor went through the side..." Aakhus ibid

"Standing in my CIC spot..." Lothrop ibid

"Doctor Ley could have explained..." Vasquez, ibid

"The Jap plane cleared..." Schneider, George S1c personal letter to Heob family, 1945

"Neither Cliff nor Harold..." Schneider ibid

"The second plane hit..." USS *Harrison* War Diary, 1-30 April 1945

"The fire was of such intensity..." USS *Haynsworth* Action Report, Period 14 March 1945 to 9 April 1945

"By means of fog from..." USS *Haynsworth* Action Report, Period 14 March 1945 to 9 April 1945

"So rapidly as only to be a hindrance..." USS *Haynsworth* Action Report ibid

"An hour later we had the fires..." Lothrop ibid

"It seemed..." Lothrop ibid

"Had burns so bad..." ..." Kelly, Edward R. TM3c, Personal Recollections

"The following material casualties..." USS *Haynsworth* Deck Log, 6 April 1945

"It had taken us an hour..." Lothrop ibid

"Total of about 35 enemy planes..." USS *Ransom* War Diary, 1-30 April 1945

"One splashing 400 yards astern..." USS *Ransom* War Diary ibid

"The *Oscar* dropped one bomb..." USS *Taussig* War Diary, 1-30 April 1945

"From a fancy red life raft..." Morison, Samuel Eliot, *History of United States Naval Operations in World War II: Victory in the Pacific*, ibid, P. 199

"The machine gun batteries were expending ammunition so rapidly..." USS *Howorth* War Diary, 1-30 April 1945

"Amidships in vicinity of torpedo tubes..." USS *Hyman* War Diary, 1-30 April 1945

"All decking and superstructure..." USS *Newcomb* War Diary, 1-30 April 1945

"Turned ship left quickly..." USS *Devastator* Report of Operations in the Invasion of Okinawa Junto, Ryukyu Islands 24 March -30 April, 1945

"Igniting films..." ..." USS *Devastator* Report of Operations in the Invasion of Okinawa Junto, Ryukyu Islands 24 March -30 April, 1945

"It was a horrible day..." Ley, Allyn Lt., Personal Letter

"It was the longest day..." Dennett, Armistead Lt., interview with author 2013

'Sailors pick through the wreckage...' Murphy, Polly; Saia, Fred, interviews with author, 2013-4

"One sailor quips..." Kelly ibid

"The performance of every man..." USS *Haynsworth* Action Report, Period 14 March 1945 to 9 April 1945

"By late afternoon on April 6..." CINCPOA Communiqué No.323 6 April 1945

7 April 1945: The Storm Continues

"In accordance with the provisions of..." USS *Haynsworth* Morning Orders, 7 April 1945

"For light in the CIC..." Lothrop ibid

"Without regard for his own safety..." Ballough, William RdM2c, Silver Star Citation, U.S. Navy, 1945

"Promptly swam..." Ballough ibid

"Seeing the peril..." Gillett, Morris CRT, *My War*, ibid, P. 103

"Fear? Yes, believe it..." Lothrop ibid

"An enemy plane bearing..." USS *Hank* War Diary, 1-30 April 1945

"Two planes were sighted..." USS *Ault* War Diary, 1-30 April 1945

"Rescue destroyers commenced firing..." ComDesRon 48 War Diary, 1-30 April 1945

"1433 Left formation..." USS *Hank* War Diary ibid

"The drama in the reports ..." author unknown, USS *John J. Weeks* Newsletter, July 2011

"On April 6 and 7..." CINCPOA Communiqué No.324, 7 April 1945

8 April 1945: Task Group 58.3

"Squadron Commander has recommended..." USS *Haynsworth* Morning Orders, 9 April 1945

"It is with deep regret..." USS *Haynsworth* Morning Orders ibid

Epilogue

"Today was almost THE day..." Plum, Robert FC2c, Personal War Diary, 1945

"Admire the guts..." Lothrop ibid

Appendix: Pilot and Crew Rescues

"There's one thing I won't forget..." Scott, J. Davis, "Jap Bait," *Flying* magazine, July, 1948, P.46

NAVY RATINGS

Adm.	Admiral
AMM	Aviation Machinist's Mate
AOM	Aviation Ordnance Mate
ARM	Aviation Radioman
B	Boilermaker
Bkr	Baker
BM	Boatswains Mate
BT	Boiler Technician
BU	Builder
Cdr	Commander
CEM	Chief Electrician's Mate
CGM	Chief Gunner's Mate
Ck	Cook
CM	Carpenters Mate
CMM	Chief Machinist's Mate
ComDesRon	Commander Destroyer Squadron
Cox	Coxswain
CQM	Chief Quartermaster
CRM	Chief Radioman
CTM	Chief Torpedoman's Mate
EM	Electricians Mate
Ens.	Ensign
ETM	Electronic Technician's Mate
F	Fireman
FC	Fire Controlman
GM	Gunner's Mate
Lt.	Lieutenant
Lt. Cdr.	Lieutenant Commander
Lt. jg.	Lieutenant Junior Grade
MaM	Mailman
MM	Machinist's Mate
PhM	Pharmacists Mate
QM	Quartermaster
R.Adm.	Rear Admiral
RdM	Radarman
RM	Radioman
RT	Radio Technician
S	Seaman
SC	Ship's Cook
SF	Shipfitter
SK	Storekeeper
SM	Signalman
SoM	Sonarman

St... Steward
TM.. Torpedoman's Mate
WT ....Water Tender
Y ....Yeoman

DEFINITIONS

AA .... Anti-aircraft
AD .... Destroyer
AH .... Hospital Ship
AK .... Cargo Ship
AM .... Minesweeper Ship
APA .... Attack Transport Ship
AO .... Fleet Oiler Ship
ARH .... Heavy Hull Repair Ship
BB .... Battleship
Bogie .... slang for unidentified aircraft
CA .... Heavy cruiser
CAP .... Combat Air Patrol
CL .... Light Cruiser
CV .... Fleet Aircraft Carrier
CVE .... Escort Aircraft Carrier
CVL .... Light Aircraft Carrier
DD .... Destroyer
DE .... Destroyer Escort
DesDiv .... Destroyer Division
DesRon .... Destroyer Squadron
DMS .... Destroyer Minesweeper
F4F/FM .... Grumman/GM *Wildcat* fighter plane
F6F .... Grumman *Hellcat* fighter plane
F4U/FG1 .... Vought/Goodyear *Corsair* fighter plane
IJA .... Imperial Japanese Army
IJN .... Imperial Japanese Navy
LST .... Landing Ship Tank
RAS .... Replenishment at sea
SB2C .... Curtiss *Helldiver* dive bomber
SBD .... Douglas *Dauntless* dive bomber
TBM/TBF .... Grumman/Ford *Avenger* torpedo- bomber plane
U-boat .... German Submarine
UnRep .... Underway Replenishment
USMC .... United States Marine Corp
USMCR .... United States Marine Corp Reserve
USN .... United States Navy
USNR .... United States Navy Reserve
VB .... Carrier Bomber Squadron
VBF .... Carrier Fighter Bomber Squadron
VF .... Carrier Fighter Squadron
VT .... Carrier Torpedo Squadron
YMS .... Auxiliary Motor Minesweeper

TASK GROUP 38.2 OPERATIONS MIKE I AND *GRATITUDE*
DECEMBER 1944

Commander Third Fleet .... Admiral William Halsey
Commander Task Force 38 .... Vice Admiral John S. McCain
Commander Task Group 38.2 .... Rear Admiral Gerald F. Bogan

Task Unit 38.2.1(Carriers)............................. **Rear Admiral Gerald F. Bogan**
    CV-6 USS *Enterprise*
    CV-19 USS *Hancock* (Flag CTF-38 Vice Admiral McCain)
    CV-12 USS *Hornet*
    CV-16 USS *Lexington*
    CVL-22 USS *Independence*

Task Unit 38.2.2 (Support) ....**Rear Admiral J. C. Jones**
    BB-62 USS *New Jersey* (Flag ComThird Fleet Admiral Halsey)
    BB-64 USS *Wisconsin*
    CA-68 USS *Baltimore*
    CA-69 USS *Boston*
    CL 54 USS *San Juan*
    CL-65 USS *Pasadena*
    CL-90 USS *Astoria II*
    CL-103 USS *Wilkes-Barre*

Task Unit 38.2.3 (Screen) ....**Capt. J. P. Womble**
  DesRon52: DesDiv 103
      DD-535 USS *Miller*
      DD-536 USS *Owen* (Destroyer flagship)
      DD-537 USS *The Sullivans*
      DD-538 USS *Stephen Potter*
      DD-539 USS *Tingey*
  DesRon52: DesDiv 104
      DD-674 USS *Hunt*
      DD-676 USS *Marshall*
  DesRon62: DesDiv 123 Capt. J. M. Higgins
      DD-696 USS *English*
      DD-697 USS *Charles S. Sperry*
      DD-698 USS *Ault*
      DD-699 USS *Waldron*
      DD-700 USS *Haynsworth*
  DesRon62: DesDiv 124
      DD-701 USS *John W. Weeks*
      DD-702 USS *Hank*
      DD-703 USS *Wallace L. Lind*

DD-704 USS *Borie* (Did not join DesRon 62 until January 26, 1945)

DesRon47: DesDiv 93

DD-531 USS *Hazelwood*

DD-534 USS *McCord*

DesRon47: DesDiv 94

DD-554 USS *Franks*

DD-556 USS *Hailey*

DD-555 USS *Haggard*

TASK GROUP 58.3 ORGANIZATION OPERATION JAMBOREE
FEBRUARY 10, 1945

Commander Fifth Fleet ....Admiral Raymond Spruance
Commander Task Force 58 ....Vice Admiral Marc Mitscher
Commander Task Group 58.3 .... Rear Admiral F. C. Sherman (ComCarDiv1)

Task Unit 58.3.1 (Carriers)
    CV-9 USS *Essex*
    CV-17 USS *Bunker Hill*
    CVL-25 USS *Cowpens*

Task Unit 58.3.2 (Support) ....Vice Admiral W. A. Lee
                                                                    (ComBatRon 2)

    BB-49 USS *South Dakota*
    BB-62 USS *New Jersey*

Task Unit 58.3.3 (Light Support) ....Rear Admiral J. C. Jones, Jr.
                                                                    (ComCruDiv17)

    CL-65 USS *Pasadena*
    CL-66 USS *Springfield*
    CL-90 USS *Astoria*
    CL-103 USS *Wilkes-Barre*
    CA-35 USS *Indianapolis*

Task Unit 58.3.4 (Screen) ....Captain J. M. Higgins
                                                                    (ComDesRon 62)
DesRon 52: DesDiv 99
    DD-668 USS *Clarence D. Bronson*
    DD-669 USS *Cotten*
    DD-670 USS *Dortch*
    DD-671 USS *Gatling*
    DD-672 USS *Healy*

DesRon62: DesDiv 123
    DD-696 USS *English*
    DD-697 USS *Charles S. Sperry*
    DD-698 USS *Ault*
    DD-699 USS *Waldron*
    DD-700 USS *Haynsworth*

DesRon62: DesDiv 124
    DD-701 USS *John W. Weeks*
    DD-702 USS *Hank*
    DD-703 USS *Wallace L. Lind*

DD-704 USS *Borie*

DesRon55: DesDiv 109
DD-682 USS *Porterfield*
DD-792 USS *Callaghan*
DD-793 USS *Cassin Young*
DD-794 USS *Irwin*
DD-795 USS *Preston II*

Task Group 58.3 Organization Operation ICEBERG
Okinawa Invasion March 14, 1945

Commander Task Group .... Rear Admiral Frederic C. Sherman

Task Unit 58.3.1 (Carriers)
    CV-5 USS *Essex*
    CV-17 USS *Bunker Hill*
    CVL-28 USS *Cabot*
    CVL-29 USS *Bataan*

Task Unit 58.3.2 (Support)
    BB-47 USS *Washington*
    BB-55 USS *North Carolina*
    BB-57 USS *South Dakota*

Task Unit 58.3.3 (Light Support)
Cruiser Division 17
    CL-65 USS *Pasadena*
    CL-66 USS *Springfield*
    CL-90 USS *Astoria II*
    CL-103 USS *Wilkes-Barre*

Task Unit 58.3.4 (Screen) .... Capt. John M. Higgins, Commander
DesRon48: DesDiv 95
    DD-517 USS *Walker*
    DD-631 USS *Erben*
    DD-642 USS *Hale*
    DD-644 USS *Stembel*

DesRon48: DesDiv 96
    DD-660 USS *Bullard*
    DD-661 USS *Kidd*
    DD-666 USS *Black*
    DD-667 USS *Chauncey*

DesRon62: DesDiv 123
    DD-696 USS *English* (flagship)
    DD-697 USS *Charles S. Sperry*
    DD-698 USS *Ault*
    DD-699 USS *Waldron*
    DD-700 USS *Haynsworth*

DesRon62: DesDiv 124
    DD-701 USS *John W. Weeks*

DD-702 USS *Hank*
DD-703 USS *Wallace L. Lind*
DD-704 USS *Borie*

Ships Sunk* or Damaged by Kamikazes
6-7 April 1945, Okinawa

Destroyers (DD) and Destroyer Mine Sweepers (DMS)

DD-417 USS *Morris*
DD-473 USS *Bennett*
DD-476 USS *Hutchins*
DD-481 USS *Leutze*
DD-528 USS *Mullany*
DD-529 USS *Bush**
DD-573 USS *Harrison*
DD-586 USS *Newcomb*
DD-592 USS *Howorth*
DD-700 USS *Haynsworth*
DD-732 USS *Hyman*
DD-746 USS *Taussig*
DD-801 USS *Colhoun**
DMS-21 USS *Rodman*
DMS-22 USS *Emmons**
DMS-28 USS *Harding*

Destroyer Escorts

DE-184 USS *Wesson*
DE-636 USS *Witter*
DE-640 USS *Fierberling*

Minesweepers (AM), Motor Minesweepers

AM-233 USS *Facility*
AM-283 USS *Ransom*
AM-318 USS *Devastator*
YMS-311 USS *Robin*

Other Vessel Types

CVL-30 USS *San Jacinto*
CV-19 USS *Hancock*
BB-46 USS *Maryland*
USS LST-447*
SS *Hobbs Liberty**
SS *Logan Liberty**

USS *HAYNSWORTH* CASUALTIES
APRIL 6, 1945 KAMIKAZE ATTACK (*PLANKOWNER)

Killed

Campbell, Barton M. CRM ....Burns of entire body surface; Transferred to USS *South Dakota* BB-57

DeLoach, Walter GM2c* ....Killed outright

Dyer, John RM3c...Burns of head and extremities; Transferred to USS *South Dakota* BB-57

Goyer, Arthur A. RM2c.......................................Burns of entire body surface; Transferred to USS *South Dakota* BB-57

Heob, Clifford S1c...Killed outright

Holiman, Bernice R. RM2c ....Burns of entire body surface; Transferred to USS *South Dakota* BB-57

Knott, John F. S1c*...Killed outright

Kubena, William R. S1c* ....Killed outright

Lenihan, Joseph P. S1c* ....Killed outright

Matschat, Robert D. S1c* ....Burns of head and extremities; Transferred to USS *South Dakota* BB-57

MacLaughlan, Hobart S1c* ....Killed outright

Satterly, Ernest W. S1c*..Killed outright

Critically Wounded and Transferred
to USS *South Dakota* BB-57 April 6, 1945

Aulbert, Lonnie Lee S1c ....Burns of head and upper extremity, fracture left femur

Davis, Carroll, RM3c..Burns of head, trunk, and arm

Holcombe, Warner RM1c* ....Burns of head and extremities

Saia, Mariano F. S1c* ....Burns of face and right arm

Studley, Milton RdM3c*............................. Burns of face and upper extremity

Vasquez, John SM3c...Compound Fracture of Skull

Wounded Transferred to USS *South Dakota* BB-57 April 7, 1945

Lembo, Frank S1c.. Burns of head and hands

Malkiewicz, Edward S1c* ....Burns of head and extremities

Wounded but remained on board USS *Haynsworth*

Bird, Ralph TM1c* ....Fracture, simple, left 5th metatarsal

Callahan, Oscar S1c*... Wound, lacerated chin

Canfield, James S1c* ....Fracture, simple, left 1st metatarsal

Davison, Jacqueline Lt. jg. .... Hematoma, right calf

Dempsey, Harold TM1c* ....Burns of face and hands
Kania, Walter SC2c ....Wound, lacerated, right elbow
Karos, Donald RdM3c ....Wound, lacerated, right forehand
Lothrop, Scott Lt. Cdr.* ....Burns of hands
McClintock, Robert Ens. .... Fracture, simple, left 4th and 5th metacarpals
Moore, Louis S1c* ....Burns of face and hands and feet
Moss, Harold A Y3c ....Sprain, left ankle
Thompson, Edward S1c* ....Burn of right ear

USS *Hancock* Sailors Rescued April 7, 1945 by USS *Haynsworth*

Heard, Haywood, S1c
Hearn, Clifton, TM3c
Hill, Frank TM3c
Johnson, Donald L., Cox ....Transferred to USS *South Dakota* BB-57
for medical treatment
McKay, Millard, S1c
Neafcy, Thomas, AMM3c ....Transferred to USS *South Dakota* BB-57
for medical treatment
Nelson, Robert, Lt. Cdr.
Tallarida, Frank F1c ....Transferred to USS *South Dakota* BB-57
for medical treatment

Left: Lt. jg. Horan rescue, 18 March 1945.
Right: Eugene Wengler ARM3c rescued, 25 Jan 1945.

The destroyers were lifesavers. All the pilots knew it," recalled 1st Lt. Philip Wilmot seventy years after the events of 1945. The approximately fifty successful rescues listed are the equivalent of half an air group for a single carrier. Safely recovering pilots and aircrews was given the highest priority by the Task Force 38/58 commanders. Enormous efforts and resources were expended to achieve the results but research to date of pilots rescued in the Pacific has given little credit to the destroyers. While many other rescues occurred during the setting of this book far from the Fast Carrier Task Force by lifeguard submarines, float planes (like OS2U *Kingfishers*), and large amphibious planes (PBM *Mariners*, PBY *Catalinas*), scant credit is given to the tin can sailors who risked their own lives to enter the Pacific to save the downed airmen. The recoveries of airmen provided evidence to the fliers that they stood a chance of surviving if they had to abandon their planes. The rescues also served to boost the morale of fliers and tin can sailors alike.

Pilot and aircrew rescues were so common that often there is no mention of them in individual destroyer war diaries. When they are mentioned, frequently names were spelled incorrectly. It was not unusual to find vast differences between the records of destroyers, Commander DesRon 62, air squadrons, carrier air groups, and aircraft carriers regarding specific rescues. Reconciling the records was a challenging but rewarding effort.

This list is not complete but does provide an overview of the rescue attempts described in the narrative. Each task group usually had two destroyer squadrons attached so at best this represents one half of the rescues associated with Task Groups 38.2/58.3 during the time the USS *Haynsworth* served. Task Force 38/58 had three to five Task Groups attached during this same period so the total number of rescue attempts is thus multiplied further.

1ˢᵗ LT Junie B. Lohan of VMF-112, rescued by the USS *Colhoun*, the day before her own demise in *Kikusui No.1* stated, "There's one thing I won't forget. I don't want any of you guys to forget it either. That's the courage of the men on those destroyers. We owe a lot to them. More than any of us can ever repay."

Of sad note are the number of rescued pilots and aircrew that were later killed during World War II or the Korean War. Their sacrifice represents their selfless service to country.

Date	DD	Pilot/sailor	Unit	Carrier	Plane	BuNo.	Crew
				1944			
26 Dec	*Lind*	unknown pilot	VT(N)-90	*Enterprise*	TBM-3D		
	Lind	unknown pilot	VF(N)-90	*Enterprise*	F6F-5E or N		
30 Dec	*Ault*	unknown sailor		*Hancock*			
31 Dec	*Lind*	Lt. Eugene Lee*	VT(N)-90	*Enterprise*	TBM-3D	68429	Robert Lundfelt ARM3c, Armando Nelson AOM2c
	Hank	Lt. jg. Jim Cuff	VT-7	*Hancock*	TBM-1C	46336	Thomas Dickie AMM1c, Victor Holland ARM3c
				1945			
3 Jan	*Haynsworth*	Lt. jg. Don Seiz	VT-20	*Lexington*	TBM-1C	46410	Clifford Gallant AOM, John F. Brady ARM3c
	Ault	Ens. L. E. Ray	VF-7	*Hancock*	F6F-5		
	Ault	Ens. Thomas Adams	VT-11	*Hornet*	TBM-1C	46058	William E. Corley AMM1c, Thomas A. Fanger ARM1c
6 Jan	*Sperry*	Lt. Rbt. McHenry	VT-20	*Lexington*	TBM-1C	17065	Edward Butler ARM3c, Carroll Fletcher AMM2c
7 Jan	*Sperry/ Tingey*	Lt. John E. Nearing*	VF-20	*Lexington*	F6F-5	58583	
8 Jan	*Lind*	Ens. P. E. King	VF-11	*Hornet*	F6F-3	42294	
9 Jan	*Lind*	Ens. John Buttler	VF-7	*Hancock*	F6F-5	71835	
	Sperry	unknown pilot	VF-11	*Hornet*	F6F-3	41783	
12 Jan	*Hank*	Ens. Thomas Jones	VT-7	*Hancock*	TBM-3	23229	Max A. Eckels ARM3c, Dean Paul

Date	DD	Pilot/sailor	Unit	Carrier	Plane	BuNo.	Crew
							Kenney AMM3c
13 Jan	Haynsworth	Robert Plum FC3c		Lind			
16 Jan	Hank	Ens. Royce Carruth	VF-7	Hancock	F6F		
25 Jan	Haynsworth	Ens. Knox Scott	VT(N)-90	Enterprise	TBM-3D	23389	Eugene A. Wengler ARM3c, William Crowley ARM3c*
8 Feb	Borie	Ens. Bruce Garlock	VF-46	Cowpens	F6F-5	72600	
11 Feb	Porterfield	Ens. Peter Kooyenga	VF-46	Cowpens	F6F-5		
17 Feb	Sperry	1st Lt. Philip Wilmot	VMF-451	Bunker Hill	F4U-1D	57834	
23 Feb	unknown	Ens. Daniel Valpey	VC-81	Natoma Bay	FM-2	56919	
25 Feb	Haynsworth	Ens. Edward Jindra	VF-12	Randolph	F6F-5	72530	
1 Mar	Ault	1st Lt. Casimah Chop	VMF-124	Essex	F4U-1D	57594	
	Ault	1st Lt. A. C. Simkunas	VMF-451	Bunker Hill	F4U-1D	82590	
	Ault	1st Lt. Fred Briggs	VMF-221	Bunker Hill	F4U-1D	82196	
	Waldron	Lt. jg. Waller Puryear	VF-4	Essex	F6F-5	71788	
14 Mar	Weeks	unknown pilot*		unknown			
15 Mar	Weeks	2nd Lt. D. Wambganss	VMF-451	Bunker Hill	F4U-1D	57918	
	Weeks	unknown pilot			SB2C (?)		
16 Mar	Waldron	1st Lt. J. Anderson	VMF-451	Bunker Hill	F4U-1D		
17 Mar	Waldron	unknown pilot					
18 Mar	Haynsworth	Lt. jg. James Horan	VB-6	Hancock	SB2C-3	19508	Leroy Cox ARM2c
19 Mar	Waldron	Ens. Wm. J. Morton	VF-83	Essex	F6F-5	72873	
	Waldron	Ens. Dennis Gray	VBF-83	Essex	F4U-1D		
23 Mar	Waldron	Ens. Herbert Gidney	VT-29	Cabot	TBM-3	68628	Norman Sokolow ARM3c, Wilfred Bond AMM3c
	Sperry	Lt. jg. Clifford Carter	VF-84	Bunker Hill	F4U-1D	57841	
	Kidd	Lt. John E. Barrows	VB-84	Bunker Hill	SB2-4E	20761	LaRoy Sell ARM1c
24 Mar	Waldron	Maj. E. Dedrick*	VMF-451	Bunker Hill	F4U-1D	57867	

Date	DD	Pilot/sailor	Unit	Carrier	Plane	BuNo.	Crew
26 Mar	Waldron	Ens. George Rawley	VF-6	Hancock	F6F	77396	
	Waldron	Ens. Wesley Midyett*	VF-6	Hancock	F6F-5	72594	
	Waldron	Lt. Frederick Bowen	VBF-6	Hancock	FG-1D	76536	
	Waldron	Lt. Richard Buck*	VF-6	Hancock	F6F-5N	77396	
	Walker	Ens. R. Meyers	VBF-6	Hancock	F4U-1D	82724	
	Stembel	Lt. jg. W. H. Keller	VF-6	Hancock	F6F-5	72632	
27 Mar	Waldron	unknown pilot					
28 Mar	Waldron	Lt. William Jacks, Jr.	VB-84	Bunker Hill	SB2C-4	21033	Howard Pederson ARM3c
29 Mar	English	Lt. Bernard Berry	VT-84	Bunker Hill	TBM-3	68281	C. T. Johnson ARM1c, Charles E. Metler AOM1c
	English	Lt. jg. M. Georgius*	VT-84	Bunker Hill	TBM-3	68445	James F. Mudd ARM2c, J. A. Holloway AOM1c
	OS2U	Ens. William Elings	VT-84	Bunker Hill	TBM-3	68440	Homer Hively ARM3c, Frank L. Baxter AOM3c
30 Mar	English	Lt. jg. Edward Laster	VT-10	Intrepid	TBM-3	68812	John Fuentes AMM1c, Lawrence M. Hebach ARM3c
31 Mar	English	Ens. R. H. Langdon	VF-83	Essex	F6F-5	71557	
31 Mar	English	Lt. jg. Nils Carlson	VB-83	Essex	SB2C-4E	20730	W. R. Sanders S2c*
3 Apr	Ault	Ens. Oliver Swisher	VF-47	Bataan	F6F-5	71723	
	Weeks	Lt. Darrel Way	VF-83	Essex	F6F-5	71884(?)	
4 Apr	English	Ens. Edward Wendt	VB-6	Hancock	SB2C-4	19830	unknown
6 Apr	Taussig	unknown Japanese pilot					
6 Apr	Hale	Lt. jg. Vernon Biddle	VF-84	Bunker Hill	F6F-5		
7 Apr	Weeks	Lt. jg. Locke Trigg, Jr.	VF-47	Bataan	F6F-5	77865	
	Unknown	Ens. John J. Gannon	VB-17	Hornet	SB2C-4E	20714	Ralph Foulks ARM3c

*Killed in Action
BuNo. = Each plane's unique serial number from the U.S. Navy Bureau of Aeronautics

George Schneider's letter written postwar
to the family of his friend, Clifford Heob S1c:

Our Countrymen would call Clifford Heob 'hero'; yet, were he to speak, he would tell you this: That each act called heroism is but the instinctive gesture of forgetting self when another stands in danger.

We who served in action know it; you who served in silence know it. But let me tell you of Clifford Heob and you will see the millions of Cliffords. Clifford was a typical American boy, born and reared in a typical American family and home; a pleasant chap, liked by all who knew him. I don't say that Cliff knew no fear—no, he was too much an American for that. Like all of us, he knew fear but knew the remedy: Faith and Selflessness.

The morning of the sixth of April was fair and warm with a few scattered clouds above, when we on the Haynsworth (DD 700), picket ship for the task force off the coast of Okinawa, were sent to General Quarters. Above us we could see two of our planes making it for two Jap planes with the result of one Jap plunging down in flames. Our guns were adding to the din when suddenly the remaining Jap dived for our ship with our plane tailing it. The chance of striking our men was too great and we held our fire as the Jap plane cleared our ship and making a short left turn, came in on our starboard beam, crashing into the Radio room directly behind the 40mm clip room where Cliff and Harold Dempsey were stationed, with the door closed. The impact was terrific, destroying all our Radio and Radar equipment, one 40mm gun, its mount and crew.

Neither Cliff nor Harold knew what had happened until they opened the door to face boiling smoke and leaping flames. I believe it was that complete selflessness of Clifford's that caused him to fumble with the earphones, just the second it took to give Harold his chance to leap out. Hands over his face, he ducked under the torpedo tubes, and dashing through the flames, reached safety, receiving face and hand burns.

I believe Clifford would have made it, too, but the dense smoke blinded him causing him to stumble over the phone wires at his feet, and pitch head first from the upper deck, through the flames to the main deck, breaking his neck and dying instantly. An hour later we had the raging fire under control.

I like to remember that although the ship was under fire from the Japs, the burial service for each man was performed under his own faith and the wounded transferred to the battleship South Dakota; that no man shirked his task nor thought of himself although the heavy fire of the enemy was continuous and the rolling sea all but swept them overboard at times.

Clifford Heob and all the other Cliffords have not died in vain; Not when, in the face of danger, they can emulate the Master and be selfless.

Maybe Cliff was a 'hero'; maybe 'hero' is but a word. But the true act of selflessness remains and is our God given heritage.

USS *HAYNSWORTH* 1944-46 PLANKOWNERS AND CREW

Young Sailors of the USS Haynsworth. (Courtesy of Marianna Steele)

* denotes plankowner and **boldface** denotes killed in action

Aakhus, Ralph RdM3
Aandal, Andrew, Lt.*
Achord, Elgene EM3c
Ackerman, Walter D. PM2*
Adair, William S1c
Addison, Vernon S1c*
Alberto, Frederick J. S1c*
Alexander, Samuel W. F1c
Allison, George A WT2c
Asay, Edward SC3c
Aulbert, Lonnie L. S2c
Ayers, Thomas A. SM2c*

Baker, Leroy MM1c
Baptie, Bryan SF1c
Barnard, Cecil R. ST3c
Barnett, Robert W. MoM2c*
Bashinger, Thomas F, Jr. FC3c*
Bateman, John D. S2c
Bauer, Edward C. Y1c*
Beasley, Harold RM3c
Bebbino, John F1c*
Bendokas, Francis J. S1c*
Beranek, Edward S1c*
Berk, Leon, Lt.
Berman, Joshua S1c*
Bichon, Henry, EM3c*

Billings, Benjamin C. S1c*
Bilski, William K. S1c*
Bird, Ralph W. TM1c*
Birkenmaier, Urban G., Jr TM3c
Black, Jonathan STM2c
Bland, Arthur B. PhM1c*
Blanton, George F. CGM*
Bly, Harold, S1c*
Bonham, Olen J. SM1c*
Brassard, Aime O. S1c*
Breckenridge, William A. TM3c*
Brodie, Thomas, Cdr., Captain 1944
Brown, James, T. GM2c*
Brush, John MoMM2c*
Berk, Leon, Lt.
Callahan, Oscar V, S1c*
Campbell, Barton N., CRM*
Campbell, James J. StM1c*
Canfield, James R., S1c*
Carlson, Edwin C F1c*
Carlson, Lawrence E. BM2c*
Casalino, Joe CTM
Cato, Wesley J. QM3c*
Cavallone, George J. S1c*
Chamberlin, Robert B, SoM1c*
Chambers, Charles F, GM1c*
Chandick, Peter S1c

Clark, Louie Maxwell, SK1c
Clarke, Paul L., StM2c*
Clarke, Robert S. TM2c*
Clement, Jack W., Cox*
Conwell, James WT1*
Cook, Phillip G EM3c
Costello, Charles E. GM3c*
Crawford, John R. F1c*
Creedon, James J FC2c*
Crowley, Claude S2c
Cummings, Harry A. Lt.

Dancer, Forrest F. BM1c*
Dato, Charles J. SC3c*
Davis, Carroll L., Jr. RM3c*
Davis, Earl W. WT3c*
Davis, Ilous StM1c
Davis, James D. Jr S1c*
Davis, Kenneth S1c
Davison, Jacqueline, Lt. jg.*
Dean, Ralph D. S1c*
Deegan, William J. EM3c*
DeLoach, Walter GM3c*
Dempsey, Harold J. TM1c*
Dennett, Armistead Lt.*
DeSalvo, Frank S. MM1c*
Dillon, Joseph N. GM3c*
Dininger, Marion W. MM3c*
Dix, William M. F1c*
Domaransky, Andrew M. GM3c*
Douglas, William W. TM3c*
Duffy, Thomas E. CMM*
Durocer, Albert J Cox*
Durrenberger, Robert F1c*
Dyer, John R., Jr., RM3c

Early, James J. BM2c*
Edds, Joe Leon S1c*
Ellett, Henry C FC1c*
Emberton, William, J. MM1c*
Eshelman, Robert P. Lt.*
Evans, Donald J F1c*

Farmer, Horace EM3c*
Ferris, Kenneth L. GM2c*

Fletcher, Eugene D. CGM*
Foster, Thomas F1c
Fraser, Melvin J. FC3c*
Frey, Preston F1c*
Friedman, Alvin EM3*
Friel, John FC2c*
Frigm, Richard J. F2c*
Fritz, Robert F1c

Gates, Leo C Cox*
George, Earl C S1c*
Gingras, Hugh E. III Lt. jg.*
Godfrey, Albert G. MM1c*
Goldstein, Philip GM2c*
Goodman, James L. FC3*
Goodman, Marion E. S2c*
Goyer, Arthur A. RM2c*
Gruber, Charles R. SoM2c*

Hall, Robert E. CFC*
Hall, Richard O. MM2c*
Hamel, Ronald S1/c
Hanson, Harold W. QM2c*
Harding, Elwood MM2c
Harvey, Bertran C. F1c*
Hendee, John M. MM2c*
Heob, Clifford, S1c
Herlinger, Richard K Cox*
Hickman, Robert W. WT3c*
Higginbotham, James L. CMM*
Hilbert, John E. MM2c*
Hilker, Richard B. SoM3c
Hitchcock, Frank Cox*
Hokes, Ben F. Sc2c*
Holcombe, Walter C .RM2c*
Holiman, Bernice. RM2c
Hoy, John R. CRM*
Hoyt, Marvin S. S1c*
Humphrey, George R., Jr. QM1c*
Hurson, Edward J. WT2c*

Israel, Lawrence Lt.*

James, Edward TM2c*
January, Richard F1c*

Jernigan, Brodie S1c*
Johanson, Ivar CY (PA)*
Johnson, Lloyd, FC2c*
Jones, James K., Jr. PhM2c
Jorgenson, Rulen Ens.

Kania, Walter A. S2c*
Karos, Don RdM3c
Kelly Edward TM3c
Kempster, Jack S2c
Kenny, Edward D. S2c
Kerr, Roy J. WT2c*
Kessler, Norton E. PhM3c*
Kidd, Arthur G. S1c*
Kirkpatrick, Scott B. S1c*
Kniskern, Ralph K RdM3c
Knott, John F. S1c*
Konetakie, Anthony T. S1c*
Kosloskie. Leon M. MM1c*
Krajczar. William S1c
Kranz, Robert J. RT3c*
Kroh, Jerald E. S1c*
Kubena, William R. S1c*

Lail, James E. RM3c*
Lakoff, Herman H. M1*
Langer, John J. MM2c*
Layden, Paul W., Jr. RT2c*
Lea, Joe W. FC3c*
Leach, Donald E. S1c*
Lechner, Charles W S1c*
Lembo, Frank S1c
Lenihan, Joseph P. S1c*
Lentz, Marvin A. GM1c*
Leo, Clarence S2c*
Leonard, Arthur S1c *
Le Roy, Arthur A. S1c*
Levy, Hyman S1c*
Lewin, Hazen W. S1c*j
Lewis, Augustus L F1c*
Ley, Allyn B., MD, Lt. jg.*
Lincoln, Abraham M. MM3c*
Lisio, Tony V. S2c*
Lizzari, Angelo J. S1c*
Loane, James F1c*

Lobay, Michael S1c*
Loeb, Harry J. F1c*
Long, Norman Jr., S1c*
Loree, Robert H. S2c*
Lorraine, Joseph D. S2c*
Loss, Edward J. S1c*
Lothrop, Scott Lt. Cdr. XO 1944-45*
Loughran, James F. S1c*
Lucente, James MM2*
Lukacs, Michael S S1c*
Luke, Otto F. MM3c*
Lutz, Clay Byron F2c*
Lyle, Jack B. Lt. jg.*
Lyman, Harry R SSM(L)*
Lyons, Edward W. F1c*

Maciak, John S1c*
Mackay, High S. SF3c*
Mackowiak, Edward F1c
MacLaughlan, Hobart M. S1c*
Maffei, Vincent S1c*
Maggi, John E. F1c*
Magliocchetti, John F. RM3c*
Mahoney, Edward J S1c*
Mailhot, Leon A. Bkr3c*
Malkiewicz, Edward R. S1c*
Mallon, John S1c*
Malone, Kenneth V. CWT*
Maloney, Martin M S2c*
Mandell, Alvin Lt. Cdr.
Mandell, Solomon S2c*
Mandola, John J. S1c*
Manley, John J. S1c*
Manna, Dominic P. S2c*
Mansfield, Joseph W. S2c*
Marchisella, Paul F. S1c*
Marcus, Alex S1c*
Marcus, Harry S1c*
Maroon, Edward S1c*
Marsh, Jack C. Y3c*
Marshall, Robert L. GM2c*
Martin, Abel S1c*
Martin, Bernard C. F1c*
Martin, Willard P. S2c*

Mascola, Saverio F1c*
Maselli, Nicholas S2c*
Masone, Dominick S1c*
Matasavage, Willard V. WT3c*
Matschat, Robert D. S1c*
Maugel, Edwin E. SoM3c*
Maxsween, Francis S1c*
Maynard, Joseph C. S1c*
McAllister, John A RM3c*
McBrayer, Earl E. SoM3c*
McBride, Leroy V. WT2c*
McCall, Charles H. Ens.
McCann, Cecil G. SF3c*
McCarthy, Michael E. RdM3c*
McCarthy, William SK3c*
McClintock, Robert Jr. Lt. jg.*
McConnell, Harry L S1c*
McCray, Raymond S. S1c*
McGarry, Joseph B. S2c*
McGee, Archie A. Jr. EM2c*
McKeen, William N. S1c*
McKelvey, Warren S. F1c*
McLaughlin, William S1c*
McMahon, William J S2c*
McNutt, Harold A. S1c*
McQueen, Roy R. SoM3c*
Medeiros, Gilbert A. S2c*
Melendez, Ernest L. F1c*
Melfa, Joseph 2 S1c*
Mennette, Michael E. EM2c*
Merry, Kenneth D. TM2c*
Mesick, Rudolph H. S1c*
Messecar, Donald R. TM2c*
Meuinier, Joseph S2c*
Meyer, Leo S1c*
Mezynski, Zigmunt E. S1c*
Michalak, Henry B. S1c*
Mier, Fredericl H. Y3c*
Miglino, Daniel A S1c*
Milgate, Lyman A. S1c*
Miller, Howard J. S1c*
Miller, Sheldon G. S1c*
Mital, Edward CM2c*
Mitchell, David R. BM1c*
Monfrede, Edward S2c*

Monks, Arnold S1c*
Mooney, Gilbert W. S1c*
Moore, Louis R. S1c*
Moore, Robert J. SoM3c*
Moore, Sheldon G. SK1c*
Moore, Thomas F. S1c*
Morgan, Samuel J. S1c*
Morin, Lionel R. CBM*
Morlock, Lawrence E. SoM3*
Morrill, Manson C. S1c*
Morrissey, George E. RdM2c*
Morton, William F. S1c*
Mosco, John D. S1c*
Moss, Harold A. Y3c
Moynihan, John A. S1c*
Munson, Edward S2c*
Murphy, Thomas, S1c*
Myreholt, Keith RM3c*

Nadeau, Frank E., Jr. S1c*
Nadel, Ralph W. S2c*
Nadolny, Edward J. S1c*
Neely, Robert A. S1c*
Nelson, Dewey V. S1c*
Neth, Frederick S. GM1c*
Newbeck, George W. S2c*
Nicotra, Nicholas S1c*
Noe, Clifton F. F1c*
Noel, Duane F. GM3c*
Norris, William J. SM2c*
Nyikos, John E. S1c*

O'Connell, Thomas A. S1c*
O'Connor, Robert J. S2c*
Olsen, Arnold R. MM3c*
Olszewski, Henry M., Jr. S1c*
O'Neill Hugh R. MM3c*
Orashen, Frank, Jr. S1c*
Orsi, Raymond A. WT3c*
Osborne, Robert S. F1c*

Parker, Marion G. S1c*
Parrott, William T. WT1c
Peavy, Roy MM3c*
Penix, Archie M. Cox*

Peres, Isaac RM3c*
Pescosolido, Joseph SF1c
Peters, Frank T. StM1c*
Petersen, Earl S1c*
Phillips, William R. Ens.*
Pick, Charles F1c
Pickens, Arthus C. F1c
Pickering, Arthur F1c
Pifcho, Daniel F2c*
Pinkney, Thomas StM1c
Piskadlo Theodore B. MoM3c*
Pizzamiglio, Gerald E. F1c*
Polichak, Paul RdM3c
Politz, Joseph J. MM1c*
Polum, John W. GM3c*
Pope, Jackson, R. Ens.*
Potter, Frank D. RdM3c*
Powell, Weldon C. S1c*

Reardon, Gerald J. TM3c*
Redmon, Don F1c*
Reeder, Claude E. RT1c*
Reser, Harrison B3c
Rhoads, Virgil G. F1c*
Richter, Richard D. F3c*
Riley, Benjamin P. Lt.*
Ring, Jack EM3c*
Ripley, William Y1c
Rittersbach, John C. MM3c*
Roberson, Frank L. S1c*
Robinette, Robert W. BM3c*
Robinson, James P., Jr. CWT*
Rome, Robert B. CEM*
Rowston, Alton J. S1c*
Rumpler, Wilbur J. S1c*
Rutledge, Michael J .Cox.*

Saia, Mariano F. RdM3c*
Samuel, Lawrence A. RdM3c*
Santasiero, Bernard MM1c*
Satterly, Ernest, W. S1c*
Savarese, John EM3c
Sayers, John F. CWT*
Scheffy, Luther Ens.*
Schlimbach, Albert R. RdM3c*

Schneider, Kenneth S1c*
Schultz, Norman F1c
Schwader, Stephen J. F1c*
Schweikert, Eugene TM3c
Scott, Thomas B. FC3c*
Scutari, Constantino O. FC2c*
Shank, Frank I. S1c*
Shattuck, Charles S1c
Shaver, James A. F1c*
Shaw, Edward MM2c*
Sikes, Robert O. SC2c*
Simons, Ralph A. Cox*
Skidmore, Ernest F. S1c*
Slagle, Rudolph W. MM2c*
Slater, Gordon K. GM1c*
Slatinsky, Robert V. CTM*
Smith, Paul C. S1c*
Smith, Sidwell L. Lt.*
Snider, Thomas L. WT1c*
Snyder Edward J. Cox.*
Sobcoviak, Frank F1c*
Sommer, John A. S1c*
Sonnenfeld, Gerard C. S1c*
Spadafore, Frank J. S1c*
Spears, David O. GM2c*
Spitzer, Ralph CQM*
Sprague, Rowland Owen BM2c*
Stambaugh, Lloyd E. M3c*
Stanley, Eugene B EM3c
Stickles, Emerson D. S2c*
Stockman, Frederick A. MM3c*
Studley, Milton H. RdM3c*
Synstegard, Rodney E. Ens.*

Tackney, Stephen Noel Cdr.
Tanner, Henry G. MM2c*
Taylor, Kenneth S. RdM3c*
Techman, Raymond R. Bkr2c*
Tewelow, Strickland B. SM3c*
Thompson, Clinton G. FC1c*
Thompson, Edward J. S1c*
Thompson, Keith R. WT2c*
Thompson, Woodrow C. S2c
Towson, John S. WT2c*
Tripoli, Cosmo M. EM1c*

PHALANX AGAINST THE DIVINE WIND

Upchurch, William S2c

Vaessen, John B. EM1c*
Valenti, John S2c
Vasquez, John SM3c
Vassey, William S2c
Virok, John J .WT3c*

Waiton, John F2c
Walker, Henry W. CMM*
Walsh, Joseph A. Y1c*
Wambles, John B. S2c
Wanamaker, George MM2c*

Ward, Don RM3c
Ward, Howard S. S1c*
Watson, Franklin MM2c
Watson, Samuel S2c
Webster, Dale S. S1c*
Weiss, Calvin M. RM3c
Wells, Gordon C. S1c*
Wilkerson, Joseph Jr. RM3c
Wilson, Eugene StM1c*
Wojiechiwski, Henry MM3c*

Yeaple, Charles F1c

DESTROYER SQUADRON 62 COMMANDERS

ComDesDiv 62...Capt. John Martin. Higgins*
                                                          Capt. W. D. Brown
Destroyer Division 123...Capt. John. M. Higgins
                                                          Capt. W. D. Brown
DD-696 USS *English* (Flag)................................ Cdr. James T Smith, 5/4/1944
....Cdr. Walter Baumberger,* 4/10/1945
DD-697 USS *Charles S. Sperry*...................... Cdr. Harry McIlhenny, 5/17/1944
                                                    Cdr. John B. Morland, 4/13/1945
DD-698 USS *Ault*...Cdr. Joseph Wylie, Jr,* 5/31/1944
DD-699 USS *Waldron*.............................. Cdr. George E. Peckham, 3/26/1944
DD-700 USS *Haynsworth*................................. Cdr. Robert Brodie,* 6/22/1944
                                        Lt. Cdr. Stephen N. Tackney,* 12/14/1944
DD-701 USS *John W. Weeks*.................. Cdr. Robert Theobald, Jr,* 7/21/1944
                                                    Cdr. William L. Harmon, 7/25/1945
DD-702 USS *Hank*......................................Cdr. George Chambers, 8/28/1944
DD-703 USS *Wallace L. Lind*...............Cdr. George DeMetropolis,* 9/18/1944
DD-704 USS *Borie*...Cdr. Noah Adair, Jr., 9/21/1944

*Promoted to admiral later in career

DESTROYER SQUADRON 62 WORLD WAR II BATTLE STARS

- Luzon Operation MIKE I and Indo-China Strikes Operation GRATITUDE (less USS *Borie)*
- Iwo Jima Operation JAMBOREE
- Okinawa Gunto Operation ICEBERG
- Third Fleet Operations Against Japan (less USS *Haynsworth)*

BIBLIOGRAPHY

Interviews and Correspondence USS *Haynsworth* World War II Crew

Aakhus, Ralph RdM3c, December, 2013

Bly, Harold RM3c, telephone and email correspondence, May, 2014

Breckenridge, William TM3c, letters of August 4, 2013 and September 8th, 2013

Dennett, Armistead Capt. USN (Ret.), Kittery, Maine, October 25, 2013

Goldstein, Philip GM2c, telephone Interview with the author, December 8, 2013

Lutz, Clay WT3c, telephone interview, March 31, 2017

Maugel, Edwin, SoM2c, letters of January 24, 2014

Peres, Isaac RM3c, telephone interview with the Author, December 6, 2013

Powell, Weldon C. S1c, email correspondence, May, 2014

Scott, Thomas FC2c, interview, Herndon, VA, September 28, 2013

Scutari, Gus FC1c, interview with author, Syosset, New York December 13, 2013

Vaessen, Jack EM1c, emails, January 19, 2014

Vassey, William S2c, Telephone interview with author, December 30, 2013

Vasquez, John SM3c, Interview with the author, Pompton Lakes, NJ, October 18, 2013

Interviews and Correspondence Non-USS *Haynsworth* Crew

Aitken, Doug Capt. USN Ret. (USS *Hadley*), Telephone interview with the author, December 10, 2013

Aandahl, Viola, spouse of Lt. Andrew Aandahl (USS *Haynsworth*), January 4, 2014

Aulbert, Rodney, son of Lonnie Aulbert S2c (USS *Haynsworth*), Telephone Interview, April 21, 2014

Domeracki, Capt. Hank, nephew of Henry Michalak S1c (USS *Haynsworth*)

Dyer, Helen, sister of John Dyer RM3c (USS *Haynsworth*), Telephone interview with the author, April 4, 2015

Eshelman, Robert, son of Lt. Robert Eshelman (USS *Haynsworth*), September 2013

Fahey, Christopher Col. USAF (Ret.), Interview with the Author, November 29, 2103

Ford, Orena, spouse of Edward Mital CM2c (USS *Haynsworth*), November, 2013

Gillett, Morris CRT (USS *John W. Weeks*), telephone October 12, 2014

Goodman, Larry, son of James Goodman FC3c (USS *Haynsworth*), September 7, 2013

Goyer, Robert, nephew of Arthur Goyer RM2c (USS *Haynsworth*), April 6, 2014

PHALANX AGAINST THE DIVINE WIND

Horan, Tim, son of Lt. jg. James Horan, Jr., (VB-6), telephone July 8, 2014

Huntoon, Bernard GM3c (USS *Holt*), interview with the author, Rutland, Vermont, July 22, 2013

Kurkorlo, James, son of Joseph Jr. S2c (USS *Borie*), email, April 23, 2014

Jones, Dianne, daughter of Oscar Jefferson Callahan S1c (USS *Haynsworth*), Telephone April 28, 2014

Jones, Lynne, daughter of James K. Jones, Jr. PhM2c (USS *Haynsworth*), Telephone, May 29, 2014

Kreuger, Linda Haynsworth, daughter of Cdr. William Haynsworth, Jr. USN (USS *Ingraham* DD-444), Telephone, August 21, 2014

Kubena, Louis, brother of William R. Kubena S1c (USS *Haynsworth*), letters, June 2, 2014.

Kulpin, Mardi, daughter of Manson Morrill S1c (USS *Haynsworth*), letter & telephone August 12, 2014

Lechner, Keith, son of Charles W. Lechner S1c (USS *Haynsworth*), Telephone August 23, 2014

Lembo, Francine, daughter of Frank Lembo S1c (USS *Haynsworth*) Telephone, May 1, 2014

Lizzari, Robert Sr., son of Angelo Lizzari S1c (USS *Haynsworth*), Telephone, April 23, 2014

Lowder, Sylvia Parker, daughter of Marion Parker GM3c (USS *Haynsworth*), 2013

Matsukado, Patty, daughter of 2nd Lt. Frederick E. Briggs USMCR (VMF-451), Telephone, January 31, 2015

Mandell, Robert, son of Lt. jg. Alvin Mandell (DesRon 62), emails, April 2014

Matschat, Chris, grandnephew of Robert Matschat S1c (USS *Haynsworth*), emails, May 17, 2014

Matschat, Nancy, Niece in Law of Robert Matschat S1c (USS *Haynsworth*), emails, May, 2014

McConnell, Linda daughter, Edward Mital CM2c (USS *Haynsworth*), emails, 2013-2016

Messecar, Margaret, spouse of Donald Messecar TM3c (USS *Haynsworth*), letters, 2013

Miller, Justin McCarthy, Col. USMC Ret., (VMF 217, VMF-321), Telephone Interview with the Author, November 26, 2013

Mulé, Philip AMM3c, (USS *Hancock*), phone interview, March 31, 2017

Murphy, Polly spouse of Thomas Murphy RdM3c (USS *Haynsworth*) 2013

Nokleby, Cory, grandson of Donald Karos RdM3c (USS *Haynsworth*) email, May 1, 2014

Pickens, Stephen and A.C., Jr, sons of A. C. Pickens F1c, email (USS *Haynsworth*) January, 2014

Richmond, Helen Dyer sister of John Dyer, Jr. RM3c, (USS *Haynsworth*), April 5, 2014

Saia, Fred, son of Mariano Saia GM3c (USS *Haynsworth*), Telephone Interview, April 22, 2014

Satterly, Margaret (Charles), Sister-in-law of Ernest Satterly (USS *Haynsworth*), Telephone interview with the author, November 28, 2013

Schauron, Bill GM1c (USS *Slater* DE-766), interview with author, Albany, NY, August 8, 2013

Siebert, Diana, Niece-in Law of Clifford Heob S1c (USS *Haynsworth*), telephone and email, May 4, 2014

Shinn, Karen, daughter of Keith Myreholt RM2c (USS *Haynsworth*), telephone and email, 2014

Stanny, Viola. Sister of 2nd Lt. Albert Simkunas (VMF-221), telephone, February 15, 2015

Steele, Marianna, daughter of John Magliocchetti (USS *Haynsworth*), telephone and email 2013-2014

Tackney, David, son of Cdr. Stephen N. Tackney USN (USS *Haynsworth*), telephone interviews 2013-14

Tackney, Michael, son of Cdr. Stephen N. Tackney USN (USS *Haynsworth*), telephone interview, January 16, 2015

Wengler, Michael, son of Eugene Wengler ARM3c (VT(N)-90), email, January 17, 2015

Wheeler, John MD, Telephone interview, July 1, 2014

Wilmot, Philip, 1st Lt. USMCR (VMF-451), Telephone Interview with the author, December 20, 2013

Zeoli, Nicholas, RdM2c, USS *Boston* CA-69, Interview by Author, Fair Haven, VT, July 26, 2013

Personal Journals, Letters and Published Accounts

Aakhus, Ralph RdM3c, Personal Letters (Courtesy Ralph Aakhus)

Clark, Louie SK1c, "The Remembered and the Un-Remembered," letter to the editor Madison Journal, May 30, 2011

Kelly, Edward R. TM3c Recollections, (Courtesy of Ed Kelly)

Lind, J. Fred, *Sea Attitudes: A Collection of World War II Memories.* Privately published

Lothrop, Scott Lt. Cdr., Personal Letters (Courtesy of Cdr. Peter Lothrop, USN, Ret.)

McKeen, William, Personal War Diary (Courtesy USS *Haynsworth* Association)

Mital, Edward CM2c, Personal War Diary of Haynsworth, (Courtesy of Linda McConnell and Orena Ford)

Morton, William, *DD700 USS Haynsworth Ship's Reunion Souvenir Booklet*, Joliet, Illinois, 1989 (Courtesy of Lynn Morton Lindemann)

Morton, William, Personal War Diary, (Courtesy of Lynn Morton Lindemann)

Myreholt, Keith, Personal War Diary (Courtesy of Karen Shinn)

O'Leary, John Louis QM2c, World War II Autobiography, unpublished (Courtesy of John O'Leary)

Parker, Marion, Personal War Diary (Courtesy of Sylvia Parker Lowder)

Plum, James Robert FC2c, Person War Diary (Courtesy of Wauneta Plum)

Schneider, George, Letter to Clifford Heob family, 1945 (Courtesy of Kim Seibert)

Studenski, Frank J. S1c, *War Diary of the U.S.S. Boston CA69*, unpublished, 1989 (Courtesy of Nick Zeoli)

Thomson, James. Personal War Diary, *USS Astoria* CL-90, 1944-45

Published Histories and Other References

The Bluejackets' Manual 1943 Eleventh Edition, Annapolis, Maryland, United States Naval Institute, 1943

Borneman, Walter R., *The Admirals: Nimitz, Halsey, Leahy, and King-The Five-Star Admirals Who Won the War At Sea*, New York, Little, Brown and Company, 2012

Buckner, Melton F., Jr., *Sea Cobra: Admiral Halsey's Task Force and the Great Pacific Typhoon*, The Lyons Press, Guilford CT, 2007

Buell, Thomas B., *The Quiet Warrior: A Biography of Admiral Raymond A. Spruance*, Naval Institute Press, Annapolis, Maryland, 1987

Bullis, Richard and Jack Melnick, *The History of United States Ship Waldron: Destroyer 699*, Self Published, 1991

Caswell, Dean Col., *Fighting Falcons: The Saga of Marine Fighter Squadron VMF 221*, VMF 221 Foundation, 2004

Cope, Jeffrey E., *U.S.S. Holt (DE-706) Destroyer Escort*, Bloomington, IN, Authorhouse, 2008

Cross, Robert F., *Shepherds of the Sea: Destroyer Escorts in World War II*, Maryland, Naval Institute Press, 2010

Cunningham, James F., *American Pastor in Rome*, Garden City, New York, Doubleday & Company, 1966

Cunningham, John. *Made in New Jersey: The Industrial Story of a State*, New Brunswick, New Jersey, Rutgers University Press, 1954

"Destroyer Growing Addition to Sea Power," Associated Press, New York, April 15, 1944

Ellis, John, *World War II: The Encyclopedia of Facts and Figures*, United States: The Military Book Club, 1993.

Friedman, Norman, *U.S. Destroyers: An Illustrated Design History*, Annapolis, MD, Naval Institute Press, 1982

Friedman, Norman, Arnold S. Lott, Lt. Cdr., USN (Ret.),and Robert F.Sumrall, HTC, USNR, *The Gearing Class Destroyer: The USS Joseph P. Kennedy, Jr. (DD850): The First Gearing Class Saved for Posterity*, U.S.S. Memorial Committee, Inc., Fall River, MA, R. E. Smith Printing, 1979

Gandt, Robert, *The Twilight Warriors*, Random House, New York, 2010

Gillett, Morris, *My War: A World War II Autobiography*, Self Published, Birchwood, WI 2014

Halsey, William, J. Bryan III, *Admiral Halsey's Story*, McGraw-Hill Book Company, Inc, New York, 1947

Handbook of Damage Control, U.S. Naval Press, 1941

Hansen, Richard, *The USS Gamble in the South Pacific-World War II*, Solving Light Books, 2014

Hanson, Victor Davis, *The Western Way of War: Infantry Battle in Classical Greece*, Alfred A. Knopf, New York, 1989

Hata, Ikuhiko, and Yasuho Izawa, *Japanese Naval Aces and Fighter Units in World War II*. Translated by Don Cyril Gorham. Originally published in 1970 by Kantosha in Japanese. Annapolis: Naval Institute Press, 1989

Heden, Karl E., *Sunken Ships of World War II: US Naval Chronology*, Boston, Brandon Books, 2006

Hobbs, David, "The Royal Navy's Pacific Strike Force" *Naval History Magazine*, Feb. 2013: Vol. 27 No. 1. Website: news.usni.org/2013/01/14/royal-navys-pacific-strike-force-0

Inoguchi, Capt. Rikihei, Cdr. Tadashi Nakajima, and Roger Pineau, *The Divine Wind: Japan's Kamikaze Force In World War II*, Annapolis, MD, Naval Institute Press, 1958

Jones, Mark C. Submarine shortage solved: French and Italian submarines as U.S. Navy training targets in the Western Atlantic, 1943-1945. The Submarine Review (June 2015): 126-139.

Kennedy, Maxwell Taylor, *Danger's Hour*, Simon & Schuster, NY, 2008

Lord, Walter, *Incredible Victory: The Battle of Midway*, Burford Books, Short Hills, NJ, 1967

Lott, Arnold, *Brave Ship, Brave Men*, Naval Institute Press, Annapolis, MD, 1986

Lundstrom, John B., *The First Team and the Guadalcanal Campaign*, Naval Institute Press, Annapolis, 2005

The 1927 Lucky Bag, J. S. Heavilin, Schilling Press, NY, 1927

The 1942 Lucky Bag, United States Naval Academy, Baker, Jones, Hausauer, Inc, Buffalo, NY 1941

Marston, Daniel, *The Pacific War: From Pearl Harbor to Hiroshima*, Osprey Publishing, New York, 2009

Morison, Samuel Eliot, *History of the United States Naval Operations in World War II: Victory in the Pacific: Volume XIV,* Little, Brown, and Company, Boston, MA. 1960

Morison, Samuel Eliot, *History of the United States Naval Operations in World War II: The Liberation of the Philippines: Luzon, Mindanao, the Visayas, 1944-1945: Volume XIII,* Little, Brown, and Company, Boston, 1959

Morton, William, *USS Haynsworth (DD-700) 1991 Reunion Journal, Reunions Inc*, Orlando, FL, 1991

Mrazek, Robert J., *A Dawn Like Thunder: The True Story of Torpedo Squadron Eight*, Back Bay Books, New York, 2008

Mueller, Joseph, N., *Classic Battles: Guadalcanal 1942*, Osprey Publishing, London, 1992

Office, U.S. Secretary of the Combined Chiefs of Staff (United States and Great Britain), *Octagon Conference, September 1944: Paper and Minutes of Meetings , Octagon Conference and Minutes of Combined Chiefs of Staff Meetings in London, June 1944*, Joint History Office, Washington DC, 1944

Olson, Michael Keith, *Tales of a Tin Can Sailor: The USS Dale from Pearl Harbor to Tokyo Bay*, MBI Publishing, Minneapolis, MN, 2007

Parshall, Jonathan, and Anthony Tully, *Shattered Sword: The Untold Story of the Battle of Midway*, Potomac Books, Dulles, VA, 2005

Reilly, Robin L., *Kamikaze Attacks of World War II*, McFarland & Company, Jefferson, NC, 2010

Reilly, Robin L., *Kamikazes, Corsairs, and Picket Ships: Okinawa, 1945,* Casemate, Haverton, PA 2010

Roscoe, Theodore, *Tin Cans: The True Story of the Fighting Destroyers of World War II*, United States Naval Institute, New York, 1953

Rottman, Gordon L, *Okinawa 1945: The Last Battle*, Wisconsin, Osprey Publishing, 2002

Scott, J. Davis, "Jap Bait," *Flying* magazine, July, 1948

Sholin, Bill, *The Sacrificial Lambs*, Mountain View Publishing, Washington, 1989

Spurr, Russell, *A Glorious Way to Die: The Kamikaze Mission of the Battleship Yamato, April 1945,* New Market Press, New York, 1981

Stout, Frank U.S. Navy Correspondent, *"Japanese Plane Attack,"* 1945

Sumrall, Robert F. *Sumner-Gearing-Class Destroyers: Their Design, Weapons, and Equipment,* Naval Institute Press, Annapolis, MD, 1995

Taylor, Theodore, *The Magnificent Mitscher*, Naval Institute Press, Annapolis, MD, 1954

Tomlinson, Thomas M., *The Threadbare Buzzard*, Zenith Press, St. Paul, MN, 2004

Turner, Peggy Seiz & Rolf Seiz, *Red Wing to Hong Kong*, Sentinel Printing, Minnesota, 2012

USS *Brush* DD-745: *Welcome on Board*, U.S. Navy, 1957

Wouk, Herman, *The Caine Mutiny*, Doubleday & Company, New York, 1952

Ziesing, Hibben Lt. Cdr., USNR, *History of Fighting Squadron 46: A Log in Narrative Form of its Participation in World War II*, New York, NY, Platnin Press, 1946

__, *Handbook of Damage Control NAVPERS 16191*, U.S. Navy, 1945

Official War Diaries, Muster Rolls and Reports

ACA Reports No. 1-4-5 Air Operations Against Japan, Ryukyu Islands and Jap Task Force, 3/14/45-4/15/45 pp 215-216

ComAirGroup 6, ACA-1 Reports of Air Operations Against Japan, Ryukyu Islands and Jap Task Force, 3/18/45 – 5/24/45

ComAirGroup 6, War History: April 10, 1944-October 15, 1945

ComAirGroup 7, ACA Reports Nos. 41-45 & 47-67 Air Operations Against Formosa, Philippines, French Indo-China, and Ryukyu Islands, January 3-22, 1945

ComAirGroup 83, Air Group ACA Reports of Air Operations Against Japan, Ryukyu Islands, and Jap Task Force, 3/18/45-5/24/45

ComAirGroup 83, War History, 1945

ComAirGroup 84, Air Group ACA Reports of Air Operations Against Japan, Ryukyu Islands, and Jap Task Force, 3/18/45-5/24/45

ComDesDiv 50, War Diary, April 1-30, 1945

ComDesDiv 96, War Diary, April 1-30, 1945

ComDesDiv 123, Action Report 10 February 1945 – 4 March 1945

ComDesDiv 124, War Diaries 1 January – 31 May 1945

ComDesRon 52, War Diary, 1-31 March 1945

ComDesRon 62, War Diaries, August 1, 1944- April 30, 1945

ComdtNY Mare Island, USS *Haynsworth* (DD700) – War Damage Report

ComTaskFor 58, Reports of Air Operations Against Japan, Ryukyu Islands and Jap Task Force, 3/18/45- 5/28/45

ComTaskFor 58, Report of Operations of Task Force Fifty-Eight in Support of Landings at Okinawa, 14 March through 28 May (East Longitude Dates), including Actions against Kyushu, Nansei Shoto, Japanese Fleet at Kure, the *Yamato*, and Operations in Direct Support of Landings at Okinawa; 18 June 1945

ComTaskGr 38.2 Report of Air Operations Against Formosa, Philippines, French Indo-China, and Ryukyu Islands, January 3-22, 1945

ComTaskGr 58.3/38.3: Commander Carrier Division One: Action Report 14 March – 1 June 1945

Office of Naval Operations, Administrative History of ComServFor, Pacific Fleet, 1945

Octagon Conference: September 1944. Papers and Minutes of Meetings Octagon Conference, Office, U.S. Secretary of the Combined Chiefs of Staff, 1944

USS *Astoria*, War Diary, March 1-31, 1945

USS *Ault*, War Diaries, January 1 –May 31, 1945

USS *Ault*, War History, 1945

USS *Ballard*, War Diary 1-30 June, 1942

USS *Bataan*, Navy Cruise Book, 1945, p. 78

USS *Bataan*, War Diaries, 13 March – 17 April, 1945

USS *Bennett*, War Diary, April 1-30, 1945

USS *Breton*, War Diary April 1-30, 1945

USS *Borie*, Deck Logs August 9-11, 1945

USS *Borie*, War Diaries, January 1- August 31, 1945

USS *Borie*, War History, 1945

USS *Bougainville* CVE-100, War Diary March 1-31, 1945

USS *Bullard*, War Diaries, 1 March – 30 April, 1945

USS *Bunker Hill*, Report of Air Operations Against Japan, Bonins, and the Ryukyus, 2/14/45 – 3/4/45

USS *Bunker Hill*, Report of Air Operations Against Kyushu & Honshu, Japan, Ryukyu Islands and Jap Task Force, 3/18/45- 5/11/45

USS *Bunker Hill*, War Diary, 1-30 April, 1945

USS *Bush*, War Diary, 1 March – 6 April, 1945

USS *Bush*, War History, 1945

USS *Cabot*, Report of Air Ops Against Japan, Ryukyus & On Jap Fleet Southwest of Kyushu, Japan 3/18/1945-4/8/1945 including AA Acts 3/19/45-4/7/1945, pp 12-13

USS *Cabot*, War Diary, 2 March – 11 April, 1945

USS *Charles S. Sperry*, Deck Log, January 6, 1945

USS *Charles S. Sperry*, War Diaries, January 1-May 31, 1945

USS *Charles S. Sperry*, War History, 1945

USS *Colhoun*, Action Report, Invasion and Occupation of Okinawa, Nansei Shoto, April 1 to April 6, 1945, and the loss of the USS Colhoun (DD801)

USS *Defense*, War Diary April 1-30, 1945

USS *Devastator*, Report of Operations in Support of the invasion of Okinawa Gunto, Ryukyu Islands, 24 March – 30 April, 1945

USS *Ellyson*, War Diary, 1 -30 April, 1945

USS *Emmons*, Action Report and Sinking of USS Emmons (DMS 22), April 12, 1945

USS *English*, Deck Log 26 February 1945

USS *English*, War Diaries, January 1-May 31, 1945

USS *Enterprise*, War Diary 1-31 March, 1945

USS *Erben*, Report of Operations During the Carrier Air Strikes On Japan & The Ryukyu Islands, 3/14/45 -5/28/45 Including AA Actions

USS *Essex*, Action Report: Support of Occupation of Okinawa 14 March – 1 June 1945

USS *Essex*, War Diary, Report of Air Operations Against Kyushu, Shikoku, & Honshu, Japan, Ryukyu Islands and Jap Task Force, 3/18/45- 5/29/45, including AA Actions, 3/18/45-5/14/45

USS *Essex*, War Diary, April 1-30, 1945

USS *Facility*, Actions Reports of April 4, 6 1945

USS *Fieberling*, Action Report, Air-Sea Action off Western Beaches of Okinawa Jima, 6 April, 1945

USS *Franklin*, War Diary, March 1-31, 1945

USS *Gamble*, War Diaries, 1 June to 31 August, 1942

USS *Hale*, War Diary April 1-30, 1945

USS *Hancock*, Report of Air Operations Against Formosa, Philippines, French Indo-China, South China, & The Ryukyu Islands, January 3-22, 1945

USS *Hancock*, Report of Air Operations Against Kyushu, Shikoku, & Honshu, Japan, Ryukyu Islands and Jap Task Force, 3/18/45- 5/11/45

USS *Hancock*, War Diaries, 1 March – 30 April, 1945

USS *Hank*, War Diaries, January 1- April 30, 1945

USS *Hank*, War History, 1945

USS *Harding*, Action Report-Report of Capture of Okinawa Gunto- Phase I and II to 30 April 1945

USS *Harding*, War Diary 1-30 April 1945

USS *Harrison*, War Diary, 1-30 April 1945

USS *Haynsworth*, Action Report, Period 3/14/45- 4/9/45, Kyushu Strikes, Support of Okinawa Jima, Bombardment of Minami Daito Jima

USS *Haynsworth*, Deck Logs, April 1-11, 1945

USS *Haynsworth*, Deck Log 1944-1945, CM2 Edward Streator

USS *Haynsworth*, Morning Orders: January 3, 8; March 17, 19. 23, 24; April 7 & 9, 1945

USS *Haynsworth*, Muster Rolls, June 1944- June 1945

USS *Haynsworth*, War Diaries, June 1, 1944- July 31, 1945

USS *Haynsworth*, Report of Operations During Strikes On Japan, Ryukyus and Jap Task Force, 3/18/45-4/9/45

USS Haynsworth, Report of Operations in the Philippines Area, 12/30/44- 1/25/45

USS *Hornet*, War Diary 1-31 January, 1945

USS *Howorth*, War Diary April 1-30, 1945

USS *Hutchins*, War History, 1945

USS *Hyman*, War Diary, April 1-30, 1945

USS *Indianapolis*, War Diaries, March 1-31 1945 and June 1-30, 1945

USS *Lexington*, Report of Air Operations Against Formosa, Philippines, French Indo-China, South China, & The Ryukyu Islands, January 3-22, 1945

USS *John W. Weeks*, War Diaries, January 1-April 30, 1945

USS *Kidd*, War Diary, April 1-30, 1945

USS *Kimberly*, War History, 1945

USS *Missouri*, Action Report Covering the Bombardment of Okinawa on 24 March, 1945

USS *Morris*, War Diary, April 1-30, 1945

USS *Mullany*, War Diary, April 1-30, 1945

USS *Newcomb*, War Diary, April 1-30, 1945

USS *Pasadena*, Deck Logs, April 6-7, 1945

USS *Pasadena*, War Diary, March 1-31, 1945

USS *Porterfield*, Special Action Report on Surface Engagement of 26 February 1945.

USS *Quincy*, War Diaries, March 1-April 30, 1945

USS *Quincy*, Muster Rolls, March 1-April 30, 1945

USS *Randolph*, War Diary, March 1-31, 1945

USS *Robin*, Report of Operations in the Invasion and Occupation of Okinawa Junto, Ryukyu Islands, 25 March – 23 June 1945

USS *Rodman*, War Diary, April 1-30, 1945

USS *San Jacinto*, War Diary, April 1-30, 1945

USS *San Jacinto*, Anti-Aircraft Action Report, April 14, 1945

USS *Sigsbee*, War Diary, April 1-30, 1945

USS *South Dakota* Deck Logs, April 6-7, 1945

USS *South Dakota*, Casualty Report, April 8, 1945

USS *South Dakota*, War Diary, April 1-30, 1945

USS *Springfield*, War Diary, March 1-31, 1945

USS *Stembel*, War Diaries, March 1- May 31, 1945

USS *Sterett*, War Diary, April 1-30, 1945

USS *Taussig*, War Diary, April 1-30, 1945

USS *Tucker*, War Diary, 1 July -4 August, 1942

USS *Waldron*, War Diaries, January 1-May 31, 1945

USS *Walker*, War Diary, March 1-31, 1945

USS *Wallace L. Lind*, War Diaries, January 1-August 31, 1945

USS *Wasp*, War Diary, March 1-31, 1945

USS *Wesson*, War Diary March 1- April 17, 1945

USS *West Virginia*, War Diary 1-30 April, 1945

USS *Windham Bay*, War Diary March 1-31, 1945

USS *Witter*, War Diary April 1-30, 1945

USS *YMS 81*, Action Report: Suicide Plane Attack on USS YMS-81, 16 April, 1945

VB-84, War History, 1945

VBF-83, War Diaries, January 1 - April 30, 1945

VBF-83, War History, 1945

VF-7, War History, 1945

VF-12, War Diary, August 1-31, 1945

VF-46, War History, 1945

VMF-112 & VMF-123 (Forward Echelons), War Diary, April 1-30, 1945

VMF-451 (Forward Echelons), War Diary, 1-31 March, 1945

VPB-21, War Diary 1-30 April, 1945

VT-10, War History, 1945

VT-11, War History, 1945

VT-30, ACA Report #37, 7 April, 1945

VT-84, War History, 1945

VT(N)-90, War History, 1945

DVD References

Blue Devils: Marine Squadron VMF-451, Dir. Terry Dodge, TLD Productions, 2008

Websites with Dates Accessed

Allen M. Sumner Class Destroyers: As Built-Interior Photographs, navsource.org/archives/05/interior/htm, numerous visits

Attack on Cam Ranh Bay, jimhooper.co.uk, September 23, 2013

"The Catholic Church, Cremation, and Burial at Sea,"
    seaservices.com/catholic-burial-at-sea, August 23, 2013

Damage Control Museum, damagecontrolmuseums.org, January 24, 2014

Destroyer History Foundation, destroyerhistory.org/fletcherclass/DesRon48,
    July 2, 2013

Federal Shipbuilding and Drydock, Co.,
    en.wikipedia.org/wiki/Federal_Shipbuilding_and_Drydock_Company,
    June 29, 2013

"47 Ships Sunk by Kamikaze Aircraft," Kamikaze Images,
    wgordon.web.wesylan.edu/kamikaze/background/ships-sunk, July 5,
    2013

HMS *Ulster-Bombed off Japan 1945*,
    candoo.com/ulsternorrie/ulster/ulster53.html, September 23, 2014

Hoplite: Ancient Greek Soldier, Britannica.com/topic/hoplite, July 20, 2013

Imperial Japanese Submarine I-123, combinedfleet.com/I-123.htm, July 20,
    2013

Military Times Hall of Valor, valor.militarytimes.com, numerous visits 2013-
    2017

Nanshin Maru, ww2timelines.com/1945/February/02171945.html, July 8,
    2013

NavSource Naval History: Photographic History of the U.S. Navy,
    navsource.org, numerous visits

Sampson Naval Training Center, rpadden.com/Sampson.htm, July 7, 2013

SS *Hobbs Victory*, hobbshistory.com/HobbsVictory.html, July 13, 2014

"Ulithi: Its existence kept secret throughout the war...",
    laffey.org/Ulithi/Page%201/Ulithi.htm, July 6, 2013

Ulithi Atoll Berthing Chart,
    memoriesshop.com/Oilers/Taluga/History/Berthing-Plan.html, August
    13, 2013

United States Navy Task Forces List, pacific.valka.cz/forces., numerous visits

United States Pacific Fleet Organization May 1,
    1945,ibilio.org/hyperwar/USN/OOB/PacFleet/Org-450501, August 17,
    2013

USN Overseas Aircraft Loss Lists (Dec 44- May 45),
    aviationarchaeology.com/src/USN.html, numerous visits

U.S. Navy Active Ship Force Levels, 1886-Present, histo-
    ry.navy.mil/branches/org9-4.html, July 27, 2013

U.S. Navy Airplane Losses; pacificwrecks.com; numerous visits

U.S. Navy Action reports, muster rolls, war diaries, and war histories;
    fold3.com, numerous visits

U.S. Navy World War II Airgroups,
    researchatlarge.com/Ships/Airgroups/CV-9.html, August 10, 2013

USS *Astoria*, mighty90.com/WWII History.html, January 7, 2014

USS *Bennett*, en.wikipedia.org/wiki/USS_Bennett_(DD-473), July 21, 2013

USS *Borie* DD-704, destroyersonline.com, September 8, 2013

USS *Haynsworth* DD-700, usshaysnworth.com, numerous visits

USS *Haynsworth* DD-700, usshaynsworth.org, numerous visits

USS *John W. Weeks* Association Newsletters, ussjwweeks701.org/pdf_files/newsletter, July 13, 2013

USS *John W. Weeks*, http://www.ussjwweeks701.org/stories_from_our_members.htm#Picket _Duty _(late_March,_1945)_By_Morris_Gillett, October 12, 2014

USS *Ordronaux*, usskpkennedyjr.org/ordronaux617/617brodie.html, July 20, 2013

USS *Wallace L. Lind*, Serial 033176, News Material Prepared by Enlisted Naval Correspondent Attached to the U.S.S. Wallace L. Lind (DD703), - 24Sept 1945, pages 1-3

USS *Whitehurst*, *"Refresh Your Memory,"* de634.org/Facts.htm, July 30, 2013

VT(N)-90, cv6.org/ship/logs/vtn90/vtn90-4501.html, January 9, 2015

Welcome on Board...USS Brush, pamphlet, 1957

"World War II Navy Boot Camps," astralpublishing.com/wwii-navy-boot-camps.html, June 4, 2012

INDEX

Clark, R.Adm. Joseph J., 248, 252, 312, 318, 350, 354, 369,

Clark Airfield, 146

Clark, SK2c, Louis, 347, 435, 440

Clarke, TM2c Robert, 324

Colhoun, USS DD-801, 353, 354, 357, 477

Comella, Lt. jg. 318

Coral Sea, Battle of, 34, 35, 36, 38, 95, 137, 286

Corley AMM1c, W., 137, 477

Costello GM3c, Charles, 87

Cotten, USS DD-669, 220

Cowanesque, USS AO-79, 276

Cowpens, USS CVL-25, 184, 185, 186, 187, 204, 214, 215, 224, 478

Cox ARM2c, Leroy, 245, 246, 478

Cruiser Division 17, 280, 281

Cuff, Lt. jg. Jim, 133, 478

Cummings, Lt. Harry A., 430

Cunningham, Cdr. James. J. Father., 365, 374, 397, 398

Davis, Bette, 94

Davis, RM3c Carroll L., Jr., 290, 317, 348, 365, 408, 431, 474

Davison, Lt. jg. Jacqueline, 474

Davison, R.Adm. Ralph, 248

Dayliner Alexander Hamilton, 20

Dean, Lt. Carrol, 172

Dedrick, Maj. Emerson, 272, 273, 274, 478

Defense, USS AM-317, 360

DeLoach, GM2c Walter, 313, 323, 339, 395, 474

DeMetropolis, Cdr. George, 147, 154, 283, 284, 488

Dempsey, TM1c Harold, 323, 337, 475, 480

Dennett, Lt. Armistead, 59, 60, 61, 102, 105, 114, 132, 194, 195, 254, 261, 310, 322, 329, 366, 367, 377, 399, 403, 430, 439

DesDiv (See Destroyer Division)

DESECRATE I, Operation, 124

DesRon (See Destroyer Squadron)

Destroyer Division 24, 108

Destroyer Division 50, 372, 373, 377, 392

Destroyer Division 95, 235, 249

Destroyer Division 96, 235, 248, 253, 260, 265, 272, 283, 289, 294, 297, 299, 301, 372, 377, 391, 392, 418, 422

Destroyer Division 99, 220

Destroyer Division 109, 186

Destroyer Division 123, 100, 170, 249, 488

Destroyer Division 124, 100, 237, 249, 422, 424

Destroyer Escort Division 69, 107

Destroyer Squadron 11, 438

Destroyer Squadron 34, 451

Destroyer Squadron 48, 235, 385

Destroyer Squadron 52, 129, 186

Destroyer Squadron 53, 261

Destroyer Squadron 55, 186

Destroyer Squadron 61, 154, 352

Destroyer Squadron 62, 14, 67, 79, 89, 98, 100, 101, 102, 103, 113, 117, 126, 128, 129, 130, 132, 133, 135, 142, 146, 150, 152, 154, 159, 166, 170, 171, 176, 177, 182, 186, 191, 199, 200, 202, 209, 213, 220, 223, 229, 235, 253, 254, 256, 264, 275, 277, 280, 281, 284, 286, 294, 388, 412, 415, 417, 422, 432, 438, 447, 488, 489

Destroyer Training Facility, Norfolk, VA, 51, 52, 53, 65, 93, 408, 428,

Devastator, USS AM-318, 361

Dickie, AMM1c T., 133, 477

Dillon, GM3c Joseph N., 87

Dönitz, Grand Adm. Karl, 84

Domarasky, GM3c Andrew, 395

Doolittle, Col. Jimmy, 31

Doolittle Raid(ers), 31, 32, 33, 41, 101, 110, 116, 188, 191

Dortch, USS DD-670, 147, 202, 220

Kyushu Island, Japan, 134, 238, 241, 242, 244, 248, 250, 266, 270, 273, 274, 278, 283, 289, 291, 292, 294, 312, 316, 372, 373, 415, 452,

Lackawanna, USS AO-40, 302
Lakoff, Cox. Herman, 395
Langley, USS CVL-27, 171, 220
Laura, movie, 93
Laws, USS DD-558, 147
Layden, RT1c Paul, 320, 321, 335
Le Shima, Island, 355
Lembo, S1c Frank, 331, 332, 348, 397, 441, 474
Lenihan, S1c Joseph P., 310, 323, 334, 339, 395, 474
Lentz, GM1c Marvin, 39
Leutze, USS DD-481, 358, 359, 360, 361, 473
Lexington, 22, USS CV-2, 34, 35, 38, 137
Lexington II, USS, CV-16, 125, 128, 136, 139, 143, 146, 151, 189, 286, 477
Ley, Lt. jg. Allyn B., 60, 61, 77, 78, 140, 144, 161, 189, 196, 226, 229, 236, 246, 325, 336, 339, 340, 341, 348, 361, 364, 365, 366, 379, 397, 439
Lifeboat, movie, 93
Lind, Fred, 196
Lizzari, S1c Angelo, 72, 197, 198, 441
Logan Victory, SS, 355, 473
Long, Maj. Herbert H. "Trigger", 328
Lothrop, Cummings, 308
Lothrop, Lt. Cdr. Scott, 15, 59, 60, 65, 86, 114, 131, 144, 148, 161, 168, 169, 190, 200, 215, 220, 239, 248, 249, 254, 271, 275, 284, 298, 300, 308, 310, 320, 309, 328, 330, 335, 342, 343, 344, 349, 369, 370, 381, 384, 393, 394, 395, 396, 397, 401, 402, 416, 430, 435, 438, 439

LOVE III, Operation, 125
LST 447, USS, 355, 356, 392, 473
Luzon, Philippines, 80, 97, 113, 128, 135, 138, 142, 143, 145, 147, 148, 151, 153, 159, 170, 176, 489

MacArthur, Gen. Douglas, 96, 113, 125
MacLaughlan, S1c Hobart, 94, 290, 323, 331, 334, 395, 408, 450, 474
Maddox, USS DD-731, 171, 176, 201, 220
Magliocchetti, RdM2c Ed, 420
Magliocchetti, RM3c John, 69, 106, 290, 369, 399, 407, 408, 416, 420, 431, 441
Malkiewicz, Edward S1c, 397, 474
Manila, City, 146
Mare Island, CA, 412, 414, 430, 432, 450
Mariana Islands, 54, 69, 95, 113, 114, 125, 432
Marion, William. F., 154
Marshall Islands, 34, 124
Marshall, Capt. W., 385
Marshall, USS DD-676, 169, 246, 252
Martin, Dean 446
Matschat, S1c Robert D., 210, 310, 323, 332, 334, 365, 374, 391, 402, 474
Matthews, Lt. jg. Harvey, 320
Maugel, SoM3c Ed, 91, 114, 115, 173, 441
McAllister, RM3c John Albert, 3, 9, 10, 13, 15, 23, 25, 45, 48, 50, 51, 65, 94, 106, 290, 369, 399, 407, 408, 410, 416, 428, 448, 450
McAllister Tugboat Company, 20
McCain, V.Adm. John S., 102, 128, 129, 130, 131, 143, 154, 154, 155, 157, 163, 170, 177, 423, 432
McClintock, Ens. Robert, 475
McGee, EM2c Archie A., Jr., 331
McHenry, Lt. Robert E., 143, 144, 477

McIlhenney, Cdr. Harry, 148, 205, 254, 255, 256, 300, 380, 488

McKay, S1c Millard, 475

McKeen, S1c William N., 250, 364, 400, 401, 403, 412, 441

McKirttrick, Capt. H. V., 65

McVay, Capt. Charles, 432

Meiji Air Base, Japan, 88

Mercury, USS AK-42, 302

Messecar, TM2c Donald R., 324, 442

Metler, AOM1c Charles E., 286, 445, 479

Meyers, Ens. Randolph, 277, 479

Michalak, S1c Henry, 71, 73, 132, 244, 245, 442

Midway Atoll, 24, 37, 39, 110, 193

Midway, Battle, 36, 39, 40, 95, 140, 193, 239

Midyett, Ens. Wesley, 277, 479

MIKE I, Operation, 128, 159, 176

Miller, USS DD-535, 147, 252, 253

Minami Daito Shima, Island, 221, 280, 281, 292, 304, 415

Mindoro, Philippines, 125

Missouri, USS BB-63, 65, 89, 272, 432, 438

Mital, CM2c Edward, 91, 114, 167, 170, 211, 254, 281, 296, 366, 396, 412, 430, 442

Mitchell, Gen. William, 122

Miyazaki, Japan, 372

Mog-Mog Island, 183, 225, 229, 230

Mohawk. (See Mitscher, Adm. Marc)

Momm, Cdr. Albert, 357

Momsen, Capt. Charles, 400

Monongahela, USS AO-42, 211

Mooney, S1c Gilbert, 283

Moore, Louis S1c, 475

Moore, Ens. Robert D., 245, 246

Morrill, S1c Manson C., 283, 284, 442

Morris, USS DD-417, 361,363, 364,

Morrisey, RdM3c George, 337,

Morton, Ens. William J., 256, 478

Morton, SoM3c William, 65, 90, 91, 92, 99, 114, 115, 118, 135, 136, 142, 143, 145, 148, 150, 153, 155, 158, 167, 170, 173, 192-198, 226, 289, 321, 273, 283, 272, 330, 331, 338, 366, 375, 409, 442

Moss, Y3c Harold A., 320, 475

Mount Suribachi, Iwo Jima, 208, 209, 212, 213

Mulé, AMM3c Philip, 166, 378, 380, 381, 447

Mullany, USS DD-528, 357, 473

Murray, Lt. George G., 326

Musashi, IJN, 21, 41, 81, 83, 144, 258,422

Myreholt, RM3c Keith, 51, 91, 165, 170, 209, 216, 223, 251, 252,256, 283, 290, 317, 321, 349, 350, 351, 442, 443

Nagasaki, Japan, 258, 427, 432

Nagumo, Adm. Chūichi, 38

Nanshin Maru #36, 196

Nansei Shoto Island Group, 220, 234, 292, 294,

Nantahala, USS AO-60, 163

Nauck, BM1c William, 236, 413

Naval Station Alameda, 31

Naval Training School for Radio, 106

Neafcy, AMM3c Thomas, 397, 475

Neosho, USS AO-23, 34, 35

Nevada, USS BB-36, 110, 113, 279,

New Guinea, 34, 95, 124

New Jersey, USS, BB-62, 89, 126, 130, 146, 149, 162, 186, 190, 214, 220, 254, 272

New Mexico, USS BB-40, 286, 422, 423

Newcomb, USS DD-586, 358, 359, 361

Nimitz, Adm. Chester, 111, 126, 142, 177, 190, 206, 269, 270, 369, 398, 399

CPSIA information can be obtained
at www.ICGtesting.com
Printed in the USA
LVHW091033200222
711568LV00006B/20

9 780359 106073